The First American

A Story of
North American Archaeology

by C. W. Ceram

A MENTOR BOOK from
NEW AMERICAN LIBRARY
TIMES MIRROR
New York and Scarborough, Ontario

This is an authorized reprint of a hardcover edition published by Harcourt Brace Jovanovich, Inc.

 MENTOR TRADEMARK REG. U.S. PAT. OFF. AND FOREIGN COUNTRIES
REGISTERED TRADEMARK—MARCA REGISTRADA
HECHO EN BUFFALO, U.S.A.

SIGNET, SIGNET CLASSICS, MENTOR, PLUME AND MERIDIAN BOOKS are published *in the United States* by
The New American Library, Inc.
1301 Avenue of the Americas, New York, New York 10019,
in Canada by The New American Library of Canada Limited,
81 Mack Avenue, Scarborough, 704, Ontario.

FIRST PRINTING, OCTOBER, 1972

3 4 5 6 7 8 9 10

*The archaeologist may find the tub
but altogether miss Diogenes*
—SIR MORTIMER WHEELER

*From the past let us take over the
fire, not the ashes*
—JEAN JAURÈS

Contents

Contents

radioactive • The fascinating laboratory • Sensational first results • But are the dates always correct? • How the hydrogen bomb interferes • The Nobel Prize for an aid to archaeology

Contents

Contents

BOOK FIVE

Contents

The First American

A Story of
North American Archaeology

Preface

*One point, emphasized throughout, is the
importance of Adventure for the promotion
and preservation of civilization.*
—ALFRED NORTH WHITEHEAD
Adventures in Ideas

This is an account of *North* American archaeology. Or
to be more precise, an account of the archaeology of what
is now the United States. I shall be telling the story of
prehistoric Indian cultures in North America.

Everyone knows that the Spaniards destroyed the civilizations of the Aztecs and Incas in Central and South America almost five hundred years ago. But the astounding discoveries of archaeologists in *North* America over the past
century are far less well known. How many Americans
realize that their own part of the New World was once the
scene of flourishing cultures, that here, too, there are "pyramids" (mounds) and mummies to study, that treasures of
enormous scientific and material value have been unearthed,
and that archaeologists can now pursue the lives of the First
Americans back to the Ice Age, back to the mammoth
hunters?

As in my other books, here, too, I am tracing archaeological discovery, largely in chronological sequence. Along
that track the panorama of cultures unfolds of its own
accord, much as the archaeologists uncovered it layer by
layer. Accordingly, this book is not intended to compete
with works of science or scholarship, but rather to lead the
reader to the writings and work of scientists and scholars.
Existing books on American archaeology presuppose an

interest in the subject; mine is meant to awaken such interest among the many who have overlooked its importance. I hope to open their eyes to the treasures of the past in our own country.

Neither is this book "popular science" in the usual sense. Rather, it is the work of a committed writer who in his own fashion follows the precept of the French naturalists: Not nature, but "science seen through a temperament."

It is this commitment that justifies bold historical leaps and summaries or omissions which the specialized scholar can hardly permit himself, or which he resorts to only with profuse apologies when he must impose some kind of order on the tremendous mass of material. Thus Alex D. Krieger of the University of Washington at Seattle says: "The territory involved is so immense that it is virtually impossible for any one person to see the field situations and examine the cultural evidence at even the most important sites."[1] And John C. McGregor of the University of Illinois adds: "The subject is still advancing so rapidly, and so much detailed information is now on hand, that in general only the broader outlines may be presented."[2] And he, it may be remarked, is speaking of only one section of the United States, the Southwest.

This principle of selectivity has also had to be applied to people. I have had to restrict the list of archaeologists whose personalities and work could be discussed at any length. Many have only been mentioned. A sizable number, whose researches are no less important (for instance, in the Northwest and Alaska), had to be omitted altogether, for to follow their operations would snarl the clear thread that, I trust, runs through this book.

On the other hand, the narrative contains many items of information not to be found in technical works. That, too, is inescapable for one who approaches the subject as a writer and not as a scientist. He must look for matters of high interest, for the extraordinary, and above all for the human factor hidden within allegedly "dry" scholarship. But I can happily repudiate any charge of having forcibly romanticized, of having overstressed the elements of adventure and detection that have so often precipitated and accompanied discoveries. The famous British archaeologist Sir Mortimer Wheeler devotes several sections in one of his books to the psychological significance of adventure in archaeology.[3] And Gordon C. Baldwin of the University of Arizona, a passionate excavator, says:

"The archaeologist works just like the detective in the mystery story who reconstructs a crime from a lone cigarette stub and a thread or two of cloth. Instead of cigarettes and thread, the archaeologist salvages fragments of broken pottery, lost implements and utensils, and bits of charcoal. From these he pieces together the story of how and when people lived and died in towns which have been long forgotten."[4]

As it happens, Baldwin has several sides to his nature; he has also written western novels for pleasure. But H. Marie Wormington of the Denver Museum of Natural History, who observes extreme scientific rigor and skepticism in her writing, and avoids the slightest romantic flourishes, is also moved to speak of the "detective methods used by archaeologists."[5] And anyone who would like to know more about the adventurous, human aspect of our subject may look into the report of an outstanding, enormously experienced American excavator, one who has personally participated in more than twenty-four "digs" since 1907: Neil M. Judd, whose *Men Met Along the Trail: Adventures in Archaeology* deals explicitly with this part of the game.

Nevertheless, the exciting moments of archaeology must never be permitted to overshadow the long hours of self-sacrificing, purely scientific detail work in the field and in the museum, hours that are toilsome and often tedious. The desire for color must never lead to any carelessness toward facts, let alone to a distortion of them. In this book I have stuck to the facts; there has been no inventing; no romanticizing. Since, however, a great many facts, especially in chronology but also in pure interpretation, are still the subject of scientific controversies, the alternatives have been scrupulously presented, as far as possible in some of the specialists' own words.

The extensive bibliography should enable the ordinary reader, the scientists in other fields, and the young student of archaeology, to approach the field in a directed way. For the European reader, and this includes archaeologists, this book may well be a guide into totally undiscovered country.

Throughout this project I have benefited enormously from the valuable advice and friendship of Emil W. Haury, the great teacher at the University of Arizona, who was the excavator of Snaketown and many other sites. He was the first to read the entire manuscript and contributed a number of important corrections. I am especially indebted to him, as I am to Frederick Johnson of the Peabody Foundation in Andover who placed at my disposal a wealth of unpublished material and likewise checked the entire manuscript. Henry Clyde Shetrone, author of what is already considered one of the "classical" works on North American archaeology, once wrote: "The author bespeaks the tolerance of his readers, particularly those who, through training and experience, are in a position to note his errors."[6] I make the same appeal.

My friends Sanford J. Greenburger and Harold Strauss helped me to make initial contacts with various specialists. Through their offices I received encouraging suggestions from H. Marie Wormington; from Carleton Coon, formerly of the University of Pennsylvania; from Gladys Weinberg, then editor of the magazine *Archaeology*. I owe other valuable suggestions to Frederick J. Dockstader of the Museum of the American Indian in New York City; Froelich Rainey and Alfred Kidder II of the Museum of the University of Pennsylvania; Richard P. Schaedel of the University of Texas; Phileo Nash, former director of the Bureau of Indian Affairs in the Department of the Interior in Washington, D.C.

Emil W. Haury arranged for me many conversations with leading specialists, among them Raymond H. Thompson, his successor as director of the Arizona State Museum in Tucson; Paul Damon, head of the radiocarbon laboratory; Bryant Bannister, director of the Laboratory of Tree-Ring Research. On questions of dating, Rainer Berger of the University of California helped me greatly by checking my chapter on the C-14 method, as did Ernst Hollstein, who briefed me on the status of German tree-ring dating.

In Flagstaff I was indebted to the generous helpfulness of Edward B. Danson, director of the Museum of Northern Arizona, and to Harold S. Colton, founder of that museum. Colton, in spite of the searing heat and his age of eighty-four, spent an entire afternoon showing me "his" ruins; George Gumerman then had the kindness to continue the tour.

I met with equally generous aid in Albuquerque from Frank C. Hibben, excavator of the controversial Sandia Cave, and from Alfred E. Dittert, Jr., of the Laboratory of Anthropology in Santa Fé.

On various questions of detail I received friendly advice from Admiral Samuel Eliot Morison; from Saul K. Padover of the New School for Social Research in New York; from Beverly E. Brickey of the City Art Museum of St. Louis; and from General Charles A. Lindbergh, who with Alfred Vincent Kidder pioneered in aerial archaeology by undertaking the first orientation flights over New Mexico.

I am indebted to Shareen Brysac for her help in obtaining many photographs. My friend Nathan Resnick, director of the libraries of Long Island University, was of the greatest assistance in procuring what were often the oddest books and in keeping watch over many scientific periodicals for articles that I would otherwise have missed.

I am grateful to William Jovanovich, the chairman of my publishing house, for the intense personal commitment with which he approached the editing of the book, and to his assistant, Ethel Cunningham.

I am grateful to all of them for their help in a field which has become so vast that it can hardly be entered without guidance.

I owe special and deepest thanks to my wife, Hannelore Marek. For more than four years, at those crucial times when an author begins to despair at the mountains of material facing him, she always found the right and patient words of encouragement. I have a similar debt of gratitude to my friend Felix Guggenheim in Beverly Hills and to my wise fellow writers in Woodstock, Robert Pick and Manuel Komroff.

C. W. C.

Woodstock, N.Y.
1971

The First American

A Story of North American

Archaeology

PRELUDE

The President and the Mounds

In 1781 a most unusual book was written in the state of Virginia, one of the thirteen states that constituted the United States of America. Later generally known as *Notes on Virginia,* its exact title read: *Notes on the State of Virginia; written in the year 1781, somewhat corrected and enlarged in the winter of 1782, for the use of a Foreigner of distinction, in answer to certain queries proposed by him respecting* . . . There followed twenty-three chapters, some long, some short.

What was most unusual about this book was its author. Burdened for more than a decade with extraordinarily heavy political duties and known to the public almost entirely as a statesman, he displayed in *Notes on Virginia* an encyclopedic knowledge presented in exceedingly polished English. The twenty-three chapters of the *Notes* provide far more than a description of Virginia; they constitute virtually an anatomy of the author's native state. Hardly any region of the world at this time had ever been represented with such exactitude, and certainly none in the new wild country that had just barely won its freedom.

The author discusses the topography and geography, the

economics and politics, the zoology and botany of Virginia. He provides data on the rivers and harbors, on useful plants and wild animals (quite incidentally, he ventures to challenge the most famous authority of his age, the French naturalist Buffon, on certain matters), its mineral possessions as well as its naval forces (three vessels with sixteen cannon and two or three armed boats, "seldom . . . in a condition for service"). In Chapter XI, under the title "Aborigines," he reports on a personal undertaking that was absolutely unique in the world at the time. We may say that this man, Thomas Jefferson, who twenty years later would become the third President of the United States of America, was describing nothing less than the first attempt at a scientific archaeological excavation.

Naturally there had long been archaeological digging in Europe. But it was scarcely conducted in a scientific manner, since chance and avarice usually guided men's spades. The physician Jacob Spon, who traveled in Asia Minor and Greece, probably coined the word "archaeology" in 1674 (from the Greek *archaios* = old); but until the nineteenth century it rarely meant more than the study of the *art* of ancient peoples, and then chiefly that of the Greeks and Romans. Johann Joachim Winckelmann (1717–1768), the German scholar whom archaeologists throughout the world still revere as the "Father of Archaeology," wrote his epochmaking *Geschichte der Kunst des Altertums* ("History of the Art of Antiquity") in 1764. It is likely that the extremely well-read Jefferson knew the work; in his day he owned what was probably the most valuable private library in America. But Winckelmann's book was a history of *art,* especially sculpture. It was in no sense a study of the whole *culture*—whereas nowadays archaeologists regard it as their supreme task to discover, describe, and interpret the general culture. And Winckelmann was not an excavator at all. He based his theories on the finds made by others at Herculaneum and Pompeii. And the diggers at these sites from 1711 on were essentially treasure hunters, bent on unearthing works of art for royal collections. Their methods of excavation would have horrified a modern archaeologist. They destroyed more than they actually rescued from the rubble of millennia, their energetic digging undeterred by even a trace of scientific caution. And then, in 1781, we find an American statesman and gentleman farmer reporting on an excavation he had undertaken out of pure thirst for knowledge and whose method was so painstaking that 173 years later the famous British archaeologist Sir Mortimer Wheeler commented: "No mean achievement for a busy statesman."[1]

Now, as it happens, Thomas Jefferson (1743–1826) was one of the most unusual men of his age in America—an age rich in excellent minds. At his side stood George Washington, Benjamin Franklin, Alexander Hamilton, John Adams, Thomas Paine.

Among them all Thomas Jefferson stands out as the author of the most momentous political document in American history, the Declaration of Independence. That, aside from his presidency, was the climax of his career, or rather of his public activities, which poured into innumerable channels. His father was a tobacco planter, justice of the peace, and colonel of the militia, who had bought his 400 acres of land for an enormous bowl of arrack punch. Thomas Jefferson grew up in the fine manor house of a deceased friend of his father's. He studied law and entered politics early, at the age of twenty-six becoming a delegate to Virginia's House of Burgesses, the first legislative assembly of citizens on American soil. On the side he engaged in intensive study of the arts, literature, and science. He made music, read the Greek and Latin classics in the original, served as his own architect in designing and building his marvelous and since world-famous home, Monticello, for decades an assembly point for the most cultivated minds in America. From Monticello the torrent of his stimulating, instructive, disputatious letters poured out—they amounted to some 18,000 by the end of his life—full of the most progressive ideas on the Negro question (although he himself still owned slaves), on religion (all his life he advocated religious freedom, the separation of church and state), on the Indian problem (in a letter to the Delawares, Mohicans, and Munries he wrote in 1808: "You will mix with us by marriage, your blood will run in our veins, and will spread with us over this great island,"[2] a tremendous idea in his time, for it was scarcely meant symbolically). And all this in a still savage country in which there were scarcely any good roads, in which the greater part of the inhabitants lived in log cabins, wore moccasins and coonskin caps, dressed in homespun cloth, and scarcely knew how to write.

In his old age he suffered from financial difficulties. He

had to sell his library to Congress for $23,000; it became the foundation of the Library of Congress, the most important library in the world today. But that sum was not enough. Monticello itself was in danger. Whereupon the cities collected a voluntary offering and saved the grand old man's home. And once more he crowned all his previous great gestures by founding the University of Virginia, at whose opening ceremonies he presided at the age of eighty-two. Shortly afterward he drafted the text for his tombstone: "Here was buried Thomas Jefferson, Author of the Declaration of American Independence, of the Statute of Virginia for Religious Freedom, and Father of the University of Virginia." He died on July 4, 1826, fifty years to the day after his Declaration of Independence had been promulgated.

During one of his few spells of personal leisure, when he had been compelled because of a number of troubles to resign from the governorship of Virginia, he wrote *Notes on Virginia*. Sixteen editions of the book appeared even during his lifetime. One limited to 200 copies was published in Paris in 1782, another in London five years later, and there was even a German edition in Leipzig by 1789.

Here, in a few pages, were the observations that make this remarkable man so pertinent to North American archaeology that he unquestionably deserves his place at the beginning of this book.[3]

Curiously, Jefferson begins with an extremely discouraging observation: "I know of no such thing existing as an Indian monument; for I would not honor with that name arrow points, stone hatchets, stone pipes and half-shapen images." But virtually in the same breath he mentions the exception: "Unless indeed it would be the barrows, of which many are to be found all over the country." And he describes them, always using the old-fashioned word "barrow" for the tumulus graves that we nowadays call "mounds": "These are of different sizes, some of them constructed of earth, and some of loose stones. That they were repositories of the dead, has been obvious to all; but on what particular occasion constructed, was a matter of doubt. Some have thought they covered the bones of those who have fallen in battles fought on the spot of interment. Some ascribed them to the custom, said to prevail among Indians, of collecting, at certain periods, the bones of all their dead, wheresoever deposited at the time of death."

In order to settle these conjectures—in other words, out

of pure desire for knowledge—he came to the following decision: "There being one of these [barrows] in my neighborhood, I wished to satisfy myself whether any, and which of these opinions were just. For this purpose I determined to open it and examine it thoroughly."

He then gives a systematic description of the locale so keen-eyed and comprehensive that a modern archaeologist could not do better. The mound in question rose out of low-lying ground, opposite several hills that contained the remains of Indian settlements. It was of "spheroidical" form, about forty feet in diameter at the base. It may originally have been twelve feet high; Jefferson draws that conclusion, for he considers the fact that the earth had been plowed there during the past twelve years, resulting in a reduction in level of as much as seven and a half feet. From traces he decides that before cultivation sizable trees as much as twelve inches in thickness had stood on the spot. And then he launches on the adventure of excavation. He does not spend a word on the feelings that must have moved him immediately before the spade was first driven into so mysterious a past. Rather, he gives his report as matter-of-factly as if he had done nothing else all his life:

"I first dug superficially in several parts of it, and came to collections of human bones, at different depths, from six inches to three feet below the surface. These were lying in the utmost confusion, some vertical, some oblique, some horizontal, and directed to every point of the compass, entangled and held together in clusters by the earth. Bones of the most distant parts were found together as, for instance, the small bones of the foot in the hollow of a scull; many sculls would sometimes be in contact, lying on the face, on the side, on the back, top or bottom, so as, on the whole, to give the idea of bones emptied promiscuously from a bag or a basket, and covered over with earth, without any attention to their order. The bones of which the greatest numbers remained, were sculls, jawbones, teeth, the bones of the arms, thighs, legs, feet and hands. A few ribs remained, some vertebrae of the neck and spine, without their processes, and one instance only of the bone which serves as a base to the vertebral column. Ten sculls were so tender, that they generally fell to pieces on being touched. The other bones were stronger. There were some teeth which were judged to be smaller than those of an adult; a scull, which on a slight view, appeared to be that of an infant, but it fell to pieces on being taken out, so as to prevent satisfactory examination; a rib, and a fragment of the under-jaw of a person about half grown; another rib of an infant; and a part of the jaw of a child, which had not cut its teeth. This last furnishing the most decisive proof of the burial of children here, I was particular in my attention to it. It was part of the right half of the under-jaw. The processes, by which it was attenuated to the temporal bones, were entire, and the bone itself firm to where it had been broken off, which, as nearly as I could judge, was about the place of the eyetooth. Its upper edge, wherein would have been the sockets of the teeth, was perfectly smooth. Measuring it with that of an adult, by placing their hinder processes together, its broken end extended to the penultimate grinder of the adult. This bone was white, all the others of a sand color. The bones of infants being soft, they probably decay sooner, which might be the cause so few were found here."

And then he sets forth a very simple decision: "I proceeded then to make a *perpendicular* cut through the body of the barrow, that I might examine its internal structure."

That one sentence marks the advent of a specialized archaeological discipline!

For our story of North American archaeology, what matters is not *what* Jefferson now discovered in his barrow but *how* he found it, the way he immediately drew conclusions, the way he brought a dead mound and its bones to life by recognizing the factor of time and hence of development: "This [the cut] passed about three feet from its center, was opened to the former surface of the earth, and was wide enough for a man to walk through and examine its sides. At the bottom, that is, on the level of the circumjacent plain, I found bones; above these a few stones, brought from a cliff a quarter of a mile off, and from the river one-eighth of a mile off; then a large interval of earth, then a stratum of bones, and so on. At one end of the section were four strata of bones plainly distinguishable; at the other, three; the strata in one part not ranging with those in another. The bones nearest the surface were least decayed. No holes were discovered in any of them, as if made with bullets, arrows, or other weapons. I conjectured that in this barrow might have been a thousand skeletons. Everyone will readily seize the circumstances above related, which militate against the opinion that it covered the bones only of persons fallen in battle. . . . Appearances certainly indicate that it has derived both origin and growth from the accustomary collection of bones, and deposition of them together; that the first collection had been deposited on the common surface of the earth, a few stones put over it, and then a covering of earth, that the second had been laid on this, had covered more or less of it in proportion to the number of bones, and was then also covered with earth; and so on. The following are the particular circumstances which give it this aspect. 1. The number of bones. 2. Their confused position. 3. Their being in different strata. 4. The strata in one part having no correspondence with those in another. 5. The different states of decay in these strata, which seem to indicate a difference in the time of inhumation. 6. The existence of infant bones among them."

In this brief paragraph Jefferson in 1781 (for the account was first penned in that year) introduces what has since become the foremost methodological tool of all archaeologists, whether they work in the Far East, in the Land of the Two Rivers (Mesopotamia), in Egypt, Yucatan, or Arizona: *stratigraphy*. That is the method of determining the age of remains from their stratification, in other words, developing their *calendar*. It sounds very simple. But even today, when atomic science and other sciences have furnished archaeologists with extremely precise methods for establishing dates, stratigraphy is the "university" of every archaeologist, in which every student must be trained with the utmost stringency and in which even the master is never done learning new things.

We shall have a great deal more to say about the art of stratigraphy later on. But it is worth noting here that this extraordinary man, Thomas Jefferson, not only indicated the basic features of the stratigraphic method, but also virtually named it, although a hundred years were to pass before the term became established in archaeological jargon. For in this classic paragraph he uses the word "stratum" for layer no less than six times. And this same scientific method had been put to a use that Jefferson could not have dreamed of. For Jefferson himself has been made the object of an archaeological excavation. Roland Wells Robbins, the enterprising American amateur archaeologist, began in 1954 looking for traces and remains of the long since vanished house where Jefferson was born. He found it and dug it up, utilizing the stratigraphic technique that had been devised by the man who played there as a child.

Under what heading should we classify his discovery, his method, the work of his spade at this Virginian mound? European historians of archaeology have not mentioned Jefferson at all, with one exception. This was Sir Mortimer Wheeler, director of several archaeological institutes and one of the most painstaking of diggers in England and India, who had this to observe:

"He describes the situation of the mound in relation to natural features and evidences of human occupation. He detects components of geological interest in its materials and traces their sources. He indicates the stratigraphical features of the skeletal remains. And he relates his evidence objectively to current theories." And we must repeat Wheeler's tribute: "No mean achievement for a busy states-man in 1784!" Wheeler is mistaken, however, about the year; it was three years earlier.

Jefferson had no idea how long ago the builders of these mounds had lived, or what kind of people they were. He knew that there were many such mounds, but he did not suspect that in the Mississippi and Ohio valleys alone thousands could be found—of the most bizarre shapes, frequently looking like animals, and of a kind unique in the world. But he had undoubtedly raised the most important question—the question of the *first American*. Where had the builders of these mounds come from? And the answer he gave was in principle the correct one: from Asia, by the northern route. But it took more than 150 years, during which the wildest theories were propounded, before we were able to prove conclusively that this was the answer to the question.

We must realize, however, that it was not the mounds—those strange architectonic testimonies to a mysterious past—that provoked the first questions on the part of the first Europeans. For North America was initially conquered not from the east, but from the south; not by the sons of the Pilgrim Fathers after 1620, but almost a hundred years earlier by the Spaniards who came up from Mexico. They encountered highly curious structures, but these did not interest them, for they were in search of gold. They discovered the Indian "skyscrapers" that they called "pueblos," but what they were looking for were more legendary places like the "Seven Cities of Cibola," where the streets were said to be paved with gold. With cross and sword they marched into the pueblos—and missed a unique opportunity. They could have extended the hand of friendship to a *prehistoric* people. Had they investigated instead of plundering they could have provided us with priceless information about an early culture (for they found pueblos that had been continuously inhabited for half a millennium). They did indeed extend a hand to those humble "heathen savages"—but that hand was dripping with blood.

Book One

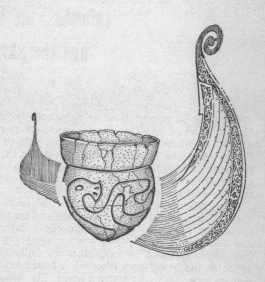

1

Columbus, the Vikings,
and the Skraelings

OCTOBER 12 is celebrated as a national holiday in the
United States of America. It is the anniversary of the day
in 1492 on which Columbus first caught sight of the "New
World." Since he thought he had reached India, he called
the inhabitants *Indios*—Indians. The name "America" was
conferred upon the new continent some time later, after the
traveler Amerigo Vespucci.

Many cities, a mountain, a river, a university, innumerable streets, movie theaters, and drugstores are named after
Columbus. Columbus Day is ordinarily a day of parades
and festivity. But never had the anniversary led to such
huge demonstrations as took place on Columbus Day in
1965. As the newspapers reported, a mammoth traffic jam
tied up New York City for five hours. The demonstrations
were conducted largely by Americans of Italian descent,
who turned out in droves to protest a theory that was far
from new, but had suddenly received fresh nourishment
and had to be taken seriously. For just two days before

36

Columbus Day, of all possible dates, the New York *Times* had published an article that infuriated these selfsame Italian-Americans by seeming to rob them of their claim to a Genoese Columbus. Yet the article, dated "New Haven, October 10," made no attempt at a sensational tone. It began with a simple statement:

"Yale University announced today 'the most exciting cartographic discovery of the century'—the only known pre-Columbian map of New World lands discovered by Leif Ericson in the 11th century." The map was reproduced alongside the article. There could be no doubt: in the upper left corner of the map the name "Vinland" was inscribed, and there is no longer any doubt today that this name referred to a part of North America. The Yale scholars had established the fact that this map was drawn "circa 1440," in other words fifty-two years before Columbus's voyage. And for dramatic effect these scholars had appointed Tuesday, October 12, as the day on which—according to the *Times*—they intended to present the map to the public for the first time. Little wonder that the Italian Historical Society of America considered this choice of date an affront and an act of sheer tastelessness.

Where had this extraordinary map suddenly come from? That the Vikings discovered North America some 500 years before Columbus has been in the schoolbooks for many decades. And there is a certain irony in the fact that some 10 million to 15 million Americans of Italian descent continue to dismiss the Viking voyages as a myth and go on celebrating Columbus's discovery every year. For, in the first place, it is not at all certain that Columbus was even an Italian, and, in the second place, it is a matter of sober history that Columbus did not so much as glimpse the *North* American continent, let alone set foot on it. He discovered only the islands off Central America. In fact, he did not even see South America until his third voyage in 1498. But a year before, on June 24, 1497, John Cabot of England had actually rediscovered North America. He had landed at Cape Bauld, Newfoundland, and sailed around Cape Race. He did not, as historians believed up to a few years ago, explore the coast of North America as far as Cape Hatteras. According to the most recent researches (as Admiral Samuel Eliot Morison has informed the author in a letter dated December 3, 1969), he found his time running short and had to turn back.

In any case, if anyone should be hailed as the discoverer

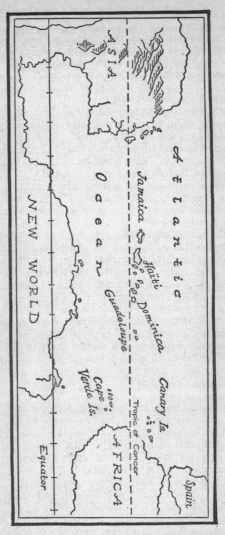

*The world as the contemporaries of Columbus saw it,
rendered from a map ascribed to Zorzi, circa 1503.
Columbus's mistaken belief that he had discovered
India prevails here: the "New" World is shown attached to Asia.*

of North America (aside from the Vikings and obscure later explorers), that man is certainly Cabot, not Columbus. To further compound the irony, Italian pride is in no way compromised by this acknowledgment. For John Cabot's real name was Giovanni Caboto and he was undoubtedly an Italian who was merely employed by the English.

As far as Columbus's descent is concerned, there are many obscurities. It was probable that he was born in Genoa, but it is by no means certain that his parents were Italians. The first event we hear of in connection with him is his participation, probably at the age of fourteen, in a naval battle off Cape St. Vincent, Portugal—and here he fought on the side of the Portuguese against Genoa! The name he gave himself was always Colón, which is distinctly Spanish; he never used the Italian form Colombo. Moreover, among all his writings there is not a single line in Italian. Even his letters to his brothers and to Genovese officials are written in Spanish, and his brothers also called themselves by the Spanish names Bartolomé and Diego. There is even a theory, though the evidence for it is rather weak, that he was the son of Spanish Jews who fled to Italy from the Inquisition's persecutions then raging in Spain.

But let us be careful: none of all this is certain, and these remarks are not intended to rob our schoolbooks and the Italian Historical Society of America of their Columbus. Even though he never saw the North American continent and believed until the end of his life that he had discovered India, the fact remains that he and no other inaugurated the "Age of Discovery." To that extent his accomplishment stands far above that of the Vikings in the history of our civilization. In order to clarify this matter we must say something here about these "Northmen." But now a last word about Columbus, to make it clear why we begin a book on "the first American" with him. Columbus was—and this, alas, is undeniable—the first slave hunter on the outlying islands of the American continent. The most deprecating thing that has been said about him is that he introduced slavery to America and syphilis to Europe. (Syphilis was a relatively mild disease in Central America. It became a frightful plague only after it had been imported into Europe by Columbus's sailors.) But at the same time he was also the first man to institute really careful studies of the country and its inhabitants. In fact, he went about this task so thoroughly that Edward Gaylord Bourne, the American anthropologist, in a lecture in 1906, called him "the founder of American anthropology." Perhaps Bourne was being somewhat excessively enthusiastic. Still, this side of Columbus, which is highly pertinent to our subject, is so little known that it calls for an example. The following quotation comes from the *Historie* of Columbus's son Ferdinand, who quotes his father "in the very words of the Admiral."

"I have taken pains to learn what they believe and if they know where they go after death; especially from Caunabo, who is the chief king in Española, a man of years, of great knowledge and very keen mind; and he and others replied that they go to a certain valley which every principal Cacique believes is situated in his own country, affirming that there they find their father and all their ancestors; and that they eat and have women and give themselves to pleasures and recreation as is more fully contained in the following account in which I ordered one Friar Roman (Ramon) who knew their language to collect all their ceremonies and their antiquities although so much of it is fable that one cannot extract anything fruitful from it beyond the fact that each one of them has a certain natural regard for the future and believes in the immortality of our souls."[1]

Such words on the part of Columbus, and the report of the above-mentioned cleric, Ramon Pane, may well have contributed to the extraordinary haste with which their Catholic majesties and the Church declared the Indians "human beings." For incredible though it may sound today, since the Bible made no mention of the existence of a "redskinned" people, there was serious doubt that they were human at all.

Back to the Vinland map. The discovery of this map was the outcome of pure chance. As Thomas E. Marston of Yale University has recorded: "In October, 1957 the antiquarian bookseller Laurence Witten, of New Haven, showed to my colleague Alexander O. Vietor and myself a slim volume, bound in recent calf, which contained a map of the world, including Iceland, Greenland, and Vinland, and a hitherto unknown account of the mission of John de Plano Carpini to the Mongols in 1245–47. Mr. Witten told us that he had acquired it from a private collection in Europe."[2]

The manuscript of the travels to the Mongols, the "Tartar

Relation," need not concern us here. The scholars labored over the map for some eight years. Then they proceeded to their dramatic publication shortly before Columbus Day. What aroused particular excitement was the text in the upper left section of the map: "By God's will, after a long voyage from the island of Greenland to the south toward the most distant remaining parts of the western ocean sea, sailing southward amidst the ice, the companions Bjarni and Leif Eiriksson discovered a new land, extremely fertile and even having vines, the which island they named Vinland."

In his foreword to the 1965 edition of *The Vinland Map* Vietor writes: "The Vinland Map contains the earliest known and indisputable cartographic representation of any part of the Americas, and includes a delineation of Greenland so strikingly accurate that it may well have been derived from experience. If, as Mr. Skelton supposes, this part of the map originated in the North, and probably in Iceland, it represents the only surviving medieval example of Norse cartography. These conclusions, if accepted, have far-reaching implications for the history of cartography and of the Viking navigations."

"If accepted" are the key words. Could there still be doubts after an eight-year examination of the map? Vietor adds the proviso: "In the absence of an unbroken record of their history, there can be no absolute and unassailable demonstration that they are not counterfeit." But he also says, "All tests that would not involve damage or destruction of the manuscript have been applied," and then he states his deep conviction (and that of his colleagues) that the map with its clear coastal contours is genuine, that it was made around 1440 and was evidently based on still older sources.

There is sound reason for scholars to move with extreme caution especially in the field of Viking research. For it was a forgery (or was it not, after all?) that once created the first great sensation in this field and gave rise to a scientific dispute that went on for decades: the so-called Kensington Stone.

Although the fact that the Vikings reached America before Columbus had already been accepted in the last century, this thesis rested upon the Old Norse sagas, which were passed on orally and not set down in writing until the thirteenth century.

There was therefore a sensation when a new "document" was suddenly added to these sagas, a testimony literally in stone that Northmen had been on the North American continent long before Columbus.

Toward the end of 1898 a farmer named Olof Ohman, a Swedish immigrant, found a large hewn stone under an aspen near Kensington, Minnesota. The stone was about two and a half feet long, sixteen inches wide and five or six inches thick. It looked like a gravestone. The farmer's ten-year-old son was the first to recognize that the stone bore peculiar lettering. A neighbor was called in to examine it, and there began the discussion about the Kensington Stone that has continued to this day, and in which people from all countries—specialists and even more laymen, the qualified and the unqualified—have passionately participated. For the writing on the stone proved to be Norse runic script and was quickly deciphered. It read:

"8 Swedes and 22 Norwegians on an exploration journey from Vinland westward. We had camp by 2 rocky islets one day's journey north of this stone. We were out fishing one day. When we came home, we found 10 men red with blood and dead. AVM [probably an abbreviation for *Ave, Virgo Maria*] save us from evil. We have 10 men by the sea to look after our ships, 14 days' journey from this island. Year 1362."

From the very first, opinion was radically and irreconcilably divided. One side maintained forcefully that the stone was a forgery; the other side held with equal forcefulness that it was genuine. The controversy evoked a rash of stories about the Viking landings. Wild exercises in imagination went into providing "proofs." The affair went so far that in 1965 Lawrence Steefel, professor of history at the University of Minnesota (and thus very close to the scene of the find), commented that the whole affair reminded him of Mark Twain's method. "In his preface to 'A Horse's Tale' the great humorist writes: 'Along through the book, I have distributed a few anachronisms and unborn historical incidents and such things, to help the tale over the difficult places. The idea is not original with me; I got it out of Herodotus. Herodotus says—at least Mark Twain says so —"Very few things happen at the right time, and the rest do not happen at all: The conscientious historian will correct these defects." ' "[3]

Without going into the detailed and often highly acute arguments on both sides, we may refer the reader who wishes further information to a number of recent books

In 1841 America's now classic schoolbook poet, Henry Wadsworth Longfellow, wrote a ballad entitled "The Skeleton in Armor." It was based on reports that a skeleton in full armor had been found in Fall River, Massachusetts, ten years earlier. The bones were thought to be those of a Viking. The ballad also suggested that the so-called Newport Tower in Rhode Island had been built by the Northmen in pre-Columbian times. The skeleton has vanished, but the tower still occasionally comes up for discussion. Out of these elements Longfellow fashioned a romantic ballad of a kidnaped bride, twenty stanzas in length. Here are three of them.

SPEAK! speak! thou fearful guest!
Who, with thy hollow breast
Still in rude armor drest,
    Comest to daunt me!
Wrapt not in Eastern balms,
But with thy fleshless palms
Stretched, as if asking alms,
    Why dost thou haunt me?

I was a Viking old!
My deeds, though manifold,
No Skald in song has told,
    No Saga taught thee!
Take heed, that in thy verse
Thou dost the tale rehearse,
Else dread a dead man's curse;
    For this I sought thee.

Three weeks we westward bore,
And when the storm was o'er,
Cloud-like we saw the shore
    Stretching to leeward;
There for my lady's bower
Built I the lofty tower,
Which, to this very hour,
    Stands looking seaward.

that present the pros and cons of the matter and vigorously advocate one side or the other. On the pro side is the work of Hjalmar Rued Holand, who became owner of the stone in 1907 and subsequently devoted almost his entire life to defending its authenticity. He has written several books about it, the most important being, by his own statement, *A Pre-Columbian Crusade to America.* Author of the leading contra book is Erik Wahlgren, professor of Scandinavian languages at the University of California (of Scandinavian descent himself, he subordinates national loyalty to science). Its title is *The Kensington Stone: A Mystery Solved.*

The present situation is this: by far the greater number of scholars in the field consider the Kensington Stone a forgery. They do not believe it dates to the year 1362 but to the late nineteenth century. Their arguments are good and persuasive. But—and this must be mentioned—they are based on circumstantial evidence. What might be called *juridical* proof of the forgery has not been offered even by a scholar so thorough as Wahlgren, for he, too, has not been able to answer the questions: *Who* forged the stone and *why?* And it remains highly interesting to reflect upon the whys, the possible motivations for such a forgery.

Whatever the truth of this matter, today we are in the happy position of being able to file this dispute away. For we can now actually prove by archaeological methods that Vikings landed and settled in North America before Columbus and Cabot. But first of all let us take a brief glance at what the sagas have to tell us.

The Vikings do not conform to any of our preconceived ideas about the rise and fall of a "culture" or a "high civilization." They were a piratical people for whom clan represented the highest of loyalties. Using superior ships and armed with excellent weapons, they sailed the seas and rivers—westward to America, southward to Sicily, eastward down the whole length of the Volga River. Wherever they turned up, cities burned, blood flowed, and corpses lined their path. Their deeds became legendary in their lifetimes and for several centuries were related at all the hearth fires in northern Europe until they were at last written down in the form we know as "sagas," which tell of the marvelous adventures that took place around A.D. 1000.

These sagas are told with remarkable dryness. They tend to be a listing of facts. There is not a trace of Homeric exuberance in them. The characters are treated with little heroic exaltation. There is no attempt to conceal their human weaknesses. Thus we learn, for example, that the Vikings in Iceland would accept being baptized only in the hot springs because they—Vikings, of all people—"hated cold water." Or we hear that Eirik the Red, when he returned home to Iceland from a newly discovered island that he wanted to settle in the next few years, reported that he had discovered Greenland; moreover that he gave this name to a land almost entirely covered with ice in order to make it "more attractive" to future settlers. The trick is still commonly practiced by real-estate agents.

The sagas that especially concern us are *The Greenlander's Saga* and *Eirik the Red's Saga*, for they describe the discovery of America and the Northmen's first contact with the aboriginal inhabitants—or, as the sagas put it, the discovery of "Vinland," Wineland.

It is important to realize that this discovery, quite unlike Columbus's, proceeded in a series of jumps, as it were. The starting point was Norway, and the successive jumps took the explorers to the Faeroe Islands, Iceland, and Greenland. The first Northman to see Greenland was probably a Viking named Gumbjörn, who had been driven westward of his course by bad weather. The first to settle in Greenland was Eirik the Red. He established himself on a bay that was called Eiriksfjord; his main farm was Brattalid. Today two main areas of Viking settlement have been studied closely. They are known simply as Western Settlement and Eastern Settlement. The latter is unfortunately named, for although it is slightly to the east of the Western Settlement it is still entirely on the western side of Greenland, directly west of Cape Farewell, Greenland's southern tip.

Eirik the Red had come to Greenland because he had been banished from Iceland for several manslaughters. His son Leif spent his early years in Norway and returned to Greenland bearing a royal command to Christianize the settlers. He succeeded very well with his mother (she built the first church in the Western Hemisphere), but not at all well with his father, who called the priests Leif had brought with him good-for-nothings and "men of mischief."

For the existence of Greenland settlements we have archaeologically verified facts; the remains of this first church were excavated by the Danish archaeologist Knud Krogh and others, and in 1967 newspapers throughout the world published pictures of the skeletons found there. Undoubtedly they are the skeletons of Vikings who lived there and set out from Greenland to discover America. It is scarcely surprising that someone immediately asserted that one of the skeletons must be that of Leif, the voyager to America, who returned home after his discovery and died there.

It was Leif who, according to the sagas, first discovered

the "New World" after it had been previously sighted by another man, Bjarne Herjolfsson. With thirty-five men, among them a "southlander"—probably a German, or at least a German-speaking man—named Tyrkir, Leif sailed westward in A.D. 1000 on a voyage of exploration. He came first to a stony coast, for which reason he called the country "Helluland" (Flatstone Land), present-day Baffin Land. Sailing southward, he discovered a richly wooded coast and called the land "Markland" (Woodland), present-day Labrador. Continuing on to the south, he reached a country which—but the name he gave it deserves a more detailed account. After the Vikings had arrived in this third region, it seemed to them so beautiful and fruitful that they stayed, built houses, and soon went on further explorations inland. One day the "German," the man named Tyrkir, was missed. Leif set out to look for him. He had not searched long when Tyrkir came staggering toward him. He made faces and behaved foolishly; in short, he acted as if he were drunk. Asked the meaning of his behavior, he offered an astonishing piece of news: he had found wine grapes. He was highly indignant when his companions doubted his story. After all, he said, he had been born in a southern country where the vine was cultivated! Leif thereupon named the country Vinland. Whether or not he had found wine grapes, Tyrkir must have been a wag. For no one has ever managed to get drunk by eating grapes. But more of that later.

At any rate, the name "Vinland" has provoked a scholarly controversy that has gone on for decades.

For wild grapes do not grow in America as far north as the latitude where even doubtful critics concede the possibility that the Vikings may have landed. Grapes are restricted to areas much farther south, in the latitude of Massachusetts. Hence Vinland was localized by ingenious arguments—although nobody could offer so much as a shred of proof—all the way along the eastern coast of America as far south as Florida. What was needed, after all the disputation, was a man who would subject the ancient accounts to close and unbiased examination once more, conducting research rather than just theorizing. That man came along.

He came, as Count Eric Oxenstierna, Viking specialist, later phrased it, "with the vigor of the pioneer and adventurer, with keen and concrete insight."[4] A tall white-maned

Norwegian named Helge Ingstad, his first step seemed neither pioneering nor adventurous. For he rode in an ordinary bus from New York to Rhode Island and began his search by taking a walk.

Helge Ingstad had already done research in Greenland and had formed his first theories there on the probable position of Vinland. When in 1950 he equipped his first expedition to search for remains of Viking settlements along the coast of North America (up to 1964 he undertook five expeditions in which he was joined by scientists from five countries), he was ridiculed in official scholarly circles—the general fate of pioneers. Searching for possibly one single settlement along a coastal strip more than 1,500 miles long was compared to looking for a needle in a haystack. Yet even his modest bus ride to Rhode Island produced a result. For in a long since abandoned coal borehole he found a piece of anthracite that compared precisely in quality with a specimen that archaeologists had found deep in the lowest stratum of a house on Greenland—the house that had belonged to the Viking Torfinn Karlsefni, who lived there around A.D. 1000. This piece of coal had been a mystery to the scientists, for there is no anthracite on Greenland. Had Torfinn brought it from Rhode Island? Why not?

But Ingstad was not hunting at random, as many people imagined. He had a plan, and from the start had been aiming at Newfoundland. For he had once again scrutinized the word "Vinland," and had asked with the openmindedness of a man without preconceived theories: Must Vinland necessarily mean "Wineland"?

What is more, he found so many contradictions in the sagas, especially Tyrkir's obviously dubious story about the "wine," that he was prompted to observe (and was the first to do so) and to demonstrate that wine can also be made from the so-called squash berry, which grows far to the north along the coast of America, and also from the currant. In fact, the currant is actually called *vinbär* (wine berry) in Scandinavian. But Ingstad went a crucial step further. He expressed general doubt that *vin* meant wine at all. He showed that *vin* had been used since the most ancient times in the figurative sense, meaning simply "rich land," "fruitful land," "land of meadows and pastures." In the fruitful parts of Norway and Denmark there are many localities whose names contain the prefix "vin," although wine had never grown in those parts.

Slowly Ingstad worked his way north, often accompanied by his wife Anne Stine and his daughter Benedicte. At times he sailed in his own boat, which had been designed by the same shipbuilder who had built Fridtjof Nansen's famous polar ship, the *Fram*. By way of Cape Cod and Boston Ingstad sailed up the coast as far as Maine and Nova Scotia. Nowhere did he find the conditions that would have

The voyages of the Vikings around A.D. 1000. The map shows that, unlike Columbus, they reached the New World by a succession of leaps from island to island.

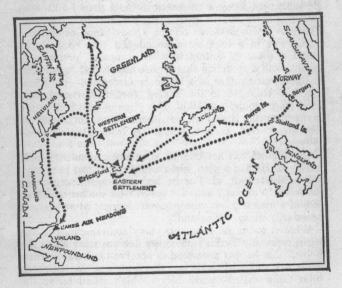

fully corresponded with the descriptions in the sagas—until he reached Newfoundland.

We cannot go into details on his many years of painstaking work. To conclude the Vinland problem it is sufficient to say briefly: on the northern tip of Newfoundland, near the tiny fishing village that bears the curious name L'Anse aux Meadows, he found ruins that were clearly not those of Indian or Eskimo settlements. Nor were they the work of late whalers. The name of the village is half French and half English and means "The Bay by the Meadows." This name, although it appears on maps only since the nineteenth century, corresponds to the description of the landing site given in the sagas.

Ingstad dug up the foundations of eight houses of varying sizes, a smithy and a charcoal kiln. The so-called "long house" had several rooms and was of considerable size, no less than sixty-five by fifty feet. Although very few objects were found, what there were proved to be highly interesting archaeologically. Worked iron (produced from bog iron, which is found in lumps close to the surface of the ground) was dug up; it had been obtained from the ore by a smelting process unknown to either Indians or Eskimos, but familiar to the Scandinavians. There was copper used in an alloy also unknown to the natives of America, who merely hammered copper. And most important of all—this find was made only on the last expedition, and the archaeologists threw their arms around one another, so overwhelmed with joy were they—there was a small spindle wharve of soapstone of a type characteristic of Greenland and Norway.

No fewer than twelve radiocarbon datings (or C-14 datings, as they are also called; see Chapter 8) were obtained from the bits of charcoal that had been found. All these gave approximately the same date: around A.D. 1000 —the very same date ascribed in the sagas to Leif's expedition.

There no longer seems to be any doubt that the "long house" had been Leif Erikson's house. From that house Leif had gone out on hunting and fishing expeditions. At the fireplace (whose precise location the archaeologists established) he had sat evenings and told his men stories of those deeds that had passed from mouth to mouth to Greenland, Iceland, and Norway, where they were ultimately forged into the sagas. He had finally rented this house to a kinsman when he himself returned to Greenland to die in his native land. And then one day, as excessive charcoal remains prove, the big house went up in flames. Had it already been abandoned? Had natives burned it down? We do not know.

Helge Ingstad, the lucky modern descendant of those Vikings and discoverer of their traces, treats the matter with a scientist's caution, for he sums up his findings in the following manner:

"To judge by all the material available to us, it is probable that the Northmen who stayed in L'Anse aux Meadows about a thousand years ago are identical with the Vinland voyagers of the Icelandic sagas. It is also probable that it was there that Leif Erikson built his 'big house.' We must assume that the Vinland of the saga was northernmost Newfoundland."[5]

An impatient reader may ask at this point when we are coming to real archaeology in America, whose story our book promises to tell. First of all, in describing the Jefferson and Ingstad excavations we have already given two examples. In the second place, we need this background because American archaeology (or rather, archaeology in America) exists in a remarkable state of dependence. Entirely unlike

A Viking battling a Greenland "pygmy." This rendering of a drawing by Olaus Magnus (16th century) is a product of pure fantasy.

archaeology in Europe it is a subdivision of anthropology —the science of man in general—whereas archaeology in Europe began as a science of monuments and written documents, and archaeologists generally think of their science as a subdivision of history.

Because of this peculiarity of archaeology in America— that it is linked with anthropology—we must begin with the first human encounters, which awakened archaeological interest only at a much later period. When we briefly discussed Columbus, we quoted the statement of the overenthusiastic scholar who called Columbus the first American anthropologist because he at any rate promptly took account of the manners and morals of the aboriginals. And if we are to compare Columbus with the Vikings, as is the fashion nowadays, we must ask: What did these bold sea-farers and first settlers have to say about the aboriginals? The answer is: remarkably little. They gave them a strange name, Skraelings, and what they relate is somewhat unclear and not very pleasant.

After Leif there came to America Torvald Eriksson, Torfinn Karlsefni, and a demonic woman named Fröydis. An expedition organized by Torstein Eriksson failed

Leif's brother Torvald sailed to Newfoundland in Leif's ship, wintered in Leif's houses, and made several expeditions. One day the Vikings came upon three boats drawn up on the sand and overturned. Nine men were hiding under them. The Vikings forthwith fell upon these men and slaughtered them; only one escaped. This incomprehensible act can be explained only as a manifestation of their characters; certainly there was no reason for it, and it bore bad fruit. A "countless fleet of skin-boats" attacked the Vikings and showered a hail of arrows upon them. One of the arrows struck under Torvald's arm into his chest. He pulled it out, delivered a brief speech to his comrades urging them to return home, and died.

The death of Torvald probably occurred around A.D. 1007. About 1020 Torfinn Karlsefni, a Viking who had come to Greenland from Norway, set out on another Vinland voyage. He sailed with sixty men, five women, and many head of cattle (the figures vary in the different accounts, but at any rate this seems to have been the largest expedition and one obviously bent on long-range settlement), spent the winter in Leif's house, and in the following summer also had an encounter with the Skraelings. The cattle began to bellow when the first Skraeling emerged from the forest. That frightened the Skraelings so much that they fled in panic, not back into the forest, but trying to find refuge in the nearby Viking houses. But the houses were guarded. The details are unclear, but instead of a fight there was a friendly meeting and even bartering. At first all that the Skraelings wanted were the Vikings' marvelous weapons, but when these were refused they contented themselves with milk, which they drank with great relish. In return they gave mainly furs.

Nevertheless, Karlsefni was mistrustful and built palisades around his house. At this time a son was born to him —*the first white American*. We even know his name: Snorre.

The Skraelings came back. This time there were more of

them, and they were more obstreperous. When one tried to steal a weapon, one of Karlsefni's warriors killed him. The Vikings immediately made preparations for battle, for they now expected attacks. In Professor Gwyn Jones's version of the saga the account runs: "The Skraelings advanced to the spot Karlsefni had fixed on for battle, battle was joined, and many fell from among the Skraelings' host. There was one big, fine-looking man in the Skraeling host who Karlsefni imagined must be their chief. One of the Skraelings had picked up an axe, he stared at it for a while, then swung at a comrade of his and cut at him. He fell dead on the instant, whereupon the big man caught hold of the axe, stared at it for a while, then flung it as far out over the water as he could. After which they fled to the forest, each as best he might, and that was the end of their encounter."[6]

According to the *Greenlander's Saga* Karlsefni was in Vinland for two years; according to the *Eirik the Red's Saga* for three years.

The last Vinland voyage that the *Greenlander's Saga* relates was undoubtedly the most dramatic. The story centers around the viciousness of the woman Fröydis. Her husband was evidently a man of weak character, for it was she who persuaded two brothers from Norway, who had come to Greenland just after Karlsefni's return, to join in the adventurous voyage to Vinland. And so they sailed to Newfoundland, where soon after their arrival Fröydis started a quarrel with the brothers. She wanted to have the brothers' larger ship. One night she visited the two brothers, deliberately half dressed. She wakened them from sleep and talked peaceably about the ships with the two surprised men. Then she returned home to her husband. Again in Jones's version: "She climbed into bed with her cold feet, and at this Torvald woke, and asked why she was so cold and wet. She answered in a passion, 'I have been to those brothers,' she said, 'asking to buy their ship—I wanted to buy a bigger one. But they took it so badly that they beat me, maltreated me—and you, wretch that you are, will avenge neither my shame nor your own! I can see now that I am not back home in Greenland, but I shall separate from you unless you take vengeance for this.'

"He could not endure this baiting of hers. He ordered his men to turn out immediately and take their weapons, which they did, and crossed straightway to the brothers' house and marched in on the sleeping men, seized them and bound them, then led them outside, each man as he was bound. And Fröydis had each man killed as he came out. Now all the men were killed, but the women were left, and no one would kill them.

" 'Hand me an axe,' said Fröydis.

"Which was done, and she turned upon the five women they had there, and left them dead."

A gruesome tale. The survivors returned home. Although Fröydis bribed her men to silence, one of them proved unable to conceal the crime. Leif extracted the truth from the others under torture. And Fröydis was outlawed.

This bloody story has been retold here only because it apparently marked the end of the Vinland voyages, at least as far as they are recorded in the sagas. This Fröydis episode tells us nothing about the matter that is important to our purposes—the natives.

What, then, were the Skraelings?

If we were to assemble all the astute explanations that have been propounded in recent decades, it would fill a thick volume. If we cite only what the sagas actually tell us, it would fill barely a page.

Actually, the problem has not been solved. The question is a simple one, but of extraordinary interest to anthropologists and ethnologists: Were the Skraelings Indians or Eskimos?

Their appearance is described as follows: "They were black, ugly men and had shaggy hair on their heads. They had large eyes and broad faces."[7]

During one of his voyages to the north Karlsefni had come upon five sleeping Skraelings and with Viking consistency had killed them. He found in their possession wooden containers filled with a mixture of blood and bone marrow. This is a known Eskimo delicacy, but Ingstad maintains that North Canadian Indians also use this article of food. The arrows that were shot at the Vikings rather suggest that the Skraelings were Indians.

The word itself explains nothing, although similar words occur in Norwegian and Icelandic: *scraela* = scream, or *scraelna* = shrink. Thus the name might be humorously translated "screaming shrunken heads," but this would still not give us the slightest clue to tribal identity. The simplest assumption is that the Vikings made no distinction whatsoever between Indians and Eskimos and called every native they met a Skraeling.

That question must remain open. So, for the present,

must the other question of how many Vikings reached America during the following centuries—or whether any did at all. (After all, the Vikings remained settled on Greenland for some 500 years before they mysteriously disappeared.) Yet history tends to show that scientific discoveries occur in curious waves. Thus it is highly likely that the "Vikings in America" problem, which has suddenly received new impetus in the past decade, will have new and surprising lights thrown upon it in the near future.

At present, however, we can only say that the landings of the Vikings in America, interesting as they are from many points of view, *did not change Western man's view of the world or have any effect on his economic patterns.* That was accomplished by Columbus. That was accomplished by the Spaniards who were destined to conquer the North American continent by moving up from the south. In the following chapters, therefore, we shall speak of these explorers.

In view of this, then, Leif's brother Torvald may have been something of a seer when he pulled the arrow from his fatal wound and spoke his last words. He said, "I notice I have put fat on my body. We have found a fruitful land, but we shall have little joy of it!"[8]

2

The Seven Cities of Cibola

ONLY one influential man in early America stood up and accused the conquerors of the monstrous crimes they had committed against the Red Man. He was Bishop Bartolomé de las Casas, who in 1552 wrote his *A Relation of the First Voyages and Discoveries Made by the Spaniards in America with an Account of their unparallel'd Cruelties on the Indians.*

This man alone acknowleged the Indians as fellow human beings with equal rights, recognized their virtues, respected their traditions, and observed their independent culture, which was—at least in the Aztec empire of Mexico and the Inca empire of Peru—in many respects higher and more refined than that of the conquistadors, who were bad representatives of their country and their church.

The conquistadors had followed hard upon Columbus, the discoverer. Starting in 1519 Hernando Cortés with a handful of heavily armed cavalrymen had in two years destroyed the flourishing realm of the Aztec Emperor Montezuma ("like a passer-by who thoughtlessly strikes off the head of a sunflower," Spengler remarks) and robbed it of fabulous treasures. Francisco Pizarro seized no less gold when he shattered Atahualpa's Inca empire in 1533. Under the sign of the cross the governors appointed by the Spanish crown killed and looted on an inconceivable scale.

Las Casas (1474–1566), who was an eyewitness to these atrocities for forty years, remarks of the Indians: "They are a weak effeminate *People,* not capable of enduring great fatigues; they care not to be expos'd to toil and Labour, and their Life is of no long continuance; their constitution is so nice, that a small fit of sickness carries 'em off." What, he goes on to ask, do the Spaniards do with these people? They baptize them first, then enslave them and send them chained—men, women and chlidren—into the fields and the mines. "The Almighty seems to have inspir'd these People with a weakness and softness of Humour like that of Lambs: and the *Spaniards* who have given 'em so much Trouble, and fallen upon 'em so fiercely, resemble savage Tigers, Wolves, and Lions, when inraged with pressing Hunger. They applied themselves forty years together wholly to the massacring the poor wretches that inhabited the Islands; putting them to all kinds of unheard of torments and punishments . . . insomuch that this Island which before the arrival of the Europeans, contained about three millions of People, is now reduc'd to less than three hundred. . . . We dare assert, without fear of incurring the reproach of exaggerating, that in the space of forty years

Rendering of an illustration on a petition for better treatment addressed by Mexican Indians in 1570 to the Spanish government, which had already caused millions of Indians to be killed.

in which the *Spaniards* exercised their intolerable tyranny in this new world, they unjustly put to death above twelve Millions of People, counting Men, Women, and Children. ...

"They laid Wagers with one another, who should cleave a Man down with his Sword most dexterously at one blow; or who should take his Head from his Shoulders most cleverly; or who should run a Man through after the most artificial manner: they tore away Children out of their Mothers arms, and dash'd out their brains against the rocks. ...

"They set up Gibbets, and hang'd up thirteen of these poor Creatures in honour to Jesus Christ and his twelve Apostles (as they blasphemously expressed themselves): They kindled a great Fire under these Gibbets, to burn those they had hang'd upon them. ... If at any time a *Spaniard* either touched with the Sentiment of Compassion, or prompted with those of Avarice, thought fit to spare one of these poor wretches [children] for his own Service: another would come transported with Rage, and fall upon him in his presence, and either run him through the Body, or cut off his Legs, so as to render him unserviceable. ... One day there came to us a great number of the Inhabitants of a famous City ... to complement us, and bring us all sorts of Provisions and Refreshments. ... But that evil Spirit that possess'd the *Spaniards* put 'em into such a sudden Fury against 'em, that they fell upon 'em and massacr'd above 3000 of 'em, both Men and Women, upon the spot, without having receiv'd the least offence or provocation from 'em. I was an Eye-witness of this Barbarity. ... Among other things they strung up more than two hundred Indians merely to escape the cruelties of a single Spaniard—well known to me—who was the worst among all these other barbarians."[1] (Industrious research has determined this barbarian's name, which las Casas does not give: Roderigue Albuquerque.)

A persecuted cacique (chieftain) named Hatuey performed an act of macabre symbolism. When he realized that he could scarcely escape, he gathered the remnants of his men together and asked them why the Spaniards were so cruel. It was not, he said, because they were by nature malignant, and wicked, "but they have a god whom they worship and whom we also ought to worship with all our might. ... Behold, he said—pointing to a basket full of gold and gems that stood beside him—this is the Christians' god! If it seems well to you, let us perform *areytos* [dances or ballet figures] in his honor. Perhaps he will be merciful to us and command the Christians to do no harm to us. Joyfully, they all cried: Very well, very well! And at once they danced before the god until they were all tired. Now Hatuey said: Behold if we keep him with us, they will take him away from us anyhow, no matter what we do, and will kill us afterwards. Let us rather throw him into that river."

And so they buried the Christian god—gold—in the river. Needless to say, Hatuey was in fact slain by the Spaniards.

The Spanish historians have made strenuous efforts to present las Casas as a liar. They maintain he was insane, a dangerous demagogue, a victim of delusions. As late as 1963 the respected historian R. M. Pidal called him "a megalomaniacal paranoiac." During his lifetime las Casas was at one time persecuted, then won several spurious victories for his Indians from Ferdinand V and Charles V, then was persecuted again. He was the most magnificent of all Don Quixotes, and an obstinate, bitterly intent seeker after justice. Perhaps some of his figures will not hold water. But recent non-Spanish research has established that in the period of the conquest between 15 million and 19 million Indians were exterminated. Though none of the figures may be exact, the fact remains: there were millions.

And one sole motive lay behind this greatest mass slaughter in the history of mankind: greed for gold. That quest for gold emanated directly from Spain, for the Crown was hopelessly in debt. Avarice transformed honest and stalwart men, who had perhaps only intended to undertake peaceful colonization, into utter monsters the moment they set foot in the New World. How had Cortés arrogantly put it when the governor wanted to assign him land for colonization? "I have come to win gold, not to plow the fields like a peasant!"

The crimes described by las Casas took place in Central America as well. The search for gold became the subject of myth. "El Dorado" was one such mythification and mystification that lured men to the south. To the adventurers who kept pouring out of the ships, this land of gold seemed a tangible reality. When Pizarro found enough gold in the land of the Incas to fill an entire room, even Peru did not seem the authentic, ultimate Dorado—and others went on searching for it. They continued right on down to the eighteenth century. It is scarcely surprising that soon after Cortés's conquest of the resplendent Aztec cities with their temples and palaces, men's eyes turned expectantly to the north. No one had any idea of what might lie to the north of Mexico—not even the Mexican Indians, as it turned out. Were there deserts, mountains, fruitful land, a continent, or an endless ocean? Why not more palaces and temples? And once again tropically overheated imaginations combined to produce a wishful fantasy: there, in the unexplored north, must lie the legendary *"Seven Cities of Cibola,"* where the streets were paved with gold and the doors of the lofty houses studded with precious gems.

The name "Cibola" also appears in the forms Ceuola or Cevola. Strangely enough, the Spaniards brought this myth of the Seven Cities with them from Europe. The story went that in the eighth century a bishop, fearing the approach of the Arabs, fled from Lisbon westward across the sea to a land where he founded seven flourishing cities. This tale was paralleled by a possibly equally old Indian legend from Mexico and Central America, a story of "Seven Caves," from which a number of tribes derived their origin. In one of the numerous early "Histories," the word "Chico-muxtoque" occurs. It is formed from the Nahuatl word *chicomoztoc*, which means approximately "Seven Caves." These two myths became a detailed narrative and ultimately merged into what seemed to be an authentic account. Somewhere in the north it should be possible to find these cities. Did not such and such a soldier know a comrade who knew somebody who had already visited one of them? The Seven Cities of Cibola passed from mouth to mouth, from tavern to tavern; Cibola became the very symbol of gold, wealth, and power.

Later, a soldier who ought to have known better, a man named Pedro de Castañeda, who was in the service of the conquistador Coronado, provided the following description:

"In the year 1530, Nuño de Guzman, President of New Spain, at that time owned an Indian, one of the natives of the valley or valleys of Oxitipar, whom the Spaniards call Tejos. This Indian told him that he was the son of a trader deceased long ago, who, while his son was still a child, was wont to travel over the interior of the country in order to sell the handsome plumes that are used for headdresses by

HENRY NOYES PRATT
(1879–1944)

> *Where these low walls run fast to desert sand*
> *And roofs long vanished leave but brazen sky;*
> *Where winds unhindered sweep a barren land,*
> *A city's walls rose golden, wide-stepped, high.*
> *Where now the rattler waits in his scant shade*
> *Drowsing across the torrid noonday heat;*
> *A living people sought long crumbled gates*
> *Called by the drum's resurgent, sullen beat.*
> *Here sat the weavers; here the potters made*
> *Olla and urn, deft spun the patterned bowl;*
> *And in the pueblo's purple, square-cut shade*
> *The gamesters watched the carven pebbles roll.*
> *And now the walls are worn to sand, and lie*
> *Low-ridged beneath the vulture's lonely flight.*
> *Silence—Only the wild, thin, far-flung cry*
> *Of a coyote quavering on the desert night.*

—"The Seventh City of Cibola"

An anthology calls Pratt "one of the West's better-known poets." He was also a magazine editor and museum administrator. The poem may stand here as an example of how the newly discovered American past stimulated the imaginations of residents in the vicinity of such ruins.

the Indians. In exchange he brought home a large quantity of gold and silver, both metals being very common in that region. He added that once or twice he had himself accompanied his father, and had seen towns so large that he could compare them in size to Mexico and its suburbs. There were seven of these towns, and there were whole rows of streets inhabited by gold and silver workers. He said besides that in order to reach these seven towns it was necessary to cross a desert for forty days, where there was no vegetation except short grass about five inches in height, and that the direction was to the north between both oceans."[2]

There are innumerable mentions of Cibola in contemporary accounts. The first person to subject these references to careful scholarly analysis and actually to locate Cibola (no cities bursting with gold and silver, but in other respects extremely strange and remarkable) wrote some 350 years after the conquest. He was the subsequently famous Adolph F. Bandelier, the great pioneer in the anthropology and archaeology of the American Southwest. At the time Bandelier wrote his first detailed account, however, there was no American periodical that cared to publish it. Thus the first scholarly report on Cibola appeared in the *German* language—although in the United States. It was published by the New York *Staatszeitung* in 1885–86.[3]

But we shall return to Bandelier later. His sources were chiefly Spanish travel narratives, among them two concerning extraordinary adventures, which even in the extraordinary period of the Conquista created a sensation, stirred widespread restlessness, and for the first time introduced Westerners not only to the aboriginals of North America itself, but also to records of their history. De Vaca guessed at, Marcos saw, and Coronado later conquered the first age-old desert cities of the North American Indians—the mysterious *pueblos*.

The first white man to cross North America from east to west, from ocean to ocean—though not at its widest girth —was not a bloodthirsty conquistador who drove the Indians before him in yokes. Rather, he was driven, harried, for a time enslaved. His passage was, as one of his later biographers calls it, a "journey into darkness."[4] Yet his diaries were later to cast the first bright light upon a mysterious land.

This man, who bore the strange name of Cabeza de Vaca (which means "head of a cow") brought the Western world the first news of the mighty buffalo and the repulsive-looking gila monster. Above all, he was the first to bring back word that America widened out enormously to the north, in other words, that this land mass was evidently a continent. How many things must be hidden there. And, of course, the Seven Cities of Cibola!

De Vaca's journey is one of the most adventurous in all the history of exploration. It lasted for eight years, although it came about by accident. That is to say, these wanderings were undertaken with no conscious aim (aside from their first chapter, which soon proved a fiasco). If de Vaca had anything in mind during all those eight years, it was the determination to survive at all costs.

He had received his curious name from an ancestor in the thirteenth century, who was merely a humble cowherd at the time the King of Navarre was battling the Moors. This herdsman showed the King's troops a secret mountain path that would enable them to attack the enemy's rear, and in order to mark the path for the rest of the army he set up a cow's head on a pole. The King won the battle, the cowherd was rewarded, and henceforth the family was entitled to bear the name Cabeza de Vaca in memory of the cow's head.

Alvar Nuñez Cabeza de Vaca, our hero (one of the unjustly obscure heroes in the history of North American exploration, for his deeds have been overshadowed by the exploits of men like Coronado and de Soto), was the treasurer of an expedition headed by Panfilo de Narvaez, who set out like so many others to conquer part of the unknown world in the north. In April, 1528, de Narvaez's fleet reached the coast of Florida near what is now Tampa Bay. But Narvaez was not one of the great leaders who was destined to make an impact upon the history of the conquest. He was autocratic without being superior, cruel without being courageous, impetuous without being shrewd. In response to the vague report that somewhere in the north ruled a tribe rich in gold, he left his ships and set out with his small company to march through the country, with no intimation of the dangers involved. This is not the place to describe the failure of that senseless expedition. There 260 infantrymen and forty cavalrymen died slowly under the frightful hardships imposed by the Florida jungle. To this day it is scarcely possible to leave Highway 41 from Miami to Tampa without stumbling into the deadliest kind of wilderness. Just as chance has preserved for us the name of the Viking child Snorre, the first white child born in North America, chance has also preserved the name of the first Spaniard who lost his life on the way to the imaginary gold lands of the north: Juan Velasquez, who drowned while attempting to ford a river.

The ships did not follow the land party. When Narvaez's shrunken company at last reached the sea again, he had new ships built (an incredible feat, for only one of his men had any experience as a carpenter, and every single nail had to be forged by hand). In September this "fleet" put to sea. Narvaez kept putting in at bays and islands, where he would encounter Indians, some hostile, some friendly. The hardships the party endured are almost beyond description. Storms separated the ships, but they crossed the mouth of the Mississippi fourteen years before de Soto. At the end of October word went out that henceforth it was to be every man for himself. All the ships were scattered; no one knows how Narvaez and his companions came to their miserable deaths.

Among the survivors was Cabeza de Vaca. There now began the odyssey that was to make his name immortal. It seemed as if the party had undergone all the torments of hell on the march across Florida and during that incredible voyage in primitive boats. But what followed was even more terrible.

De Vaca was not alone. Cast ashore like some Crusoe on the coast of Texas, probably on Velasco Peninsula southwest of present-day Galveston, there were three other survivors with him, as ragged and hungry as he. They were Andres Dorantes, Alonso del Castillo Maldonado, and—surely the most remarkable of the four—the black man Estevanico, a Moor from Azamor. Apparently Dorantes' slave, he was destined to play an outstanding part in the later stages of the adventure.

Cabeza de Vaca, which means "head of a cow," soldier and adventurer, sometime slave and medicine man, was the first person to cross southern North America from east to west (from 1528 to 1536). Later on, one of de Vaca's fellow adventurers, the Moor Estevanico, led others to within sight of the legendary "Seven Cities of Cibola."

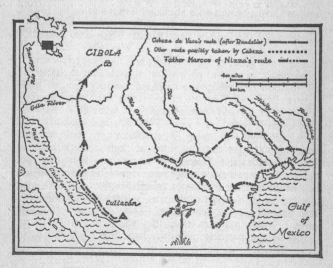

The four men were desperate, but they threw themselves resolutely into the fight for life. Perhaps they would not have done so, perhaps they would have simply lain down to die in the wilderness—starving as they were and with no aid in sight—had they ever suspected that their wanderings would go on for eight years. Would it have altered their feelings to know that after eight years they would win the glory of being the first Europeans to cross the continent of North America from Florida to California?

We can only touch on a few of the high points in this long journey. Many attempts have been made to trace it on the map (we give two examples here), but the chances of drawing up any conclusive cartographic account are slim, for de Vaca's descriptions of the landscape would fit many different places, and his distances are recorded by the extremely variable standard of a day's trek. Bandelier, the great anthropologist who traveled in de Vaca's footsteps during the 1880's, declares categorically: "I shall prove that Cabeza de Vaca and his companions never trod the soil of New Mexico, nor brought to New Spain direct information touching the Pueblo Indians of that territory. . . ."[5]

The castaways made contact with Indian tribes almost immediately. Some were friendly, some hostile. They met tribes with the widest variety of customs and languages—but all were miserably poor. The four companions were held as slaves, beaten with sticks, and made to do the lowest and hardest work; some of the Indians amused themselves plucking out the hair of their beards. Their only means of communication was sign language (for they seldom remained long with the same tribe), and the Moor Estevanico in particular was soon so good at this that an exchange of information became possible. Their fortunes changed constantly. Mistreated slaves in one tribe (for a while they belonged to a family whose members were all one-eyed), they made friends in the next. Two factors dominated their lives (although with some exceptions, as we shall see in a moment): hunger and the idea of flight, escape back to Spanish civilization. Game was scarce, and they were not experienced hunters or fishermen. Hence they were always dependent on their owners or friends. For months they kept alive by eating roots, earthworms, spiders, and lizards. Several times they fell terribly ill. They were covered with sores in which maggots bred; they shivered with fevers induced by the myriads of mosquitoes. But what was probably worst of all, they were separated, and this happened often. One of them would be lost while hunting for food; another would be given away as a slave to another tribe. And it was no doubt a miracle that they found each other again. Once Dorantes vanished for ten months. Castillo and the Moor were lost. Then the three came together, and finally de Vaca also rejoined them; by then they were already deep in the western part of Texas in the year 1534. The joy of such reunions for these poor, emaciated men cannot be described. Above all, it seems almost incredible that the spark which kept driving them on never went out completely. Through wilderness and desert they struggled on and on, never losing sight of their goal, convinced that sooner or later they must come across Spaniards again.

The Indians lived from hand to mouth. When their hunger was at its worst, they (and the four Spaniards with them) pinned their hope on the ripening of the prickly pear, the juicy fruit of the opuntia cactus. When it ripened at last, "the time of full bellies" had arrived. The fruit was nourishing; it could also be dried and preserved for a long time. The four men soon realized that only at the time of the ripening pears, when their bodies had somewhat recovered strength, could they possibly think of carrying out their carefully prepared flight to the west.

At this time two things took place, one that made their lives somewhat easier for a time at least, and the other actually assuring their return to civilization.

First and foremost, de Vaca managed to educate a friendly tribe to an appreciation of trade, primitive barter, with other tribes. He himself won respect as a trader, and henceforth was able to move about freely. Here are his own words:

"My stock consisted mainly of pieces of seashells and cockles, and shells with which they cut a fruit which is like a bean, used by them for healing and in their dances and feasts. This is of the greatest value among them, besides shell-beads and other objects. These things I carried inland, and in exchange brought back hides and red ochre with which they rub and dye their faces and hair; flint for arrow points, glue and hard canes wherewith to make them, and tassels made of the hair of deer, which they dye red. This trade suited me well. . . . I was not bound *to do anything* and *no longer a slave*."[6]

On one of these trading expeditions he found Dorantes

again—a slave. When the prickly pears ripened—they were then with the Mariames tribes and had already been wandering for six years—they worked out still another plan for flight. They arranged to meet outside the Indian camp in the dark of night. But Castillo did not come, and someone said that at the last minute he had been carried off to the Lampados tribe. The three lurked along the trail of the roving tribe; they succeeded in getting word to Castillo, and on the following night he joined them.

Then began the most astounding part of their eight-year ordeal, which was fraught with miracles, the greatest miracle of all being their survival.

In the past several years the four Spaniards had often spoken to the Indians of the great white God and his omnipotence, and the Indians had sometimes asked them to prove their God's power by having him heal their sick. This was an awkward situation, for none of the four had the slightest knowledge of medicine. In fact, they knew less about it than the native medicine men, who were familiar with many healing plants. In their perplexity they could think of nothing to do but pray. They made the sign of the cross over the patients and blew breath into them. And God helped, as de Vaca noted; he helped them again and again.

They reached the Chavavares Indians, who had already heard that there were three white men and one black who were great medicine men. Strangely, a great many of the Chavavares were suffering from frightful headaches. De Vaca made the sign of the cross over them, "and the Indians instantly felt relieved." Now, of course, both the centuries-old tradition of the Catholic Church and modern psychiatry agree that "miracles" or "faith-healings" are possible. The Church attributes them to God, the Virgin, or the saints, and modern science to the patient's own intense belief.

In any case, de Vaca repeatedly speaks of his trust in God, repeatedly thanks the Almighty, and evidently tried hard to remain humble in spirit. But he must have felt strange indeed when without an ounce of hope he had bent over a man who for days was clearly on the brink of death, made the sign of the cross over him in the slow, ceremonious way that, he had already discovered, so impressed the Indians—and next day the candidate for the grave rose to his feet and was well again.

Soon they were famous among all the Indians for their

wonder-working. Once again de Vaca faced a crisis when a wounded man was brought to him with an arrowhead lodged deep in his chest. De Vaca ventured his first operation; he removed the arrowhead and sewed up the man's chest with deerhide thread. The operation was successful.

It was plain that their lives hung in the balance. These cures could not possibly turn out well every time, and in the background stood the medicine men, devoured by envy and fury. But the Spaniards' reputation kept on mounting, and they were escorted with high honors from tribe to tribe. They reached wealthier districts where, in fact, corn was cultivated. Suddenly they had ample game to eat. When they could not consume the quantities of food that were brought to them, and tried to refuse it, they aroused anger and anxiety—for the game was not payment, but a sacrifice which could not be returned. Hereafter they had only brief periods of poverty and hunger. When they reached the great Sierra Madre, they came upon a tribe "who for the third part of a year eat nothing but the powder of straw, and that being the season we passed, we also had to eat of it."[7]

The farther west they made their way the more legendary their fame became. Already they were being called "children of the sky." As much as seventy years later other chroniclers reported that among the tribes the four had met on their journey religious notions of a Christian sort, notions of an omnipotent white god, still persisted.

At last, in the eighth year of their wanderings, they came to a river where a tribe told them about other white men —and had nothing good to say of them. At first they did not believe the stories and thought there must be some misunderstanding, for by now their journey seemed to them to be leading on into an eternity from which there was no returning. Then they found two pieces of worked iron— *Spanish* iron. And then they heard that mounted Spaniards were encamped a short distance from where they were. It was the middle of March, 1536, on the Rio de Potatlan in Sinaloa.

Captain Diego de Alcaraz stared with astonishment and the utmost distrust at the four strange figures, clad in deerskins, with wildly luxuriant beards. "They stood staring at me a length of time, so confounded that they neither hailed me nor drew near to make an inquirie."[8]

Alcaraz, a savage, cruel trooper, was on a slave-hunting

expedition. When he saw the eleven Indians accompanying de Vaca, he wanted to capture them at once—not knowing that de Vaca's main escort, which had temporarily been left behind, consisted of 600 warriors. De Vaca violently opposed his intention and promptly sent his Indians out of reach. While the four in their excitement tried to tell their whole eight-year adventure, all at once within an hour, starting with the failure of Narvaez's expedition, Alcaraz seriously considered whether he ought not put them in chains. Were they not in all likelihood wretched deserters who were trying to serve up elaborate lies?

The nearest Spanish governor thought otherwise. A large honor guard accompanied the four to the governor's residence, and their journey to Mexico City turned into a triumphal procession. Their one regret was that they could not wear the heavy Spanish boots with their brand-new outfits. Their feet, worn from eight years of tramping across the continent, could no longer tolerate anything but Indian moccasins. At the end of June the viceroy greeted them. De Vaca had to tell his story, to tell again and again all the miseries he and his companions had endured, to tell of the wretchedness of all northern Indians, of the dreariness of the wilderness and the endless expanse of this continent. Only half the story was believed—for what everyone *wanted* to hear was stories of a land of gold, and de Vaca had nothing to say about that.

In 1542 the first version of his travel story, called *Relacion* for short, was published in Zamora. This account of a trek more than 5,000 miles long bears the stamp of truth hardly equaled by any other Spanish document of the age. But the picture that emerged from it was extremely perplexing to those who still believed in a mighty kingdom in the north, those "Seven Cities of Cibola," and also perplexing to those who had a simplistic and uniform notion of the Indians as miserable, virtually subhuman creatures.

For de Vaca's picture of them showed tremendous variations in their character and way of life. His phenomenal memory had registered the smallest details, and *everything* had interested him. He was a born explorer and anthropologist. With tribe after tribe he records their customs, their religion and its rituals, their social order, their appearance, their clothing. When he speaks of their food, he even gives recipes. His is the first European description of the North American buffalo, the most important animal

The first description of the buffalo was furnished by Cabeza de Vaca. This is probably the first pictorial representation of it, published by F. Hernandez in Rome, 1651.

of the northern prairies for both Indians and the early whites. Actually, de Vaca saw only three specimens that had drifted to the south.

"All over this country there are a great many deer, fowl and other animals which I have before enumerated. Here also they came up with cows; I have seen them thrice and have eaten their meat. They appear to me of the size of those in Spain. Their horns are small, like those of the Moorish cattle; the hair is very long, like fine wool and like a peajacket; some are brownish and others black, and to my taste they have better and more meat than those from here. Of the small hides the Indians make blankets to cover themselves with, and of the taller ones they make shoes and targets. These cows come from the north, across the country further on, to the coast of Florida, and are found all over the land for over four hundred leagues. On this whole stretch, through the valley by which they come, people who live there descend to subsist upon their flesh. And a great quantity of hides are met with inland."9

The first Indians he had encountered on the Florida expedition were dangerous warriors, tall, strong, agile, armed with enormous bows. He reports that one of their arrows penetrated nine inches into the trunk of a tree near him.

But then he met tribes of small stature possessing only primitive weapons, actually Stone Age men. What astonished him most was the multiplicity of their languages. Tribes that lived close together could communicate with one another only by sign language. But in his truthful fashion he remarks concerning these people: "If they were not large, our fears made giants of them!"

He gives the names of tribes: Chorruco, Doguenes, Mendicas, Guevenas, Guaycones, Quotoks, Camoles, Mariames, Atayos, Acubadoes, Chavavares, and so on. He reproduces them phonetically. But were these the names that the tribes gave themselves, or what other tribes called them? To what extent did his ear distort what he heard? The modern anthropologist has not found the slightest trace of most of these tribes. What de Vaca has recorded is therefore all the more important. He describes lax marital customs: women were exchanged or bought or kidnaped, and could be casually divorced if they proved unfruitful. The price for a woman might be a bow—certainly not very high. Among the Mariames and the Yguazes marriage within the tribe was inconceivable. They got drunk on a kind of mescal liquor—contrary to later accounts that praised the total abstinence of the Indians—and went in for drug orgies. Property was loot, theft even from friends a commonplace. On their treks the sick were simply left behind, but children were often breast-fed until they reached puberty. There was open homosexuality and genuine transvestitism—both phenomena wrongly judged by anthropologists and physicians of the last century to be symptoms of decadence in advanced cultures. The "feminine" partner dressed as a woman and performed only female work. It must be remembered, of course, that de Vaca could make only limited observations; it would not do to draw general conclusions from his account.

They encountered many other tribes: Tarahumare, Tepecano, Tepehuane, Nio, Zoe, and others, including the Opates who employed poisoned arrows that were later to take the lives of many Spaniards. But never, not once, did they come across the one thing for which the Spanish conquistadors thirsted: riches. They had a chance to see a few emeralds, which may have been only malachite, and a few turquoises. These were scarcely worth mentioning. Also, when they crossed the Rio Pecos they saw a few miserable pueblos. But they encountered rumors of actual "cities" in the north, gigantic pueblos crowded with countless people and full of gold and silver. Again and again they came upon such vague reports. And although in his *Relacion*, just as he had previously done in his statements to the viceroy in Mexico City, de Vaca explicitly speaks of *hearsay*, never asserting that he saw any of these things himself, his truthfulness did not prevent the bedazzled Spaniards from believing what they wanted to believe. In fact, accusations were made that he was keeping his real knowledge secret and that he had hoarded immense treasures somewhere.

De Vaca put an end to all such stories by returning to Spain, to his native city of Xeres de la Frontera, and to Seville. Even there people uneasily regarded him as the possessor of enormous riches. The King recalled him to mind when he needed an honest governor for the Rio de la Plata region of South America. De Vaca accepted the governorship, but the post proved an ill-fated one. He was involved in intrigues, was even brought to trial, but was acquitted. He died in Spain in 1557. Dorantes and Castillo remained in Mexico; both married rich widows. The dates of their deaths are unknown.

There remains the last of the four, Estevanico, the Moor. For him fate held in store one more great adventure, which gave him a brief triumph and then sudden death. The Moor was to be the first person actually to set eyes on the "Seven Cities of Cibola."

The viceroy of Mexico, Don Antonio de Mendoza, issued the order for the search. Probably Coronado was to have headed the expedition, but in view of de Vaca's discouraging report, Mendoza decided it was better to undertake a careful reconnaissance before launching a large and expensive operation. He chose for his purpose Fray Marcos of Nizza (also known as Marco de Nica), a distinguished Franciscan monk who had already participated in Pizarro's conquest of Peru. Thus the friar had seen everything that the rough Spanish soldiery was capable of; he had witnessed the murder of the Inca King Atahualpa and had presumably held aloft the Christian cross on that occasion.

There were three special reasons for choosing a priest rather than a knight, as the first thorough historian of this period, Adolph F. Bandelier, stresses: (1) a priest was much cheaper to hire than any knight would have been; (2) one could expect a priest to report more truthfully

than a soldier hungry for booty; (3) a priest's cross was
often more convincing and impressive than the sword, especially in those areas that had never before been trod by
Spanish soldiers.

What better guide could Marcos have selected than the
Moor Estevanico, who knew that wild country and was
acquainted with both the savage and the gentle tribes and
who, above all, was so adept at sign language? (Let us
digress for a moment on this celebrated sign language,
which played a part in so many Indian novels later on. Of
course we know little about how developed it was at the
time of the Spaniards and nothing whatsoever about it in
the many centuries before. But we do know what an extraordinary medium of communication it became later on,
making possible the ever-expanding trade relations among
the by then *mounted* Indians. Thus Wilhelm Wundt, the
social psychologist, reports that sign language could convey
information as complicated as "White soldiers, led by an
officer of high rank but low intelligence, have taken the
Mescalero Indians prisoner.")[10]

The Moor had probably been Dorantes' slave. But during that long odyssey of the four men, competence had determined rank. He had not only been accorded equal rights
but had become a friend. Now, however, he was suddenly
something more than that. He had become the *leader* of
a group that was to a large extent dependent on him. Undoubtedly this went to his head. He now exaggerated his
natural bent for histrionics. Eager to set himself apart out-
wardly, he adorned himself with ribbons and cockades, stuck
bright feathers in his hair, and in particular draped himself with all kinds of noisemakers, rattles and bells. In this
fashion he pranced along at the head of the small expedition. There was no doubt about it: among some tribes his
reputation as one of the great medicine men who years ago
had performed miracles promptly revived, while on other
tribes this black man, the first they had seen, in his fantastic getup, made a deep impression. It would be highly
interesting to know what the Indians thought of him. There
is a record of one unfortunate effect—unfortunate for the
last days of the expedition. He had the greatest impact upon
the native womenfolk, who voluntarily threw their lot in
with him. For a short time after the expedition began he
traveled about with a kind of harem. But while several of
the tribes tolerated this, others showed concern for their
property rights. That led to some unpleasantness right from

the start. And there is no doubt that Fray Marcos, whose cross required him to preserve morality, strongly disapproved of this conduct on the part of his "leader."

The two men were seldom together, however. Estevanico took the part of advance guard. He transmitted to the Indians the glad news of the arrival of a great white man who had been sent by an almighty white King and a still mightier white God, who would be bringing them unimaginable love and to whom they had to submit. He rattled his jester's bells, distributed presents, and was successful; the Indians helped him to prepare rest huts supplied with provisions all along the way, where the priest, following at a slower pace, could be received with honors.

History has long vacillated in its view of this expedition of 1539, and of Fray Marcos himself. Undoubtedly following the viceroy's commission to the letter, he did not come as a conqueror with a sword but as an explorer bearing the no less conquistadorial cross.

But his narrative of the whole journey, the *Descubrimiento* ("Discovery"), is contradictory, especially on the decisive point. Thus we have Don Pedro de Castañeda, Coronado's chronicler, asserting that Fray Marcos had been a mendacious coward, who in reality never came any closer than 162 miles to Cibola. It is curious that a man so thorough as Bandelier, who must have subjected these early sources to the most intensive research, and this in the nineteenth century, when evidence was easier to find, should stand so completely behind Marcos:

"For more than three centuries the character of the man whose name stands at the head of this monograph has been strangely misrepresented, his actions mistold, his words misconstrued. The result of it has been that almost everything connected with the early history of discoveries in the North American Southwest has been correspondingly misunderstood. It is my purpose to follow the path which for the first time, in 1881, Mr. F. H. Cushing opened, when he sought and found among the Indians of Zuñi the truth about Fray Marcos' remarkable journey,—a path which, upon the basis of documentary research, I trod afterwards in 1885 and 1886,—and to present the tale of the first trip undertaken to Cibola as accurately as possible, with the aid of written and oral evidence, of printed books and manuscripts, as well as of geographical and ethnological facts."[11]

As we have already said, Estevanico had formed an advance guard which was joined by more and more Indians, including a great many women, so that his retinue may soon have outnumbered that of Marcos. Whatever the case, increasing numbers of Indians joined both groups. These spoke of large cities and wealthy tribes in the north, so that Marcos made the following arrangement with Estevanico:

"To go to the North fifty or sixty leagues, to see if in that direction there might be observed something great, or some rich country and well settled; and if he found anything or heard anything of that kind, to stop, and to send me a message by some Indians. That message was to consist of a wooden cross of a white color. In case the discovery was of *medium* importance, he was to send me a cross of one span in length; if *important,* the cross was to be two spans in length; and if *more important than New Spain,* he should send me a large cross."[12]

The Moor carried out his most important duty; he arranged for continuous communication between himself and Marcos. But the distance between the two parties steadily increased. The onrushing enthusiasm of the first group inspired the second. Fantastic reports came thick and fast, and Marcos's group must have been utterly electrified when an Indian runner arrived brandishing a gigantic cross. Could that cross really mean: "More important than New Spain"? More important even than Mexico City?

What was more, the Indian and his companions who appeared soon afterward reported such wonders that Marcos wrote: "I refused to believe it until I saw it myself, or obtained further proof." But why should he continue to doubt? "Cibola was as well known here as Mexico in New Spain, or Cuzco in Peru; and they described fully the shape of the houses, the arrangement of the villages, the streets and squares, like people who had been there often, and who obtained there, in return for their services, the objects of luxury and convenience which they possessed."[13]

The newest report, that there was still a desert to be crossed, a journey of fifteen days, no longer alarmed Marcos. But the Moor had evidently gone out of his mind. Now that he was in sight of the Promised Land, instead of waiting for Marcos, who, if we are to believe his account, advanced with caution and dignity, the black man was obviously seized by an obsessive desire to be the discoverer of the "Seven Cities"—he himself, all alone! But suddenly, facing still another new tribe, his rattles and charlatan tricks, his silly prancing, seemed to fail him. The inhabitants of the first large pueblo, seeing their first foreigner, took up their weapons.

An exhausted, bleeding Indian brought the news to Marcos, who was lagging far behind.

It is an ancient trick of the writer's craft, going back as far as Sophocles, that a terrible event is best reported by a messenger in terse, dry language and high-sounding phrases at a far remove from the naked experience, to which nothing but stammering is suitable. For by the rules of the craft it is not the narrator who should be wrought up. Rather, the audience should be shocked by what he narrates.

Hence nothing gives quite so persuasive an account of the disappointment, the dismay, perhaps the fear of death that seized the men around Marcos as the restrained report of the bleeding Indian who had been an eyewitness of Estevanico's first triumph and last hour. Marcos sets down his words:

"He told me that one day previous to reaching Cibola, Estevan sent, as he was wont to do always, his gourd, in order to show them in what quality he was coming. The gourd had a few strings of rattles and two plumes, one of which was white and the other red. When they reached Cibola and presented the gourd to the person whom the lord has placed there in charge, he took it into his hand, and, seeing the rattles, with great wrath threw the gourd on the floor, and said to the messengers that they should forthwith leave the town, that he knew what kind of people those (the strangers) were, and that they should tell them not to enter the place lest they should all be killed. The messengers returned and reported to Estevan what had happened, who said that this was nothing—that those who at first displayed anger always received him in the kindest manner. So he continued his road until he reached the city of Cibola, where he met people who refused to allow him to enter, and placed him in a large house outside, taking from him all he carried of objects for exchange, turquoises, and other things received from the Indians on the journey. There he was all night, neither food nor drink being given to him nor to his escort. On the following morning this Indian (the one who was telling the tale) felt thirsty, and went out of the house to get a drink of water at a stream near by, and a short while afterwards he saw Estevan endeavoring to escape, pursued by the people of the city, who were killing some of the people of his company. Seeing this, this Indian concealed himself and crept off stealthily up the said stream, and finally crossed over to take the road through the desert."14

Additional eyewitness reports confirmed the massacre. The jaunty Moor had been killed; only a few wounded men managed to drag themselves back to Marcos. The people of Cibola had killed some 300 of Estevanico's followers and had hermetically sealed their borders, even to Indian traders.

This account is completely true. A year later one of Coronado's officers heard exactly the same story when he questioned the natives. A "legend" about the incident was preserved among the Zuñi Indians down to the nineteenth century, as F. H. Cushing discovered. According to one account the Moor's body was cut into many pieces, which were sent to other pueblos in order to provide the chiefs with proof of his vulnerability and his death.

The Indians accompanying Marcos wanted to run away. Marcos distributed all his possessions among them, prevailed on some to stay, and ventured on some distance farther, on and on, until two of his trustiest Indians led him to a spot *from which he could see Cibola*.

There it lay before him, the city that had figured in the dreams of so many Spaniards. He gazed at it for a long time. Then he erected a stone cross, and had the effrontery to take "possession" for the Spanish crown of all the land lying before him, which included the pueblos of Cibola, Totonteac, Acus and Marata (beyond which even greater cities were supposed to lie). He gave it the name of the New Kingdom of Saint Francis. Then he resolved to turn back—a sensible decision.

"I was sometimes tempted to go thither, knowing that I did not risk more than my life, and that life I had already offered to God on the day when I began the journey. But finally I feared, considering the danger, and that if I should die there would be no knowledge of this land."15

But what kind of "knowledge" did he bring back with him? The man whose truthfulness Bandelier vouches for could not, as we shall see, have been entirely in his right mind when he caught his first glimpse of Cibola. (It was, as we now know, the "land of the Zuñis," on the upper Zuñi River in New Mexico, and consisted of a group of pueblos that were undoubtedly the Seven Cities of Cibola, but immeasurably exaggerated by rumor, imagination, and wish-fulfillment fantasies.) Even if we take into account his enormous excitement, and even if we know how the present-day tourist, suddenly spying in the distance, under the blazing sun, one of those ghostly looking gray beehive structures several stories high, which constitute a pueblo, can scarcely judge how many inhabitants such a "city" is likely to hold—even so, it is incomprehensible that Marcos should have dared to give the following report to the viceroy:

"With my Indians and interpreters I followed my road till we came in sight of Cibola, which lies in a plain on the slope of a round height. Its appearance is very good for a settlement—the handsomest I have seen in these parts. The houses are, as the Indians had told me, all of stone, with their stories and flat roofs. As far as I could see from a height where I placed myself to observe, *the settlement is larger than the city of Mexico.*" He goes even further: "In my estimation [it] is the largest and best of all yet discovered."[16]

This was a wholly delusory depiction of the Zuñi pueblos by a man who had come from Mexico City, which then —around 1540—may have had no more than 1,000 Spanish inhabitants but still held innumerable natives. Above all, it contained the remains of the tremendous Aztec palace and temples which—we must, alas, already betray this truth to the eager reader—could not be matched *anywhere in all North America.*

But this totally false report led directly to the conquest of what is now the Southwest of the United States. Coronado, who was to become the best known of all the conquistadors, began fitting out his expedition. He was followed by innumerable others, and in their train came many well-meaning priests, but also clerks, notaries, judges, and executioners. One hundred and forty years were to pass before the Zuñis once more rose to defend themselves against Spanish oppression.

The conquistadors passed on their trade from one to another. The comrades in the battles of one expedition became the leaders of the next:

> Cortés–Narvaez
> Narvaez–Cabeza de Vaca
> De Vaca–Estevanico
> Estevanico–Marcos of Nizza
> Marcos–Coronado

For what better adviser could Francisco Vasquez de Coronado have had than Marcos when in 1540 the viceroy sent him forth with 250 mounted men, seventy infantry-men, several hundred Indians, and a supply train of cattle, this time to make the actual conquest of legendary Cibola?

In a history of the conquest the name of de Soto cannot, of course, be omitted, or the names of the many leaders who came after him, probing deeper and deeper into the country and more and more harshly imposing the Spanish dominion of sword and cross. But let us follow our red thread—the traces of the first Indians of North America. For the present the last Spaniard we need mention is Coronado, whose sword slashed the mysterious veil that for so long had concealed the truth about the Seven Cities of Cibola.

To this day his traces may be found, and every school-child in the Southwest learns about him as the man who crossed Arizona and New Mexico. He or his subordinates —for he subdivided his expedition and sent his lieutenants out in various directions—advanced as far as what is now Kansas. His men were the first whites to behold the marvel of the Grand Canyon, although they regarded that deepest incision in the earth's surface merely as an annoying obstacle hindering their march to the north.

But to return to Cibola: the expedition was disappointing from the start. "All marched cheerfully," but the road was bad, and it "troubled the soldiers not a little, seeing that everything which the friar [Marcos] had reported turned out to be quite the opposite."[17] Horses died of exhaustion; Indians and Negroes began to desert the party. By the middle of June, 1540, when they came to the last area of desert before reaching Cibola, they were so hungry that one Spaniard, two Negroes, and even a few Indians ate plants that proved to be poisonous—with fatal results.

But finally they had put the worst of the hardships behind them, and the first messengers from Cibola reached them. Proofs of friendship were exchanged, but Coronado was mistrustful. He sent a reconnaissance patrol ahead to see whether any trap awaited them. The leader of the patrol did in fact find "a very bad place in our way where we might have received much harm. He immediately established himself there with the force which he was conducting."[18] His premonition was not mistaken. During the night the Indians appeared like shadows to occupy the trap. When they saw that they had come too late, they nevertheless attacked the Spaniards "like valiant men." The Spanish drove them back without any losses on their side. Coronado, informed of this episode, decided to attack Cibola at once, for—gold or no gold—what he needed immediately was provisions.

Next morning he and his men stood on a height and gazed at Cibola.

They saw the beehivelike complex of gray houses, with the Indians scurrying from story to story on ladders. Parleyers accompanied by interpreters, who were to announce to the Indians that the Spanish king had taken possession of the city, were showered with arrows.

Coronado launched a frontal attack.

A superior force of Indians met them in the open. But here again that phenomenon took place which was to be repeated often during the period of the conquest: a handful of men, for mysterious reasons convinced of the justice of their cause and for scarcely less mysterious reasons certain of their own invincibility and therefore fighting like devils, could drive literally thousands of Indians before them, kill hundreds, and themselves lose no more than half a dozen fighting men. That is what happened, and the Indians fled back into their city. But they did not give up. Climbing the ladders to their terraces, they showered the attackers with arrows and stones. Coronado ordered the assault and himself took the van—a conspicuous target in his armor, which glittered with gold. Twice he was knocked to the ground by stones, was grazed by them several times, and an arrow penetrated his foot. But Cibola, the legendary city, was conquered! The result of the first quick survey by the exhausted and famished Spaniards is recorded thus: "There we found something we prized more than gold or silver, namely, much maize, beans, and chickens larger than those here of New Spain, and salt better and whiter than I have ever seen in my whole life."[19]

The truth about Cibola now lay plainly before them. No mighty monarch reigned here; the doors were not studded with either gold or gems; and the Indians ate from the ground and not from golden dishes. In bitter words Coronado reported this to the viceroy, adding a contemptuous reference to Brother Marcos's false information. Cibola, it quickly became clear, was the general name for a group of Zuñi Indian towns. But was there any sense in continuing the march? Coronado would not have been a conquistador if he had hesitated.

Among the many pueblos that Coronado or his lieutenants conquered, one is particularly important for us because, centuries later, to be sure, fledgling American archaeology first tried its wings there.

The conquistadors were actually invited to this important pueblo, which was later generally called Pecos, by a friendly chief who unlike most Indians wore a handsome mustache. For this reason the Spaniards immediately called him Captain Bigotes, or as it has traditionally been rendered, "Captain Whiskers."

Captain Hernando de Alvarado set out on a scouting expedition with twenty soldiers. Within a few days they made an extraordinary discovery: they came upon *ruins*— "very large, entirely destroyed, although a large part of the wall was still standing, which was six times as tall as a man, the wall well made of good worked stone, with gates and gutters like a city in Castile."[20]

Only a short distance farther on they came upon more ruins, which had a foundation of granite blocks. Then they arrived at the town of Acoma, built upon an unassailable

An ancient ceramic vessel, with fanciful decoration, from Pueblo Acoma, N. Mex.

cliff, with only a single entrance. But through the mediation of the mustachioed chief, the Spaniards were given a friendly reception and invited to inspect the town. Three days later they reached the legendary Rio Grande and found numerous settlements on both sides of the river.

Alvarado hastily sent out crosses of peace to indicate that he had come in friendship, for his first scouts brought word that he was facing some seventy settlements in the valley of the Rio Grande. The captain also dispatched a report to Coronado informing his superior that the country was fertile, rich in maize, beans, and melons and much better suited for wintering the army than Cibola. "Captain Whiskers," however, urged that they continue on. They passed what were later to be called the San Francisco Peaks (the highest in New Mexico, snow-covered except for a short time in the summer). In the heart of the mountains they at last reached Cicuyé, as Pecos was then called.

This was a far more impressive city than any they had previously seen. Here is the first description of it, given by Castañeda, the chronicler of the Coronado expedition:

"Cicuyé is a village of nearly five hundred warriors, who are feared throughout that country. It is square, situated on a rock, with a large court or yard in the middle containing the estufas [the Spanish word for kiva; see below]. The houses are all alike, four stories high. One can go over the top of the whole village without there being a street to hinder. There are corridors going all around it at the first two stories, by which one can go around the whole village. These are like jutting balconies, and they are able to shelter themselves under them. The houses do not have doors below, but they use ladders, which can be withdrawn, and so go up to the corridors which are on the inside of the village. As the doors of the houses open on the corridor of that story, the corridor serves as a street. The houses that open on the plain are right back of those that open on the court, and in time of war they go through these inner doors. The village is enclosed by a low wall of stone. There is a spring of water inside, which they are able to divert. The people of this village boast that no one has been able to conquer them and that they conquer whatever villages they wish."[21]

Rather than follow the fortunes of further expeditions—there was one especially foolish one in search of a mysterious new land of gold called Quivira—let us examine the earliest truthful accounts that accumulated concerning these "first Americans." (The Spanish assumed these were the "first," without suspecting how long a history already lay behind the Pueblo Indians.) But let us also emphasize that what we are describing here is only a particular cultural stage in a particular area of North America—a stage that had been reached in the Southwest at the time the Spaniards arrived there. We shall consider later how far back in time this culture extends.

The word "pueblo" is Spanish and means simultaneously "people," "settlement," "town," "village." In the Southwest, and especially in Arizona and New Mexico, the Spaniards applied it to the Indian settlements of several stories, usually built of adobe, that is of sun-dried bricks made of clay or mud mixed with straw or grass. The Spaniards used the word indiscriminately for "fortified" citadels built on one of the numerous mesas or for open, unprotected villages in the plain. Whether with hindsight these settlements ought to be called towns or villages is a question that can be left to the sociologists, for the difference consists in the extent of organization within these agglomerations of people. By that standard some pueblos can be, in fact, must be, called towns, while many others were merely unimportant villages.

Until the nineteenth century the Spaniards also spoke in general of the "Pueblo Indians," as if those who lived in pueblos were a special, unified tribe or people. In reality the inhabitants of the pueblos, as we now know, were members of extraordinarily varied tribes. They spoke widely different languages and had different historical backgrounds. Nevertheless, they did have one thing in common; they were all tillers of the soil. Thus they had passed beyond the prehistoric stage of pure hunters and food gatherers. And the pueblos, although their layout could vary greatly, also had one thing in common: the semiunderground kivas, which were extremely important to their architectural scheme. Kiva is a Hopi Indian word for a room, usually circular, supported by beams and entered from the roof, which served a wide range of purposes. But the significant thing about it was that all women were absolutely forbidden to enter it. The kiva was an assembly room, conference room, prayer room, ceremonial room, schoolroom for youths, and had the aura of all mysteries that are reserved for men alone.

"They do not have chiefs as in New Spain, but are ruled

by a council of the oldest men," Castañeda wrote. "They have priests who preach to them, whom they call papas. These are the elders. They go up on the highest roof of the village and preach to the village from there, like public criers, in the morning while the sun is rising, the whole village being silent and sitting in the galleries to listen. They tell them how they are to live, and I believe that they give certain commandments for them to keep, for there is no drunkenness among them nor sodomy nor sacrifices, neither do they eat human flesh nor steal, but they are usually at work."[22] Here, then, we are confronting a far more civilized society than the kind that Cabeza de Vaca described farther to the south.

It is important to realize that every pueblo was an independent "republic"—to use the modern word. There was little trade among the various tribes; but then there were scarcely any objects of trade, except perhaps for turquoise, which was regarded as virtually sacred and of which one region might have richer deposits than another.

In many of the pueblos women played a dominant part. Great weight was laid upon kinship in the female line. Some women were feared as "witches"; they as well as the mighty medicine men were believed to possess power over the elements.

The nature religion of these Indians centered around sun worship and was expressed most attractively in their dances. The modern tourist can still see a few of these dances that have probably changed hardly at all from their original forms. On the other hand, there are still some pueblos even today where the ritual dances are supposed to take place in secret and obtrusive watchers can have their cameras smashed—which serves them right. There are the sun dances, the dance of the sprouting corn, the rain dance. The dancing is accompanied by flutes and drums, the dancers decked out in many bizarre, brightly painted symbolic masks, which the tourist can see reproduced nowadays as "kachina dolls." In fact, mass-produced replicas of them are on sale.

Some tribes practiced the art of sand painting under the direction of the priests. Skillfully tracing figures on the ground in all the colors that various types of sand and tinted flour provide, they brought this unique type of art to perfection. Their basketry and pottery had attained an extraordinarily high degree of artistic development. Many of the patterns that the Spaniards saw at the time have vanished, many have been preserved to this day, and many have been affected by ideas brought in chiefly by the missionaries.

These Indians were not only tillers of the soil. They hunted also. For game there were deer, bears, buffaloes, mountain lions, and small animals. Most of the tribes did not fish, however; they regarded fish as sacred and did not eat them.

Curiously enough, they developed irrigation techniques only to a limited extent, although every drop of water was precious, and drought could very easily have disastrous consequences. When, for example, we look around today at the gigantic ruins of Pueblo Bonito, almost red-hot in the blazing sun, it is hard to imagine how any people could have survived there unless—and this is the simplest explanation—other meteorological conditions prevailed there at the time this pueblo was inhabited.

The fields were often miles away, moreover. The Spaniards found this utterly puzzling, but the distance between pueblo and fields has since been explained on the grounds that the Indians regarded the security of their dwellings as of foremost importance. Therefore, they built their pueblos at the strategically most suitable spot.

The Spaniards thought the clothing of these Indians quite sensible. Men and women had leggings and moccasins of tanned deerhide. The men wore a tunic and trousers, the women a woven blanket thrown over the right shoulder and under the left and held by a broad sash. In winter they used skins made into a kind of overcoat, but they also had clothing of cotton woven by both the women and the men (this last surprised the Spaniards).

The men cropped their hair in front and used a headband to form a topknot. Women usually wore their hair parted in the middle. Both sexes loved adornment. Their most prized ornaments were the turquoises, which were often of considerable size but seldom pure. Or else they used pierced shells that they strung in chains from their ears or around their necks.

The number of descriptions increased considerably in the course of time, especially after the missionaries set to work, and the Spaniards soon thought they knew their "Pueblo Indians" quite well. After 140 years the Spaniards were convinced that nothing could shake their power and their ability to exploit the Indians by the artful encomienda system. But then, in 1680, the hitherto submissive Pueblo tribes suddenly rose up in a rebellion of such ferocity and fire that there is scarcely any parallel to it in the whole history of the North American Indians. Under the leadership of an evidently extraordinary medicine man named Popé they took up arms, united, first slaughtered the Spanish outposts, then the fortifications, overran everything, killed 400 of the hated conquerors, and chased more than 2,500 of them as far as Mexico.

Spanish retaliation was fearful, of course. But it was more than a decade before the Spaniards were able to restore the old order among the Pueblo Indians.

Concerning the first period of Spanish rule, the modern historian A. Grove Day remarks in his book, *Coronado's Quest:* "To such a self-sufficient people, the invading Spaniards had little to offer in the way of 'civilizing' implements or influences. True, they implanted in the country a diversity of domestic animals (the Indians had only the dog and the turkey), particularly the horse and the sheep. But the exchange between red man and white has never been one-sided. If anything, the Pueblo Indian has given more than he has received. His lore and craftsmanship and painfully won wisdom of existence have passed into the American heritage. His way of building a home, for example, created a style that is still furnishing inspiration to architecture in the western states. The Indian culture, like his dwellings, has remained firmly rooted in the soil that Coronado's army trod. Today, any visitor to the American Southwest may see this enduring race living virtually as they lived when Coronado came, four centuries ago, and white man first whispered the magical name of Cibola."

It was not until the nineteenth century that anthropologists and archaeologists first took an interest in the pueblos and discovered that the inhabitants of these adobe skyscrapers were by no means the *first* Americans but that whole peoples had lived in those parts before them and had passed away.

3

Hymn to the Southwest—
From Bandelier to Kidder

"ONE day of August, 1888, in the teeth of a particular New Mexico sandstorm that whipped pebbles the size of a bean straight to your face, a ruddy, bronzed, middle-aged man, dusty but unweary with his sixty-mile tramp from Zuñi, walked into my solitary camp at Los Alamitos. Within the afternoon I knew that here was the most extraordinary mind I had met. . . . I was at first suspicious of the 'pigeonhole memory' which could not only tell me some Queres word I was searching for, but add: 'Policárpio explained that to me in Chochiti, November 23, 1881.' "[1]

So Charles F. Lummis describes his first meeting with Adolph F. Bandelier, who became his lifelong friend. The two men traveled thousands of miles together through the Southwest.

"We trudged side by side—camped, starved, shivered, learned and were glad together. . . . There was not a decent road We had no endowment, no vehicles. Bandelier was once loaned a horse; and after riding two miles, led it the rest of the thirty. So we went always by foot; my big

86

camera and glass plates in the knapsack on my back, the heavy tripod under my arm; his aneroid, surveying instruments, and satchel of the almost microscopic notes which he kept fully and precisely every night by the camp-fire (even when I had to crouch over him and the precious paper with my water-proof focusing cloth) somehow bestowed about him. Up and down pathless cliffs, through tangled canyons, fording icy streams and ankle-deep sands, we travelled; no blankets, over-coats, or other shelter; and the only commissary a few cakes of sweet chocolate, and a small sack of parched popcorn meal. Our 'lodging was the cold ground.' When we could find a cave, a tree, or anything to temper the wind or keep off part of the rain, all right. If not, the Open. . . . He was in no way an athlete— nor even muscular. . . . He could find common ground with *anyone*. I have seen him with presidents, diplomats, Irish section-hands, Mexican peons, Indians, authors, scientists and 'society.' Within an hour or so he was easily the Center."

Bandelier spoke English, French, Spanish, and German with equal facility. This talent also extended to dialects and Indian languages. When he arrived in Isleta, New Mexico, he knew three words of Tigua. Within ten days he understood the language and could make himself understood on all matters. The material he collected as an observer and friend of many Indians was simply immense. He had difficulty in publishing it, to be sure. Inserted into his book, *Contributions*, I found a small printed notice by the president of the Archaeological Institute of America asking for donations that would enable Bandelier to continue his work. "The Council is unable at the present time to make any further Appropriation from its own funds. . . . About one thousand Dollars are needed." Incidentally, I received the book from the New York State library with the pages still uncut, that is, I was its first and only reader in seventy-five years. But although Bandelier scarcely became known in the East, "his" Southwest has shown its gratitude to him.

If the value of a monument can be judged by its size, he has received one of the biggest: 27,049 acres of land in New Mexico have been named after him. Millions of tourists pass through his world of pueblos today, through the Bandelier National Monument.

The Southwest is the name of a region that many people regard as the most beautiful in North America, if not in the world. The term "Southwest" includes all of Arizona and New Mexico, half of Utah and half of Colorado, part of Nevada and California in the west, and parts of Kansas and Texas to the east. But the term applies chiefly to the area surrounding the Four Corners, the only geographical point in North America where four states meet. This area is larger than France, West Germany, and Austria put together. In fact, Denmark, Holland, Belgium, and Luxembourg would have to be added to equal it.

To describe the landscape we have to invoke the greatest geographical curiosities in the world for comparisons, employ the most excessive epithets, and we soon realize that only superlatives do justice to this scene. There lies the driest of deserts in the most oppressive kind of monotony. There is the deepest crack in the earth's surface anywhere in the world, the mile-deep Grand Canyon, whose walls provide a record of geological history. There are mountains whose snowy peaks can guide the most distant wanderer in the desert. (Colorado alone has dozens of 14,000-footers.) There is Death Valley, which to this day claims its annual toll of victims, where the lowest point in the Western Hemisphere is to be found, 282 feet below sea level. There rises the Petrified Forest, that uncanny assemblage of ancient tree stumps millions of years old, which seem to be frozen for all eternity. There are the most torrential rivers in America, whose very names—Gila, Colorado, Rio Grande, Pecos—summon up all the romantic images of Western and Indian tales.

And, in two respects, the Southwest has the oldest cities in North America: the oldest white settlements, those of the Spaniards, and the oldest habitations of the red aboriginals. "Red," incidentally, is a dubious term; it is comparable to the prejudiced description, "yellow," which is often applied to Asian people. The Spaniards called the aboriginals *gente colorada,* which simply means "colored people" as opposed to the white Europeans (who quite like Indians are lighter complexioned in the north than in the south). But since *colorado* also means "red," the term "redskin" evolved. Anyhow, the description is no faultier than "Indians"—since the natives of North America have nothing to do with India.

This Southwest, which proved to be no Dorado for the gold-seeking Spaniards, actually became the Dorado of the archaeologists. For there they found traces of the *oldest Americans,* around whose caves the mammoth, the camel, the ground sloth, and the extinct buffaloes and horses of the last Ice Age still slunk. (Thereafter there ceased to be horses and camels in America for 10,000 years. The mustangs on which the Sioux and Apaches dashed over the prairies were descendants of a few horses that ran away from the Spaniards and multiplied with incredible rapidity. Camels were experimentally introduced during the Civil War, but proved unfeasible.)

It is remarkable that this wildest, most beautiful, most sublime region has not yet found its great writer. The stories of Willa Cather communicate some of the brilliance of the Spanish period, but only of cross sections. There are many lesser writers, to be sure, and many who sentimentalize this world for popular consumption, from Zane Grey to the movie industry. But the lack of a literature is also understandable. Faced with these deadly deserts in the south, these vivid cliff formations, those mesas—flat-topped hills, often wooded, that lie like islands or giant ships in the sea of shimmering sand, spat out by the giant snake of the Rocky Mountains, which wind down into the south— and faced with the yawning gulf of the canyons, which seem to draw our gaze into primordial depths of the earth, it is understandable that words can fail one.

Let us be clear about one thing. In his best film Walt Disney showed us *The Living Desert.* But the early men who roamed this region knew this beyond doubt; they wrested their existence from this desert. Anyone who thinks that the desert is silent has never crossed it. It sings; it rustles; it whispers. Even the most delicate lizard (not to speak of the poisonous gila monster) that scurries around the edge of a rock starts grains of sand rolling. The wind passes through the fantastic rock bridges as through the strings of a harp. The mountain lion roars his message, and the coyote howls in the dark-blue night.

The iridescence of the tiny desert flowers fades quickly, but the hundred greens of the mesas and the mountain regions remain. Two hundred varieties of cactus, the driest and the juiciest, display 200 colors. But plant life is outshone by minerals that look as if life had been breathed into them at the Creation. The Painted Desert looks like the palette of a painter god; these rocks stretch under the sun and shade like chameleons that change their colors twelve times from morning to evening. Here the velvety indigo of a shadowy valley harmonizes with the glaring orange-yellow and the painfully flaming red of the parched cliffs.

It was through such a world that the Early Hunter tramped with his atlatl, that ingeniously conceived javelin, on the track of the giant animals still inhabiting the region 12,000 years ago. Against the background of these same colors, this same sun, the fruit gatherer and early agriculturist and first Basket Maker withdrew into his cliff dwellings, dug out his pit houses, or built his first pueblos. Here the Spaniards hunted in vain for treasures; here the first pioneers laboriously established themselves. (To this day the Southwest has barely more than 3,000,000 inhabitants; we do not know how many people lived there 10,000 years ago, but there were certainly far fewer.) And here are now to be found the largest reservations of the Red Man, above all those of the Navajos and Hopis.

And this was the region in which Bandelier began the first archaeological investigation of western America.

Bandelier was not the first and only investigator. The Spanish missionaries gathered a good deal of folkloristic material, some of which still lies, unutilized, in the archives of Seville. And in the nineteenth century several expeditions of military explorers, notably Captain John Charles Frémont, crossed the Southwest in an east-west direction, to say nothing of the many bold individuals and hunters, some as ready with their pens as Francis Parkman and Clarence King, or Friedrich Gerstäcker and the runaway Swiss priest Karl Postl, both of whom wrote in German— the latter producing tales of the great Wild West under the name of Charles Sealsfield. The latter two are more important to Europe than to America, although in 1969 Postl was rediscovered and given his due praise by an American biographer. By the 1850's the first railroad-survey engineers arrived. From 1863 on the legendary scout Kit Carson, after whom Carson City, Nevada, and other cities are named, "pacified" the vast Navajo region. In 1869 the one-armed veteran, ethnologist and geologist, Major John Wesley Powell, started out with nine men and four boats on his daring exploration of the Colorado River and the Grand Canyon. Three men and two boats were lost, but the scientific findings, including first archaeological materials, were of the highest value.[2] In 1876–77 E. A. Barber described old Indian pottery in detail and with pictures, probably for the first time.

The reader interested in further study must note the following names for the period from the Civil War to shortly after the turn of the century: once more, J. W. Powell (the great friend of the Indians, who became first director of the Bureau of Ethnology in Washington, which from 1879 on published his famous, extensive annual reports), William H. Holmes, Washington Matthews, Victor and Cosmos Mindeleff, J. Walter Fewkes. These are only the most important. A special place must be reserved for Richard Wetherill and his brothers, ordinary cattlemen, whose adventurous discovery of Mesa Verde we shall describe later.

Frank Hamilton Cushing was also an unusual character. The story goes that he was only one and a half pounds at birth and from infancy on suffered from frail health. But he showed talent early and was only seventeen when he published his first article on Indian folklore. At twenty-two he accompanied Colonel James Stevenson to Zuñi, where the Spaniards had expected to find Cibola. Cushing remained there while the expedition moved on. He stayed four and a half years, became a member of the tribe, wore Indian clothing, ate their food exclusively, and shared their work and pastimes. After a year he could speak their language and received the name of Té-na-tsa-li, which means "Medicine Flower" and implies "growing on distant mountains with secret powers." His aim, however, was to become a member of the Indians' most secret council (there were several less secret circles), which was called the Order of the Priest of the Bow and comprised twelve degrees.

We have already spoken of how Bandelier, on foot and armed only with a pocket knife, traveled through the land of the Apaches, who were then still very dangerous. (Apache is a name assumed with pride by these Indians, though given them by their opponents. It means "enemy.") The fate of Cushing, as he obstinately attempted to penetrate more and more deeply into the secrets of the tribal hierarchy, shows what might have lain in store for either of them.

When he tried, despite the strict prohibition, to take part in the secret holy dance called Keá-k'ok-shi, the Indians became violent. Thereupon the slight but courageous Cushing drew his knife, drove it into the wall, and swore that he would cut off any arm that was raised against him, and that he was ready to tear apart and cut into pieces anyone who once more tried to do harm to his books.

The men of Zuñi were frustrated.

But after he had been allowed to participate in the dances for a while, a meeting of the Great Council was held. Cushing was informed that by their laws he might have to be thrown to his death over the edge of the mesa. Other solutions of a like nature were being considered—and Cushing came through alive only because he threatened the Indians with the vengeance of the Great White Father in Washington. Finally, however, they accepted him as kí-he, a friend.

Cushing had to travel to the East several times seeking cures for his various illnesses. Yet, despite his ill health, Cushing was appointed to head the Hemenway Southwestern Archaeological Expedition, financed by the wealthy philanthropist Mary Hemenway of Massachusetts. Bandelier, too, participated. Unfortunately, Cushing fell ill again, which was one of the reasons the expedition met with no great success. Moreover, he was fundamentally an ethnologist rather than an archaeologist, and above all "he was no administrator," as E. DeGolyer, the editor of his books on Zuñi, remarks.[3] DeGolyer emphasizes his other qualities: "He was a visionary, a poet, and a genius with a sense of the dramatic and a flair for publicity."

We have said that the Southwest has produced no great writer to sing its praises. But Cushing, although a descriptive ethnologist, could turn phrases that were not without poetry. Indeed, his language has been matched in our time perhaps only by a drama critic who became a nature writer, Joseph Wood Krutch.[4] Here is Cushing on Zuñi land:

"Down behind this hill the sun was sinking, transforming it into a jagged pyramid of silhouette, crowned with a brilliant halo, whence a seemingly midnight aurora burst forth through broken clouds, bordering each misty blue island with crimson and gold, then blazing upward in widening lines of light, as if to repeat in the high heavens its early splendor."

Or he describes a view of a pueblo that may still be seen today, almost a century later, provided the tourist does not come barging right up to it in his car:

"A banner of smoke, as though fed from a thousand crater-fires, balanced over this seeming volcano, floating off, in many a circle and surge, on the evening breeze. But I did not realize that this hill, so strange and picturesque, was a city of the habitations of men, until I saw, on the topmost terrace, little specks of black and red moving about against the sky. It seemed still a little island of Mesas, one upon the other, smaller and smaller, reared from a sea of sand, in mock rivalry of the surrounding grander mesas of Nature's rearing."

In contrast to Cushing, Bandelier's investigations were aimed far more at establishing cultural relationships, which at this period meant beginning to uncover historical developments. Bandelier saw "strata." In Pecos he drew comparisons with the Mexican architecture of Uxmal, although J. W. Powell had counseled him "not to attempt to trace relationships"—a strange piece of advice, for what was more natural? He measured the ruins of Pecos with what was for the time unwonted precision; in fact, his measurements scarcely had to be improved later on. And with his gift for languages he translated and commented on the old Spanish sources carefully and critically as no one had done before, thereby establishing their scientific usefulness.

He was in many respects a remarkable man. The son of an army officer, he was born in Berne, Switzerland, in 1840. His friend Lummis, who wrote his obituary,[5] says there that "it is a State secret that on his mother's side he came of royal blood." In any case his mother was a Russian aristocrat. After some wanderings the family emigrated to America and settled in Highland, Illinois, where Bandelier had his first schooling, then briefly attended university in Switzerland (it is not certain what he actually studied; curiously, it seems to have been either law or geology). He returned to Highland and put in some dreary years as an office clerk. During this time he began his private studies— on such a scale, as it later developed, that one may well wonder how in those days he could have managed to obtain the books he needed in such a one-horse town. There, too, he began corresponding with the most prominent anthropologists, ethnologists, and sociologists of his age. Among them was Lewis Henry Morgan, author of the seminal work entitled *Ancient Society, or Researches in the Lines of Human Progress from Savagery, through Barbarism, to Civilization.* This study, published in 1877, won world fame and exerted a profound influence on the materialistic philosophy of Marxism, especially Friedrich Engels' *The Origin of the Family, Private Property, and the State.*

In his isolation Bandelier regarded the older man as an

intellectual father and at first succumbed completely to Morgan's theories of the social structure of Indian peoples, even though Bandelier's own studies often ran counter to these theories. But Morgan exerted authority as a practical investigator as well as theoretician. He had lived among Indians and in 1847 had been adopted by the Senecas under the name of Ta-ya-da-o-wub-Rub. Bandelier was never able to shake off entirely Morgan's influence. Their correspondence, first published in 1940, throws highly interesting light on this matter.[6] But Bandelier went his own way wherever the interpretation of the experiences and observations of his own travels was at stake. In 1879 the Archaeological Institute of America was founded, and Morgan, who only a year later became president of the American Association for the Advancement of Science, wrote (on October 25, 1879) to the first president, Charles Eliot Norton, words that did not always sit well with this eminent institution: "Europeans would thank us more for your work done *here* than in Syria or Greece!" At any rate, Bandelier, on Morgan's recommendation, made his first journey to the Southwest, going to New Mexico. Later on, he also went to Mexico and South America, but these trips do not concern us here. At the behest of the two institutions he spent years in deserts, mountains, and, subsequently, museums (in Santa Fé, Mexico City, New York, and Washington) and collected a wealth of material. Although he is credited with some disrespectful remarks on religion in general, he converted to Catholicism—for practical reasons, it is said. Thus the story goes that even before his conversion he went about New Mexico dressed as a priest, the better to get on with the missionaries, most of whom were Jesuits. But this may be legend. At any rate, the "Father of Archaeology" in Europe, Johann Joachim Winckelmann, had also taken this step in order to gain the favor of a cardinal.

When Bandelier, in the course of his trip to Spain, died in Seville in 1914, the magazine *El Palacio* in Santa Fé, long his headquarters, headlined its story: DEATH OF BANDELIER AN IRREPARABLE LOSS.[7]

Bandelier's scientific reports, his notes, even his journals, kept every night with painstaking accuracy in his tiny handwriting (the first volume was not published until 1966), remain to this day of immense value for the student and for everyone first encountering this wild landscape of the Southwest. They provide a remarkable guide to the study of the first Americans. But a book of his of another genre altogether is of far more general interest. It is a novel—and a book, moreover, that is not even mentioned in most of the extensive bibliographies on the archaeology of the Southwest. Bandelier's novel has been totally forgotten—an undeserved fate for a book such as this.

It is an altogether unique book: a novel about prehistoric man, with all its action set in prehistoric times. As far as I have been able to determine, there are few examples of its type in serious literature. In saying this, I am disregarding cheap science fiction, which mingles prehistory with feats of astronavigation. In 1907 the novelist of grand adventures, Jack London, published *Before Adam*. Its entire action also takes place in prehistory. But the novel serves chiefly as an argument for London's unswerving belief in the correctness of the theory of evolution. He conjures up a people "without weapons, without fire, and in the raw beginnings of speech," virtually still apes "in the process of becoming men." Certainly no such people existed in North America; the process of becoming men took place on other continents. In 1915 London took up the theme once more. In Chapter XXI of his militant novel, *The Star Rover*, he has a prisoner in a strait jacket take a brief hallucinatory "trip" into prehistory. These books cannot be compared with Bandelier's historically based work, any more than the romances of the Austrian writer A. T. Sonnleitner and the Dane Johannes V. Jensen. The former wrote chiefly for young people, and the latter is so drenched in Nordic mythology that the word "historical" hardly applies.

It is not unusual for a scientist to write a novel. What is unusual is for the scientist to use his own science as the background, as the source of his plot and dramatic involvements. The English physicist C. P. Snow's novels—the outstanding example of our times—have nothing to do with his science, which is revolutionary, whereas his art remains profoundly conservative. He and many others like him live and have lived schizophrenically, scientists on the one hand, artists on the other, at home in the "two cultures," whose separation Snow in particular has theoretically lamented, but which he himself neatly separates.

Not so Bandelier. He wrote his novel within the framework of his science. In his foreword he explains his intention and his method as follows:

"By clothing sober facts in the garb of romance I have hoped to make the 'Truth about the Pueblo Indians' more accessible and perhaps more acceptable to the public in general.

"The sober facts which I desire to convey may be divided into three classes,—geographical, ethnological, and archaeological. The descriptions of the country and of its nature *are real*. The descriptions of manners and customs, of creed and rites, are from *actual observations* by myself and other ethnologists, from the statements of trustworthy Indians, and from a great number of Spanish sources of old date, in which the Pueblo Indian is represented as he lived when still unchanged by contact with European civilization.

"The descriptions of architecture are based upon investigations of ruins still in existence on the sites where they are placed in the story.

"The plot is my own. But most of the scenes described I have *witnessed*."

In other words, Bandelier had worked into this novel his anthropological, ethnological, sociological, botanical, zoological, geographical, and historical researches and observations, the products of his many years in the pueblo regions.

That, indeed, makes for the unique quality of this historical novel: the personal experience that Bandelier was able to project into the past—with good reason, as he thought, for he was convinced that most of the customs and good manners he had witnessed had been the same hundreds of years before, long before the time of Columbus. He was careful, however, not to specify the century precisely. But he felt sure that, for example, the meeting of the powerful secret society called the Secret Order of the Koshare, which he describes in Chapter XI, followed an immemorial pattern and was no different in the past from what it was in the 1880's, since these rites were governed by the strictest traditions. And when he extols the high level of the social structure, we may assume that in the old days it was even higher, even more complex, because not yet subverted by the influences of the Christian missionaries, which undoubtedly left their mark, although not so great a one as the missionaries must have hoped.

The material that Bandelier gathered in his 490 pages, each scientific detail embedded in a well-constructed story, is absolutely enormous. There is scarcely a book in which

(The New York Historical Society)

(The American Museum of Natural History)

ANCIENT AMERICAN BATTLE-MOUND.

Thomas Jefferson (1743–1826), a portrait by Rembrandt Peale, 1803. Jefferson's investigation of a mound in Virginia ushered in scientific excavation in North America. This lively, imaginative drawing of a different ancient battle mound dates from 1858, by which time many of the mounds were overgrown or eroded.

(E. B. Sayles, The Arizona State Museum)

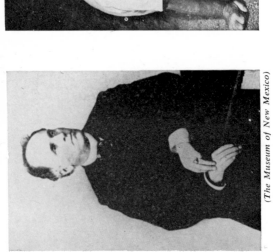

(The Museum of New Mexico)

Above, left, Adolph F. Bandelier (1840–1914), the pioneer of Southwestern archaeology. Right, left, Alfred V. Kidder (1885–1963), who introduced those rigorous scientific methods that have been continued and improved upon by Emil W. Haury (far right) (b. 1904), noted for his excavation at Snaketown, Ariz.

A museum model of Pueblo Aztec in New Mexico, here reconstructed up to the third story. ("Aztec" refers not to ancient Mexico but to a small town in the northeastern corner of New Mexico.) The circular structure in the foreground is the male meeting room, the Great Kiva (41 feet in diameter). In A.D. 1252 the pueblo of nearly 400 rooms was mysteriously abandoned.

Earl H. Morris (left), who won fame as the excavator of Aztec, shown in excavation in Canyon del Muerto (Death Canyon). Visible are 22 skulls, baskets, and vases, and several mummies, of which the second from the right is especially well preserved. The shapeless bundles on the left are also mummies, still wrapped in their original woven mats.

Mummy from the Aztec ruins, still half wrapped in matting, along with ceramic grave goods. The scalp is in poor condition, but the hair is fairly well preserved.

Mummy from a cave in Grand Gulch, Utah, with well-preserved breech-
clout.

Two Indian assistants at the excavation of Pueblo Bonito in New Mexico, which in the twelfth century A.D. housed more than 1,200 people. On the floor the pottery is *in situ*, in the very position in which it was exposed. Note the careful plastering of the walls.

The radiocarbon laboratory at the University of Pennsylvania, at which fairly precise dating of artifacts and objects can be obtained. The method was developed by Willard F. Libby, who was awarded the Nobel Prize for this achievement in 1960.

(University of Pennsylvania)

Dr. A. E. Douglass, inventor of tree-ring dating, removing a sample with a hollow drill that is manufactured solely by one Swedish family enterprise. This method is the only one that permits datings of old structures and even of charred remains *precisely to the year.*

(Western Ways Photo by Charles W. Herbert)

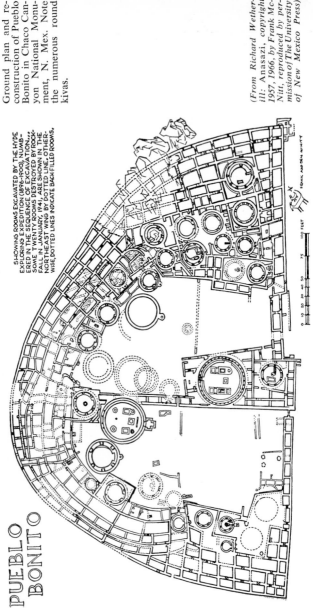

Ground plan and reconstruction of Pueblo Bonito in Chaco Canyon National Monument, N. Mex. Note the numerous round kivas.

(From Richard Wetherill: Anasazi, copyright 1957, 1966, by Frank McNitt, reproduced by permission of The University of New Mexico Press)

PUEBLO
BONITO

SHOWING ROOMS EXCAVATED BY THE HYDE
EXPLORING EXPEDITION (1896-1900), NUMBERED IN THE SEQUENCE OF EXCAVATION...
SOME TWENTY ROOMS DESTROYED BY ROCK-
FALL IN JANUARY, 1941, ARE SHOWN IN THE
NORTHEAST WING BY DOTTED LINE, OTHER-
WISE, DOTTED LINES INDICATE BACK-FILLED ROOMS.

0 10 20 30 40 50   75   100 FEET

FRANK AND S.H. WHITT

(United States Geological Survey)

The upper sketch was made by the well-known Western explorer, William Henry Jackson, who visited the ruins in 1877. Dr. Douglass performed his first precise tree-ring datings in this gigantic 800-room pueblo and found that it had been built A.D. 919–1130.

(Harper and Row)

Northern part of the Taos Pueblo as it looked in 1886. Today, the Taos Indians still live in the complex and like their ancestors reach their entrances on the roofs by ladders. D. H. Lawrence wrote respectfully of Taos, as did the Swiss psychoanalyst C. G. Jung (see Chapter 10).

The five Wetherill brothers. Richard (center) earned special fame for his discovery of the cliff dwellings of Mesa Verde, Colo., and his explorations in the vicinity of the Four Corners. This photograph was probably taken in 1893, a few years after Richard happened upon the fabulous Cliff Palace.

Reconstruction of an everyday scene in a cliff dwelling at Mesa Verde, Colo. Most activities took place out on the terrace, the rooms being used only for sleeping and the storage of supplies. In the foreground one of the Pueblo Indians' two domestic animals: the turkey (the other was the dog).

(Mesa Verde National Park)

Cliff Palace, Mesa Verde, an intricate structure built into a natural cave. The visitor is sitting on the edge of one of the many kivas, which when intact was accessible only through a hatchway in the roof.

(Dorothea S. Michelman)

Square Tower Ruin is another of the some 800 cliff dwellings of Mesa Verde. The four-story tower converts this cave settlement into a fortress. Today it is not accessible to tourists.

(Dorothea S. Michelman)

Several of the large storage jars used by the Hohokam in Arizona. The sharply curved rim of the vessels is typical of the late period from about A.D. 900–1200, at which period animal motifs appear as decoration, such as the salamander on the jar at left. The lady displaying them is Wilma Kaemlein, Curator of Collections at the Arizona State Museum.

Stone cosmetic palettes of the Hohokam, dating from A.D. 700–900. They served for mixing the paints used by the men, rather than the women, for adorning their persons. These palettes, usually six to nine inches, were frequently carved in the form of animals.

The Hohokam *etched* animal motifs on fragile marine shells—such as the horned lizard on the shell at the left—500 years before Albrecht Dürer popularized the etching process in Europe. The unfinished shell at the right shows that the process begins with a drawing being made on the shell in a substance resistant to the acid (derived from a species of cactus).

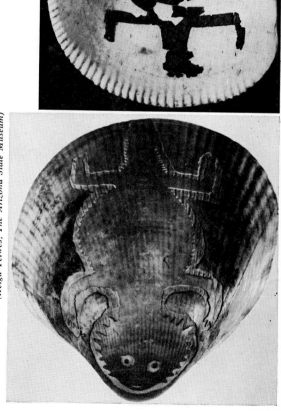

(*Helga Teiwes, The Arizona State Museum*)

(*Helga Teiwes, The Arizona State Museum*)

The greatest accomplishment of the Hohokam in their thousand-year history: extensive canal systems built to irrigate the desert. The painting depicts the Indians at work—without shovels and wheelbarrows.

(Paul Coze)

the modern reader can find so much lore presented so readably.

The title of the book is *The Delight Makers*. The reference is to the members of the Secret Council who assembled in the kiva. Bandelier uses the word "delight" in the sense of "bliss," "inward joy," and with a nod toward the older meaning of the word, which, Webster tells us, once had an active sense: "the power of affording pleasurable emotion or felicity."

A word on the literary qualities of this book. As a first novel, it is a respectable achievement. It has the strengths and weaknesses of the novels of the entire nineteenth century. The plot and its complicated intrigues might have come from Walter Scott; the love of telling detail could have been borrowed from Charles Dickens. The novel deals only with the Tehuas and the Queres in New Mexico and has, it must be admitted, a provincial air—although the word "provincial" sounds very odd in conjunction with Indian surroundings. But ultimately all comparisons are pointless. The book is unique and remains outside the categories of literary criticism. Not that the literary critics have taken the slightest notice of it up to the present day.

D. H. LAWRENCE

"White people always, or nearly always, write sentimentally about Indians. Even a man like Adolph Bandelier. He was not a sentimental man. On the contrary. Yet the sentimentality creeps in, when he writes about the thing he knows best, the Indian."

—"Indians and Entertainment," in *Mornings in Mexico*

Although for the modern reader this book is bathed in a faint romantic glow, Bandelier was not aiming at romanticism. It is true that the greatest and most profound of the German romantics, Novalis, says, "Everything turns romantic as soon as it is moved far away." But Bandelier, whose novel was first published in 1890, then reprinted twice, in 1916 and 1918, before it was forgotten, had earlier taken a severe view of romancing. This we know because of a lecture of his, delivered on February 3, 1885, at the New York Historical Society, on "The Romantic

School in American Archaeology," in which he roundly condemned the archaeologists of his time for that approach. His final sentence has an odd ring in light of the fact that he had already begun his novel, which was unquestionably a piece of historical fiction: "The days of historical fiction are past; the progress of science in auxiliary branches is alone great enough to carry the history of America upward to those heights when it shall become a critical, and therefore *practically useful,* branch of human knowledge."

But archaeology was already entering on this new phase, and a new respect for science was in the air. In 1928 the *Dictionary of American Biography* recorded: "No American archaeologist has depended as did Bandelier upon historical sources; and no American historian has checked his work so fully by a study of archaeological material."

This article on Bandelier is signed with the initials A.V.K., which stand for Alfred Vincent Kidder, who was twenty-nine years old when Bandelier died in 1914 and who was destined to carry on his labors and to place the archaeology of the Southwest on so sound a scientific footing that his work has earned the epithet of "classic." Its major theses remain unshaken and have become axiomatic.

In 1907 a note was tacked to a bulletin board at Harvard University stating that Dr. E. L. Hewett of the Archaeological Institute of America was seeking three students of anthropology as volunteers for an expedition to the Indian lands of the Southwest. Three young men who had barely dipped their noses into the science promptly volunteered: Sylvanus Morley, John Gould Fletcher, and Kidder. Chance had it that all three would win fame. We have already spoken of Kidder's contribution. Morley became the internationally known expert on the Mayas; Fletcher made a name for himself as a poet. Hewett accepted all three. Probably older and more experienced students failed to leap at the adventure. Forty years later Kidder wrote of this first assignment in the Southwest:

"We met Dr. Hewett, after a sixty mile wagon ride from Mancos, Colorado, at 'Moke Jim' Holly's ranch in McElmo canyon close to the Utah line. It was a three-room adobe in a little patch of alfalfa, the ultimate outpost on the long desert road to the little Mormon town of Bluff City on the San Juan. We slept in the lee of the Hollys' haystack. Next morning Dr. Hewett—and what a foot-traveller he was in those days—tramped us miles down the blazing hot canyon. We panted after him up the mesa at the McElmo's junction with the Yellow Jacket. From this towering prow we could see Mesa Verde and Ute Peak in Colorado; the Abajos and the distant Henry Mountains in Utah; the tall, red buttes of Monument Valley and the blue line of the Lukachukais in Arizona. None of us had ever viewed so much of the world all at one time, nor so wild and barren and broken a country as lay about us.

"Dr. Hewett waved an arm. 'I want you boys,' he said, 'to make an archaeological survey of this region. I'll be back in six weeks. You'd better get some horses.' "

It was of course insane to make such a request of three young students. But there was method behind it:

"Dr. Hewett, in one of his books, has said that he set us this appalling task to *try us out*. And it *was* a trial. . . . The tale is worth telling: of our struggles to hitch the team of horses we hired and to keep the ancient wagon from falling apart; of our abandonment of that vehicle and our purchase of three mares, each with a shambling colt; of our amateur efforts to survey the mass of canyons with a small pocket compass and to map and describe the many ruins we found."[8]

Yet Kidder was an ebullient student who, as he tells it, had come to anthropology and archaeology by accident: the lectures fell at more convenient times than those in medicine, the field he had originally meant to study, but which would have meant the end of his free weekends.

Kidder's academic career proved rich in honors. He benefited greatly from the opportunity to travel while still a student to Greece and Egypt, where he familiarized himself with the high standard of European excavations. In particular, he observed the work of George A. Reisner, the prominent Egyptologist, whose course Kidder took immediately after his return to Harvard. Kidder of all people called Reisner a "dandy"; yet he must have taken him as a model, for all contemporaries agree that in dress and manners Kidder was always a "perfect gentleman."

He dug at many sites in North America, but chiefly in Utah, Arizona, and New Mexico. His long spell of excavation in Central America, in the land of the Mayas, need only be mentioned here; but it was there that he learned the vital importance of teamwork among different scientific disciplines. For a single excavation he gathered archaeologists, ethnologists, physical anthropologists (specialists in the study of human physical characteristics), philologists, physicians, and geographers under the same tent.

Visiting the Greek museums with their great wealth in vases must have impressed him with the value of pottery for characterizing a cultural period, even if all that is left are the smallest potsherds.

But along with this he recognized the importance of chronology, that the archaeologist must constantly link the pottery and shards, in fact, every single find from skeletons to buildings, with chronology and hence with the history, the course of development of cultures. The archaeologist, he wrote, must never forget his "proper business, which is the study of the long, slow growth of human culture and the formulation of the problems of the development of society."[9] In saying this Kidder was far ahead of his time, at least in North America, where as late as 1938 an anthropologist with a bias for pure facts could say, "Theory in Anthropology is a dirty word!" Actually, Kidder's scientific methods and theories were slow to win acceptance. Not until the thirties was his approach applied to research in the Mississippi Basin. "Not until the forties were the same techniques used on the Atlantic slope," comments John Witthoft of the University of Pennsylvania in a critical survey of the course of North American Archaeology.[10]

Kidder's influence was also enlarged through the many students who worked under him. "We students, of course," one of them has said, "had more questions than answers, but he was always patient with us and helped give us *perspective* that we value along with our more formal teaching."[11] Moreover, he showed personal courage in a way that set an example to others in the field. He appears to have been the first archaeologist who went up in a plane—piloted by Charles Lindbergh, the pioneer aviator—to take archaeological aerial photographs of ruins.

Today Lindbergh recalls:

"In our Pecos-area survey projects, my wife and I (in a single-engine tandem-open-cockpit 'Falcon' biplane) cruised back and forth over areas of New Mexico and Arizona, hunting for marks of early civilization. When we saw the crossing lines of village walls, we would photograph them and mark this location on our map. . . . We found that the ruins of ancient Pecos villages could be more easily located from the air than from the ground. From the air we could see dimly but definitely the square or rectangular lines on the earth that marked where walls had stood. . . . I remember Dr. Kidder well, and with great friendship and admiration."[12]

Kidder's most important excavation, in the course of which he laid the groundwork for the methods of American archaeology, took place in the ruins of Pecos and lasted, except for a three-year suspension during the First World War, from 1915 to 1929. In 1924 Kidder summed up his labors there in a book that has by now become a classic: *An Introduction to the Study of Southwestern Archaeology.* He died at the age of seventy-eight, in 1963. His memory has been kept green by the annual Pecos Conference, which he convoked for the first time in 1927, and by a prize, the Kidder Award for Achievement in American Archaeology. One hundred bronze medals have been deposited in the Peabody Museum, and one of these is awarded every three years by the American Anthropological Association. Here is planning on an archaeological time scale! The medals are to be meted out for 300 years!

The Pecos pueblo lies to the southeast of Santa Fé, New Mexico, on a rocky ridge in the heart of a broad valley bordered by hills and mountains and, in the north, by a high, usually snow-topped range. Today the ruins are not very impressive. As one approaches them from the road the direct view is blocked by the yellow, clumsily massive adobe walls remaining from the Spanish mission church, which rear sadly into the sky. Among the ruins of the pueblo, scarcely more than shoulder height, the chamisa bush glows a brilliant orange in the spring. Here and there a futuristic-looking cholla cactus towers out of the ruins with its needle-sharp spines.

The visitor must summon up all his imagination to picture the pulsating life of many hundreds of families who for centuries inhabited this beehive town, when the walls still rose story upon story.

And yet the history of Pecos is quite close to our time. Bandelier met the direct descendants of the last people to leave Pecos.

The oldest Spanish narrative that tells us something about the character of the people of Pecos comes from Castaña de Sosa's expedition. In the latter part of December, 1590, one of his lieutenants, accompanied by only a few men, trustfully entered Pueblo Cicuyé (as Pecos was then called)

seeking food and shelter. Weakened as they were by cold
and hunger, the Spaniards had to behave peacefully. The
morning after their arrival they left their weapons behind
and went strolling among the Indians in an effort to cement friendship. Suddenly the Indians fell upon them. The
Spaniards barely escaped with their lives. They lost most
of their weapons but managed to rejoin Sosa, who set out
at once to recover the weapons—for iron weapons were
the Spaniards' most essential possession. Sosa, too, made
conciliating approaches. But the Indians drew up their ladders and showered him and his men with arrows.

Sosa had no more than nineteen soldiers and seventeen
native servants. He did have the advantage of two small
brass cannon, but he did not use these effectively. It must
be said that the Pueblo men acted in a cowardly manner.
While Sosa was marching up and down outside the walls
for a good five hours, repeatedly shouting that all he demanded was the return of his weapons, the Indians retained
their courage; they threw stones and shot arrows. But when
Sosa at last made preparations to storm the town, they
laid down their arms, calling out, *"Amigo!"* And during
the next few days they vanished, individually and in groups,
leaving the town to Sosa. Only then did the Spaniard find
that he had been dealing with a town of probably *2,000*
persons. He discovered the broad areas of cultivated land,
the canny irrigation, the enormous hoard of food (he estimated it at 30,000 fanegas; a fanega contains fifty-five
liters). He found quantities of winter clothing, capes of
buffalo leather and cotton, mantillas "gaily colored," decorated with fur and feathers.

The next man to subjugate this area was Oñate. He
visited Pecos on July 24, 1598. Thereafter reports remain
sparse for a long time. When the aforementioned great
pueblo revolt broke out under the leadership of the medicine man Popé in 1680—that revolt which inflicted an
annihilating setback upon the Spaniards for ten years—the
people of Pecos scarcely took part. Pecos was only on the
fringes of the revolt. Nevertheless, the young men of the
town at least killed the hated priest.

Then Pecos gradually withered away. The town was prey
to repeated attacks by the savage, predatory Comanches,
who systematically decimated the population of Pecos. One
counteraction by the entire arms-bearing population of the
town was so bloodily smashed that only a single man
escaped alive. In 1788 an epidemic of smallpox further

depopulated the town; only 180 persons survived it. Fewer and fewer people roamed like phantoms among the many hundreds of rooms in the pueblo. In 1805 there were still 104 left. In 1845 an observer named Gregg reported:

"Even so late as ten years ago (about 1830) when it contained a population of fifty to a hundred souls, the traveller would oftentimes perceive but a solitary Indian, a woman, or a child, standing here and there like so many statues upon the roofs of their houses, with their eyes fixed on the eastern horizon, or leaning against a wall or a fence, listlessly gazing at the passing stranger; while at other times not a soul was to be seen in any direction, and the sepulchral silence of the place was only disturbed by the occasional barking of a dog, or the cackling of hens."[13]

In 1837 only eighteen adults continued to live in the ghost town. The people of Jemez Pueblo, the only Indians in the vicinity who spoke the same language, invited the eighteen to move in with them. But the people of Pecos proudly refused. Then, in 1839, an epidemic of mountain fever broke out among them. Only five survived it. They went to Jemez. These were the "last people of Pecos." Only their Christian names are known: Antonio, Gregorio, Goya, Juan Domingo, and Francisco.

One unusual feature of Pecos that strikes the visitor at once is an oval defensive wall, almost a thousand yards in circumference, which is still recognizable as such. The remains of towers have also been identified. Normally pueblos had no surrounding walls; once the ladders were drawn to the upper stories the beehive structure itself was a fortress. And Pecos had a spring! "A never-failing spring of pure, cold water. Such an ideal combination of easily defensible building site and abundant water supply could not fail to appeal to the ancient village Indian, and the Pecos *mesilla* was settled in *very early times.*"

What caused Kidder to decide to devote a long period to excavation of Pecos was above all the vast quantity of potsherds. Because of their varied character these would certainly be traceable to different epochs. Moreover, Kidder wrote, the large cemeteries of Pecos "had never been despoiled, and the graves promised a rich harvest of skeletal materials and mortuary offerings." Exploiting all this material was only a question of good organization. "We were most anxious to discover burials; so a reward of twenty-five cents was offered to the workmen for every skeleton uncovered. The next day one appeared, the following day six; the reward was reduced to ten cents; this brought fifteen more, and in the course of a week or so we were forced to discontinue the bonus or go into bankruptcy."

In fact, by this fourth season of excavation Kidder had

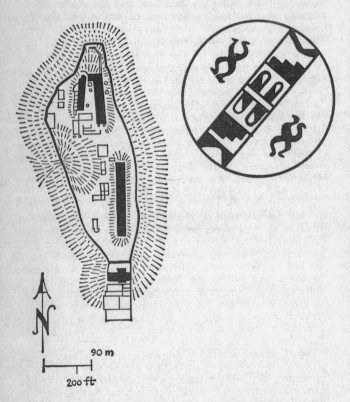

Artist's version of Bandelier's first sketch of the ruined town of Pecos. The black bands in the upper part of the drawing represent the Pueblo buildings; the cross-shaped structure is the ground plan of the much more recent Spanish mission church. After Bandelier, Kidder dug at this site. The drawing on the right shows the decoration on a bowl he excavated.

uncovered no fewer than 700 skeletons, and by the end of the excavation this number had risen to 1,200. He also collected hundreds of thousands, literally hundreds of thousands, of shards. His wife took charge of the cleaning and preliminary ordering of these—while also looking after her five children.

Kidder was quite clear about his aims. Pecos "gave rise to the hope that remains would there be found so stratified as to make clear the *development* of the various Pueblo arts, and thus enable us to place *in their proper chronological order* many other Southwestern ruins. . . ."

This hope was fulfilled in the course of excavating the building itself. "We had expected to find on the mesa top the remains of a single large pueblo showing, perhaps, signs of repair and rebuilding, but founded on the rock and permitting the easy examination of its walls from top to bottom. Instead of this it had developed that the *historic town was erected on the broken and tumbled walls of earlier houses,* and that these *again had been built over at least two still more ancient ones.*" Ultimately it turned out that *six* "towns" had been built one on top of the other in Pecos. (Kidder uses the word "town" for the complex of buildings.)

Nor was that all. Drawing upon the results of his own and others' investigations throughout the entire Southwest, above all from the region around Four Corners along the San Juan River, Kidder was able to confirm what the inquisitive farmer Wetherill had first discovered in Grand Gulch and Mesa Verde decades before: before the pueblo builders a far more primitive people must have lived in the region—tillers of the soil, a people not yet acquainted with pottery, but producers of excellent baskets—the "Basket Makers."

Into what depths of the past had Kidder penetrated? For the present he could do no more than determine the order of the strata and name them.

He set up a chronology consisting of eight major cultural divisions, beginning with the Basket Makers and ending with the Pueblos, who still survived. But his arrangement did not satisfy him. In 1927, therefore, he invited those among his colleagues who were working on the same problems to the first Pecos Conference in order to devise a new terminology. The results of this conference became known as the Pecos Classification. For decades these were the accepted categories. Since, however, a revision worked out by Frank H. H. Roberts, Jr., is now more and more coming into use, we present both side by side. Roman numeral I represents the oldest period, extending back long before the time of Columbus.

Pecos Classification	Roberts's Modification
Basket Maker I	. . . .
Basket Maker II	Basket Maker
Basket Maker III	Modified Basket Maker
Pueblo I }	Developmental Pueblo
Pueblo II }	
Pueblo III	Great Pueblo
Pueblo IV	Regressive Pueblo
Pueblo V	Historic Pueblo

Roberts's chart is not only a modification, but an improvement, though a slight one, insofar as it provides some characterization of the eras.[14] (The reader who is interested in greater detail will find it in the note.)

Establishing such a historical succession is all very well, of course, but it tells us nothing whatsoever about how long, say, the Basket Maker III or Pueblo II cultures lasted or in what century of the Christian chronology the Basket Makers developed into pueblo builders. Was it 500 years ago, or 800, or 1,000 years?

Not relative chronology, but an absolute, datable chronology of some kind is what really gives us history.

Among the archaeologists present at the first Pecos Conference there was one outsider, the physicist and astronomer Dr. Andrew E. Douglass, who had some remarks to make on this problem. In Chapter 8 we shall show that he *solved* the problem and by using methods in no way archaeological set up the framework for an absolute chronology for North American archaeology, especially for the archaeology of the Southwest.

But before we go into this, let us turn to the *excavation* of a pueblo. For this we shall consider the ruins of Aztec (*New* Mexico, not old Mexico), a site where the rise and downfall of a pueblo can be shown taking place within a limited time span and where certain typical elements occur in conjunction with quite unique and mysterious elements. But we choose this pueblo also because it is not associated with Kidder. For the reader should be aware that there were others beside Kidder who were carrying out valuable investigations of the ruins in the Southwest, contemporaries of his who contributed essential pebbles to the mosaic that Kidder almost completed in his *Introduction*. And finally, because in Aztec the diggers very early encountered pre-historic pueblo *man*. For strange to relate, though there is hardly an American who does not know what an Egyptian mummy is, few people know that in North America *hundreds of mummies have been found*.

4

The Rise and Fall of Pueblo Aztec

ALTHOUGH the excavation of Aztec is associated chiefly with the name of Earl H. Morris, it was actually an amateur who reported the first excavation of the site. At the time, in the 1880's, the amateur was a schoolboy not quite ten years old. In an amazing demonstration of the powers of memory, he gave his report some fifty years later.

His name was Sherman S. Howe, and he was one of the first pupils in the newly established one-room school of Aztec, which had also obtained its first schoolteacher at the time. All we know about that schoolteacher is that his name was Johnson. But he must have been more than the usual drillmaster. For he aroused the interest of his pupils in the visible past around them and implanted curiosity in their minds. Armed with spades and picks, determined to make discoveries, he set out with them for the ruins on a Saturday. Half a century later Howe recalled the boy he had been:

"It was snowing a little and quite cold. We went into

a second-story room, more than half full of dirt, and began digging down at the corner of the room. We struck the second floor at about five feet, and broke a hole through about two and one-half feet in diameter, but could see nothing but a black dungeon below. There was a prolonged debate about the depth of it, what might be at the bottom, and how a person could ever get back if he did go down there. Some thought it might be full of rats, skunks, bats, or rattle-snakes. We could imagine a hundred things. I believe the dread of ghosts was the worst."[1] Who would be the first to climb down in? What would he find? Young Sherman pressed forward. . . .

The Aztec ruins, today a national monument accessible by excellent roads, lie along the Animas, a river that flows from Colorado south into the northwest corner of New Mexico and joins the San Juan River. The river valley is about two miles wide and exceedingly fertile. Wild roses grow luxuriantly in shady places. Although the valley is 5,600 feet above sea level, there is ample rainfall.

The name of the ruins and the present town is, of course, misleading. No Aztecs ever lived in Aztec. But in the nineteenth century the blind historian William Prescott had published his fascinating *Conquest of Mexico,* a book that even then found its way into the smallest American libraries. Therefore people knew about the power and the glory of the Aztec empire of Mexico; they had formed a notion of its splendid temples and palaces that Hernando Cortés destroyed. And so whenever the layman encountered ruins that were even moderately impressive, he was inclined to attribute them to the Aztecs. Who else?

But the ruins in our "Aztec" on the Animas in *New* Mexico were older than those whose name they bore. In fact, the people known as Aztecs had not yet set out on their road to power in what is now Mexico City when the pueblo people were already facing decline.

The oldest written reference to them is found on a map made by the Spaniard Miera y Pacheco around 1777. He records the "ruins of very old towns" between the Animas and the Florida rivers. There are just a few more mentions in the nineteenth century by various travelers. When the western railroad line reached only as far as Canyon City, Colorado, Lewis H. Morgan forged on in a covered wagon. Morgan, the great anthropologist and Bandelier's teacher, brought back with him the first scientific drawings of the

Aztec ruins. He found rooms still completely intact, with sound roofs over them, even on the second story. But from a homesteader he learned the bad news that a quarter of the stone walls had not been destroyed by nature. The settlers of the surrounding farms had used the well-hewn sandstone blocks for building their own houses. (In defense of those homesteaders let us remember that in medieval Rome no ignorant farmers but highly cultivated popes and princes used the ancient Colosseum as building material for their palaces.)

Every so often the ruins were visited and looked at, but they continued to decay until 1916, when Earl H. Morris began his systematic excavation. Along with this, he protected the building from further vandalism and initiated reconstruction work. At this time no one as yet had any idea of how large the original structure was, or when it had been built, what people had lived there, and what else might still be hidden under the ruins. In general, little more was known than had been discovered by the schoolboy Sherman Howe thirty years earlier.

Schoolmaster Johnson was not going to have the youngest of his pupils descend first into the underworld. One of the older boys was let down on a rope. A musty odor of decay wafted upward. Hesitantly, the others followed. The surprise for which they geared themselves turned out to be a negative one. The flickering light of their candles glided over smooth walls, a smooth ceiling, a perfectly smooth floor. The room was large but utterly empty; there was not the smallest piece of trash, not a trace of ashes, not a chip of broken pottery. Then, in one wall, they made out a doorway. They crowded through it. It was exactly the same here: a similar room in similar condition. It seemed as though the people who had lived here centuries ago had carefully cleaned house before leaving it, just as a person would clean today if he hoped to rent his house on favorable terms.

"Mr. Johnson seemed disappointed and puzzled," Howe recalls. But then they looked eagerly for further adventure. One of the walls showed curious traces of labor. Without more ado, they broke a hole through it.

The first candle they held into the yawning blackness went out in the stale air. They waved their hands until enough fresh air had been fanned in. Then they lighted the candle again, and now, when the first glints of light danced over the walls and floor of this new room, the boys saw something that would have made the heart of any Tom Sawyer pound:

Against the wall a skeleton was leaning!

The boys stood numbed. "It must be that we were struck dumb with awe, and that we were debating in our minds whether to stand our ground or retreat."

Mr. Johnson could not have known that many other skeletons had been found in the United States. But something told him that here were the remains of someone native to this continent long before Columbus crossed the sea. One of those aboriginal inhabitants had been buried here—not very ceremoniously, apparently, for he had simply been leaned against the wall half-dressed, and the room had then been sealed up.

As they timorously looked closer, the boys and their teacher saw that the head had been broken off and was resting on the ground in an unnatural position. Dried scraps of skin lay on the floor, looking like leather, and mingled with these pieces of skin were strands of dark hair. As they recovered from their shock, they felt venturesome again. But hours had already passed. Johnson decided to put an end to the expedition for the present, but promised the boys to continue next Saturday.

But next Saturday the whole scene looked altogether different. In their excitement the boys had told their parents about the ghostly discovery, whereupon the hearts of these sober farmers also swelled with the urge to explore. A whole band of men now climbed through the first hole and at once set about with picks pounding holes in all the walls, hoping to find other rooms to explore. The boys crawled through ahead of them. And this time there were plenty of surprises. Once again, in Howe's recollections:

"I got into that room and stood, trying my best to take it all in and see everything I could, while that excited crowd was rummaging it, scattering and turning everything into a mess. There were *thirteen* skeletons ranging from infants to adults. The infants were two in number. The skulls had not knit together. One of them had two teeth. All were wrapped in netting similar to that around tea chests that come from China, and tied with strings made from fiber of the yucca plant. There were large pieces of cotton cloth. Most of it was plain, resembling our ten-ounce duck. It was in good state of preservation except that it was somewhat colored with age. Some of the cloth had a colored

(red) design in stripes. There was also some feather cloth, and several pieces of netting of various types. There were several baskets, some of the best that I have ever seen, all well preserved. There were a lot of sandals, some very good, others showing considerable wear. There was a large quantity of pottery. . . . Some of the pottery was very pretty and new looking."

There was too much to grasp at a single glance. The lighting was dim, and too many people were milling about. Only gradually did Howe and the others become aware of the smaller objects.

"There were a great many beads and ornaments. I cannot give a description of these, as I had no opportunity to examine them closely. I remember seeing quite a lot of turquoise. There were a number of stone axes, polished, and much nicer in appearance than the average type found in this vicinity. There were also skinning knives, so-called, and sandal lasts; cushions or rings they wore on their heads for carrying burdens—some made of yucca, nicely woven or braided; some made very plain, in coils of yucca strips, tied in various places to hold the strips together; some were made of juniper bark wrapped with strings, and some were made of corn husks. These may have been used also as jar rests to support vessels with convex bottoms which would not stand upright very well without some kind of support."

What happened next was, from the archaeological point of view, pure vandalism. But who could have taught these ordinary farmers, who now felt like treasure hunters, any better way to proceed? For weeks thereafter it became the local weekend sport after church to climb down into the ruins to "collect." But what was done with these precious, so miraculously preserved evidences of a prehistoric people? Howe recalls that very well:

"When we had finished this work, the stuff was taken out and carried off by different members of the party, *but where is it now?* Nobody knows. Like most of the material from the smaller pueblos around the larger buildings, it is gone. I, being only a small kid, did not get my choice of artifacts. I had to take what was left, which made a nice little collection, at that. But it, too, is about all gone!"

But there was still plenty left, far more than Johnson and his boys suspected. And Earl Morris uncovered it.

It is remarkable how many of the subsequently famous

anthropologists and archaeologists arrived at their vocations in their earliest youth.

Frank Cushing was nine years old when he received his first pre-Columbian arrowheads from a farmer who turned them up while plowing. By the time he was fourteen he had a collection of several hundred, and began digging. Julio Tello at the age of ten took note of some obviously artificial holes in an Indian skull that led him to his later studies on Indian methods of surgery. Roland T. Bird began his career at the age of nine, as his father's helper, and ultimately became the great dinosaur specialist who provided the American Museum of Natural History with eighty tons of dinosaur bones and other fossils. Frank C. Hibben, the future excavator of the Sandia Cave, was doing service as a water carrier at the age of nine, at the excavations of "mounds."

But the outstanding child prodigy was undoubtedly Earl Morris. On reaching the age of sixty-three he proclaimed that he was celebrating his sixtieth anniversary as an archaeologist. Born in 1889, he was little more than three years old when he undertook his first excavation. He recalls:

"One morning, in March of 1893, Father handed me a worn-out pick, the handle of which he had shortened to my length, and said: 'Go dig in that hole where I worked yesterday, and you will be out of my way.' At my first stroke there rolled down a roundish, gray object that looked like a cobblestone, but when I turned it over, it proved to be the bowl of a black-on-white dipper. I ran to show it to my mother. She grabbed the kitchen butcher knife and hastened to the pit to uncover the skeleton with which it had been buried. Thus, at three and a half years of age there had happened the clinching event which was to make of me an ardent pot hunter, who later was to acquire the more creditable, and I hope earned, classification as an archaeologist."[2]

He kept this black-and-white decorated bowl until his death in 1956. As an excavator he did a good deal in the land of the Mayas, like Kidder, but again like Kidder his true love was the Southwest. He was the digger par excellence, the man for physical work in the field, and it was only with an effort that he forced himself to toil at the desk. His collections, almost all of which have been preserved in the University of Colorado Museum, are enormous in quantity, but scarcely half of them have been evaluated, and he himself interpreted only a relatively small part of them. For many of his excavations the only record remaining is his diaries, although these were kept with great precision and with excellent illustrative material. It was not until after his death that the University of Colorado in 1963 began publishing he Earl Morris papers, which include evaluations of his finds, under the direction of Joe Ben Wheat.

Here we confront one of the truly central problems of modern archaeology, not only in America, but throughout the entire world. The past several decades have seen so much excavation that the scientific evaluation of the discoveries can no longer keep pace. In 1961 I obtained permission to see the ordinarily inaccessible cellars of the Athens National Museum. No doubt about it: the most useful Greek "excavation" today could be (and certainly should be) conducted in these cellars where countless treasures repose, treasures that have not even been catalogued yet and which even archaeologists who have worked in Greece for years have never seen. As for the situation in American archaeology, Joe Ben Wheat, curator for Anthropology at the University of Colorado Museum, comments:

"Such collections often are known to a few archaeologists by reputation, even by footnote or brief-reference type of publication; but by and large, they remain just as buried and unknown as if they had never been excavated. If the not inconsiderable cost of excavation, storage, and curation is ever to be justified, then these collections must be assiduously re-excavated from the museum and placed on record. From the point of view of knowledge, this is even more important, for most of this material *could not be duplicated today*."[3]

In any case, in 1915 Dr. N. C. Nelson, then archaeologist of the American Museum of Natural History, went to have a look at the Aztec ruins. He and his colleagues agreed unequivocally that they must be excavated. Morris was selected to carry out the "dig." And Aztec became *his* Aztec. He dug there from 1916 to 1921, then sporadically in 1923, and again in 1933–34. What he had turned up by 1923 was so impressive and obviously important even to the unpracticed eye that Aztec was declared a national monument. On February 8, 1923, Earl Morris was appointed its first custodian at a salary of $1,200 a year— starvation wages even then. But he wrote cheerfully:

"My attitude toward this piece of work is not that of one

who labors because of the financial consideration involved. My interest in it is the same as if I were doing it on my own initiative."[4]

From the start he encountered great difficulties. The condition of the ruins varied greatly and the masses of earth that had to be removed—often it was soft, but often as hard as cement—were enormous. Morris conceived a fantastic plan for utilizing a sluiceway in order to wash the useless earth down from the higher northern side. That did not work. A narrow-gauge tramway also proved a failure. Finally he returned to the old method of horse-drawn wagons which could be fully loaded directly at the excavation and would transport the "rubbish" far away, to a site that was free of ruins.

The rooms he excavated had collapsed in such a variety of ways that every room had to be dug out by special methods. He discovered many kivas (twenty-nine were excavated in Aztec), those semiunderground secret assembly rooms. Most important of all, he uncovered the "Great Kiva," which rose considerably above the southern part of the plaza.

This Great Kiva is the finest and most impressive of these structures to be seen in the United States. For in 1933 and 1934 Morris restored it, so that anyone can now see it as it was centuries before Columbus when it served for secret assemblies, rites, and dances.

It is circular, with a diameter of forty-one feet along the inner floor. (This does not make it the largest: the big kiva in Chaco Canyon, for example, has a diameter of sixty-three feet.) A bare three feet above the floor it bulges to a good forty-eight feet in diameter. The room consists of two structural members; they might be called rings. The inner ring, the kiva proper, is situated eight feet underground; the outer ring consists of fourteen rooms, which open on the inner part. One of these rooms also forms the exit to the plaza.

When we enter this dusky room today, we cannot but be struck by its religious atmosphere. The well-shaped fireplace seems like an altar; carefully faced pits, whose purpose is still unknown, seem like empty sarcophagi; the stone shafts divide up the room like a church. Nowhere else in North American ruins can we feel so powerfully the religious spirit of a long-vanished people. In these surroundings, too, it is easy to imagine the fantastically garbed medicine men engaged in their ecstatic dances.

This kiva is not a primitive hole in the ground; it is architecture. Morris had already proved that the same was true for the pueblo itself. The building was not a random accumulation of crude adobe structures. Rather, the blocks of hewn sandstone were carefully fitted and their yellow-brown expanse relieved by a long ornamental band, five layers broad, of green stone.

Today three stories can still be distinguished even though so much has collapsed. There are still almost twenty rooms whose ceilings are completely intact. In fact, there may be more, for Aztec has not yet been completely excavated. The pueblo was strong and self-contained; it had only a single entrance. So-called "windows" merely lead from one room to another; none open on the outside. According to the latest data of 1962, 221 rooms have been found in the lowest story, 119 in the second story and 12 in the third. This adds up to 352 rooms, but there can be no doubt that when it flourished the pueblo was far larger. One estimate suggests that this building town was inhabited by 1,500 persons; but this is far from an exact figure. The population may have been much greater. (In 1964, for example, Roland Richart recorded the excavation of another fourteen rooms in the section called the "East Ruin.")

We have already described the geographical situation of the pueblo. What is significant about this position is that Aztec lay about halfway between the large pueblo group at Chaco Canyon (farther south, in the northwest corner of New Mexico, close to where Highway 44 now runs) and the equally large pueblo in Mesa Verde (to the north, in the southwest corner of Colorado, close to the present town of Cortez). Both are unlike in their architecture and particularly in their pottery, which is extremely varied in color and ornamentation.

How did Aztec arise? Was it the product of the emigration, or expulsion, of sizable groups from these other civilized centers? Or was there merely an exchange of ideas and techniques between an earlier population and the groups at Chaco and Mesa Verde? Or, again, did small warlike tribes conquer the valley of the Animas and impose their manner of life upon the inhabitants? None of these questions has been answered. All that is certain is that first a Chaco style prevailed in architecture, pottery, and burial rites. But very few graves have been found for this early period, which, in fact, is true for the entire Chaco region.

The utterly mysterious aspect of the building of Aztec,

however, is that it was built *twice*, with about a hundred-year interval between the two phases of building.

Only a few decades ago archaeologists would never have ventured to hope that exact dates could ever be obtained for such periods as these. Now, however, we can provide dates precisely to the year, utilizing the system of tree-ring dating. Here we can give only the *results;* we will explain the *method* later in our chapter, "The Endless Tree."

Today we know that the first Pueblo Aztec was built between A.D. 1110 and 1124; we even know that the greater part of the work was done during the years 1111–15.

Around 1110 the first group of future inhabitants reached the site and began the building. Next year there must have been an influx of much larger groups, for this year about half the pueblos were completed. No matter how many people were engaged in the work, their achievement seems staggering when we stand before the ruins today. Around 1115 the third wave of immigrants appeared and nearly completed the work. There are indications that the building was carried on up to four stories. The decade to 1124–25 saw the building of annexes, which were probably necessary as families increased, or because of the custom of using old houses as refuse dumps.

It is, of course, highly tempting to try to imagine the life of these people, and projections based on the archaeological finds are quite possible, even desirable. European scholars are extremely cautious about such descriptions—*too* cautious, for unless the archaeologist conceives of his work as ultimately bringing dead objects to life, he remains a mere collector of objects.

John M. Corbett has attempted such a reconstruction of the life for the first period of Pueblo Aztec:

"Aztec, at the height of the Chacoan occupation, must have been a fascinating sight. On a sunny summer day, the plaza and rooftops would have been a busy swarm of activity—mothers nursing and tending their young, grinding corn for tortillas, preparing meat for the stew pot, making baskets, and molding clay pots for later firing. Old men basked in the sun or instructed the young boys. Most of the men and older boys were busy tending the corn, beans, and squash in the fertile fields surrounding the pueblos. This was exacting work, since each plot, clan by clan, had to receive its carefully husbanded share of water from the irrigation ditch that ran along the slope of the high terrace just to the north of the pueblo. At times during the day, hunters would straggle in happily if burdened with game, sadly and slowly if empty-handed after a fruitless chase. Occasionally a wandering group of strangers would pass by with items to trade. They were made welcome and fed, and the whole plaza took on a festive air.

"At night the pueblo must have presented a vastly different appearance: dark, mysterious and quiet. Here and there a small dying fire cast a flickering glow upon a brown adobe wall. In one or two of the kivas, a faint light through the hatchway in the roof indicated preparations under way for a ceremony, or perhaps a special highly secret meeting of one of the clan societies. If you looked closely you might make out one of the sentinels, silhouetted briefly against the night sky as he shifted position. But the pueblo was silent—a silence broken by an occasional dog's bark or baby's wail—until, shortly after the morning star appeared, the hunters crept quietly out of the pueblo, and as the star faded, the broadening morning light heralded the approach of another day in the life of Aztec pueblo."[5]

Not a word in this idyllic description mentions any possible threat. Yet, if things went on so peacefully, it is inexplicable why this flourishing community suddenly dissolved, mysteriously vanished without a trace. Whatever happened must have taken place in a very short time. Yet the inhabitants must have had the time to pack their things quietly, for they took everything of value with them. Morris and others after him found no evidence of external catastrophe. No great fire drove them away. No plague-stricken bodies sent them running off in panic. There are no signs whatever that some warlike tribe expelled them from their houses. There are no traces of battle or slaughter, and no possessions of new occupants have been discovered.

Around 1130 the pueblo was empty, as deserted as a ghost town. Owls rested in the "window" openings; rats scurried through the rooms; the wind blew more and more sand into the cracks until the floors were covered with as much as eight inches of it. Only now and then would a crash sound among the lifeless walls as a ceiling collapsed after the rains had cut channels through it.

For a hundred years the pueblo remained deserted!

What is more mysterious is that this exodus almost coincided with that of the Chaco tribe. But in Chaco Canyon the supply of water had demonstrably shrunk to such an extent that the thousands of inhabitants could no longer feed themselves. And their emigration extended over several decades, beginning around 1100. Possibly it was a group of early emigrants from Chaco who moved north into the fertile Animas valley and there founded Aztec, establishing dominance over the much more primitive original inhabitants of Basket Makers.

But the problem of water, which drove the builders of Chaco to nomadism, did not exist in Aztec, or not acutely. The Animas was a river that never completely dried up. A few things suggest the possibility that the river may have changed its course and thus so deranged the system of irrigating the fields that repairs were either not possible or not attempted. We do not know. In all probability the thousands of Aztec men with their women and children moved southward, rejoining the Chaco people if these were really their tribe, and on learning that they were also leaving, continued on with them to the mighty Rio Grande and the land of the Hopis, where all traces of them are lost in the darkness of history.

But now we confront a second enigma.

About a hundred years later the ghost town was occupied by a new tribe. To be exact, the new settlers arrived between A.D. 1220 and 1260. Once again we find signs of a brief period of energetic building, the period between 1225 and 1250. This represents the labor of an entire generation. Children were born during this period and had time to found families.

Archaeologically, it has been proved beyond the shadow of a doubt that Aztec lay completely empty during the intervening century. For the new arrivals, finding rooms blocked with sand, broken stone and beams, built new rooms on top of the rubble instead of clearing it out. They also made many of the rooms smaller by putting up new walls and reducing the size of doors. Their style of building, their tools and pottery, unquestionably betray influences from the north, no longer from the Chaco Valley to the south but from Mesa Verde to the north. They also restored the Great Kiva, although they did work carelessly and without proper regard for the style. But at any rate they used it again. Other, smaller kivas of a different shape were built. Massive beams were pulled out of the old pueblo and used in other places, and in addition to hewn sandstone this new tribe built with cobblestone. One curious structure with three walls is what is now called the Hubbard Mound. From the whole arrangement of the religious centers it can be deduced that during this period the "priests" or medicine men were more dominant than ever before.

What struck Morris as the greatest difference between the Chaco and the Mesa Verde periods was the character of the graves. In the latter period, there were no fewer than 149, mostly under the floors of the rooms, which continued to be lived in after the burial. Many of the bodies were buried with great care, and large quantities of artifacts were given to them to accompany them on their last journey. But this practice did not last long. Suddenly there comes a period in which the burials take place with the greatest haste and scarcely any grave goods are laid beside the dead. And then a disastrous fire destroyed almost the entire eastern wing of the pueblo. Was this an accident? Or had enemies after all penetrated into the pueblo this time and burned the place deliberately? Or did the inhabitants themselves set fire to their home before they departed?

For they did depart!

Exactly as the "Chaco people" (we use this term for lack of a better) had done a century earlier, these new arrivals left after a generation, though they had just finished restoring the pueblo at the cost of infinite labor. From about 1252 on they, too, vanished into the unknown, just as their predecessors had done.

Once again no plausible external cause can be found, unless it was again a shrinking water supply. Perhaps the population early observed the omens of a catastrophic change in weather conditions, a more and more conspicuous lack of rainfall, and fled prematurely. For the really great drought, a drought of almost inconceivable duration that struck the region like one of the plagues of Egypt, did not come until two decades later and lasted precisely from 1276 to 1299. Those twenty-three years depopulated the entire San Juan Valley, which had once been so fruitful and which perhaps could have become the cradle of a North American civilization.

Today only ruins remain of Aztec, and nothing but the well-restored kiva suggests the onetime culture that stamped its character upon the lives of these peoples.

5

Mummies, Mummies . . .

A six-year-old girl once wrote in her diary: "I want to dig for buried treasure, and explore among the Indians, and paint pictures, and wear a gun, and go to college."[1] And in fact she realized almost all these desires: she went to college and studied anthropology; she made discoveries among the Indians, dug for "treasures," and at times—in the Navajo country—she also wore a gun. For this adventure-minded little girl ultimately became the wife of Earl Morris.

She was an astonishing woman. A tomboy in manner, she was extraordinarily intelligent, could endure the most incredible hardships, yet had a keen eye for the finest particulars in her husband's work and in the wild landscape of the Southwest. She has also left us an enchanting record of her work: her book *Digging in the Southwest*, which was published in 1933. Since it is neither a scholarly report nor a purely literary work, it has found no place either in bibliographies of technical archaeological writings or in histories of American literature. It has been forgotten just like Bandelier's *The Delight Makers*, and just as unfairly. For like the latter work, it once again has documentary value today, illustrating as it does the restraint with which many archaeological problems of the Southwest were regarded in 1933.

For some 300 pages Ann Axtell Morris chats about her experiences on digs with her husband. She is witty, sprightly, critical, and every so often she takes a gentle poke at the excessive pedantry of professional colleagues. But she also writes with the greatest admiration for their achievements. The book still makes marvelous reading. For the young student and the nonspecialist there is no better and more amusing introduction to the pioneering days of archaeology in the Southwest. Here is an example of her approach; she is describing the wrangles that specialists get into over definitions.

"I remember an occasion when the cream of Southwestern practicing archaeologists were gathered in one spot at a given time and spent two priceless days of their conjunction in arguing on, 'When is a kiva not a kiva?' They not only failed to agree on that negative proposition, but, what was an infinitely greater loss, they never decided positively what a kiva is. And this, be it to their shame and discomfiture, when every man, woman, and child of them can *instantly recognize a kiva as far away as it can be seen.*"

But in order to illuminate the difficulties of a definition she adds a tart footnote: "A typical kiva is a subterranean, circular, ceremonial room strictly limited to the use of men. Upon occasion they are found above ground, less often rectangular in shape, infrequently secular in function, and sometimes giving welcome to the ladies."[2]

Our reason for introducing this particular lady in our brief chapter on mummies is that she herself devotes several sections of her book to this subject, commencing with the excavations in "Mummy Cave." (This cave must not be confused with Mummy Valley in Kentucky, where mummies have also been found, including the well-preserved body of a woman which after its discovery in 1875 became famous as Little Alice. It was subsequently stolen and sold, was later supposed to be exhibited at Mammoth Cave, but then disappeared completely.) But before we use the word "mummy" one more time, the term will have to be clarified. For in North American archaeology there is a certain disinclination to use it. In the index to his *Southwestern Archaeology* John C. McGregor does not even list the word. Whenever it does crop up, it is usually set in quotation marks to indicate that the term is dubious.

This reluctance is exaggerated and often wrong-headed. Normally, the word "mummy" makes us think of the well-preserved bodies in ancient Egyptian coffins or sarcophagi. The Egyptians certainly raised mummification to an art. Their aim was to preserve the body so that after death the *ka*, the spirit or soul of the deceased, would be able to slip back into his "husk." The technical procedure of mummification might take as much as seventy days. The intestines were removed, the brain extracted, the body steeped in special baths of chemicals, then wrapped in innumerable linen strips before it was at last laid to rest. It has been calculated that the price for the whole operation must have been the equivalent of between $1,000 and $2,000. Behind it all stood a firm belief in a new life after death.

For many decades mummification was regarded as one of the insoluble secrets of the Egyptians. Today we understand the process fairly well. Above all, we know that their embalming chemicals often destroyed more than they preserved and that the excellent state of many Egyptian mummies was due not so much to the treatment but to the dryness and germ-free quality of the burial places. Thus we have many examples in Egypt of the bodies of poor people, whose families could not afford the cost of mummification and who were therefore simply buried in the sand, which have been better preserved than the expensively prepared mummies. And it is noteworthy that whenever such dried bodies, buried without elaborate preparation, have been found, no Egyptologist has ever hesitated to call them "mummies." The same term is also applied to the bodies in the catacombs of Europe, in the Capuchin monastery in Palermo, Sicily, and in the lead cellars of the cathedral of Bremen, Germany. Brockhaus's Encyclopedia defines a mummy as "a corpse preserved from decay by natural drying or artificial preparation."

Thus we are quite justified in using the term "mummies" for the bodies of pre-Columbian human beings found especially in the Southwest, insofar as the favorable climatic and soil conditions have kept their faces, hair, and skin in a well-preserved condition. There is all the more reason to use the term since among certain tribes, at least, belief in a future life underlay the careful burials of these bodies. If there had been no such belief, the rich gifts of grave goods, weapons, ornaments, and implements would have been largely pointless. (Even mummified dogs have been found. It is clear from the careful way they were laid to rest that they were not simply tossed into a hole in the ground. Indeed, beside two dogs, one of which closely resembled a present-day spaniel, two red-painted deer bones have been found—food for the journey into the beyond. It is said that the mummy of a tan "collie" was shown at a dog show in Boston and won a blue ribbon!)

Naturally, mummies are far rarer than skeletons. For the special conditions for preservation did not exist everywhere.

The burial methods of the pre-Columbian Indians in the Southwest alone must have been as varied as their religious ideas. At present we shall not go into this subject, for archaeologists have found a bewildering multiplicity of such methods in the eastern part of the United States, in the lands of the mound builders (we will recall Thomas Jefferson's finds of skeletons). The scope of this book hardly permits us to enter upon a full-scale review of this matter. There are so many single finds, distributed all over the whole vast continent, that their interpretation must be considered an affair among specialists. Nevertheless, we can offer a few examples that will suggest just how mysterious the whole field is.

What is the archaeologist to think when, for example, he finds skull graves—nothing but heaped-up skulls—and not a trace of the bodies that belonged to them? And what should he think when in an entirely different place he finds nothing but bodies and not a single skull—and the finds in these two sites do not belong together?

Or how are we to understand the case of a corpse cut into two halves at the waist and then carefully sewed together again?

And what strange event must have led to "the burial of the hands." Earl Morris came upon this example in Tseahatso Cave, not far from the Mummy Cave. His wife has described the find:

"The circumstances were as follows: At the bottom of the cist, resting on a clean bed of grass, lay the two hands and forearms of an adult. The bones were held together by dried ligaments; the palms lay upwards. And this was every bit of the original human being there was to be found. The severed elbows touched the wall of the cist, and the two cists across the partition walls were empty, thus proving that the burial was complete as found. Moreover, there were burial furnishings, and here is where the almost ludi-crous aspect of the matter comes in. For on these two poor lonely hands were bestowed two pairs of the most exqui-sitely woven sandals patterned in black and red that have ever come out of Southwestern soil. Not mittens but *san-dals!* On top of these were three necklaces, two of which had abalone-shell pendants, while the third was a unique masterpiece. It was made of eighteen white shell rings, each about three inches in diameter and each lashed to a neck cord so as somewhat to overlap its fellow. As effective an ornament as could well be devised—but a *necklace,* not a bracelet! There was a basketful of long crescentic beads, large basket covering the whole, and finally—ab-surdity of absurdities—there was an enormous stone *pipe.* Shoes without feet, necklaces without a neck, and a pipe without a mouth—truly metaphysical triumphs over physi-cal negation."

The remaining parts of the body could not be found. Naturally the Morrises and others after them pondered this strange burial of hands. One explanation was that the man had been killed in a landslide; his body could not be freed; there were only his hands protruding above the ground from his outstretched arms. And so his fellows had cut these off and in his funeral honored the parts as the whole.

A more easily elucidated tragedy also turned up in this area. At the bottom of a cist was found an enormous basket containing the corpses of four children. On top of these lay the bodies of another fourteen infants and older children. There were no signs of violence. It seemed clear that some terrible infectious disease had within a few days carried off most of the children in the community.

In this case there was no violence, but there was in other cases, although we can say that the pre-Columbian peoples of North America probably (in sharp contrast to the "highly civilized" peoples of middle America, such as the Aztecs) were unacquainted with war, that "continuation of politics by other means" which makes its appearance only after agricultural communities become real states. Politics, and thus war, begins with the state; for war is more than tribal feuds, predatory expeditions, struggle for watering places and pastures, an occasional slaying or vengeful killing. To be sure, all such phenomena are primitive prototypes of war, but they are a far cry from that permanent militarism that mankind has developed only in its high civilizations ever since their beginnings among the Assyrians, Persians,

Greeks, and Romans. The civilized Spaniards introduced militarism into North America. Our pueblo peoples seem to have been peaceable; they took up weapons only in emergencies, for self-defense—and were usually defeated.

PHILIP FRENEAU
(1752–1832)

American poet, newspaper editor, and ship's captain. Freneau was for a time a political supporter and associate of Jefferson, and must have been aware of Jefferson's archaeological excavation. The entire poem runs to ten stanzas.

> In spite of all the learned have said,
> I shall my old opinion keep;
> The posture, that we give the dead,
> Points out the soul's eternal sleep.
>
> Not so the ancients of these lands—
> The Indian, when from life released,
> Again is seated with his friends,
> And shares again the joyous feast.
>
> His imaged birds, and painted bowl,
> And venison, for a journey dressed,
> Bespeak the nature of the soul,
> Activity, that knows no rest.
>
> His bow, for action ready bent,
> And arrows, with a head of stone,
> Can only mean that life is spent,
> And now the old ideas gone. . . .
>
> —"The Indian Burying Ground"

Consequently, finds of mummies or skeletons that indicate a massacre are relatively rare. Morris found a group of skulls, all bearing the deep marks of heavy stone axes; even children and infants had been slaughtered in this way. In the body of an old woman also killed with a stone axe he found as well the remains of an arrow that had evidently first struck her. It had pierced her side from below, and it seems as if the woman must have tried to pluck it out, but she was only able to break off the stone tip. The hardwood shaft remained in her body—and then the deadly axe struck her. (We shall have occasion to speak of a massacre on a much greater scale in Chapter 22, "The Towers of Silence.")

Both in the early period of the Basket Makers—the pueblo builders' predecessors—and later on, the dead were simply buried under the rubbish heap that accumulated outside their cave dwellings, sometimes carefully, sometimes carelessly. Sometimes the gravediggers did not bother to dig a proper grave, either because they were short of space or simply because the ground was too hard. In such cases they often forced the bodies into the smallest possible holes in grotesquely distorted postures. In doing so they were playing a mean trick on future archaeologists. For when the scientific digger came upon a hand, he would have no idea which way to dig in order to locate the chest or legs.

For this reason a find like the one Morris made in Aztec is much more gratifying. Under the floor of a room he found the carefully interred body of an adult male. He called this find "the Warrior's Grave." The body was wrapped in feather cloth and then in rush matting. Along with numerous minor grave goods lay something quite extraordinary: a shield, thirty-six inches long and thirty-one inches wide, unusually rich in ornamentation covering the greater part of the body. The shield was tightly woven, the outer rim coated with pitch and sprinkled with tiny selenite splinters, dark red toward the center and with a greenish-blue border. A superb piece of work. Beside it lay axes, undoubtedly weapons rather than tools, one of which was marvelously shaped out of hematite. There was also a long knife of red quartzite. The man had been unusually tall and strong of frame, and his expensive burial showed that he must have enjoyed great prestige.

We do not know what this warrior died of. Perhaps of some dreadful creeping disease. For we must once and for all dispel the myth of the healthy life of primitives, that myth which underlies the everlasting "back to nature" cries that were first sounded in our Western world 200 years ago by the French philosopher Jean-Jacques Rousseau and which can still be heard. There is no basis at all for them. Followers of Thoreau may continue to preach this creed, but it must be remembered that Thoreau himself, and people of his ilk, are merely interesting eccentrics in a world dominated by civilization.

Infant mortality has always been extremely high among "primitive" peoples, of course. But aside from that, we are fairly safe in assuming that the life expectancy of pre-Columbian man in North America was scarcely more than thirty years. (Even today the life expectancy of a Pueblo Indian who still lives in the old way is no more than some forty years, whereas that of the White American in the nearest town, perhaps no more than twenty-five miles away, is more than sixty.) Many deformations and signs of disease have been discovered in the remains. And we must also remember that the specialist in paleoautopsy can detect only those diseases that leave traces in the bones; organic diseases leave no traces at all, and epidemics can only be conjectured—as in the case of the children's grave described above.

Earl Morris once sent a mummy he had dug up in 1931 to the Santa Monica specialist Dr. Roy L. Moodie, for it seemed to him that the body showed some signs of illness and he wanted a professional opinion. Moodie's report indicated:

"It seems that the cadaver was a young man about twenty-seven years old who possessed three separate and distinct sets of infirmities.

"First: he had received a great jagged fracture of the forehead which had miraculously just missed touching the brain. This wound had become infected and had discharged pus for weeks—no wonder, since antiseptics were totally unknown. Eventually it had healed leaving a dense white scar.

"Secondly: his teeth were in fearful shape. He suffered from caries, pyorrhoea, attrition of the first molars and secondary dentine. All of this must have been exceedingly painful, but was relatively unimportant in comparison to his other troubles.

"Thirdly: he was afflicted by a terrible disease called osteitis fibrosa, wherein the whole bony framework as well as the marrow was gradually being replaced by fibrous tissue. Although it had not started until he was mature, already one of the long heavy thigh bones was considerably bent, and other bones were enlarging and rotting away within his living body."

At first Dr. Moodie believed that the man had died of pneumonia, but then he corrected his view. He concluded "that death may have come about through toxemia, a condition resulting from the many tumors which were almost like cancer. . . .

"And lest we have exaggerated sympathy for our mummy, he cites a mummy of a young girl from one of the Channel Islands off the California Coast whose body was riddled by thousands of tumors the size of a lima bean, over a hundred of which were on the head."[3]

Canyon del Muerto (Canyon of the Dead), Antelope House, White House, Mummy Cave—what is now the region of the Canyon de Chelly National Monument in the northeastern corner of Arizona—was the area in which Morris probed for nine years and made many finds: ruins with towers, cave dwellings, hundreds of rooms, graves containing mummies and skeletons. His finds covered more than a millennium of pre-Columbian history in the Southwest. The Basket Makers, and later the pueblo peoples, were living here at the time the Roman Empire was breaking down in Europe.

Some of the canyons are so narrow and deep that the sun does not reach into them until ten o'clock, and disappears again by two. The atmosphere can become so uncanny, especially after sunset when noises drowned out by the day's activities suddenly become audible, that even the archaeologists report being overcome at night by anxiety feelings that brought them to the verge of hysteria.

The Navajo Indians who worked as their helpers were in any case convinced that ghosts haunted the valley. These Indians had a superstitious fear of the dead. If a mummy was found, they instantly laid down their tools and left the rest of the digging to the archaeologists.

How did the scientists feel about these bodies whose wrinkled faces were suddenly brought to light after centuries of slumber, sometimes after more than a thousand years? Did they feel themselves grave robbers, ghouls? (This was a moral question that bothered many Egyptologists during the nineteenth century, when they first began removing the pharaohs from their tombs.) Were they overcome by the breath of eternity? Did they feel their spines tingling with metaphysical shivers such as Howard Carter reported so vividly when he first looked into the face of Tut-ankh-Amen? Or were they merely cool analysts of archaeological findings, hard-headed processors of the past?

They felt and were all of these things, depending on circumstances.

The Morrises never seemed to feel excessive piety. For days they used a long box, which contained one of the best preserved of their mummies, for a breakfast table. And they took mischievous pleasure in inviting their best Navajo workmen to join them at this table—Navajos who would have run away in horror had they suspected the nature of the table on which they were eating those canned peaches they liked so well.

But on the other hand this sort of thing could happen: one day in Tseahatso Cave, they dug up the mummy of a man who had belonged to the Basket Makers. The body was probably a thousand years old. Beside it lay four atlatls, baskets, sandals, hanks of human hair, bits of flint—all by now common finds. But in this case something more significant had been included with the grave goods. It was well known that the Basket Makers had carved flutes, but few had been discovered in good condition. And here lay four wonderfully preserved specimens!

The archaeologists could not resist.

In the presence of the mummy, former owner of the instruments, they raised the flutes to their lips and tried to coax musical notes from them. At first they could produce no sound. But then Morris found the correct embouchure, and across the glorious landscape clear notes rose into the pure air.

Ann Morris comments:

"It seemed as if, in their reliving, the old Flute Player himself should likewise be stirred to life. We did not rationally expect him to rise from that dusty grave, but because he did not, he somehow seemed to be infinitely farther away than before. Familiarity with some of our best mummies had bred a feeling of neighborliness for them. But now, all of a sudden, one and all they receded back into time, and we were aware of the tremendous aloofness of Death."[4]

In discussing the Southwest we have been more or less following the chronology of the discoveries, from the first sight the Spaniards had of the pueblos to the first excavations, interpretations, and attempts to establish the course of historical evolution.

The time has come now to jump forward somewhat, to explain how the first successes in *dating* were achieved, to say *when* the Basket Makers lived, *when* the pueblos were built. Hence in the next two chapters we will be more engaged with physics and biology than with archaeology. Consequently, we must first say something about the *purpose* of North American archaeology, and also about the two scientific methods that to this day are still the alpha and omega, the basic equipment of the archaeologist: the interpretation of "layers and shards."

Book Two

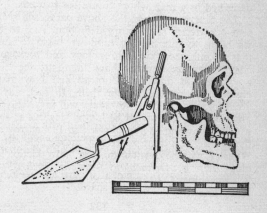

6

What Is Archaeology, and Wherefore Do We Study It?

ANTHROPOLOGY is the science of man, archaeology the science of what man has left behind him. Or, as the archaeologist Stuart Piggott has quipped: "The science of rubbish." As for the archaeologist himself, he has been cleverly described as a man whose future lies in ruins.

The first sentence of the above paragraph seems to present a perfectly satisfactory definition. And so it is—until we begin to interpret it, until we begin looking into all that is embraced by anthropology and archaeology nowadays, until we discover how differently the two sciences are taught in different countries and how many subdisciplines are included under them. In fact, any writer on archaeological matters nowadays will invariably offer some prefatory words on what he himself regards as archaeology, usually throwing in the phrase "in the narrower sense of the word." On that score we may quote Sir Mortimer Wheeler, who has written the best "introduction" to archaeology there is, *Archaeology from the Earth*. "What in fact is archaeology?" he asks. And answers, "I do not myself really know."

132

But let us keep our feet on the ground. Archaeology means the excavation, the collection, and the interpretation of vanished cultures from historic times back to prehistoric times. It springs from man's desire to find out about his past to compare it with his present, to measure himself against it. A measure of ancestor worship is a prerequisite for all archaeology. What is more, ever since the great archaeological finds of the nineteenth century, since the discovery of the tombs of the pharaohs, the Maya ruins in Central America, Heinrich Schliemann's excavation of a hitherto legendary Troy, and Arthur Evans's bringing to light the equally legendary "Palace of Minos" on Crete— along with the tremendous treasures turned up in the course of these projects—archaeology has acquired an aura of romantic adventure.

As I have already suggested in the Preface, this aura is deserved. Ann Axtell Morris speaks of archaeology as "that lovely game which is played in the earth's out-of-the-way corners and furnishes all the excitement of treasure-seeking decently concealed under the respectable cloak of science."

The outsider, who usually learns about the scientific results only from journalistic accounts, tends to forget that behind those results are three principal agencies: work, work, and still more work. Enormous labor in the "field," the battling with adverse circumstances, frequently political in nature, as well as with heat, cold, dust, mud, disease-bearing insects. All that is followed by long close study of minutiae in the laboratory and the museum. Then come scholarly disputes that may go on for years. Not inspiration but perspiration is required. And yet, on the other hand, only a completely unimaginative scholar could put the case so bluntly. Let us conclude these remarks with the motto of Johann Joachim Winckelmann, the "Father of Archaeology," whose *History of the Art of Antiquity* in 1764 threw open the first gates into the past: "We must conceive with passion and develop with deliberation."

In the United States archaeology is a relatively young science. In Europe it goes back to the Renaissance, when admirers of the past began collecting works of ancient art, rediscovering the languages of classical antiquity, and glorifying antiquity to the point of making the ideals of the Greeks the standard for all education. That is, the first step was *accumulation,* the second *understanding,* the third *imitation.* Western civilization began to take an interest in the past unmatched by any other of the great civilizations; people were possessed by a hitherto unknown mania for putting this past into some kind of chronological order. To this day, in fact, no Westerner confronting a ruin can repress the question: "How old is it?" The question, "Who built it?" always comes second.

Thus two sources of European archaeology have naturally been art history and philology. From the outset they went hand in hand, for most of the things found earlier in Greece and Italy, and in the nineteenth century in Egypt and Asia Minor, were works of art that frequently bore inscriptions. Thanks to this archaeological teamwork, we received knowledge of the cultural history of mankind extending back more than 5,000 years, as far as the Sumerians. Everything for which the written word supplied evidence was considered "history." Archaeology uncovered such marvels as the temples of Olympia and Delphi, led us into the still further past through such sensational discoveries as those of the tomb of Tut-ankh-Amen and the royal graves of Ur, and by deciphering the hieroglyphs and cuneiform scripts made amazing contributions to our knowledge of the "ancients." It was obvious that this kind of archaeology must of necessity become a handmaiden to history, for the historians were the ones to piece together the lifeless factual materials and formulate a sweeping vision of humanity's development over the millennia. In the course of this enterprise, the moralistic element, the educational principle Schiller had enunciated in his famous Jena lecture of 1789, "What is universal history and wherefore do we study it?" receded more and more. According to Schiller, the historian should focus on those facts alone that "have exerted a significant, undeniable and easily traceable influence upon the present form and condition of the generation now living." To the present-day archaeologist, who seeks the truth and nothing but the truth, any such program seems at best secondary.

The situation of American archaeology is entirely different. In the glossary to his book, *America's Buried Past,* the archaeologist Gordon C. Baldwin (who incidentally has written several western novels, something a European archaeologist—what a pity—could scarcely indulge in without ruining his reputation) tersely states his definition: "Archaeology: The study of man before written records." This is not a careless formulation, for he repeats it in the

In the United States today there are more than 10,000 amateur archaeologists who are ardently concerned with America's past. That has not always been the case. In 1847 Congress debated whether George Catlin's portraits of Indians ought to be bought for the Smithsonian Institution. Congressman James D. Westcott of Florida reacted fiercely:

"I am opposed to purchasing the portraits of savages. What great moral lesson are they intended to inculcate? I would rather see the portraits of the numerous citizens who have been murdered by these Indians. I would not vote a cent for a portrait of an Indian."

And as late as 1892 Congressman H. C. Snodgrass of Tennessee objected to a proposed grant of $35,000 for ethnological research:

"I believe that it is a useless expenditure. I do not believe it will add anything to science or education to expend thirty-five thousand dollars to send a set of political employees over the country to dig into Indian mounds and publish accounts of whatever they may find there."

—The quotations are from
Geoffrey T. Hellman, *The Smithsonian: Octopus on the Mall*

text: "Archaeology is the science of uncovering man's past from the things he left behind. In other words, it is learning all about *prehistory*, the peoples and their arts and crafts *before written history*."

Here is a puzzler for the European. By this definition, the excavation of King Assurbanipal's library of clay tablets at Nineveh would not have been archaeological work. Baldwin's definition is bound to strike all Europeans as totally irrational. In a sense it is, for it will not do to strip half the meaning from a word that has had a clear denotation for a century.

But, as we have said, the situation in North America was and is different. The North American archaeologist deals entirely with *prehistory*, not with "history evidenced by written records," for the Indians before Columbus had no writing. And they also had no temples and palaces, let alone a Venus of Milo, or a Hermes by Praxiteles. Thus North American research into the past could not be inspired by works of art and inscriptions; it could not grow out of art history and philology. From the start it sprang from a preoccupation with man, from anthropology. "This book is concerned with archaeology as a part of anthropology," writes James Deetz in his excellent *Invitation to Archaeology*. In North America that is the natural view.

Anthropology, for its part, began with the material assembled by the Spanish conquistadors, later by the first travelers, still later by the first trained ethnologists. The kind of anthropology that attained a first peak in Europe with measurements of skulls and that dealt by preference with the human body became the special discipline of "physical anthropology" in North America. There followed an altogether extraordinary fission of the disciplines, which by now had reached a considerable degree of confusion. There is political, social, historical, psychological anthropology; irrationally enough, there even exists a Christian and of course a Marxist anthropology. It rather reminds one of Hitler's requiring his scientists to develop a non-Jewish, German physics.

What interests us here is the kind of anthropology that has taken archaeology under its wing. That is what is called "cultural anthropology," and it ranges all the way from dealing with prehistoric man to projects such as Hortense Powdermaker's, who, after studying a Stone Age culture in Melanesia, trained her scientific magnifying glass with the same cool methodology upon the social structures of contemporary Hollywood.[1]

Now as it happens, archaeology is taught at 137 universities and colleges in the United States (the count as of 1968). But oddly enough, these courses are not always under the departments of anthropology. They are just as often taught in the departments of sociology, geology, art history, general history, and at the University of Southern California and a few other institutions they are actually given in the department of religion. Robert Ascher of Cornell University, in a highly critical study, comments: "My interpretation is that the organization of the field of archaeology in the university is anachronistic. It reflects the origin and earlier history of the subject, but not archaeology today."[2]

This confusing situation, in fact, is simply the consequence of too rapid development. There is a good example of that. During the twenties two professors at the University of Kentucky, the zoologist W. D. Funkhauser and the physicist William S. Webb, started to go in for excavation as a hobby. In other words, they became Sunday archaeologists. In July, 1927, the university inaugurated a Department of Anthropology and Archaeology. Whom did it appoint as its first professors? The zoologist Funkhauser and the physicist Webb. Incidentlally, they made some significant discoveries concerning the prehistory of Kentucky.[3]

Nowadays, that sort of thing could no longer happen.

From the start it was clear that historical conceptions, the theories of culture and civilization that have been developed by Spengler and Toynbee, say, could not usefully be applied to North America. But beyond that there grew up among archaeologists at North American universities a particular, almost principled dislike for all grand conceptions. Whenever anything like philosophical thinking reared its head, it was immediately regarded with suspicion. For instance, it took five years before the greatest stimulator of modern anthropological thought, Claude Lévi-Strauss, was even translated into English, although by that time his "structural anthropology" had already spread so fast from the forum of the Collège de France in Paris that it had become the subject of violent controversies among intellectuals in the smallest cafés.

In America the concept of "culture," for example, was regarded as so ambiguous as to have virtually no value. In fact, a whole book has been published merely to define the definitions.[4] Especially for the host of locally oriented, overspecialized fact finders, every larger conception that goes beyond the borders of their own state is automatically suspect. Franz Boas and Alfred L. Kroeber, Margaret Mead and Ruth Benedict, who always regarded their researches in terms of worldwide references and who above all possessed the educational background that made such a broader view possible, are altogether exceptional. When Ruth Benedict, in a study on Indian peoples, cites Nietzsche's conceptions of Apollonian and Dionysian, calling the Pueblo peoples Apollonian, she is using a language thoroughly alien to North American professional literature in the field. Her book *Patterns of Culture* is unique and has justly made her world-famous; its influence rebounded to Europe and has affected European thinking—something that can be said of very few such works. And this partly accounts for the total ignorance Europeans have of the pre-Columbian history of *North* America.

This general attitude may well be what prompted Sir Mortimer Wheeler to burst out against his American colleague W. W. Taylor:

"Archaeology is primarily a fact-finding discipline. It has indeed been stated by an American writer that 'Archaeology per se is no more than a method and a set of specialized techniques for the gathering of cultural information. The archaeologist, as archaeologist, is really nothing but a technician.' I have no hesitation in denouncing that extreme view as nonsense. A lepidopterist is a great deal more than a butterfly-catcher, and an archaeologist who is not more than a potsherd-catcher is unworthy of his logos. He is primarily a fact-finder, but his facts are the material records of human achievement; he is also, by that token, a humanist, and his secondary task is that of revivifying or humanizing his materials with a controlled imagination that inevitably partakes of the qualities of art and even of philosophy."[5]

However, Wheeler wrote these lines in 1956. In the interval there have been extraordinary developments in North American archaeology. Five hundred and thirty-six museums (according to a 1967 count) have permanent exhibits showing the history of the Indians from their beginnings to the present. One museum alone, the Ocmulgee National Monument Museum, contains some 2,000,000 relics from the Mound Builders to today. The literature on the subject is increasing at an alarming pace; the catalogue of the Laboratory of Anthropology in Santa Fé lists more than 10,000 publications just on the archaeology of the Southwest. Only computers will be able to sort out this material.

In view of this new plethora of facts the formation of larger views becomes imperative. And during the past decades more general surveys have been published than in the preceding fifty years. The pebbles are being fitted together into a mosaic; American prehistory is becoming comprehensible as a whole. And a problem such as the diffusion theory—whether and to what extent Asia may have influenced the development of the American cultures—is nowadays being discussed the world over. All this calls for a reconsideration of old theories and a general revision of the whole conception of archaeology in America. Gordon R. Willey and Philip Phillips breached the wall of provinciality in 1958 when they published their much-discussed book, *Method and Theory in American Archaeology*.

Today, we see emerging the very special task of *North* American archaeology, its potential gift to the archaeology of the world and to prehistory in general.[6]

The early history of the Old World is for the most part buried under the rubble and shards of advanced civilizations. No direct relationship exists any longer between the Early Hunters and food gatherers, the dwellers in caves and pit houses, and present-day man. But in North America, scattered over a vast continent, the early history of man lies in the topmost stratum, and in the pueblos the scientist sees a functioning population whose pattern of life was, in essentials, much the same as that of early man. North America's last Stone Age man died in San Francisco in 1916—a fantastic story that will be told in the Epilogue to this book.

Paul S. Martin (who with George T. Quimby and Donald Collier provided one of the first comprehensive accounts as early as 1947, in *Indians Before Columbus*) has some cogent things to say about the special situation of American archaeology:

"My reader may say: 'Very well. The Greeks and Romans contributed to our civilization; but what is the good of investigating Indian cultures?'

"My answer is twofold: The American Indians have contributed to our way of life by giving us ideas in architecture (Pueblo and Maya) and by giving us many valuable food plants such as potatoes, tomatoes, peanuts, corn, beans, squash (to name only a few).

"The second part of my answer is slightly more involved. We should be glad to investigate Indian civilizations, even if we assumed that they had contributed nothing to ours, because America and the Indians were pretty much cut off from the Old World and the differing cultures were developed here more or less independently, after the Indians (Mongoloid peoples) had emigrated here via Siberia. In short, the New World constitutes a kind of *gigantic test tube, a great laboratory* where all sorts of events were taking place. . . . This is one of the few such 'laboratories' that we know of, since it is impossible to place societies in a test tube and watch what happens."

Martin concludes—and before turning to some of the special methods of archaeology we shall conclude this chapter with his words:

"And so the value of archaeology lies in developing a new way of looking at life, in searching for truth and beauty where it leads us, and in helping us understand our times and our problems. We need to broaden our understanding of man's hopes and desires and our knowledge of man's nature. Perhaps if all of us put our heads together we can discover the causes for the rise and decline of civilizations and perhaps save our own from disappearing."[7]

7

Strata and Shards

DURING the twenties the El Navajo Hotel in Gallup, New Mexico, was the meeting place of all the archaeologists who gathered in the area for the annual Indian festivals. One day "Ted" Kidder joined a merry group at the hotel and asked with a grin:

"What would you do if you had to work in Pecos? I've just been trenching a refuse slope, and I find the *earliest* pottery on *top* and the stuff that was made last on the *bottom*."

His colleagues stared at him in amazement, for that statement literally turned the basic laws of stratigraphy upside down.

They remained perplexed until Kidder explained that the last inhabitants of Pecos had obviously—or rather, it was not obvious but became clear only after much thought and a careful examination of the environs—dug a new deep trench at an old site, throwing the topmost shovelfuls to one side and the lower ones on top. In this way they had precisely reversed the otherwise inviolable order of archaeological layers, the "strata."

141

But, Kidder continued, that had not been his knottiest problem in Pecos: "I got one grave that had *all six varieties of pottery at once in it*—every kind of bowl that was ever made at Pecos from the beginning to the end!" And grinning still more broadly, he offered the only possible explanation: "Evidently some prehistoric collector has been on the job ahead of me."[1]

In our opening account of Jefferson's excavation of the mound we offered an explanation of the importance of stratigraphy, the science of strata. Let us emphasize once again that this extraordinary President of the United States was the first man in the history of archaeology, including European archaeology, to apply the technique deliberately.

It seems so simple: when you dig, the earliest materials always lie on top, the oldest on the bottom. When, therefore, you find several strata of cultures and can distinguish them and number them by pottery types, you have a relative chronology. "Relative" means that you do not know how long the culture of any one layer persisted, or when the oldest was laid down according to Christian chronology.

But how, the layman may ask, do these strata arise in the first place? The answer is that they come into being in the course of centuries primarily through a wide variety of natural causes, such as geological upheavals. Thus stratigraphy first became tremendously important to geologists. The forerunner of the science is rightly considered to be William ("Strata") Smith, who in 1816 published his *Strata Identified by Organized Fossils.* But strata also arise in much shorter periods of time wherever people have lived. People build huts or houses. Storms, landslides, floods, fire,

Cross section of Crooks Mound (Hopewell culture). Here is a burial mound in which the stratigraphic elements are particularly clear. The skeletons were found in the third stratum from the top.

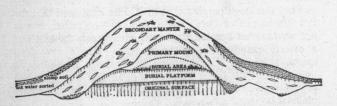

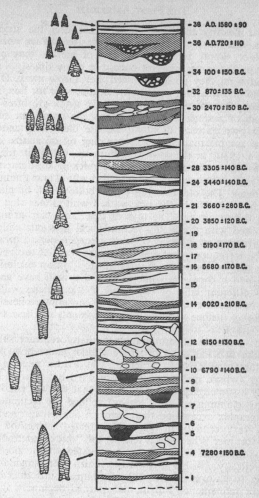

- 38 A.D. 1580 ± 90
- 36 A.D. 720 ± 110
- 34 100 ± 150 B.C.
- 32 870 ± 135 B.C.
- 30 2470 ± 150 B.C.
- 28 3305 ± 140 B.C.
- 24 3440 ± 140 B.C.
- 21 3660 ± 280 B.C.
- 20 3850 ± 120 B.C.
- 19
- 18 5190 ± 170 B.C.
- 17
- 16 5680 ± 170 B.C.
- 15
- 14 6020 ± 210 B.C.
- 12 6150 ± 130 B.C.
- 11
- 10 6790 ± 140 B.C.
- 9
- 8
- 7
- 6
- 5
- 4 7280 ± 150 B.C.
- 1

The stratigraphy of a cave in the Absaroka Mountains near Yellowstone Park. The finds in thirty-eight strata indicate that the cave was inhabited for more than 9,000 years. In the lowest strata the weapons are only points used on javelins and spears propelled by atlatls (spear throwers). The upper strata contain finely shaped arrowheads.

or war destroy them. Often men abandon the stricken places, but most of the time, in order to salvage what is useful or simply following the law of inertia, they build again on the same site. Not once, but many times!

And what they no longer need they throw away. Often they go on discarding refuse on the same spot for hundreds of years. But in fact "archaeological" strata are often the product of a single generation. They can come into being in our own garbage dumps if we use them long enough. Let us assume that we began dumping refuse at the same spot in 1930. In the lowest stratum we will find, for example—if we dig according to the rules of stratigraphy— mostly pots and pans of iron, mingled with a few aluminum specimens. The old auto tire at the bottom will be plainly distinguishable from the type with a white inner ring that we will find on top. The toys of that time were primitive compared with the highly technological toys our children are throwing away today. During a certain period tin cans will be infrequent; that was during the war. At the bottom there will be numerous bottles, on top almost exclusively cans; and if there are some bottles, they will have an entirely different kind of cap. And plastic articles will appear only in the topmost layer. One can amuse oneself by imagining further variations in the contents of these short-term strata.

The principle of stratigraphy is, therefore, very simple. But the two examples given by Kidder show how many problems can arise in practice. The British general Pitt Rivers (whose real name was Lane Fox, but who in 1880 gladly assumed his new name, since that was the condition for his claiming a sizable legacy) refined the technique of stratigraphic excavation that Heinrich Schliemann had applied very crudely in Troy. He created a method that Sir Mortimer Wheeler later to call "three-dimensional." Drawings ought to be so exact, he insisted, that it should be theoretically possible afterward to return every single found object to its original site. Wheeler himself introduced still further refinements. But he also warned beginners against the capriciousness of strata: "The first rule about stratification is that there is no invariable rule."[2]

In North America stratigraphy has developed since Kidder to the point of complete mastery.[3] The famous Snaketown excavation of 1934–35, carried out by Emil W. Haury, Harold and Nora Gladwin, and E. B. Sayles was so precise that after fresh digging thirty years later Haury could say with pride that the new results were "complementary and not contradictory."[4] During a recent excavation of a cave in Wyoming precisely *thirty-eight* separate strata were distinguished and could be dated from 7280 B.C. to A.D. 1580![5]

After all, not only man himself, but most of what he has created, is perishable. That applies particularly to the artifacts of prehistoric man, to his utensils of wood, bone, basketry, and textiles. When we consider how easily such things decay, it seems a miracle that archaeologists have nevertheless been able to find so much.

There is one exception. Pottery is almost imperishable!

As early as the last century archaeologists realized what a key to understanding the past was provided by pitchers, vases, and bowls, even when nothing remained but shards piled up in heaps at the entrances to the sites of prehistoric dwellings. (North American archaeologists have four terms for such accumulations: dump heaps, kitchen middens, refuse piles, and trash mounds.) Consequently, they were jocularly dubbed "pot hunters," though nowadays this has become a term of opprobrium for unscrupulous searchers and nocturnal diggers, in short, grave robbers, who, no matter under what disguise, are digging only to find objects they can turn into money. But even "classical" archaeology at first looked down upon this new branch of research:

"Half a century ago Godley, an Oxford scholar, ironically laughing at his fellow scholars, who were then just appreciating the value of archaeological evidence for the ancient world, wrote:

> *For 'tis not verse, and 'tis not prose,*
> *But earthenware alone*
> *It is that ultimately shows*
> *What men have thought and done.*"[6]

In fact, the importance of pottery to archaeology cannot be exaggerated. With pottery humanity's *culture* begins. Vessels of clay, originally shaped by hand and dried in the sun, later fired, are perhaps the first products of technology, and the ornamentation on the clay is perhaps the first *artistic expression*—aside from cave and rock paintings.

Almost always, pottery coincides with the commencement of agriculture, with the establishment of fixed abodes.

Pottery vessels quickly assumed a wide range of functions. They were used for eating, drinking, and storage; but they were also employed as urns in which the ashes of the dead were preserved, and as grave goods intended to accompany the dead on their journey. Clay figurines, idols, formed in the human image, were the first expressions of religious art. Often the clay came from places that were kept strictly secret, places that might lie hundreds of miles away. Such was also the case with the clay for peace pipes —for the Indians, of course, gave the Old World not only tobacco, but the pipe that goes with it.

Pottery, subsequently fired, glazed, and ornamented to the point of highest artistry, accompanies all the cultures of humanity. Its simplicity or subtlety is evidence of the state of the culture. And the strata of potsherds often provide us with the only useful stratigraphy we may have for a given culture.

The wonderful development of pottery can be traced in every museum that has arranged its objects according to a fairly correct chronology. First come the crude utilitarian or accidental forms, thick-walled, with rough surfaces, scarcely ornamented. Then follows a markedly skillful handling of the clay, which suddenly seems to be molded much more easily; the forms are rounder, more regular. The first ornaments, which in the earlier periods are simple lines and dots looking as if they had been scratched by a child's uncertain hand, gradually appear firmer, surer. They break away from their origin in basketry and are employed more freely, more playfully. Then the first colors appear, white, black, red. Then the pots, bowls, and vases become more and more thin-walled, are fired harder and more evenly, attempt many more colors, more and more difficult ornamentation.

No other objects of human labor provide so vividly and persuasively the evidence for the development from primitiveness to culture, from crudeness to refinement, from utilitarianism to—we are at this point already justified in saying—works of art. By taking a hundred steps in a museum we can trace this development. We should do it slowly, reflectively, and with some sense of awe.

How was pottery invented? And when?
The Old World, it seems, has known it for more than

7,000 years, China for perhaps 4,000, America since 2500 B.C. But a special problem immediately arises: pottery of that age can be found in Middle America and farther south, and also in the northeastern part of North America (archaeologists distinguish the "nuclear" and the "woodland" traditions).[7] These two types of pottery differ and *twice* arose separately, *independently of the Old World.* Naturally, Asiatic influences may have affected it later on. And it is also natural that the types of pottery should have spread through the American continents, mingling, exerting reciprocal influences. There is even a certain probability

The most artistic and fancifully ornamented pottery of the Southwest was made by the Mimbres. This stylized mountain lion on a bowl dates from the tenth to the twelfth century A.D. *When such a bowl was placed in a grave to accompany the dead, it was often deliberately smashed, "killed."*

that pottery was invented not just twice but three times in North America alone. It seems likely that it was once again invented at a much later period, around A.D. 400, in the vicinity of the San Juan Valley in the Southwest, somewhere near the Four Corners. (But this whole question of originality is still extremely controversial.)

Oddly enough, there are historians, especially in Europe, who seem unable to get along without pointing to "influences." For some reason, they refuse to acknowledge that phenomenon in cultural history which is constantly presented to them in the history of technology: to this day individual inventions are made *simultaneously* several times and in several places. Pottery was newly invented at least twice in North America. (Given the overwhelming abundance of pottery that has been found in North America, we are impelled to ask how long it would have taken to produce such articles in prehistoric times. Not until 1925 were serious experiments undertaken to provide an answer to that question. The production of small ornamented bowls required two hours, plus about twelve hours of drying time. Firing took from thirty-six to eighty minutes.)[8]

But how?

Charles Lamb's humorous essay, "A Dissertation Upon Roast Pig," was once familiar to generations of American schoolchildren, and perhaps still holds its place in the anthologies. In it Lamb propounded the theory that the art of roasting meat was discovered in the days of long ago by a little Chinese boy named Bo-bo, who playfully set fire to his father's hut, incidentally burning nine suckling pigs. Thereupon "an odor assailed his nostrils, unlike any scent which he had before experienced." So far, so good. Lamb's satire rested on his assertion that for generations thereafter the Chinese (quite logically) made a practice of shutting pigs in their huts and burning the huts down in order to produce good roasts.

If we now say that real Indian pottery began with the process of firing, we may well assume an Indian Bo-bo, an innocent child who one day perhaps, also in the far distant past, playfully rolled a bowl that had been merely dried in the sun into the hearth fire. And then the mother, at first alarmed, discovered with pleasure that the bowl had not been spoiled, had not cracked, but had become much harder and more useful than before.

That is the purely materialistic viewpoint: "Social facts determine consciousness." But the idealistic viewpoint would have it that a thoughtful mind drew the intellectual conclusion that if the warm sun makes the soft clay hard, the hotter fire would make it still harder: "Consciousness determines social facts."

The same explanations can be offered for the origins of the first ornamentation, although in this case they are not so sharply separated. For example: the wicker carrying basket wrapped around a vase not yet completely dried left grooves which were later, out of custom, imitated on bowls and vases that did not need carrying baskets. But—here comes the argument of those who are not strictly materialists—the first ornaments that man invented were probably those he imprinted upon his own body. It is known that the North American Indians used body paints and tattooing extensively, and some have argued that the impulse to ornamentation prompted them to transfer these techniques to utensils. And what about the wealth of shapes? Undoubtedly utility determined the shapes at the beginning, but the *instinct for play* must not be ignored. Man was and is a *homo ludens*, as Johan Huizinga, the Dutch cultural historian, has called him in one of his most famous works.[9]

Finding pottery is one thing, interpreting and classifying it another. The archaeologist in general confronts six questions:

Where, in what surroundings and stratum, has the piece been found?

What is the nature of the material?

What is the method of manufacture?

What is the style, the form?

What kind of ornamentation has been used?

What chance is there to date the object?

On the question of dating there has been developed lately, particularly at the University of California, a method that permits establishing a date in terms of absolute chronology for the origin of every piece of pottery. This is the method of thermoluminescence: a measurable radiation effect produced by firing old pottery once again. It arises from the radioactivity of the minerals in all clays.

In 1963 E. T. Hall of Oxford University gave a brief description of the method. At the time he still had some reservations concerning its value, but in 1970 he wrote:

"All pottery and ceramics contain certain amounts of radioactive impurities (e.g. uranium and thorium) to a concentration of a few parts per million. These materials emit alpha-particles at a known rate depending upon their concentration in the sample. When an alpha-particle is absorbed by the pottery minerals surrounding the radioactive impurity, it causes ionization of the mineral atoms: electrons are released from their tight natural binding to the nucleii and may settle at a later time at metastable states of higher energy. Thus energy is stored. At ordinary temperatures these electrons remain in these metastable states or traps. If at any time the material is heated, for example during the firing of a pot, to a sufficiently high temperature, the trapped electrons will be released, with the emission of light.

"From the time when the pottery was fired, when all the traps were emptied, up to the present time, a process of filling will occur as the alpha-particles are absorbed by the material, and the longer this time the more will have been filled, thus the greater will be the thermoluminescence.

"To date a piece of pottery, therefore, we must make the following measurements:

(i) measure the light output when the sample is heated up;

(ii) measure the alpha-radioactivity of the sample;

(iii) measure the susceptibility of the sample to the production of thermoluminescence by an artificial known irradiation from a radioactive source.

"By a combination of these results it is possible to derive the absolute age, or time since firing, or to compare the result with those of pottery of known age in order to date the sample."[10]

But interpretation?

That is no business for amateurs. In 1965 I myself, no novice in the archaeology of the Old World, for the first time visited the excavation site of an ancient Indian culture, the Hohokam culture in Snaketown, Arizona. It has been excavated chiefly by Emil W. Haury. As we walked over millions of shards, Haury would pick up a piece here, a fragment there, usually no bigger than two fingernails and to my eye revealing nothing more than a point or a broken line. But Haury would murmur: "Period so-and-so, mixture, period so-and-so, but this one is much older, see!" It seemed like— But cheery Ann Axtell Morris, who has commented on almost everything, remarks in a reporting on her own first field trip in 1923:

"A person just had to 'feel' it. That sounded pretty unsatisfactory, and it was not until some years later that it all suddenly dawned, somewhat like the acquisition of a foreign language to which one has been exposed for some time. Identifying pottery types 'takes' like a vaccination. One night you are completely at sea, the next morning you have got it! Time invariably does the trick. It is not a case of dots or dashes, or lines or spaces or shape or clay. It is a subconscious combination of all these together with an indefinable something else that speaks more loudly than words."[11]

Another and more important woman scientist, A. O. Shepard, attempted in 1954 to write a little handbook on the problems of ceramics and their classification. Merely dealing with essentials resulted in a book of 414 pages.[12]

This leads us to the two most important contributions in the physical sciences that North America has made to the archaeology of the world.

8

The Tick of Time

"WE archaeologists," Froelich Rainey, director of the University of Pennsylvania Museum, has said, "are too little aware of the revolutionary technological changes affecting our world and I think the physical scientists are too little aware of the forces of history. Here, we are at least crossing over between the two worlds of science and the humanities in a very practical day-by-day experience. There is enthusiasm and excitement on both sides and a new awareness of the attitudes in another kind of discipline."[1]

Rainey spoke these words in 1965, when many physical scientists from a wide variety of disciplines had already eagerly come to the aid of archaeology, with remarkable results. But the results in the near future will be even more remarkable; this can already be predicted with perfect confidence.

In 1963 two British scientists attempted to take stock of the many methods, especially dating methods, that had been developed up to that point: Don Brothwell of the British Museum and Eric Higgs of Cambridge. They called their book *Science in Archaeology: A Comprehensive Sur-*

vey of Progress and Research. This solid volume of 595 pages contained fifty-four different articles by various authors on a multitude of methods for answering archaeological questions by employing the resources of the physical sciences and modern technology. Only twenty years before neither an archaeologist nor a physical scientist would have dreamed of such possibilities.

Yet the progress of these new techniques has been so swift that a book on the same subject today would have to be considerably bulkier. In 1952 Frederick E. Zeuner's *Dating the Past* was regarded as the standard text on the subject. Today it has only historical value, and the second edition (1970) of the big compilation by Brothwell and Higgs contains 125 more pages.

We are here describing the history of North American archaeology. Therefore we must limit ourselves for reasons of subject as well as space to the two methods that have been developed solely in North America by North Americans. It so happens, however, that these two methods are the two most important, the two with the greatest promise for the future. They are radiocarbon dating (also called the C-14 method) and dendrochronology (also called tree-ring dating).

Of all the new dating methods, radiocarbon dating, developed by Willard F. Libby of the University of Chicago, created the greatest stir—and rightly so, as we now know.

Libby was born in 1908 on a farm in Colorado. He intended to be an engineer but changed his plans after beginning his studies, and turned to chemistry. Even at that time the study of chemistry was unthinkable without physics and mathematics. He thus was not stepping outside his field when he became more and more interested in radioactivity. Between 1941 and 1945 he participated in the creation of the atom bomb; he speaks of this period in general terms as a time of "war research." After the war he accepted a professorship at the University of Chicago, and here he laid the foundations for the new method of dating.

It is almost impossible to quote Libby directly, for his writing is usually extremely technical. But E. H. Willis, a member of one of the first radiocarbon laboratories set up at Cambridge University after Libby had begun his work, once attempted a brief summary of the method:

"Libby, in postulating the idea that the cosmic ray-produced radiocarbon might provide a valuable means of age determination, supposed that the C-14 atoms would be readily oxidized to carbon dioxide and would mix freely with the atmospheric carbon dioxide. As a consequence of the rapid turnover of the earth's atmosphere, radiocarbon-labelled carbon dioxide would achieve a uniform global distribution, and might be expected to be taken up in the

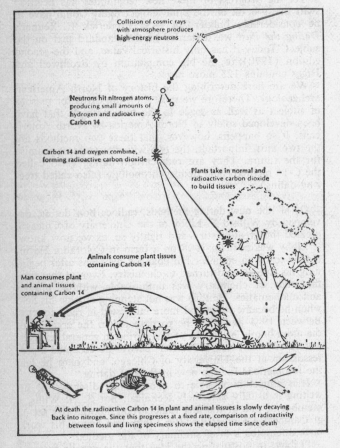

Collision of cosmic rays with atmosphere produces high-energy neutrons

Neutrons hit nitrogen atoms, producing small amounts of hydrogen and radioactive Carbon 14

Carbon 14 and oxygen combine, forming radioactive carbon dioxide

Plants take in normal and radioactive carbon dioxide to build tissues

Animals consume plant tissues containing Carbon 14

Man consumes plant and animal tissues containing Carbon 14

At death the radioactive Carbon 14 in plant and animal tissues is slowly decaying back into nitrogen. Since this progresses at a fixed rate, comparison of radioactivity between fossil and living specimens shows the elapsed time since death

How Carbon 14 enters into all organic substances.

same proportion by all plant life during the process of photosynthesis. All animal life, derived directly or indirectly from plant material, would also be expected to contain the same universal specific activity. Sea life would be similarly affected, since the carbon dioxide of the atmosphere is in exchange equilibrium with the oceans which in turn reach equilibrium with the atmospheric carbon dioxide. He argued that these equilibria are reached quickly compared with the half-life of C-14. Upon the death of an organism, further uptake or exchange of radiocarbon would cease, leaving the trapped radiocarbon to decay exponentially with time."[2]

The matter can perhaps be put more simply: it is known theoretically that the atmospheric part of our planet is constantly being bombarded by cosmic rays. These rays, upon impact with our atmosphere, produce neutrons that react with the atmospheric atoms of nitrogen, creating tiny quantities of Carbon 14 (C-14). This C-14 forms a chemical bond with oxygen and reaches the earth as carbon dioxide.

Tiny quantities of this carbon dioxide are thus compounded of C-14 rather than ordinary carbon, but the plants of our earth do not differentiate. They absorb both kinds of carbon dioxide and turn them by photosynthesis into food. Since animals and men eat plants, C-14 enters into every animal and every human being.

All this would be largely of academic interest if C-14 were not radioactive.

The conclusion Libby drew was that all organic matter is radioactive, and he reasoned further that there must be a way to measure this radioactivity. Since radioactive substances decay at fixed speeds, the pattern was consistent. It is therefore possible to determine that after a specific time the amount of radioactivity in a substance will be reduced exactly one half, and after an equal length of time to one fourth—and so on. This measurement is called the "half-life." For C-14 it is about 5,568 years. Or so it was at first assumed, then corrected.

The important fact is that a plant's quantity of C-14 remains constant as long as the plant is alive; any losses are replaced by continual intake. But the moment the plant dies (or the man or animal that has previously consumed plants) the radioactive decay begins. If, then, the Geiger counter can be used to measure the exact quantity of C-14 remaining, the age of the dead organism (not how long it lived, but how long a period of time has passed since its death) can be determined. In other words, the historical age of any organic material can be measured.

Libby announced this discovery in 1947 after he had tested many organic materials. It may at first make us rather uncomfortable to realize that we are ourselves radioactive, that the milk we drink, the meat we eat, the salad we spear with such boredom, the table at which we sit, and the bed in which we sleep are all radioactive (and every child today learns in school how dangerous radioactivity is). But we need not worry; the quantities are inconceivably small. Consequently, Libby's chief problem was to develop a highly sensitive method of measurement. Theoretically a tree that was felled 5,568 years ago ought to produce only half as many ticks in the Geiger counter as one felled today. And in practice that proved to be more or less the case. For in an astonishingly short time Libby succeeded in constructing the necessary refined—or we should say, super-refined—measuring instruments.

At this point the archaeologists first began paying close attention. Had a dream at last come true? Had a way been found for determining by purely physical methods the age of objects that could not have been dated by the methods known hitherto?

Seldom have fundamentally different sciences struck up a collaboration so rapidly as they did here. The reason was that not only the archaeologists were hoping for a great new aid. Libby himself immediately realized that archaeology alone could provide him with exact proofs of the validity of his measurements. All he need do was to try out his method on objects whose extreme age had already been established beyond question. It was obvious that ancient Egypt could provide such materials, for written sources and astronomical data had enabled Egyptologists to develop a chronology correct almost to a decade.

As early as January 9, 1948, there took place the first conference among representatives of various sciences, and by February the American Anthropological Association had appointed a special committee to undertake a systematic study of the usefulness of Libby's method for archaeology. Frederick Johnson of the Peabody Foundation in Andover acted as chairman. The other members were Froelich Rainey of the University of Pennsylvania Museum, Donald Collier of the Chicago Museum, and later Richard Foster Flint, the Yale University geologist. These four appointed other assistants, who were assigned specific areas of experimentation.

And then a torrent of materials from all over the world poured into Dr. Libby's laboratory. Never had a technical laboratory seen so bizarre a collection. Libby's office soon resembled a curiosity cabinet. There were bits of mummies from Egypt's great period, charcoal from a fire at which some prehistoric man had warmed himself, the tooth of a mammoth that had become extinct during the last Ice Age, a sandal from an Indian grave in Ohio, a piece of plank from the funeral ship built for a pharaoh's last rites, a half-charred bone with an arrowhead still stuck in it, a morsel of beam that had once supported the roof of a Hittite temple. . . . As it turned out, more than half of the samples Libby tested during his first period of work were of American origin—109 of 216 samples. That was not surprising, since American colleagues were naturally the first to turn to Libby, begging for help with datings they had fruitlessly struggled with and debated over for decades—for example, dating the earliest traces of man in America, especially so-called Folsom man, of whom we shall be hearing a great deal in this book.

Nevertheless, the samples from the Mediterranean world were the ones that provided the first confirmations of Libby's theories. He first tested a piece of acacia wood from a beam that had been found in the tomb of Pharaoh Djoser. The historians had assigned this pharaoh a date of approximately 2700 B.C. Libby's dating came out slightly older than 2000 B.C. That was too large a margin of error. He did better dating the piece of plank from the funeral ship of Pharaoh Sesostris. Here the error was only four and a half per cent.

Then, however, something happened that seemed to discredit seriously Libby's method but turned out to confirm it brilliantly. James H. Breasted, the great American historian and archaeologist, founder and first director of the world-famous Oriental Institute of Chicago University, *the* authority in his time for Egyptology, sent bits of wood from a pharaoh's sarcophagus which, he informed Libby, must be of very great age. Given Egyptian conditions, that meant thousands of years old. Libby's test showed that the wood was modern! Was physics right, or the word of a great authority? Breasted, by no means an obstinate man, examined his sarcophagus once again and this time gave it close scrutiny. And he found out that he, the great expert, had actually been victimized by a modern forgery![3]

This was a major vindication. But then again there came a series of faulty results. Some archaeologists began to murmur that they had been taken in prematurely by a grand hope. Libby fostered this view by admitting from the start that his measurements always included an uncertainty factor averaging about ten per cent. He expressed this by adding a plus and minus to every date. Thus, a piece of wood is 2,000 years old ±100 or ±200. But this factor could be calculated within reasonable limits and was not too grave a matter. For in prehistoric datings, in which thousands of years are always involved, fixing the date within a century represented enormous progress. Libby now knew that he was on the right track; what remained was to improve his apparatus.

If we enter a radiocarbon laboratory today—and there are now several dozen of them over the globe—we feel as if we are stepping into the quarters of one of those monstrous mad scientists of the movies who, surrounded by mysterious and intricate gear, are preparing the downfall of a government or of the whole human race.

One entire room in such a laboratory seems to consist of nothing but glass and metal pipes, cylinders, conduits, intertwined in the weirdest shapes. And these pipes are steaming and hissing; liquids and gases rise up and go down; the pointers of meters quiver under invisible influences. In brief, to the layman the room looks like a witches' kitchen. And the strangest items of all are the strongboxes, made of steel, big as pianos, obviously weighing tons, which in their hidden interiors conceal the real soul of the laboratory: a combination of counters for measuring radioactivity.

For unfortunately we cannot merely place a Geiger counter near a piece of old wood and count the ticks in order to determine the remaining radioactivity and thus the age of the substance. That is not possible, because the energy of C-14 radiation is too feeble and also because in many cases other radioactive substances affect the reading.

The first thing to be done is to extract the pure carbon from the material to be examined. Oddly enough, the simplest way to do that is to burn it. The carbon separates out in gaseous compounds that can easily be reduced to a solid.

When the archaeologists heard about this aspect of the matter from Libby, their hearts sank. What? The whole measuring procedure was possible only by destroying the samples? The thought horrified them, for just at the end of the forties the Dead Sea Scrolls had been discovered, those scrolls containing unknown biblical texts. Dating them had become the supreme problem for Christian studies. Suddenly here was a means of precise dating. But was it not unthinkable to sacrifice a single one of these rolls whose preciousness could not remotely be measured in terms of any monetary value?

Here, certainly, was a real problem. Libby began calculating how much of a given material he needed. In the case of wood, in order to carry out at least two measurements (and from the start Libby insisted that several measurements were essential to check results) he would need at least twenty grams of carbon. To obtain them he needed at least sixty-five grams of wood. The amount differed according to the material involved. To date peat or linen, for instance, 200 grams were needed, for bones, even more.

This was a problem that does not matter in the case of many materials, because so much is available that the destruction of a few grams is insignificant. But there were other problems that for a short time greatly perturbed Libby himself. The inaccuracies that had arisen at the beginning of his experiments because of the interference of other radiation were eliminated as the physicists quickly learned to take proper protective measures. Nevertheless, every so often some measurement would turn up that was completely wide of the mark. In these cases it sometimes turned out that the fault was not Libby's but that of the archaeologists who had supplied the material. Here is a very simple case. The archaeologists had excavated the remains of a house. They found several beams, sawed out a piece and sent it to Libby for a check—only for a check, since from other indications they already knew how old the house was. Libby's dating indicated an age 200 years older than the archaeologists had determined! In one such case subsequent examination of the excavation site revealed the following circumstances. The house had undergone repairs ages before, and the repairers had used a piece of scrap wood from a building that had been erected 200 years earlier. And out of the whole beam the archaeologists happened to send this particular patch to Libby!

Similar problems came up because the stratigraphy of a site had not been recorded with the utmost care, so that Libby received pieces that the archaeologists *thought* belonged to the oldest stratum, but which in reality had come from a much more recent stratum.

There is another source of error for which neither Libby nor the archaeologists can be blamed. It is inherent in the material. It has turned out, for example, that the flesh of certain aquatic animals shows fewer traces of the radioactive substance than the shell. Or that certain plants do not take in as much C-14 as other plants in different environments. Such sources of error can be corrected only by ample experience.

One highly curious result emerged from measurements of relatively young trees alongside a superhighway. According to the radiocarbon dating they were several hundred years old—an obviously ludicrous result. What had happened? Exhaust gases, which are becoming a worse problem every year, are pouring vast quantities of carbon compounds into the air. This "dilutes" the carbon compounds normally present in the atmosphere and thus considerably diminishes the percentage of radioactive C-14, thereby creating the illusion of a decay process that has not actually taken place. The opposite phenomenon is also possible. From 1954 on the laboratories in America suddenly showed considerably altered results; all the materials tested suddenly seemed ten per cent or more "younger" than expected. For a brief time this phenomenon could not be explained at all. Finally, one of the scientists thought to place the blame on the hydrogen-bomb tests that had been repeatedly undertaken from 1954 on. He proved to be right. After every explosion a strongly radioactive cloud drifted from west to east over America, influencing the measurements.

By now many more sources of error are known, but they are being eliminated one by one. Nevertheless, many of the initial measurements (up to the mid-fifties) have had to be repeated. For example, views of the half-life of C-14 have also changed. It is now assumed to be not 5,568 but 5,730 years. Accordingly, all the old measurements undertaken before 1961 have had to be recalculated because they were about three per cent too low. Further improvements are expected in the near future. Whenever possible, therefore, pieces of the original samples are saved, so that the measurement can be repeated a few years hence. It eases matters that nowadays the measurements no longer need destroy as much material as at the start. For example, it has been possible to test the Dead Sea Scrolls without sacrificing too large a sample.

Moreover, as we have remarked at the beginning of this chapter, a good number of other dating procedures are now available. And every conscientious archaeologist attempts to apply all possible methods. These must corroborate one another before the result is accepted.

Of all the methods, however, radiocarbon dating remains the most important as far as chronological range is concerned. When Libby began, he thought that materials older than 25,000 years would not be susceptible to measurement. Today the threshold has already been pushed back to 70,000 years, that is, to around the time of Neanderthal man.

For some time all dates obtained have been systematically collected on punch cards by an organization called Radiocarbon Dates, Inc., c/o John Ramsden, P.O. Box 22, Braintree, Massachusetts, where they are available to every scientist. Moreover, a list of dates is published annually under the title *Radiocarbon*. This publication was started by the *American Journal of Science*.

Willard F. Libby received the Nobel Prize in 1960. He is the only scientist to have been awarded this prize for work essentially connected with archaeology.

9

The Endless Tree

In spite of the enormous importance to archaeology of radiocarbon dating, the new physical method still could not do one thing: fix the exact *year*. But a method for doing so had actually existed long before radiocarbon dating. We are discussing it after rather than before Libby's discovery because for a long time this method was applied only within a limited geographical area, namely, the American Southwest. Moreover, its full capacities have been realized only in the past two decades, chiefly in the Laboratory of Tree-Ring Research in Tucson, under the auspices of the University of Arizona.

Like all great and simple ideas, tree-ring dating or dendrochronology was conceived of several times before it assumed the pre-eminent practical importance it now has. Every Columbus is preceded by Vikings. It is therefore scarcely surprising that the basic idea was propounded by the man who anticipated so much else that advanced technology was to make a reality: Leonardo da Vinci. There is a note in his journals to the effect that dry and wet years can be traced in tree rings.

Tree-ring analysis was also proposed in 1837 by the author of the *Ninth Bridgewater Treatise*, Charles Babbage (who developed the principles on which all modern computers are designed). He speaks of a method for determining differences in tree rings and envisions the possibility of 'cross-dating' (we shall learn in a moment what that is). "The application of these views to ascertaining the age of submerged forests," he writes, "or to that of peat mosses, may possibly connect them ultimately with the chronology of man." And Frederick E. Zeuner, the historian of chronology, does not hesitate to state: "Indeed a remarkable case of vision in science."[1]

But the real inventor of the method, the man who exploited its usefulness to archaeology to the utmost, was an American, a physicist and astronomer who originally, as director of the University of Arizona's Steward Observatory, was occupied with an entirely different subject: the influence of sunspots on terrestrial weather.

He had developed his method in principle as early as 1913, but not until 1929 was he able to take a retrospective view and begin an article with the following proud statement.

"By translating the story told by tree rings, we have pushed back the horizons of history in the United States for nearly eight centuries before Columbus reached the shores of the New World, and we have established in our Southwest a chronology for that period more accurate than if human hands had written down the major events as they occurred."[2]

This remarkable man, Dr. Andrew Ellicott Douglass, continued working in his laboratory until his ninetieth year; he died in 1962 at the age of ninety-five. The starting point for all his later work was his observation that sunspots have affected the climate of the earth. To put the matter crudely, every eleven years, when sunspots reach their maximum, there have been many storms and much rain on earth, hence ample moisture for the vegetable kingdom. But in order to prove that this connection had existed for a long period of time, Dr. Douglass needed more than the sparse meteorological data of the past, since regular records of weather stations were a matter of relatively recent date.

In a moment of happy inspiration he remembered an observation he had made as a boy, an observation every one of us has made. If we examine the surface of a sawed-off tree, we see rings. It has been known since time immemorial that these are annual rings. But what the casual glance does not perceive, and what led Dr. Douglass to his decisive idea, is the fact that the rings are not of equal thickness. Some are narrow, some broad. Frequently, a few broad rings follow a series of narrow ones, and vice versa. They also differ in color. Was it possible, Douglass reflected, that the fat rings represent "fat years" and the lean rings "lean years"—in other words, moist and dry years?

That was easy to prove. He could rapidly compare the outer rings of a newly cut tree with the weather reports of recent years—and found that his assumption was correct. Therefore the same thing would be true if he went back to the pith of the tree. In other words, if he had before him a tree 300 years old, he should be able to tell precisely what kind of weather had prevailed in a specific region 300 years ago.

Studying this matter in Arizona, he found an unquestionable connection between sunspots and the growth of the trees. Every eleven years there had been a "fat period," a time of ample moisture. Oddly, there was one exception. Between A.D. 1650 and 1725 he found only drought! Could that be possible? Had there been no or few sunspots for seventy-five years? Or was there a flaw in his theory?

Then something quite incredible happened. The British astronomer E. Walter Maunder had heard about his work and wrote to him. Preoccupied with the phenomenon of sunspots for many years, Maunder had determined from entirely different sources that around 1700 there had been a long period of no sunspots. He gave the dates, and they corresponded precisely with the seventy-five-year period that Douglass had determined from his tree rings!

It is not quite clear what prompted Douglass to push his researches further and further back into the past. Perhaps he was simply irritated by the barrier presented by the trees at his disposal. For in Arizona, where he was working with pine trees, he could not go back beyond the year 1450; he simply could not find any trees older than that.

For a man of the Southwest who knew his way about in this land of many ruins it was no great leap for him to say to himself: I must have a few slices from the old trees that the first Spaniards felled here around 1650 and even before to build their missions and churches.

Douglass received help as early as 1914 from Dr. Clark Wissler of the American Museum of Natural History in New York. Wissler even gave him still older samples, from the beams of the prehistoric Pueblo Bonito in New Mexico.

But Douglass was not satisfied. He had meanwhile discovered that for his analyses he did not need a whole slice from a beam. A "core"—a sample rod extracted from a beam with a hollow drill—could tell him as much as a slice.

He wrote to archaeologists throughout the Southwest asking for such samples—slices, cores, even half-charred remains could tell him something, he declared. Among the persons he addressed was Earl Morris, who was working in the Aztec ruins fifty miles north of Pueblo Bonito, and Neil Judd, who was digging in Pueblo Bonito itself. Both of these "great houses" had been built at about the same time; so much was evident from the similarity of the artifacts found in them. But were they really *exactly* of the same date?

Both sites were pre-Spanish—that was clear, too. But since there had never been any kind of written calendar in North America, neither Judd nor Morris had the remotest idea to what year in the Christian chronology the building of their pueblos should be assigned. Then Dr. Douglass wrote them: "I thought you might be interested to know that the latest beam in the ceiling of the Aztec Ruins was cut just exactly nine years before the latest beam from Bonito. Most of the other wood shows contemporaneous occupation."[3]

"I thought you might be interested," Dr. Douglass had casually written. In fact this news had the effect of a bombshell on Judd and Morris. They found it simply astounding that someone claimed he could distinguish an age difference of only nine years in prehistoric beams with absolute certainty. Would such a wizard be able to tell them in what century, perhaps even in what decade, those nine years lay?

Here Douglass was confronting the crucial problem of dendrochronology. He solved it. The astonishing thing is that in his own accounts of his method he makes no fuss at all about this decisive discovery. It seems to him something to be taken for granted.

To put the matter briefly, he discovered the possibility of "cross-dating" or "overlapping." For example, a tree felled in 1960 has, say, 200 annual rings. That means that the tree began growing in 1760. The 200 rings vary in width and provide a faithful picture of the climatic conditions from year to year. Now the dendrochronologist seeks out an old church with very old beams from the same vicinity. One of these beams has, say, 100 rings. A graphic representation of the varying widths of the rings is made on a long tape. These tapes are placed together, one above the other, and adjusted until, if the scientist is lucky, the outer rings of the beam from the church correspond with the inner rings of the tree that began growing in 1760. Let us say that this overlapping in our case amounts to fifty rings, hence fifty years. That means that the church beam with the hundred annual rings was cut in 1810, and that the tree from which it was taken began growing in 1710. Thus we have dated our church beam. In addition—and this is the most significant aspect of the matter—we have taken a further step of fifty years back into the past. Now we need only find still older beams which likewise overlap, and the chronology can be extended backward ad infinitum. We have, in effect, an "endless tree."

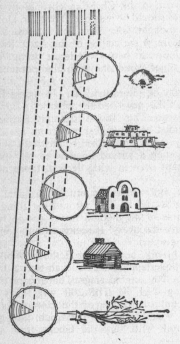

Illustration of tree-ring dating (dendrochronology). By overlapping of the wood samples, starting with a recently felled tree, the scientist can determine to the very year the dates for the building of the blockhouse, the Spanish mission church, the pueblo, and finally the prehistoric pit house.

How far back?

It certainly sounds incredible, but we may anticipate the answer here: in the Southwest such an endless tree has been constructed extending back *before the birth of Christ*.

It is clear that dendrochronolgy is very simple in principle. In practice, however, it is extremely complicated. We see that as soon as we visit a tree-ring laboratory. These laboratories, incidentally, are the sweetest-smelling in the world. While the C-14 laboratories must be described as veritable witches' kitchens, the tree-ring lab seems like a string of classrooms reserved for the study of higher mathematics—except for the wonderful odors of woods that permeate the whole place, woods from all over the world, from sandalwood to resinous pine. A glance at the innumerable diagrams and a peer through the microscope at the sometimes minute samples of half-charred wood immediately reveal some of the difficulties. For no tree does us the favor of growing at exactly the same pace as its neighbor. Innumerable influences blur the rings, cause checks to their growth, adhesions, overlays, and these are often so hard to recognize that misinterpretations are easily possible. And of course any mistakes will make the *entire* scale wrong and particularly interfere with the establishment of an overlapping. In decades of work many "dirty tricks" of tree growth have been discovered, and the methods of evaluation have been continually refined. In 1934 Fay-Cooper Cole, the great teacher of anthropology at the University of Chicago, established a tree-ring laboratory there and soon tried out a new method of evaluation known as the Gladwin method. It eliminated some of the inadequacies of the Douglass method but unfortunately introduced new sources of error of its own. But let us return to the twenties and the first great triumphs of tree-ring dating.

Dr. Douglass once compared his method with the Rosetta Stone, that famous stone inscribed in three languages that provided the key for deciphering the Egyptian hieroglyphs. Today this comparison is justified; at that time, when Douglass sat brooding over fragments of wood from Pueblo Bonito, it was not yet valid. For he was still entirely in the dark about the chronology of Bonito. But he received assistance, for science was beginning to take an interest in this new tool. The National Geographic Society, to which archaeology owes so much, the American Museum of Natural History, and the Carnegie Institution in Washington were the first to lend Dr. Douglass support and to provide funds. It was obvious that he had to find a site that lay historically between the early Spaniard period and the—let us give it that name here—the Bonito-Aztec period. No fewer than three expeditions were dispatched in 1923, 1928, and 1929 to find this site.

Before the end of 1928 Dr. Douglass was able to present an unbroken ring sequence extending back to A.D. 1300. One fragment of wood, but only a single one, actually pointed back to 1260. Alongside this fixed chronology Douglass constructed, from more than thirty ruins, a floating chronology of no fewer than 585 years. "Floating" in this sense meant that these 585 years represented a continuous period but that he did not know where to place them within our Christian chronology. He knew only that they must begin at some point *before* the year 1260. The problem was to close this gap.

In 1929 this problem was solved. But the success was won only by overcoming difficulties from an unexpected quarter.

Douglass and his assistants, who had turned up in virtually all the pueblos of the Southwest with their drills, aroused the suspicion of the Indians. The scientists tried to win them over by living with them for a time. They made efforts to learn the Indians' language and complicated code of courtesy. But all these efforts were at first of no avail. After all, suppose a man of a different skin color and strange manners came into our house and insisted that for scientific reasons we couldn't understand he wanted to bore holes into our cherished beams and walls. We would probably think him insane and simply throw him out.

At one time, because he was forbidden to bore his holes, Douglass had no choice but to crawl into a low cellar, where he spent seven hours lying on his stomach counting rings in the floor joists.

At last a bright assistant hit on a solution. By chance he discovered that the Indians of the region were mad about purple velvet, of all things. Whole bales of purple velvet were promptly procured, and after the scientists had additionally consented to cap every drill hole with a turquoise, in order to keep the spirits from getting in or out, the expedition was allowed to bore wherever it pleased.

The most useful cores were obtained in eastern Arizona, in the ruins near Showlow. Here Emil W. Haury, then a young man, later to win fame as the excavator of Snaketown, found a piece of wood that all at once brought Southwestern archaeology into line with Christian chronology. The piece was not very pretty; it was half charred. The group catalogued it under the number HH 39—and after they had analyzed it this number became the most celebrated in the history of North American tree-ring dating. To make a long story short, this piece overlapped the existing tree-ring sequence by no fewer than twenty-three years and permitted dating to the year 1237. With that as a clue, Douglass and his assistants had an easy time achieving further back-dating—to the year 700!

In the course of this work it turned out that there had been no gap at all between the fixed and the floating chronologies. The scientists could have established an overlap from the beginning had they only realized it and had sufficient material at their disposal early enough. But an enormous wealth of material had been lost in previous excavations. For the archaeologists had not paid the slightest attention to the bits of wood that often crumbled in their hands; they had thrown these away as useless. In addition,

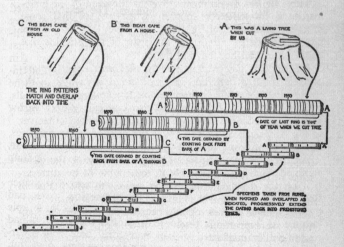

Again, illustrating the process of tree-ring dating by the technique of overlapping.

this particular segment of history showed an unnatural type of tree-ring development, which was therefore hard to analyze. For it was now discovered that between A.D. 1276 and 1299 there had been an altogether unusual period of drought. (Later on this drought, lasting for a whole generation, served to explain the then incomprehensible signs of a vast migration on the part of the Pueblo Indians.)

In any case, in December, 1929, Dr. Douglass was able to announce that he had obtained a continual tree-ring chronology back to A.D. 700—an "endless tree" of 1,229 years!—and that in addition to Pueblo Bonito he had been able to date accurately some forty other pueblo ruins.

Here are a few examples of his datings:

Pueblo Bonito	919–1130
Aztec	1110–1121
Mesa Verde	1073–1262
Mummy Cave (Tower House)	1253–1284
White House	1060–1275
Oraibi	1370–1800
Kawaikuh	1284–1495
Showlow	1174–1393

These figures by no means give the life span of the pueblos, as is immediately apparent when we see that some of them embrace only a very brief span of time. These are merely dates *within* the life span of the pueblos that could be established beyond doubt.

We must realize that these are the most exact archaeological datings that have been obtained anywhere in the world where written documentation is wholly lacking.

Can it be that these datings also conceal errors? And why in our account have we consistently limited ourselves to the American Southwest? Was the method inappropriate elsewhere for some reason?

As for possible sources of error, Dr. Bryant Bannister summed them up impeccably in the course of his dissertation on the dating of the Chaco region, to which Pueblo Bonito also belongs. He published the dissertation in 1965, by which time he had already become director of the Laboratory of Tree-Ring Research in Tucson, Arizona. The reader will immediately observe that these sources of possible error are the same as those with which the radiocarbon daters have to contend:

1. The association between the dated tree-ring specimen and the archaeological manifestation being dated is direct, but the specimen itself came from a tree that died or was cut prior to its use in the situation in question.
2. The association between the dated tree-ring specimen and the archaeological manifestation being dated is not direct, the specimen having been used prior to the feature being dated.
3. The association between the dated tree-ring specimen and the archaeological manifestation being dated is direct, but the specimen itself represents a later incorporation into an already existing feature.
4. The association between the dated tree-ring specimen and the archaeological manifestations being dated is not direct, the specimen having been used later than the feature being dated.[4]

Strictly speaking, these are problems that the archaeologist should be dealing with—since he must be alert to all the circumstances—rather than the dater. In one ruin, for example, the archaeologists were able to demonstrate that the tree trunks had been transported by the Indians the incredible distance of 175 miles. Naturally, the growth of their rings differed radically from that of the trees in the vicinity, so that at first they could not at all be fitted into the chronology of the ruin. Then again, the following unusual case was tracked down. As Bannister describes it, "Douglass documents one case in which a fourteenth century log was probably reused continually until it was discovered in 1929 in a recently abandoned section of Oraibi."[5]

These examples lead us to the last question: Why have we confined ourselves to the American Southwest? That is simply because at first the method actually proved itself only in the Southwest—or rather, because only in the Southwest were the conditions for dendrochronology ideal.

Libby's radiocarbon dating was an American gift to archaeologists of the whole world—at once.

Douglass's dendrochronology was initially useful only to the Americans themselves. Every region must develop its *own* tree-ring sequence. Therefore, it would have been useless for Douglass to take what seemed the obvious step and go looking for older trees in California, where the redwoods and giant sequoias were waiting to be analyzed. Those trees had lived up to 3,000 years, but they had grown in an entirely different climate from that of the Arizona and New Mexico trees and therefore could not show the slightest overlapping with them. (In the fifties Dr. Edmund Schulmann, also of the University of Arizona, discovered still older trees in California: the bristlecone pines, which are up to 4,500 years old—the oldest living organisms in the world. They proved to be excellent checks for radiocarbon dating, which in this case obviously functioned without error. Using *dead* wood, C. W. Ferguson of the same university succeeded in obtaining an unquestionably accurate backdating to the year 5200 B.C.[6]

Finally, experience taught that not all climates and trees are equally favorable for dating purposes. It was one of the luckiest strokes that Douglass had begun his work in Arizona, for of all trees the Arizona conifers (pine, fir, piñon) lent themselves best to this analysis.

Nevertheless, the method soon conquered other regions. J. Louis Giddings, the late grand old man of Eskimo research, applied Douglass's method to Alaska and pushed a continuous chronology back to A.D. 978. And in 1967 Charles C. DiPeso reported that in the course of the extremely complicated stratigraphic work at the Las Casas Grandes ruins in the Mexican province of Chihuahua he had discovered a history extending over many hundreds of years, and by means of tree-ring dating had drawn up a chronology from A.D. 850 to 1336—at which time the town was burned down.

In the course of this Las Casa Grandes excavation the first results were only a floating chronology of 586 years. The services of a computer were needed before it could be "tied in" to an "endless tree." But it must be stressed that even a floating chronology is tremendously valuable to archaeologists. Bryant Bannister had already proved that in Turkey, others in Scandinavia. For even if no tie-in to the Christian chronology exists, it is illuminating for the excavator if he can date exactly the time relationships of the various strata in a ruin to one another or, provided the floating chronology is long enough, if he can determine the life span of one or several cultural strata. For even the most careful kind of stratigraphy will only give him the succession of the strata.

In Germany, shortly after the war, Bruno Huber, the Munich professor of forestry, succeeded in obtaining a dating series for the Berchtesgaden region extending back to the year 1300. Again in Germany an enthusiastic amateur, Ernst Hollstein, a school superintendent in Trier, took up the method in 1961. He pursued it first as a hobby, then with the support of other scientists, and by and by his work was recognized as so original that the government relieved him of his official duties for eighteen months so that he could devote himself to his "hobby." He studied particularly oakwood in the Rhineland and was soon after to date the west aisle of the cathedral of Trier (1042–1074), the nave of the cathedral in Speyer (1045) and the choir seats in Cologne Cathedral (1308–1311).

Thus, through the labors of a man in Tucson, Arizona, who at first was solely interested in sunspots, there emerged and spread through half the globe the most "absolute" system of archaeological dating.

Book Three

10

Along the Road . . .

WITHOUT more ado, we can now co-ordinate the development of the Basket Makers up to the highest forms of pueblo life with Christian chronology—which Kidder, dependent on stratigraphy alone, could not yet do at the Pecos Conference in 1927, since tree-ring dating was only in its beginnings at that time. In table form the sequence is as shown on the facing page.

Of course, this is only an outline. It records the *common elements*, although the picture may have been considerably more complex. During any of these periods there may have been an array of different tribes with different languages. In the pueblo periods the open-minded observer would in fact be struck by the variations among the cliff dwellings, the mesa pueblos, and the valley pueblos. And the transitions are never sharp. Consequently, we are only indicating the basic characteristics here.

Basket Makers I to III. The Basket Makers I appeared around or before the birth of Christ in the vicinity of the Four Corners. They are hypothetical; we can say nothing about them except that they laid the ground for everything that so clearly distinguished the Basket Makers II. The

	↑	Pueblo V (period to the present)
1600		
1540	Spaniards conquer the pueblos	
1500		Pueblo IV
1400		
1300		
1200		Pueblo III (the Great Age)
1100		
1000		Pueblo II
900		
800		Pueblo I
700		
600		
500	Atlatl replaced by bow and arrow	Basket Makers III
	Beginning of pottery	
400		
300		Basket Makers II
200		
100		
Birth of Christ	↓	Basket Makers I

latter are tribes whose life we can picture with some accuracy. They lived in caves or in extremely primitive pit houses, were farmers who already planted corn and squash, had long skulls, reddish-brown skins, and thick dark hair. They attained a degree of artistry in basket weaving that is simply astonishing. Of course, they had no pottery at all, so that baskets had to serve them for every purpose, for transportation, storage, even for cooking. (Nowadays only Boy Scouts learn how to go about that. The baskets, made watertight on the inside with resin, cannot be put over the fire, of course. Therefore the cooking procedure is reversed; the water is heated from inside rather than from outside by dropping red-hot stones into the basket.) Storage baskets could be all of 100 inches in circumference and were often wonderfully decorated in reds and blues.

It was in their sandal making that these fanatical artists in wicker revealed their greatest skill. With basketry and leather straps, pebbles, shells, and feathers, they produced such fantastic specimens of craftsmanship, forever invent-

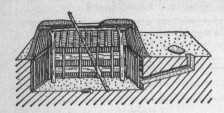

Reconstruction of a pit house from the vicinity of Flagstaff, Ariz. The entrance doubled as a smoke hole. The shaft on the right served for ventilation and could be closed.

ing new forms, that it is hard to find several pairs of sandals that are exactly alike. Yet archaeologists have been able to distinguish plainly the sandals they made for daily use and what might be called "Sunday sandals" for festive occasions.

They also developed the first type of cradle carried on the back, such as can still be seen in the Navajo country. Every white woman feels it a sin and a shame when she sees the infants tightly wrapped and condemned to complete immobility. But careful studies have shown that the children do not suffer from this treatment and that it is a great advantage to the mothers. It must have been a different matter altogether when the head wrappings were so arranged that the long skulls were deformed into flattened skulls, as was done in a later period.

Their weapons were stone knives and wooden clubs. For small animals they used throw sticks, but did not develop a genuine boomerang. Their most important weapon

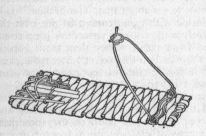

This sandal was worn in 300 B.C., perhaps even earlier. The toes were held by the binding on the left; the cord on the right was wound around the ankle. The Early Hunters and food gatherers invented innumerable variants of this type.

was the atlatl, the thro*wing*-stick, which they had taken over from earlier hunters. (A description and picture of this first of mankind's "miracle weapons" will be found in Chapter 21.) The geographical distribution of the Basket Makers II cannot be exactly determined, since their principal products, baskets and sandals, were of such a perishable nature. Still, it can be said that they spread from Four Corners along the present boundary of Utah and Arizona far to the West and into Nevada.

The Basket Makers III distinguished themselves from their ancestors by high inventiveness or the ability to assimilate rapidly foreign influences and inventions. After A.D. 450 we observe the introduction of pottery among them; somewhat later the atlatl was replaced by bow and arrow. Their menu was enriched by beans. We are able to assign a tree-ring dating of A.D. 475 to the first houses characteristic of this era. These pit houses are round or egg-shaped, sometimes surrounded or lined with stone slabs. They extend into the ground from one to five feet and have a diameter of nine feet to twenty-five feet. The walls are often carefully plastered.

Pots of widely varying shapes are now found for the first time in sizable quantities in the deeper strata of the graves and rubbish heaps. There are baked and unbaked pots with distinct developments in design, so that stratigraphic ordering is possible. The first small clay figurines are also found, always female.

Fairly close to A.D. 700—in other words, a century before Charlemagne was crowned Emperor in Europe, 300 years before the first Vikings landed in America—the pithouse dwellers became builders of "towns." The culture of the pueblos began.

Let us once again describe the stages as formulated by the Pecos Conference. Basket Makers II represents the "agricultural, atlatl-using, non-pottery-making stage."

Basket Makers III: "Pit- or slabhouse-building, pottery-making stage. . . . Pottery is characterized in general by coarse lines, simple designs, many basket designs, and some crude life forms, generally a relatively coarse paste, and globular forms." Toward the end of the period bow and arrow are introduced (though many scholars assign this act to the next period).

The same classification defines Pueblo I as follows:

"The first stage during which cranial deformation was

practiced, vessel neck corrugation was introduced, and villages composed of rectangular rooms of true masonry were developed (in some areas)."[1]

These features of the pueblo culture were developed in Pueblo I, that is, from A.D. 700 to 900. During this period the population spread in a southwesterly direction, into what is now New Mexico, and also westward perhaps as far as the Grand Canyon.

During the Pueblo II period the real pueblos, consisting of groups of houses, were constantly expanded. This meant an enormous increase in the density of the population, a concentration of families into family groups, and the establishment of the first *societies* with a hierarchic order—that is one directed by the priests—which centered in the kivas. These, like the pit houses of the past, continued to be built half or entirely underground, as if to preserve the air of secrecy and concealment. The custom of cranial deformation in rigid cradle boards suddenly arose, but no satisfactory explanation for this development has been suggested.

We can fairly exactly place the beginning of Pueblo II at A.D. 900, as marked by the appearance of ceramics with black-on-white decoration. Then the first clay jugs with true handles turn up. (Such trivialities are highly significant for the development of a society. They suddenly make many of the activities of life easier—as, say, the invention of the match made everyday life in the nineteenth century so much easier.) The distribution of the various types of pottery permits us to deduce constant communication among the pueblos, even after sizable groups moved farther to the south or east, as far as the Pecos River. By tree-ring datings and characteristic pottery we can again date the end of the Pueblo II period with considerable precision—to about 1100. It is pure chance that these developments fall in so closely—though never exactly to the year—with round numbers in our Christian chronology.

There follow some 200 years that we call scientifically Pueblo III, or in a more poetic vein the Great Age of the Pueblos, or even the Golden Age. In the course of it there arose those beehive dwellings of several stories, holding hundred of families, those stacked complexes of homes that call to mind one of the most modern apartment buildings of our times, Habitat, at Expo 67 in Montreal. There are indications, although the matter remains highly uncertain, that the buildings rose to six and perhaps even to seven stories. White Americans did not build the first seven-story apartment house until 1869, in New York—and this was considered so daring an experiment that the whole world looked on with bated breath.

All arts and crafts were refined during this period. In addition to basketry came the first polychrome ceramics in the most artistic shapes. The ceramics of the Mimbres culture are probably the most amazing of all, advancing far beyond geometrical decoration. Suddenly insects, fish, and birds appear, their characteristics fantastically exaggerated so that they become fabulous creatures, whereas on the other hand a grasshopper, for example, might be delineated in the finest detail. All in all, it was "in many cases *the best pottery produced during any period,* with a general marked decrease in the importance of corrugated wares."[2]

The marvelous ceramics are accessible to everyone in the great American museums; the number of pieces runs into the millions. As for the amounts to be found in private col-

Bird, fish, dog, bear, and buck—black-and-white decorations on Mimbres (New Mexico) bowls.

lections, these simply cannot be estimated. Naturally, the degree of artistry varies. Undoubtedly, the Indians practiced barter. Not all the pueblos sprang up at the same time, so that a rising pueblo might take over and continue designs and methods that were already being replaced by more refined variants in the pueblo of their origin. Nor did practices that were very old simply die out. Before the archaeologists properly realized that, they were surprised to discover that at the time huge Pueblo Bonito was at the height of its glory, pit houses were still being built in the same area.

Specialization must have developed within this society. It seems fairly certain that artistic inlay work with turquoises, small copper bells, stone carvings representing animals or birds, necklaces composed of 5,700 shell beads—each one pierced with a hardwood drill—could not have lain within *everyone's* abilities. Unfortunately we know very little about the clothing; except for some tiny remnants, which nevertheless show that it was artistically woven, all of it has succumbed to the passage of time.

The present-day tourist who wanders from ruin to ruin in Arizona and New Mexico passes among the ghostly shadows of the twelfth and thirteenth centuries, years during which the fever of the Crusades raged in the Old World. For toward the end of the twelfth century came the great drought. By 1300 or thereabouts the Golden Age was gone; the "cities" were abandoned and decayed. In the Rio Grande Valley, at Pecos, in the Hopi and Zuñi regions in the west, culture continued to survive for some time. That leads us to Pueblo IV, the period that we now consider to have ended with the day in 1540 on which Coronado conquered the first pueblos, the so-called Seven Cities of Cibola. The rude soldiery wrecked much in searching for treasures that the pueblos had never possessed, and soon the missionaries began corrupting the complex religion of the Pueblo people with Christian teachings. We call the period from 1600 to the present Pueblo V—to the present because in spite of the Spaniards and in spite of the later torrent of pioneers, who were followed by the real-estate speculators, many pueblos still survive.

On August 25, 1916, the National Park Service was founded. It had been preceded by the Antiquities Act of 1906, which allowed the federal government to intervene if necessary to save ancient monuments of America's past from decay or destruction. Even so, to this day powerful interests, on grounds of economic necessity, are forever seeking to penetrate into areas where the building of dams for power plants would inflict irreparable damage upon the landscape and further invade the rights of the Indians. In recent years, however, such projects as the proposal to dam the Grand Canyon and Glen Canyon have evoked violent protests on the part of the public.

The bill establishing the National Park Service defined its aims as follows: "To promote and regulate the use of the Federal areas known as national parks, monuments and reservations specified by such means and measures as conform to the fundamental purpose of said parks, monuments and reservations, which purpose is to conserve the scenery and the natural and historic objects and the wildlife therein and to provide for the enjoyment of the same in such manner and by such means as will leave them unimpaired for the enjoyment of future generations."

Here we are interested in the archaeological aspect of this act. In this realm the Park Service, which like the Bureau of Indian Affairs is a branch of the Interior Department, has performed extraordinarily well. The moment a historic or prehistoric site is declared a national monument, it becomes subject to the special protection of the government, and the Park Service sees to the preservation of the ruins, while at the same time providing access to them, supplying guards and knowledgeable guides for them. It has sponsored all those mini-museums scattered along the highways in the Southwest.

The guides are friendly rangers, mostly aspiring archaeologists, unlike the importunate Egyptian dragomans who pull at your clothes with one hand and with the other demand their baksheesh. And the small museums often contain enchanting little exhibits, finds made at the site, so that the visitor can see the whole picture and understand the direct relationship between the stone tool, arrowhead, ornament or skull, and the nearby ruin. Literature on the ruin is also provided, written by specialists with reference to the particular site, in good clear language, well illustrated, low in price.[3] Usually there is also a small sales counter where colored slides can be bought—better ones than most people are able to take themselves—although at some sites I found explicitly marked spots from which the best photographs can be shot at specific times of day. Often there will also be carefully made replicas of the originals found on the site and very little of the trash usually offered in tourist shops.

In addition, these museums have the courage to present "living showcases," which so few European museums offer —perhaps because they tend to shun what might be falsifying reconstructions. Here the layman sees the abstract information of books and pamphlets, which he may find difficult to visualize, translated into a series of vivid realistic scenes: a little theater of life in prehistoric days. He sees the bustling pueblo existence of the early "Red" Men; he sees the hunters struggling with the buffalo, then is shown how the animal is speared and sent plunging over the cliffs. There are miniature versions of those impressive life-sized models shown in the big museums, above all the New York Museum of Natural History. It is no wonder that these museums are thronged with hordes of children and teenagers—while European museum attendants mostly stand gazing into yawningly empty rooms.

The Park Service also provides highly instructive demonstrations. Near Kayenta in northern Arizona, within the Navajo National Monument, are three large ruins: Betatakin, Keet Seel, and Inscription House. (In 1661 the Spaniards left an inscription there, which unfortunately is no longer legible.) Betatakin is one of the most attractive cliff dwellings in the Southwest. Deep in the canyon, built into an enormous shell-like cave in a red sandstone cliff of enormous height with colorful striations made by running water, is an agglomeration of "apartment" houses and towers where a pueblo tribe lived. They occupied Betatakin from 1242 up to the drought period around 1300. Some 150 rooms can be counted, including six kivas, thirteen open patios. Betatakin, which means "Hillside House," was rediscovered in 1909 by Byron Cummings and John Wetherill, and carefully restored in 1917 by Neil M. Judd.

The descent into the canyon to the ruins, among Douglas firs, piñons, and junipers, takes about one and a half hours. But a shorter path leads to a spot from which a magnificent view across the gorge to the whole cave complex can be enjoyed. If you stay long enough in the shifting light of the moving sun, the buildings take on a haunting sense of life.

Along this path the Park Service has planted a sampling of plants that at one time eased, or even made possible, the lives of the Indians who occupied the pueblo These give the most direct answer to the question every visitor sooner

This pitcher was made by the Anasazi between A.D. 1100 and 1200. Six inches high, it is at once handsome and functional, decorated in black and white.

or later asks himself: To what extent did these Anasazi (the word simply means "the old ones") understand how to utilize the products of nature? Here are some examples of the plants and their uses:

Big Sagebrush (*Artemisia tridentata*), with a very tart smell, is still chewed by the Hopis. A dense gray-green bush that grows waist-high, it has tiny leaves, which are boiled as a medicine for rheumatism and colds.

Cliff Rose (*Cowania stansburiana*), shoulder-high, gray-green bush. An infusion of it was used for washing wounds. Today it also provides food for cattle and sheep.

One-seed Juniper (Mexican cedar or *Juniperus monosperma*), firewood and lumber. Edible berries. A green dye is also made from the bark and berries.

Narrow-leaf Yucca (*Yucca angustissima*), the useful plant on which the prehistoric Indian depended most. Knee-high, long, lance-shaped leaves, used for sandals and baskets. Split, they yield fibers for many purposes. The spines are used as needles. The fruit is edible. The root supplied soap (still used by the Hopis and Navajos).

Piñon (*Pinus edulis*), tree, with extremely nourishing nuts that keep well. Resin useful for waterproofing baskets. Provides a black dye for woolen clothing.

Buffalo Berry (*Shepherdia rotundifolia*), silvery gleaming large shrub. Edible berries. The Navajos still use these berries to make a salve for sheep whose eyes have been irritated by sandstorms.

Prickly-pear Cactus (*Opuntia erinacea*), small cactus with disklike leaves. The fruit is boiled to a jelly or, after the long spines are removed, dried in the sun for later use.

Nowadays there are dozens of possible ways to take possession of that landscape of ruins. Even the booklet entitled *Southwest* in the Golden Regional Guide Series, which can be bought at every drugstore, suggests four one- to three-week tours. We are not writing a guide. Therefore, we shall mention only a few of the sites and then turn once more to a closer look at one of the most important ruins, Mesa Verde, because the story of its discovery, which is the real theme of our book, is so unusual.

In the southernmost part of Arizona lies the lively city of Tucson, which only a generation ago was an unimportant small town. Here are located the University of Arizona, founded in 1891, and the Arizona State Museum. During the past three decades the museum's anthropological-archaeological department has been stamped by the personality of Emil W. Haury, the great teacher and scholar, head of a "Field School" for practical archaeology, excavator of Snaketown and the Ventana Cave. Part of this great center are the radiocarbon laboratory and the Laboratory of Tree-Ring Research discussed in the last chapter.

The museum's collections are so well arranged that viewing them is probably the best preparation for anyone about to set out on explorations of the ruins to the north.

On the way to Phoenix, exactly sixty-nine miles north of Tucson, we come upon the first ruins, Casa Grande, at one time a four-story, blocklike building of yellow adobe, the heart of a settlement that flourished 600 years ago. The way there, and then beyond Phoenix as far as Flagstaff, goes by what are now excellent roads through two of the most beautiful and typical Arizona landscapes: first through the desert, in which, at night, the headlights pick out nothing but the tall, saguaro multibrachiate cactuses (each arm, it is said, takes some seventy years to grow), and then up into the country of fantastic, fiery red and yellow cliff statuary. Before Flagstaff we come to Montezuma Castle, one of the best preserved cliff dwellings. It hangs, looking utterly absurd, halfway up a cliff in a gigantic cave. A few

*Prehistoric pueblos and cliff dwellings in the Southwest, in-
cluding the still inhabited Taos in the north. The other still
inhabited pueblos to the south, as far as Albuquerque and
beyond, are absent from this map.*

lifeless windows stare down; it can be reached only by ladders. The friendly supervisors have posted a sign asking
anyone who has the *luck* to see a rattlesnake to kindly report it to them! It had already been abandoned by 1450.
Naturally, Montezuma Castle has nothing to do with the
last emperor of the Aztecs who was defeated by Cortés and
stoned by his own people in 1520. The same applies to
nearby Montezuma Well, a round lake that would seem to
have been produced by the impact of a meteorite. From its
deep gorge the weird body of water glints up at us like an
eye of the earth's interior. Here, too, the Indians built
almost inaccessible cliff dwellings in the side walls.

The Museum of Northern Arizona, with its Research
Center in Flagstaff, constantly enriched for many years by
Edward B. Danson, is a center of multifarious anthropological, archaeological, ethnological, geological, and biological researches. It was founded by a remarkable philan-

thropist and scientist, Harold S. Colton. We must pause for a moment to speak of him.

Colton, the son of a Philadelphia banker, born in 1881, initially studied zoology and chemistry and became a professor at the University of Pennsylvania. In 1912 he went to Flagstaff for the first time; the town then had 2,000 inhabitants. In 1916 he set out on his first archaeological expeditions in the vicinity, using horses and mules. Ten years later he settled permanently in Flagstaff and founded the museum of which he became director for thirty-two years. He also made something of a hobby of architecture, drawing detailed plans for buildings of gray-brown basalt— and creating a style that was much imitated in Flagstaff (and in Flagstaff alone). I met this tall, lean, hawk-nosed gentleman with the neat goatee when he was eighty-four years old, and was staggered by his intellectual alertness and physical vigor. One afternoon he drove me more than a hundred miles to "his" ruins. In the course of his career he located 156 prehistoric sites, published more than 200 papers on a wide variety of subjects, and attempted the classification of 400 types of Southwestern pottery. His academic qualifications and honors are so numerous that *Who's Who* takes twenty lines to list them in abbreviated form. He is already almost a legendary figure in the archaeology of Arizona, and will remain so.

Colton's estimate of the Pueblo population of Northern Arizona.

A.D.		
	600	3,000
	800	10,000
	1000	23,000
	1150	19,000
	1400	7,400
	1890	2,000
	1950	4,000

The large increase between 1890 and 1950, after the population had reached its lowest point, is true of not only the Arizona Indians, but all the Indians in the United States. Contrary to widespread opinion, they are not dying out, but increasing.

One of his most readable and informative books on prehistoric northern Arizona is entitled *Black Sand*. It is chiefly concerned with the effects of a disaster that took place northeast of Flagstaff in 1064–65. A volcano—Sunset Crater—erupted and spewed black ashes over a territory of 800 square miles, suffocating all life. One might hope for an American Pompeii, but the Sinaguas who lived here dwelt in miserable pit houses. So there are no villas lying under the black sand. But what looked like blackest death after the catastrophe proved to be the germ of new life. The black land was more fertile than ever before, and the Indians, who had fled, in time poured back. However, news of the magical fertility spread, and there followed a unique "run" on the black earth. Whole families poured into the region, especially from the south. What is more important, they brought new ideas, new practices, a new and superior culture. The people and the land changed. In the second generation after the eruption the pit-house dwellers were living in three-room houses.

When the Hopi Indian today looks up at the crater, he knows that some of the 250 kachinas—the helpful and punitive spirits—are looking down at him, for that is where they live. In a crack in the lava lies Yaponcha, the mighty god of wind. Was it he who for a century and a half after the "fortunate" disaster slowly but steadily blew away the fertile soil, so that in the first half of the thirteenth century the maize grew ever thinner, the fields became parched, and the people had to emigrate again?[4]

Eighteen miles north of Sunset Crater lie the four-story Wupatki ruins; twenty-one miles south are the ruins of Walnut Canyon.

Sinaguas also lived in Wupatki. (The name, from Spanish *sin* = without, *agua* = water, was coined by Colton and suggests the difficult conditions of life for these Indians.) Within the Wupatki National Monument, taken in its broadest sense, there are 800 ruins. Wupatki proper was inhabited from A.D. 1120 to 1210, ninety years, as was Nineveh, described in the Bible as so glorious and terrible. But at Wupatki there were only dwellings, not palaces, and kivas instead of the temple, and the town was not razed but abandoned. Nevertheless, there remain two buildings unusual in the Southwest and highly important.

In 1933, when the Museum of Northern Arizona began its first excavations, the archaeologists came upon a circular wall with a step, probably meant to be a row of seats, running around it. This seemed, of course, to be another kiva.

*Specimens of polychrome pottery from the vicinity of Ka-
yenta, Ariz.*

But the ceremonial features normally present in kivas were completely lacking, and there were no indications that this circular arena had ever been roofed. Was this possible? A kiva, a "secret" ceremonial room, open to all eyes under the glaring rays of the sun? To this day the archaeologists have not been able to determine the precise function of this structure. It is the only known example of its kind. For lack of a better term it has consequently been dubbed an "amphitheater."

The second structure is a ball court. It is not the only one of its kind, but it is probably the northernmost ancient ball court on the American continents, and it testifies to what extent culture, dances, and games infiltrated from south to north. For these ball courts are Mexican. The Spanish soldiers were the first white men to see them and also the first to lay hands on the curious elastic balls the Indians used for their games—the first *rubber* balls any white man had ever seen. Moreover, two of the balls have actually been found in Arizona.

We remain within the world of ruins, and then of still inhabited pueblos, if after a side trip to the Sinagua cliff dwellings of Walnut Canyon we once more drive north,

Decoration on pottery from Chaco Canyon, N. Mex.

turning eastward from Highway 89 at Tuba City into Hopi Land. First of all, we come to Oraibi, the *oldest still inhabited town* in the United States. It has been lived in continuously since the twelfth century. Here, in other words, is a town *older than Berlin, just as old as Moscow.*

Northeast from Tuba City the Navajo Trail—today no longer an Indian trail but a good highway—runs to Kayenta. President "Teddy" Roosevelt, who loved the still Wild West, spent days covering this stretch on horseback He stayed a night in Kayenta at the lonely farmhouse of one of the Wetherill brothers and found the place interesting enough to write a newspaper article about it. As little as ten years ago scarcely more than a dozen travelers a month visited this town, except, perhaps, for an archaeological expedition exploring the nearby Betatakin ruins. Today there are many plush motels in the neighborhood.

If we pass the de Chelly Canyon (in the New Mexico direction), where the Morrises dug for so long, then take the side road through Four Corners, drive up the terrifying serpentines to Mesa Verde, Colorado, and then push on into the broad expanses of New Mexico, southward by way of Farmington, we will then turn off Highway 44 to reach Pueblo Bonito. This tremendous pueblo complex proved from the start to be most fascinating to archaeologists because its strata, pottery, and tree rings allowed them to trace *history* for the first time.

There are no fewer than 800 rooms in tiers of four and five stories, resting upon massive walls. Built between 919 and 1130 upon numerous relics of a much earlier period, the pueblo at one time housed an estimated 1,200 persons. Its excavation was begun in 1897, first by George H. Pepper, then by Neil M. Judd. Since then it has been repeatedly explored and sifted up to the present day. Some 100,000 tons of earth were moved by hoes, shovels, and wheelbarrows. The first power scoops—in those days called steam shovels—while laborsaving, were somewhat hazardous to science. Ann Morris quotes a driver exclaiming, "Well, well; here's half a mummy. Isn't that interesting?" The pueblo covers an area as large as that of the Capitol in Washington. Fifteen more ruins are to be found in the vicinity at distances of from seven to forty miles. The richest turquoise ornaments were found in Bonito, among them a necklace consisting of 2,500 turquoise beads!

An abundance of ruins and still inhabited pueblos mingle in the broad Rio Grande Valley between Albuquerque and Santa Fé as far as Taos. (The magic of Santa Fé, that city whose architecture still bears the imprint of its Indian and Spanish past, really deserves lengthy description. The museums in Albuquerque and in the old Spanish governor's palace in Santa Fé are worth seeing.) In 1948 the first systematic photographs were taken of twenty-five pueblos from Acoma in the south to Taos in the north. Stanley A. Stubbs evaluated them, comparing them with ground surveys, and in 1950 published an account of them in his *Bird's-Eye View of the Pueblos.*[5]

Taos is probably the pueblo that attracts the most tourists; for this reason it is also the most highly commercialized pueblo. It is 600 years old and came into being as a result of the flight of tribes from the great drought in the San Juan Valley. In 1680 Taos was also the starting point of the already mentioned great pueblo revolt against Spanish rule under the leadership of the medicine man Popé. Today some 1,200 people live in Taos. One of the most distinguished visitors to the pueblo was the Swiss psychologist

Vases, pitchers, and bowls from Canyon de Chelly, Ariz.

(Above) Religious ceremony in the Great Kiva of Aztec: a modern reconstruction   *Paul Coze and Petley Studios*
(Overleaf) Cliff Palace in Mesa Verde, Colorado

Bradshaw Color Studios

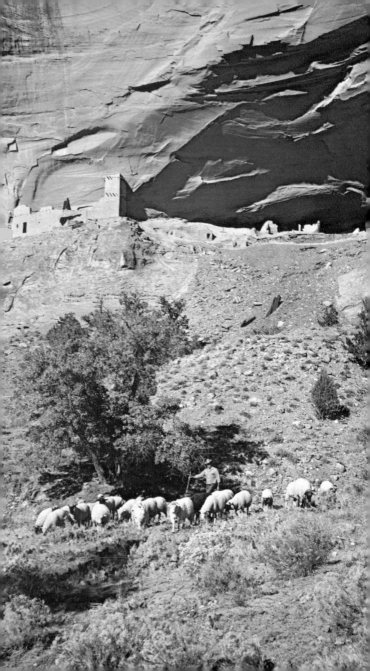

(*Left*) Mummy Cave in Canyon de Chelly, Arizona   *Josef Muench*

(*Above*) Montezuma Castle—a misleading name, for it is not Aztec and was built at least 300 years before Montezuma lived
Bradshaw Color Studios

(*Below*) The Betatakin ruin near Kayenta, Arizona.
Bradshaw Color Studios

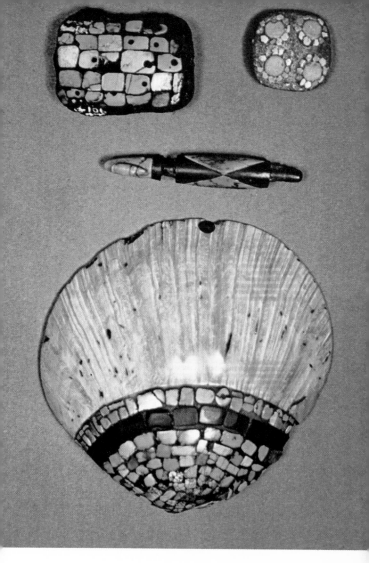

(Left) Hohokam pottery from Snaketown, Arizona, 100 B.C. to A.D. 1100
Arizona State Museum

(Above) Turquoise mosaic inlay work. Ornaments from Hawikuh, New
Mexico   *Museum of the American Indian*

(Overleaf) Diorama of a mammoth hunt in Arizona 12,000 years ago
Arizona State Museum

Carl Gustav Jung. The fact has been little noted in scholarly books. So we are justifiably eager to know what this world-famous man, specialist in the primitive psyche and the theory of archetypes, had to say about the Indians. Jung speaks of his meetings in 1924–25 with "Chief" Ochwiay Biano. (Jung at least gives him this title, although the Pueblo Indians never had a "chief." Nowadays they have an official "governor" who represents them in dealings with the whites; but within the world of the pueblo the far more important and influential "caciques" to this day often remain totally unknown to white officialdom.) Biano expressed his contempt for all whites, and concluded: "We think that they are mad."

Jung asked why he thought so.

"They say that they think with their heads," Biano replied.

"Why, of course. What do you think with?" Jung asked in surprise.

"We think here," the Indian said, indicating his heart.

Jung was stunned. "I fell into a long meditation. . . . This Indian had struck our vulnerable spot, unveiled a truth to which we are blind."

Later he sat on the fifth story of the pueblo and had a second conversation with Ochwiay, which gave him an insight into the mysteries of Eleusis, so that he suddenly understood certain passages in Pausanias and Herodotus. After a brief talk about religion the Indian told him conclusively, "The sun is God. Everyone can see that." Then a second Indian suddenly appeared out of the blue and in a "deep voice, vibrant with suppressed emotion spoke from behind me into my left ear: 'Do you not think that all life comes from the mountain?'" Looking at the river, which was indubitably pouring down from the distant mountains, Jung could only reply: " 'Everyone can see that you speak the truth.' Unfortunately," he adds, "the conversation was soon interrupted, and so I did not succeed in attaining any deeper insight into the symbolism of water and mountain."[6]

Another psychologist has observed more deeply and commented more profoundly. But he was, in addition, a writer, who lived for a long time in New Mexico—D. H. Lawrence. His three brief studies, "Indians and Entertainment," "Dance of the Sprouting Corn," and "The Hopi Snake Dance" are very much worth reading.

GOETHE (1749–1832)

America, you're better off than
Our continent so antiquary,
You have no castles falling down,
No marble statuary.

Unburdened by anxieties,
Yours is a present life,
Free of useless memories
And futile strife.

Goethe's poem loses its point in present-day America—
now that the white man is recognizing his Indian heritage,
appeasing his guilt feelings by preserving Indian monuments, and learning to be proud that the New World is
also an old world.

The social and religious traditions that still retain their
vitality in the pueblos extend far back into the times before
Columbus. Richard Erdoes writes about their society:
"Women have a position of great power in Pueblo Society.
To them belong the houses and everything in them. A
woman will say, as a matter of fact: 'This is my grand-
mother's house!' Even when a man comes home loaded
with game he has hunted, it becomes his wife's property as
soon as he lifts it across the threshold. . . . A man goes to
live with his wife in *her* house. If he marries a woman from
another village, he will move there. A widower will return
to his mother's home.

"A child will often take the mother's surname. A boy
belongs to his mother's clan. It is always different from his
father's, because people from the same clan may not marry
each other. The most important man in a boy's life is his
maternal uncle—his mother's brother. It is he who introduces him to his clan and sponsors him when he is initiated
into his religious society.

"Certain types of work are reserved for women, others
for men. Besides doing much of the house building and
repairing, the women tend the gardens, do the light field
work, prepare the food, and make pottery and baskets. The
men do the hunting, heavy field work, and *weaving*. Every
Hopi groom is expected to weave a complete set of clothes
and blankets for his bride.

"Such a society, in which the people trace their descent

from their mothers, is called matrilineal. If a woman wants to divorce her husband, she will simply put his blanket and shoes outside the door. This tells him that he is no longer wanted."[7]

In this description the author is deliberately simplifying these relationships a great deal. In actuality they are so complicated and so integrated within an intricate and obscure religious framework that ever since Morgan's and Bandelier's times there have been literally thousands of publications dealing with this subject alone. To what extent Pueblo society confirms J. J. Bachofen's classical view of "matriarchy" (1861) is a matter of opinion.

Nevertheless, if we start with the period of the Basket Makers we must observe that in 2,000 years the Indians developed neither wheel nor plow and were unacquainted with iron. They did not have horses, cattle, sheep, or pigs; the only animals they had domesticated were the dog and the turkey. They did not develop a script, let alone an alphabet. The thousands of so-called pictographs (the word actually means "picture writing") found drawn and painted on rocks have very meager communicative content. The only real Indian script was devised by the crippled, intellectually brilliant Cherokee Sequoyah, who was born in Tennessee in 1760 and died in Mexico in 1843. Over a period of twelve years he developed a kind of alphabet so that his people could match the abilities of the white man. It was a genuine script—teachable, readable, writable—but it did not win acceptance.

In spite of all these deficiencies a "high culture" would have been possible for the Pueblo Indians. That has been proved by the Mayas and Aztecs in Mexico and by the Incas in South America, all of whom developed highly complicated political structures, erected monumental buildings, and made remarkable discoveries in astronomy and mathematics. (The Mayas developed the best calendars in the world and invented the zero.) The Pueblo tribes stood on the verge of such accomplishments. What did they lack that the Central American Indians had? What kept them from taking the first step?

As early as 1924 Kidder commented: "Few races have gone so far toward civilization as did the Pueblos while still retaining the essential democracy of primitive life. . . . There were neither very rich nor very poor; every family lived in the same sort of quarters, and ate the same sort of food. . . . Pre-eminence in social or religious life was to be gained solely by individual ability and was the reward of services rendered to the community."[8]

Moreover, why did they not respond more vigorously to influences from the south? The extent of these influences is still the subject of controversy today. Did the Pueblo Indians *want* to continue in that state of primitive democ-

A sample of the writing invented by Sequoyah, a Cherokee, who hoped thereby to make the white man's culture accessible to the Indians. It is the only authentic Indian script (half alphabet, half syllabary) ever devised in North America; but it dates from after A.D. 1800.

racy that Kidder describes, and in which they were simply happy?

During the fifties the British archaeologist Jacquetta Hawkes and her husband, the writer J. B. Priestley, traveled among the pueblos. She was filled with astonishment, and asked, "Did it really happen without any spark from the Old World? If it did, then it's enormously important. Man appears as a creature with an innate urge to develop urban civilization, to build altars and temples and palaces. If I were an American archaeologist, I should think of nothing else but proving whether this is or is not the truth."[9]

And D. H. Lawrence says of the pueblos: "That they don't crumble is a mystery. That these little squarish mud-heaps endure for centuries after centuries, while Greek marble tumbles asunder, and cathedrals totter, is the wonder. But then, the naked human hand with a bit of new soft mud is quicker than time, and defies the centuries."[10]

After all these facts, let us conclude this chapter with a faintly romantic tale, which might bear the title "The Lost City of Lukachukai."

Anyone who thinks that research into the pueblos and cliff dwellings has been finished is badly mistaken. There are surely hundreds of caves and ruins that remain undiscovered as well as uninvestigated. However, one dream still cherished by men in the thirties is scarcely likely to be fulfilled any more: the discovery of an entirely legendary city, perhaps another kind of "Cibola." But Morris was still concerned with pursuing such rumors. He went to look for "the lost city of Lukachukai."

These rumors are not very old—so far as we know. They appear to have cropped up only at the beginning of this century. Ann Morris writes with a mysterious air: "The details of this particular story are in the possession of Earl and myself. . . ." But then she adds ironically: "It is a case of our knowing a man who knows an Indian who knows . . ."[11]

Like all authentic rumors, the stories pointed toward the unknown—in this case the then inadequately explored regions south of Four Corners, which were supposed to harbor a whole mountain range, sometimes called Chuska, sometimes Tunicha, sometimes described as massive and sometimes as insignificant, and absent from any map. Nowadays Highway 666 runs along this area on the east.

In any case, the result of all this was to narrow the search to a region that the Navajos called *Lu-ka-chu-kai*, which means "the place of the white reed." When all the stories were co-ordinated, they pointed to a site within an area of only fifty square miles. That should certainly be findable!

But this was no simple task because of the nature of the region, a wilderness like few others. Rock formations without a road or path and abysses filled with torrential waters during the rainy seasons, blocked exploration. And yet, along with all the legends there was one precise and credible account.

In 1909 two Franciscans, Fathers Fintan and Anselm, traversed this wild mountain landscape. One noon they reached a high peak and decided to rest. Their guide, a young Navajo, suddenly disappeared. But he soon returned. And he brought back with him an olla, an unusually large, magnificently decorated ceramic water jar—completely undamaged!

By chance Father Fintan had spent some time helping to assemble the pottery collection of the Brooklyn Museum. He recognized the rarity of the piece and quickly asked, "Where does that come from?" Whereupon the Navajo made that sweeping Indian gesture that embraces the whole horizon and refused to say. But he volunteered that at the spot where he had found the jar there were innumerable others lying around. What was that? Simply lying on the surface? And undamaged? Certainly, the Indian replied. What was more, there were big houses there, and a high, high tower. And was everything unbroken? Yes, and besides, there were many jars still full of corn, and along with them a great many metates, those shapely little stone vessels for grinding corn, and many fine blankets and splendid sandals. The Anasazi, the "old ones," must have left their homes suddenly, the Indian said, and undoubtedly they would be returning some day.

The Franciscans described the jar to the Morrises, who concluded that it probably belonged to Pueblo III, the Golden Age of the Southwest. The tall houses and the tower also pointed to that period. Here was a bonanza for archaeologists—the more so if everything was actually unbroken.

The Fathers tried to buy the olla, of course. But as soon as they proposed this, the young Navajo froze up. Neither money nor arguments shook him in his refusal. The jar belonged to the Anasazi, he declared; he had borrowed it only to show it to his friends, and naturally he would have to bring it back. (This attitude recalls the story of a Mr. Kennedy who years ago, bit by bit, stole no fewer than 400 Indian relics from the New York Museum of Natural History—not to enrich himself, or to satisfy a collector's mania, but to give them back to the Indians!)

The Indian disappeared again. In half an hour he returned, and the three continued on their way. The Fathers met Morris and told him the whole story. They would return some day, they said. Their campsite could not be missed, and the "lost city" must be within less than half an hour's walk of it, so it should be easy to find.

They were mistaken about that. Ann and Earl Morris had careful descriptions, but in spite of several strenuous efforts they were unable even to find the campsite. Emil W. Haury spent half a summer in this region of canyons in 1927 and examined many ruins, but none corresponded to the legendary "lost city." The myth has been dismissed. The name Lukachukai no longer appears in modern books on archaeology. A few years ago, along Highway 666, I met a number of Navajos who still wore the stiff hat and short braids of the older generation, which is now dying out. When I insistently questioned them, they said that they had never heard the name.

In point of fact, beyond the state border, in Arizona, in the shadow of towering Matthews Peak, which is more than 9,000 feet high, a small town has adopted that mysterious, sonorous name: Lukachukai.

11

The Inquisitive Brothers
of Mesa Verde

ONE hot afternoon two men were riding at a trot through the parched southwestern landscape of Chaco Canyon. Farmer Richard Wetherill and his cowhand, Bill Finn, were out looking for some clue to who had killed the favorite horse of Wetherill's daughter Elizabeth. As they approached a river bed they encountered a group of Navajo Indians, several of them armed.

What happened next was never fully clarified, not even in the subsequent judicial investigation held under unusual circumstances. According to Finn's testimony, Chis-chilling-begay, a Navajo with whom they were acquainted, approached them and struck up a conversation. They parted. The sun was blinding; no one could see clearly. A shot was fired and passed over Finn's head. Another shot struck Wetherill's raised hand, which was holding the reins, and passed through into his chest. He tumbled from his horse, killed instantly.

Such incidents were not unusual in 1910. We would have no reason to tell the story if Richard Wetherill had not been one of the most picturesque personalities in the Navajo country—perhaps the last of his kind—and surely the most exceptional amateur archaeologist who ever lived in the Southwest.

Wetherill, too, suffered the lot of every great amateur in science. Reluctantly acknowledged by the professionals, he was at the same time always being slandered—as a pot-hunter, as a Navajo trader who had enriched himself at the expense of the Indians, as a cattle thief who was haled into court four times. As for his "enrichment," after he

Unusual decoration on a bowl from Mesa Verde, Colo. Most of the Mesa Verde people's decoration was strictly geometric. (Before A.D. 1300.)

died his widow found $73.23 in his bank account, along with I O U's amounting to several thousand dollars from the Navajos.

We are indebted to Frank McNitt, the editor of a small Massachusetts newspaper, who with a zeal bordering on fanaticism undertook many journeys to the Southwest to collect all available facts about Richard Wetherill and restore the honor of his name. Thanks to McNitt's book, *Richard Wetherill: Anasazi* (its documentation is absolutely convincing), we now know how great a part this farmer and his brothers played in the archaeology of the Southwest.

There were five brothers: Richard, Benjamin, John,

Clayton, and Winslow. This is not the place to sketch the pioneering life of these five Quakers; we are interested primarily in their discovery of Mesa Verde.

Of course these men were amateurs, but they were not untutored. They made drawings, took photographs, pushed into the wildest country, clambered into the most inaccessible canyons, and provided the first dependable accounts of the Basket Makers and the cliff dwellings of Mesa Verde.

Mesa Verde is, as the name indicates, a great plateau covered with lush vegetation about fifteen by twenty miles in area. It rises to a height of 2,000 feet above the surrounding country in the southwest corner of Colorado.

Lest I seem to be falling into a kind of boastful patriotism and exaggerating what can be seen in Mesa Verde, I shall quote the account of a witness whose motives cannot be suspected—once again the British archaeologist Jacquetta Hawkes, whose eyes have been schooled by all the wonders of the Old World. After she first climbed the steep road to Mesa Verde she wrote:

"We drove along through the low woods at the stately pace prescribed by the regulations; all seemed quiet and monotonous, the level plateau unbroken. With the suddenness of utmost delight it was there before us. We were at the edge of a deep canyon—the earth had opened before us. The upper parts were vertical walls of sandstone, banded buff and brown; lower down, these broke into steep slopes dark with vegetation. This natural grandeur so suddenly revealed was marvelous enough, but there, opposite to us on the far side of the canyon, was a *hanging city,* a little pale gold city of towers and climbing houses filling a vast oval hollow in the rock. The dark points of the pines rose up to its foot, the immense black shadow of the cave roofed it with a single span, but the fronts of the houses and towers were in bright sunlight, all their angles revealed and the doors and windows showing as jet-black squares. It was like an intaglio sharp-cut in an oval bezel. The limestone rose sheer above it to meet the forest and then the unbounded blue. It looked so infinitely remote, there across the gulf, so remote and serene in its rock setting, that it seemed like some dream or mirage of an eternal city."[1]

Mesa Verde must have had a similar striking effect on those who first saw the ruins. The first was probably Captain J. N. Macomb in 1859, although a certain Father Francisco Atanasio pitched camp in the vicinity as early as 1776.[2]

On a cool December morning in 1888 Richard Wetherill appeared upon the scene. With his cousin Charlie Mason he was looking for lost cattle. In point of fact, these were not his first ruins; he had discovered others in the vicinity of his father's farm considerably earlier. One night in 1885 an enterprising young lady had spent the night at the farm, a Miss Virginia Donahue, who ignored all injunctions to return home as quickly as possible and instead went hunting arrowheads and pottery with the Wetherill brothers. She paid a second visit to their farm the following year, and on October 6, 1886, the brothers and the girl found their way to one of the most impressive ruins, the "Balcony House." But Richard and his cousin were alone when they made their most important discovery—what is now called the Cliff Palace. It is the largest of all cave "towns," with 200 dwelling rooms and twenty-three kivas. On December

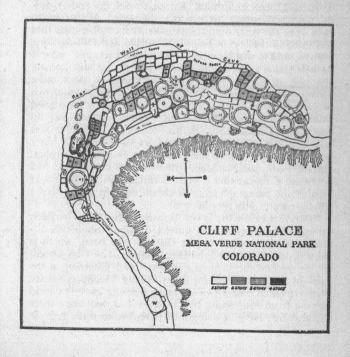

CLIFF PALACE
MESA VERDE NATIONAL PARK
COLORADO

18, 1888, they found the Spruce Tree ruin, and the following day the Square Tower ruin.

The apparently pre-Columbian tribe that lived here was called Anasazi, and the Indians dubbed Richard with the honorable nickname of "Anasazi." The Wetherills continued to explore the region on their own and to put their knowledge at the disposal of others. They became the indispensable guides to everyone who came to the region and showed a serious interest in ruins. When in 1893 the Swedish archaeologist Gustav Nordenskjöld published a preliminary scientific account, *The Cliff Dwellers of Mesa Verde,* he owed much of his information to those remarkable brothers, above all Richard.

Today we know that the history of Mesa Verde began around A.D. 500 and that, like the history of so many other pueblos and cliff dwellings in this area, it had come to an end by A.D. 1300.

The distances Richard covered on foot and horseback must have been enormous. Through meetings and friendships with scientists his expertise increased. He seems to have been the first to postulate the existence of a tribe that had lived in the region before the pueblo and cliff-dwelling peoples, and it was he who called this "preceramic" people Basket Makers, the name by which they are still known, although archaeologists and others sometimes speak more generally of "Anasazi." His first detailed description of this people probably dates from 1894. The article is not signed with his name, but McNitt, his best biographer, has no doubt of its authorship. In his student days Kidder was warned against "Wetherill's invention of a people." Later he brilliantly confirmed their reality by his own researches. (In 1897 Mitchell Prudden, with Wetherill's assistance, had published a report that should have banished all doubts.)[3] Here is one paragraph from Wetherill's article, which shows what a careful observer he was:

"Two feet below the lowest remains of the Cliff Dwellers, we have found remains of quite a different tribe. This difference is determined by the shape of the head, which is natural, long-headed or dolichocephalous. The Cliff Dwellers, as we find them, have a perpendicular flattening at the back of the head, making it artificially brachycephalous. We have taken ninety-two skeletons from the cave at depths varying from four and a half to seven feet, including three cliff dwellers lying at a depth of from two to three feet. In the central portion of the cave the skeletons were lying close enough to touch each other."[4]

First photographs of the ruins were brought to the East by William Henry Jackson, starting in 1874. Jackson, *the* photographer of the West in its pioneering days, even made clay models of the cliff dwellings, which created a stir at the Centennial Exposition in Philadelphia. No one had ever before heard of such cave dwellings in North America. In fact the models and photos created such a sensation that for a while they diverted visitors from the real attraction of the exhibition, Alexander Graham Bell's fantastic invention, the telephone.[5]

Mesa Verde was declared a national park, and J. W. Fewkes undertook the initial archaeological organization of the site. Today there is a permanent archaeological station there, with an impressive museum. The necessary steps to

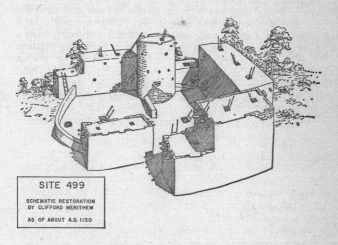

SITE 499

SCHEMATIC RESTORATION
BY CLIFFORD MERITHEW

AS OF ABOUT A.D. 1130

Reconstruction of one of the smaller Mesa Verde structures, one that shows all the characteristics of the larger complexes: multistories, defensive tower, all entrances gained from the roofs, underground kivas. Not enough wood remained to permit tree-ring dating, but consideration of the types of pottery found here, whose ages are known from other sites, led to the conclusion that the site was occupied chiefly between A.D. *1100 and 1150.*

protect the ruin had been taken. But only a few years ago the public was alarmed to learn that this most beautiful of Indian "cities" was imperiled. Supersonic Air Force planes were flying over the cliff dwellings and producing cracks in the old buildings that had withstood all the trials of nature for centuries. In 1967 the government was forced to deal with the problem. The New York *Times* published detailed reports. There was, for example, the testimony of a Navajo named Guy Yazzie Teller who actually saw one of the cliffs collapsing and burying a ruin after the jets had flown over.[6]

To round the story out, there is this incident told by Alfred V. Kidder, who made his own explorations of Mesa Verde decades after Wetherill had put it on the map. Kidder writes:

"A number of years ago, Jesse Nusbaum and I were exploring cliff dwellings on the west side of Mesa Verde. We saw one that was high up on the canyon wall opposite us, and decided to look into it. But it was a terribly hard climb—up a sheer wall and across a narrow ledge, with a long drop below. But we finally made it. With great elation over our discovery and the successful climb, we peered down through an opening in the rocks at our ruin. And right there before our eyes was an upended slab of stone. On it we read these words: 'What fools these mortals be. R. Wetherill.' "[7]

The "simple farmer" Wetherill knew his Shakespeare.

12

Those Who Have Vanished: Cochise, Mogollon, and the Hohokam

"FROM Cochise came Mogollon, which developed to Hohokam, to Basket Makers to produce Pueblos. . . ."[1]

What is this? Had the archaeologists suddenly discovered a historical line that seemed untraceable when Pueblo research was in full swing? Did North American Indian culture extend still farther back into the past, and, above all, did it extend much farther south?

The quotation above, from John C. McGregor, dates from 1965 and merely corroborates something Harold S. Gladwin and Emil W. Haury had already suspected thirty years earlier—a theory that Haury then developed in 1943.[2] But twenty-seven years later Haury no longer thinks in terms of so linear a development. He continues to believe that the Mogollon came from the Cochise (with cultural influences from Mexico), but he now believes that the

207

Hohokam were a group of immigrants who introduced an entirely new culture into the Southwest—a hypothesis that does not exclude later Mexican influences, as we shall see.

Leaving aside a rather marginal Patayan culture, we can say today that the Cochise and Mogollon cultures (located in southern Arizona and also called "desert cultures") coincided. Paul S. Martin, who has specialized in the Mogollon, wrote in 1959:

"The term 'Mogollon' has been adopted to signify the addition of agriculture, house building, and pottery-making. . . . This term connotes one of the longest continuous cultural growths in North America, with roots reaching back to about 6000 B.C. and," he continues surprisingly, "with trunks, limbs, and leaves reaching perhaps up to the present time—a span of perhaps about 8,000 years."[3]

Nowadays we are no longer so lavish with millennia in pushing the time back into the past. The facing table may give the reader a sense of the temperal relationships; it represents the conclusions of recent research.

This table is based upon a summary by McGregor, who has leaned upon Harold S. Gladwin (1936) for the Hohokam classification and on Joe Ben Wheat (1955) for the Mogollon arrangement.

As far as the Hohokam are concerned, they can now be dated far more precisely by means of a still novel method adopted by Robert L. DuBois of the University of Arizona, who has taken the remains of old fireplaces for his test material. The method is called "archaeomagnetism," and it has as its basis the fact that the compass needle never points precisely north, and varies over the ages. Thus there would be different readings for the magnetic North Pole at the time of Christ, of Columbus, and at present.[4]

The radiocarbon method had dated a bit of Hohokam charcoal to 425 B.C., with a possible error of 100 years plus or minus. The new method gave the date 300 B.C. for the oldest fireplace that has so far been found.

Real Hohokam *cultural* development took place between A.D. 500 and 1100–1200, after which they slowly vanished as a "people." But four earlier phases can be distinguished clearly, and more precisely than the following table would indicate. Thus there are no fewer than seven cultural phases in the history of this "vanished" people, phases that brought in many innovations and changes of all sorts. But, remark-

	HOHOKAM	MOGOLLON
	Modern	
A.D. 1700		
1600	Recent	
1450		
1300	Classic	
1200		
1100	Sedentary	
1000		Mogollon V
900		Mogollon IV
700	Colonial	Mogollon III
600		
500		
400		Mogollon II
Birth of Christ	Pioneer	
		Mogollon I
300 B.C.		

ably enough, one thing remained constant: their architecture.

These Hohokam stood out from the first as a very special and remarkable people, and in this chapter we shall confine our attention to them, for "synthesis demands not only compression but rigorous selection."[5] The word "Hohokam," a Pima Indian word for "those who have vanished," seemed for a long while to be valid.[6] It was way back in 1927 that Harold S. Gladwin, guiding spirit and director of the Gila Pueblo Archaeological Foundation of Globe, Arizona, first came upon actual traces of this people. He then spent years locating thousands of prehistoric sites before he fixed on Snaketown (twenty-eight miles south of Phoenix) as the probable center of their culture. From the start there was no lack of controversial discoveries. For example, Gladwin disagreed with Kidder in his identification of the massive, many-storied ruin of Casa Grande as a Hohokam monument. However, in the course of his experimental trenchings Gladwin came upon a "mound" that was ten feet high and 165 feet in diameter, in which he struck

Hohokam design.

a solid and obviously worked block of stone. At this point
he began to reconsider Kidder's view. But then he dug
deeper and found that the "prehistoric" block was "a
square block of concrete with an iron pipe embedded in it,
which turned out to be a U.S. Land Office marker!"[7]

In any case, in 1934 the first archaeological camp was
established at Snaketown, a small Indian settlement of
about fifty persons. From the start there was a whole staff
of specialists at the site, and many Pima Indians were employed as helpers. Emil Walter Haury, then only thirty,
became director of the excavation. As it turned out, he
organized an excavation that was in every respect a model
of its kind. Incidentally, he also directed the first Mogollon
excavation, the published account of which is "now a land-
mark in the archaeological works of the Southwest," as
Martin remarks.[8]

An archaeologically minded tourist coming to Snaketown
around 1966 and gazing across the broad field over which
two excavations have been made (for Haury deepened the
diggings in 1964) would probably have been disappointed,
even though on April 3, 1965, the National Park Service
declared the area a National Registered Historical Land-
mark. This, by the way, was the occasion for a solemn ceremony in which no fewer than 500 Pima and Maricopa
Indians participated, Indians who may be (a big may be!)
the descendants of the Hohokam.

The landscape is barren, parched, dusty. When the rare
rains fall, the land turns to mud and becomes almost impassable. The Gila River, which once irrigated fruitful

Grotesque Hohokam painted ceramic jug, reconstructed by archaeologists from many fragments. It had lain buried for more than 950 years.

fields in this region, is nowhere to be seen. The eye discerns a few faint outlines of mountain ranges on the horizon. Scattered salt bushes and dead-looking mesquite shrubs intensify the impression of aridity, the sense of being in an African semidesert. And curiously enough, the one large shade tree in this dusty plain, parched, picturesque, and looking utterly in character here, is an African tree, a tamarisk, which a biologist planted here experimentally two generations ago, and which has actually thriven.

Nevertheless, a tribe settled in this area around the time of the birth of Christ. It managed to survive here only because it transformed the desert by almost inconceivable labors.

At the age of thirty Haury had already made a reputation. This tall, spare, quiet man had studied at the University of Arizona, where he was later to become the foremost teacher of archaeology. He took his doctorate at Harvard, contributed, as early as 1929, to the development of tree-ring dating as a research assistant, and had already done some digging. Gladwin, initiator of the Snaketown excavation, had the highest regard for Haury and his second important assistant, E. B. Sayles, and said as much in the preface to his conclusive report of 1937:

"Haury's analysis of the fine arts and his methodical

Saw-toothed Hohokam arrowheads.

sectioning of rubbish deposit, Sayles' care and ability in the excavation . . . are, we believe, *model examples of American technique at its best*."[9]

In the present brief account of the amazing Hohokam we are summing up the results of both excavations, that of 1934–35 and that of 1964–65.

The oddest part of the story of the discovery of the Hohokam is the fact that in 1887–88 Frank Hamilton Cushing, whom we have already met in Chapter 3 as "Medicine Flower," collected no fewer than 5,000 samples of Hohokam culture. Haury comments: "From the ruins he examined, Cushing concluded that the desert had been the home of a 'greater if not further advanced ancient people than the Pueblo people to the north.' "[10] That was, as we shall see, in some respects an overstatement. But it was nevertheless an astonishing prediction on the basis of material that at the time could scarcely be interpreted.

There are various reasons for the fact that the Hohokam

went virtually unnoticed for so long. In the first place, unlike the other early peoples of the Southwest, they cremated their dead. A few fragments of bones and skulls have been found, so badly damaged that little could be discovered from them. Consequently, we have no real idea of what they looked like. A second custom of theirs is still more singular: they often intentionally smashed their most valuable and artistic ceramics, as if they deliberately wanted to wipe out their traces from the eyes of posterity.

In addition, they left behind scarcely noticeable remains of impressive buildings. Their greatest achievement, the one that distinguished them above all the other peoples of the region, was the building of gigantic irrigation projects extending over many square miles. And the largest part of these was erased by nature. The eternally drifting sand filled the channels, although here and there one of the 6,000 Pima Indians can still be seen today working beside a 2,000-year-old irrigation canal, continuing what his presumptive ancestors began: the cultivation of corn, squash, beans, cotton, and tobacco.

For the Hohokam were no longer mere hunters and food gatherers. But how it is they ventured to advance into the desert and what impelled them to do so remains their secret to this day.

Still and all, conclusions can be drawn. Haury has amassed more than 1,500,000 potsherds and other relics. Tens of thousands of the shards have already been washed, arranged, and catalogued, and now await further research. Once we have realized what a key to the past pottery provides, we will understand that it is possible to form some picture of the "vanished people," and even to determine one essential feature of their characters—that they were a *peaceable* folk.

After completing his second excavation, Haury flew in a helicopter over Skoaquik—the Pima name for Snaketown, and an apt one, for there are certainly rattlesnakes enough in the region. The aerial view for the first time revealed the tremendous size of this "urban" settlement. It covered 300 acres. He and his men had dug up 167 house ruins. How many had there been?

If a Hohokam's house burned or a desert storm blew it down, he usually built his new house in the ruins, but sometimes alongside. These dwellings were a good deal more than pit houses. They were dug only about a foot into the ground. Rammed posts, with others placed slantwise against them, supported a roof and walls made of branches, which were then plastered with mud. The method of building did not change; in 1935 Haury was able to photograph the last house of this style, built and occupied by a Pima Indian. Over the centuries the upper part would have been destroyed by the wind. What lasted were remnants in the holes, or at least the holes themselves, in which the posts had been sunk. The scientists learned that the best instrument for detecting the location of such houses was not the eye but the ear—"by listening to the singing of the trowel as it was drawn over the packed soil. A change in pitch indicated that a different surface, the soft scab of a posthole, was in contact with the blade."[11]

Thus it proved possible to determine the approximate density of population in Skoaquik-Snaketown. Throughout its existence the city had comprised about 100 houses, each of which lasted approximately twenty-five years. In purely statistical terms this meant that 400 new houses were built every century—and this over a span of 1,200 years (as Haury calculates). From the helicopter, therefore, Haury was able to look down on the remains of some 5,000 dwellings!

In among them lay curious mounds. When these were investigated, it turned out that the smaller ones especially were pure mounds of rubbish. This means that the neat Hohokam housewives did not simply throw their refuse out in front of the house, as most other prehistoric peoples did. But other mounds had obviously been built deliberately. The largest had a carefully designed platform more than fifty feet in diameter. The highest, Mound No. 29, exhibited stratigraphically the above-mentioned seven phases of the culture, and in addition permitted the first certain dating. For in the stratum of the fifth phase the scientists found pottery they were already familiar with!

This type of pottery came from the northern pueblos and had already been dated as precisely as if each piece were stamped with its year of manufacture; in this case the date was A.D. 500. But this find was still more important for another reason. It meant that the Hohokam had had trade relations with the North. Would this be true also for the South?

The very existence of mounds with a platform pointed unequivocally to influence from Mexico. For there, and still farther south, stood the temple pyramids of the Mayas. But the archaeologists found an even more significant feature: a ball court. As we have already indicated in connection with the Wupatki ruins, such courts were undoubtedly inspired by the peoples to the south, for whom the ball game must have been the national sport. We know only that the game was played with a "rubber" ball that had to pass through a ring installed on a high side wall. The material for the ball was probably obtained from the guayu bush. There is no point to our wracking our brains about the rules of the game. The Spanish accounts are too meager to permit any deductions. Curiously enough, there is a description, accompanied by a pen drawing, by a German —the engraver and traveler Christoph Weiditz. It dates from the beginning of the sixteenth century.

"In such Wise the Indians play with a blown up Ball, hitting it with the Hinder Parts and the Hands. For moving on the Ground they wear a hard Leather over the Hinder Parts, so that it may receive the Impacte of the Ball, also such leather Gloves."[12] The drawing corroborates this curious rule: two players are shown protruding their "hinder parts" with the ball flying between them. The game must have required a good deal of agility.

These extraordinary Hohokam maintained relationships not only with North and South but also with the West. Among the ruins have been found seashells that could only have come from the Gulf of California. There is something very special about these seashells.

Here is a little anecdote to demonstrate that field work —hard, patient labor conjoined with scientific planning

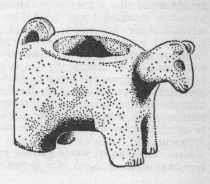

A Hohokam incense burner, or possibly a medicine cup.

and only rarely aided by a lucky accident—can lead to such a wealth of finds and knowledge.

When Haury started out for the excavation, his students gave him a "good digging" token, a small silver trowel engraved with a quotation from Shakespeare's *Julius Caesar:* "You are not wood, you are not stones, but men!"—perhaps a classic motto for the way an archaeologist should regard his finds.

Whether for the fun of it or out of some superstitious belief that they might be able to conjure up the "vanished" people, Haury and his seventy-two-year-old Pima friend of long standing, Williams, went out somewhere in the middle of the field and threw the silver trowel into the air. Flashing in the sunlight, it fell to the ground. And at that spot Williams solemnly thrust his spade to begin the dig. . . . We must disappoint the expectations of those of our readers who are inclined toward magic: this spot proved to be the least productive of all the places they were to probe during the entire excavation.

But to return to the shells. These were most astonishing, for they were ornamented with all sorts of motifs—horned toads, snakes, as well as a wide variety of geometric designs. It proved possible to date them "around A.D. 1000," but there remained the mystery of how the Indians had worked the brittle material. The figures and designs were not painted on the shells or scratched into them; they were in relief, slightly raised or incised. Some sort of etching process must have been involved, but here again the scientists were baffled. Could the desert have furnished any chemical suitable for etching? The only possible acid was the fermented juice of the fruit of the saguaro cactus. Could an Indian somehow have stumbled on this property and turned it to use for creative, artistic purposes?

If so, it would mean that this Indian had actually invented an entire *process.* He would also have had to find a substance which resisted the bite of the acid. And such a substance was available: resin or pitch. The Indian would have had to draw his design on the shell with pitch, then steep the shell in acid solution, whereupon the unprotected parts would be eaten away. After a while the pitch would be carefully scraped off, and there would be the elegant decoration.

Here, undoubtedly, was a genuine individual invention. The most amazing aspect of it is that this was, so far as

Clay Hohokam incense burner, found in a grave dating from about A.D. 1000. It represents a mountain bighorn sheep. At its widest point the vessel is seven inches in diameter.

we know, the first artistic use of the etching process in history. A Hohokam Indian invented it in A.D. 1000, that is to say, *about 450 years before European armorers applied this process, more than 500 years before the German painter and graphic artist Albrecht Dürer, working in Nuremberg in 1515,* made use of the method to enrich the potentialities for artistic expression.

Has this hypothesis been proved? It has, for in 1965 Haury found a seashell with a drawing of an animal traced in pitch on its inner side. This shell was a piece from the workshop, which for some reason had never been placed in the acid bath.

But these Hohokam, who never advanced beyond primitive huts in their domestic architecture, demonstrated other artistic abilities. We shall refrain from discussing the touching little copper bells, because their origin is not definitely established.[13] But there are the cosmetic trays or tablets.

Many museums possess ancient Egyptian cosmetic palettes, on which the elegant ladies of the pharaoh's court blended their cosmetics. The Hohokam had something similar: finely wrought stone slabs, up to six inches long, their flat part often resting on an artfully carved base representing a horned toad, lizard, a snake, or a bird. These motifs, too, seem to have been introduced from the South, especially the snake in all its variants, although of course the Hohokam had enough snakes around to have hit upon this motif independently. The combination of snake and bird has remained as an emblem in the Mexican flag to this day. Among the Hohokam, however, the probability is that the palettes were not used by the women for cosmetics but by the men for mixing the body paint with which they adorned themselves for their religious dances.

Hohokam pottery is varied, richly and colorfully ornamented. When it came to finding Hohokam ceramics, James Lancaster, a member of Haury's staff, was remarkably lucky—which seems to contradict what we said a while back about the relation between labor and luck. Granted, Lancaster was a professional, but all his previous experience had been in mesa and canyon country, not in the desert. Nevertheless he proved to have the keenness of the neophyte, the luck of the beginner.

In succession, he found eighteen thick-walled earthenware vessels, probably "incense pots" in which fragrant or narcotic substances were burned during the religious ceremonies. This is a custom that existed throughout the world and has continued in modern times in the Catholic Church.

A little later, when he cautiously opened a modest trench only two feet deep, he came upon a little ceramic treasure: clay animals. There was a whole herd of deer—nineteen of them—five inches high, heads raised in an attitude of attentive listening. There were also three vessels in human form, forty clay shards, shell bracelets, and other items.

Luck continued with him, "as if he had kinship with this ancient tribe," Haury remarks. He found fifty vessels carved out of soft stone, including such ingenious forms as an animal whose back formed a bowl, male figures holding a pot ornamented with three toads realistically scrambling up its sides. These superlative products of Hohokam craft were all broken; it was apparent, moreover, that they had been deliberately shattered. Were they secret ritual objects that had to be "killed" after use?

This people, so artistic in small things, were also creative on a large scale. We are referring to their system of canals, without which their extensive agriculture could not have been possible, above all their growing corn. And maize was

Clay figurine, five inches in height. Hohokam work, from A.D. 900–1100.

the foundation upon which most of all North American cultures arose.

This system of *mile-long* canals was created bit by bit by the labor of innumerable generations. One canal three miles long, dug by hand with the most primitive wooden and stone tools, could be dated back to the period *before* the birth of Christ, long before the Hohokam had begun their career as craftsmen. The canals had to be carefully adjusted to the lay of the land. How was this done without any optical surveying instruments? They had to be constantly supervised, changed, improved; regulatory devices had to be installed—and this over a span of centuries.

And nature was against them. The water level of the Gila River was never constant; the quantities of rain could never be predicted, not even by the best medicine men. Disasters were inevitable. After carefully studying the network of canals, Haury ventured to sketch the following picture:

"At the height of Arizona's midsummer heat, cumulus clouds build up into dark towers. Sweeping in over the desert, they cause intense local downpours. One of these hit the upper terrace sometime before A.D. 900. The canal, filling within minutes, burst its banks, and the water gouged out a deep gully near the head gate as it raced toward the lower terrace. Traces of this event pointed up more clearly than any theory how hard the Hohokam had to labor to keep their canals flowing. They conquered the desert only through continuous effort."[14]

What was the end of this remarkable people?

For undeterminable reasons the "city" of Snaketown died around A.D. 1100. (This is Emil W. Haury's latest estimate, stated in a letter from him to the author dated January 12, 1970.) The people still survived. Small groups built modest settlements in other parts of the valley and continued practicing their skill in irrigation. In the fourteeth century came an invasion of other tribes from the East and the North. It was a *peaceful* invasion; in fact, the Hohokam had been a nation without wars for 1,000 years. Infiltration by people of the Mogollon and Anasazi cultures took place. Apparently they came in great numbers (the pottery tells us all this). The scientists call these the Salado people. About this time the four-story, fortresslike Casa Grande was built.

But Haury believes that the Hohokam lived on, that their tribe is still extant in the present-day Pimas. The life style, type of house, pottery, and irrigation are too similar to these distant forebears to be matters of chance. Nowadays, to be sure, even Pimas drive Fords. But it is significant that the Pimas who worked as Haury's helpers became more and more convinced in the course of their labors that they were digging in the homes of their ancestors. And when the excavation was finished, they gave a party for the scientists to express their gratitude. They handed presents around—marvelously woven basketry. And then they sang songs in six-man choruses: Christian hymns in the Pima language!

Before we turn our attention to the father and mother of these cultures—maize—let us ask: Do the Hohokam have any lessons for us? Haury concludes the report he wrote for the *National Georgraphic* magazine, intended for a wider public, with a philosophical observation:

"After so many years of association with the vanished Hohokam, I am convinced that their achievement is instructive for our own time. Their secret of success was profoundly simple: they came to grips with, but did not abuse, nature. They became a part of the ecological balance instead of destroying it. They accepted the terms of their existence in a difficult environment, and they continued for well over 1,000 years.

"For our own generation, with its soiled streams and fouled air, its massive and abrupt changes in environment, its shortages of water, its rampant misuse of shrinking open space, the achievement of Snaketown holds a profound meaning."[15]

13

The Story of Maize

By now it has become virtually axiomatic among historians that every high culture begins with the tilling of the soil and that agriculture is the prerequisite for any higher development.

We know today that the earliest forms of agriculture arose in Mesopotamia. Here, too, the first high cultures of humanity suddenly emerged from obscurity, after the long, historyless twilight existence of primitive peoples. These cultures sprang into being with a swiftness that is totally mysterious, in view of the hundreds of thousands of years that preceded them, and without explicable cause. First came the Sumerians, then the Babylonians and Assyrians along the Tigris and Euphrates, while about the same time the Egyptians were creating a culture in the valley of the Nile, the Indians in the valley of the Indus, and the Chinese along their great rivers.

These cultures achieved domestication of many plants and animals. They invented the wheel, lever, and plow, and soon devised writing.

Nothing of the sort is true for the cultures of North America, not even for the cultures of the Incas in the

Andes, the Mayas in Central America, and the Aztecs in Mexico, which we also tend to regard as high cultures (so Spengler and Toynbee regard them). The American peoples invented neither the wagon wheel (in Central America the wheel does appear on *toy* animals) nor the plow and developed no alphabetic writing. And they failed to do something of equal importance in North America: they domesticated very few animals, or plants.

Our present-day overevaluation of purely technical matters in the development of early man is well illustrated by the list of fifteen basic achievements appearing in a popular work on "great inventions." The first seven on the list are:[1]

1. The wheel	5. The smelting of metal
2. The lever	6. Writing
3. The wedge	7. Weaving
4. The screw	

This is a purely technological approach. In terms of cultural history it is nonsense. It is significant that the man who drew up this summary seems completely blind to the importance of domestication. Thus the invention of the wheel would scarcely have had any meaning had those early peoples not had draft animals to hitch to carts (the wheelbarrow is, oddly enough, a very late invention). It is very strange to see the screw listed as Number 4; screws could hardly have been useful before the development of metal working, which follows it on the list. To further confuse matters, the art of weaving cloth and making baskets is much more ancient than metal working; it is even older than pottery, which is omitted altogether, although it is of crucial importance to every early culture. And to place writing before weaving is simply dead wrong. The chronology of this list is a muddle.

If, moreover, we apply this list to the American cultures, we see that most of them, including those that rose to a high level, did without the first six items. They acquired only Number 7, weaving, and almost simultaneously arrived at the indispensable invention of pottery.

Certainly, also, the prime importance of domestication ought not to be overlooked. For domestication of animals and plants is essential if human life is to move to a higher plane. Domestication freed early man from the insecurity of hunting and food gathering. By attaching previously wild animals to human households and cultivating previously wild plants so that they yield more food more consistently, man becomes master of his survival. He has learned how to outwit nature, to dominate animals and plants and ultimately to *exploit them systematically*.

It is noteworthy that the biblical story of the Creation shows this tremendous evolutionary leap on the part of humanity being accomplished in a single generation. Adam and Eve lived in Paradise until they were *condemned* to labor in the fields. But their children, Cain and Abel, ruled over a domesticated nature: Abel was a herdsman, Cain a tiller of the fields. Obviously, the first authors of the Bible could no longer even imagine any human form of existence without domesticated animals and plants and regarded that pattern as imposed by God almost from the beginning.

In reality it took hundreds of generations before man succeeded in accomplishing this first and most important subjugation of nature. Probably he did so at various places on earth, but again Mesopotamia seems to have been the first center. Why the principal domestications apparently took place everywhere at about the same time, and why all important domestications were concluded between 3000 and 2000 B.C. with no more following down to the nineteenth century remains an unsolved riddle. (Not until the nineteenth century was there a vast increase in the varieties of existing domesticated species. Still later, there appeared new domesticated animals—mink, silver fox, and chinchilla —while in recent years the process is being extended into the realm of the microcosm, with the domestication of algae and even microbes.) And we must also say that the question of how these first subjugations of animals and plants took place continues to be a riddle, even though for the past fifty years science has presented us with a new theory every decade. Some of the latest theories have even contended that here and there *self*-domestication must have taken place (this idea also being applied to man, but that is not pertinent to our subject), that certain animals, say, voluntarily submitted to man. One example offered is the dog, which was the first of all domesticated animals (as early as the tenth millennium); in the dog's case this is easily imaginable. Remarkably enough, North America in particular provides one highly interesting example of likely self-domestication. But before we discuss that, let us note that in North America before the time of Columbus, only the dog and the turkey were domesticated—an amazingly scanty score, given the wealth of animal life on the Amer-

Left, tobacco, together with the oldest representation of a cigar, from Mathias Lobel's Stirpium, *Antwerp, 1576. Right, the oldest printed picture of an ear of maize, from Oviedo's* Historia Natural, *Seville, 1535.*

ican continents. (Incidentally, the possibility is not excluded that the dog was brought along by the first immigrants over the Bering Strait, *already domesticated*.)

The case of the turkey is rather special. In the first place, most of the tribes did not keep the turkey for eating, but for the sake of its feathers, which they prized for ornamentation. And second, evidence is piling up that the turkey actually is an example of self-domestication. If that should prove true of the dog, this would mean that the North American peoples achieved not a single genuine animal domestication—which overturns a prime rule in the history of cultures. As we shall see, it was different with plants.

But to return to the question of the turkey's self-domestication: much has been learned about this through an experiment that Jean M. Pinkley has humorously described in an article entitled "The Pueblos and the Turkey: Who Domesticated Whom?"[2] Her thesis is stated almost at the outset: "To say that the Indian domesticated the turkey is 'putting the cart before the horse.' The Indian had no choice; the turkey domesticated him."

The experiment dates from 1944, when the National Park Service—which has made many efforts to restore fauna that have become extinct in a given area in historical times—in collaboration with the Colorado State Game and Fish Department set out the first turkey cocks and hens in Mesa Verde, the canyon in the extreme southwest of Colorado that contains such a wealth of ruins.

A mere ten birds were placed in the new area in the first three months: three cocks and seven hens. Since the biologists assumed that the birds would need assistance until they became familiar with the territory, especially in winter, food was supplied. That was the beginning of a disaster.

For a few years all went well, that is, the birds seemed to be surviving. Then more birds were brought in, and what happened in the fifties might have been taken from a story by James Thurber, as far as the comic aspects went, or from the famous Hitchcock film *The Birds,* insofar as it resembled a nightmare.

What witnesses reported sounds almost incredible. The birds rapidly developed into a major nuisance. Within a few years they became accustomed to all the noises produced by people and cars in Mesa Verde, with its many visitors. Turkeys took to strolling on the roads and forcing drivers to make dangerous stops and swerves. The birds discovered that the porches of houses offered excellent shelter on rainy days. They hopped up on the porches and refused to leave. Insatiably gluttonous, they seized every opportunity to steal food, and even entered into a pact with the jays, who discovered sources of food first and then would alert their allies by loud screeching. Since they were enormous birds, they dropped great quantities of excrement, with the result that the paths became off limits for people in light summer shoes. There was no comparison with the filth that little pigeons deposit in Venice's St. Mark's Square. Children could no longer play out in the open; droppings the size of baseballs landed on their heads. Women who were hanging their washing were attacked and the laundry soiled. Doors had to be kept locked because the birds walked boldly into living rooms and made a mess of everything.

For some incomprehensible reason the park managers once more set out another breed of turkeys. These needed no time at all for habituation; they promptly allied themselves with the old, experienced turkeys. By now the situation was completely out of control, and with the hordes of turkeys on the roads, driving in the area had become hazardous.

Something had to be done. "Our lawns, porches, roofs,

walks and driveways resembled barnyards. The birds were arrogant, defiant, noisy, dirty pests, and we decided for their own good and for the sake of our sanity, that steps had to be taken to drive them back into the wilderness, to force them to become 'wild' turkeys."[3]

After a conference with the biologists the park attendants went out with rifles; this was in the winter, when the park has few visitors. They waited until the birds had assembled in groups and then fired close over their heads. Startled, the turkeys flew up, fluttered as much as 300 feet away, and assembled again, obviously somewhat disturbed. The attendants moved closer and shot again. This time the birds fluttered as before, but settled only 150 feet away and showed only slight signs of anxiety. The attendants shot for the third time without effect; the birds merely beat their wings angrily. They were obviously ruffled but had realized that there was no danger and did not budge.

What next? The biologists recommended cherry bombs, the kind of noisemakers used on the Fourth of July that can be rather dangerous in unskilled hands. When the bombs exploded among the turkeys, they hopped up and down like mad for a moment—but remained where they were. Desperately, the attendants threw more bombs, until finally one fell without going off immediately. One of the older gobblers promptly pecked at it and was blown into turkey heaven. The effect on the others? None whatsoever.

The attendants now flew into a veritable fury. For several days they gathered piles of stones and pelted the birds from far and near. The turkeys showed anger when they received direct hits and screeched with rage. But otherwise they remained where they were and played with the stones. The attendants then tried water hoses and doused the birds; the turkeys enjoyed it. The men chased them with sticks until the men, not the birds, were ready to drop with exhaustion. They took to their patrol cars and roared along the roads with sirens howling; the birds chimed in with zest. "The more we persisted, the more the turkeys enjoyed it. . . . If turkeys were not as bird-brained as they are, I would suspect them of deliberately frequenting the meadows to have their pictures taken so they could laugh at the antics of that two-legged creature known as man!"[4]

Enough. Somehow, over a longer time, the men finally mastered the plague of the birds. But what is the conclusion to be drawn from this unusual and involuntary experiment?

It is conceivable that something like this had happened

The turkey was the only other animal domesticated by the North American Indians, aside from the dog. But did they really domesticate it? (See text.) The design, from Mimbres pottery, dates to between A.D. 1100 and 1300.

once before. When the Indians of the Basket Maker II culture developed the beginnings of agriculture and laid out their first small plots (social groupings would not have been much larger than families and clans in those days), they must soon have discovered that they had to assign two or three persons to stand guard over the ripening crops. In the Mesa Verde region, where there were no permanent water-courses, birds and tillers of the soil had to occupy the same localities, simply because these were the places where the water was. Thus the birds became accustomed to the gestures and noises of people. Now these early farmers were still largely dependent on wild fruits, nuts, berries, and seeds of all kinds. And it seems a likely assumption that when they went out food gathering, the birds were not frightened off, but became even more habituated to the presence of humans. They were already despoiling the crops of the Indians and probably stealing what they could out of the Indians' storage baskets and caves. Judging by the recent episode in Mesa Verde National Park, the Indians could scarcely have driven off the birds, even if they set all their children to shooing them away.

These conditions probably worsened when the Indians of the Basket Maker III culture became more sedentary, settling in small pit-house colonies. For now the birds knew precisely where food was to be had when the harvesting and gathering were over and the perilous winter was at the door.

The outcome: "There was nothing left for the Indians to do but to corral them at night and herd them during the day."[5] Infuriating as the turkeys could be, it is a wonder that the Indians did not destroy all the birds before they discovered how useful they could be for their meat, bones, and feathers. But they did make that discovery. And so there took place the domestication of the turkey, which in this case may well be termed a case of self-domestication. And turkeys proved to be enormously valuable to the peoples of Mesa Verde. For here the turkey was actually eaten —though elsewhere, as we have mentioned, this was not done. The Mesa Verde Indians used the bones to make tools and ornaments, the feathers for adornment and blankets.[6] But that was the second step in the development. In regard to the first, the narrator of the recent Mesa Verde story remarks in retrospect: "My sympathies lie with the Indians; they were truly exploited."[7]

But the domestication of plants in America was another matter entirely. Yet here, too, there is scarcely any comparison with the achievements of the Old World.

Victor R. Boswell, horticulturist of the United States Department of Agriculture, tells an amusing story about a friend who was suddenly gripped by a horticultural passion. He decided that he wanted to see the plants he had been eating all his life actually growing, and although a city dweller, he started a garden in his backyard. One day he showed Boswell his flourishing garden. "So far," he said, "I've grown *only American vegetables*. Next year I want to go in for foreign things."

Boswell let his eyes roam over the fine green rows. He noted the kinds there were and could not keep from saying, "Those tomatoes, snap beans, peppers, lima beans, and potatoes are the only truly American vegetables you have. All the others are foreign—onions, radishes, lettuce, spinach, beets, chard, cabbage, broccoli, collards, carrots, parsley, turnips, peas, asparagus, soybeans, and mustard, eggplant, and the rest. The foreign plants in your garden outnumber the native ones by about five to one."[8]

With greater precision he might have added that only a special kind of bean was *North* American; tomatoes, peppers, and potatoes came from Central and South America.

On the other hand, the backyard gardener had left out two really American food plants, squash and the most important of all, the plant that actually provided the basis for all American cultures· maize. But maize and squash need more room than the ordinary backyard gardener has at his disposal.

In importance as a staple, maize is second only to rice,

which feeds more millions throughout the world than any other grain. Columbus himself sent a few golden ears home —although these were probably hardly as golden as some of our favorite present-day sweet corn. In the time of Columbus there already existed innumerable varieties, including some which were quite small and unimpressive, but they ranged through almost all the colors of the rainbow. To this day Central America produces more varieties than the entire United States.

Maize soon conquered large parts of Europe under various names: *kukuruz,* Turkey wheat, or *Welschkorn.* In Italy it was eaten as *polenta,* in Rumania as *mamaliga.* In Germany, however, it never became more than a feed for animals. During the famine years after 1945 a German cabinet minister, whose point of view had evidently never expanded beyond that of a German farmyard, was misled by this fact into a political blunder. He referred to the cornmeal being sent in the well-meant food shipments coming to Germany under the Marshall Plan as chicken feed unfit for human consumption. The Americans were distinctly annoyed, for since colonial times they have eaten maize in so many different forms that only the Mexicans surpass them in ways of preparing it. Incidentally, the usual term in America, "corn," is actually the generic word for grain of any kind; but the original Indian word *maize* seems to be gaining ground lately, at least in scholarly use.

The great cultures of the Old World based their economies on wheat and rye, barley, oats, and millet, but especially on the first two cereals, from which bread could be baked. The baking of bread was invented in ancient Egypt. The story of this vital food has been fascinatingly told by Heinrich Eduard Jacob in his masterpiece, *Six Thousand Years of Bread.*

When man began to settle in fixed abodes, to form large communities, and to create his first cities, he needed *grain* as the basis for his already specialized social life. Everywhere, without exception. And everywhere, wherever scientists have applied their spades and dug into the past, they have come upon the traces of this supremely important food. Perhaps the most moving discovery was made in Pompeii, where after removing the dense layer of ashes and lapilli that the eruption of Vesuvius in A.D. 79 had showered upon this prosperous city, they found just-baked breads still in the bakers' ovens!

At first thought it may seem strange that the archaeologists, whom the layman conceives as digging primarily for treasures, objects of art, and written documents, have always been more interested in these remains of early man's food. But the reason is simple enough. If we can trace back where grain came from, that is, where the wild plant was first domesticated and transformed into a cultivated plant, we will have discovered the place, or rather the region, in which it was possible for man's first large-scale societies to form.

In fact, this biological detective work has been crowned with success in the case of most varieties of grain. Almost all the wild forms have been traced to the lands of the eastern Mediterranean. The ways they spread and often the speed of their spreading are sometimes incredible. The same is true later on for the American food plants. The South American potato was brought to Queen Elizabeth I of England by Sir Francis Drake and conquered the continent of Europe—but was *introduced* at a much later period to *North* America, and then in the guise of the "Irish" potato. The tomato, also from South America, had long been eaten with pleasure by Europeans, especially by the Italians; but in North America it was considered poisonous as recently as 100 years ago! Only the experiment-minded President Jefferson set a few tomato plants in his garden at Monticello. They were first introduced into Salem, Massachusetts, by an Italian painter in 1802, and in New Orleans they did not appear until 1812.

Few difficulties were encountered in localizing squash and beans. In fact, the wild plants so closely resemble the cultivated plants that even the nonspecialist will recognize them.

But until very recently the origin of maize seemed to be a total mystery. This plant seemed to have sprung as a cultivated grain directly from the hand of God. For in spite of a botanical hunt over the entire continent, far down into South America, no one could find the wild plant from which it had developed. Or rather, from which it *must* have developed, for maize is the one type of grain that is totally dependent on man for cultivation and protection. *Maize does not reproduce itself;* it must be sown by human hands. If a field is left to itself, the overripe grains will fall to the ground and sprout, but they sprout in such numbers that the new plants choke out one another.

Where, then, did maize come from?

Obviously, it did not occur to the botanists to look for the wild plant in northern Canada or in southern Tierra del Fuego. Maize needs warmth and at least fifteen inches of rain annually. The search therefore began in places where the climate was suitable for it and where high civilization suggested a long tradition of maize growing: in southern Mexico, in Yucatan, and in Guatemala—that is to say, in the vicinity of the most important civilization that ancient America produced, that of the Mayas.

After a long search a grass was found that seemed related to maize. It was called teosinte. The controversy over teosinte raged for years, until scientists at last regretfully agreed that teosinte had to be ruled out as the ancestor of maize. For several biologists maintained, with plausible arguments, that for teosinte to have developed from a grass into a plant bearing such heavy fruit as maize would have taken no fewer than 20,000 years!

In any case, is intellectual anticipation of a final product conceivable if not the slightest pre-existing model of the end product can be seen? The answer is certainly no. Until Darwin, Mendel, and Burbank apprehended the first laws of genetics, systematized them, and showed how they could be turned to use, the results of selection, breeding, and cultivation were pure chance. The notion, therefore, that the first tillers of American soil could have thought, If only we select this grass often enough in such and such a way, cultivate it thus and thus, perhaps after hundreds of seasons it will bear heavy ears of grain for our children's children, is sheer absurdity. There had to be a wild plant that *obviously* showed some such prospect for the future, at least in a small way.

The controversy continued. An exciting clue turned up in the form of a "petrified" ear of maize that had been discovered in a curiosity shop in Cuzco, Peru, in 1920 and ultimately found its way to the Smithsonian Institution in Washington, where it nearly vanished among some 50 million other collector's items. This ear of corn, to be sure, looked terribly, terribly old. On the other hand it amazingly resembled, down to fine details, a present-day ear of corn, a fact some of the scientists found particularly baffling. After long discussions they decided on an unusual step. They cut the "fossil" in two in the hope that its internal structure might provide more information. The supposed fossil was made of baked clay. And in the interior was a hollow space in which three baked clay balls skittered around. As Hibben laconically comments, "Some clever Peruvian had long ago manufactured this 'petrified' ear of corn as a rattle for his baby."[9]

Finally, the great Luther Burbank turned his attention to the matter. In fifty years of work that made him world-famous, Burbank had bred hundreds of new and better types of vegetables, fruits, and flowers that remain associated with his name. He now began on a series of experiments with teosinte and after only eighteen generations of careful breeding had developed a primitive form of maize —only to discover that he had erroneously started with a hybrid, a cross of teosinte with maize. He died in 1926 without having solved the problem.

The whole question entered a new phase in 1948 when the archaeologist Herbert Dick, then still a student at the Peabody Museum of Harvard University, made a surprising find in Bat Cave in New Mexico. In the course of a stratigraphic excavation, a dangerous operation that required the use of dust masks, he came upon several strata containing different varieties of maize. And these varieties showed distinct signs of evolution. In the lowest stratum, some six feet deep, the smallest and leanest ears were found, no longer than an inch and a half, but unquestionably a form of maize. A C-14 dating gave the astonishing age of 3600 B.C. What was more, the biologists were able to prove that these oldest specimens of maize so far discovered were forms of popcorn and pod corn, which still exist. (The principal types today are popcorn, pod corn, flint corn, dent corn, soft corn, sweet or sugar corn, and starchy sweet corn.) Paul C. Mangelsdorf of Harvard now took up the study from the standpoint of biology, while Richard Mac-Neish of the Peabody Foundation in Andover continued the archaeological hunt.

It would lead us too far afield to trace in detail this prolonged and extremely subtle piece of research. MacNeish searched thirty-eight caves in Tehuacán, Mexico, and not until he attacked the thirty-ninth did he find what he was looking for.

As a result of this project, biologists and archaeologists now regard the problem, which appeared so utterly mysterious only a few years ago, as virtually solved. Mangelsdorf,

MacNeish, and Galinat published a joint report, which concluded with the following summary:

"Remains of prehistoric corn, including all parts of the plant, have been uncovered from five caves in the Valley of Tehuacán in southern Mexico. The earliest remains, dated 5200 to 3400 B.C., are almost certainly *those of wild corn*. Later remains include cultivated corn and reveal a distinct evolutionary sequence that gave rise ultimately to several still-existing Mexican races. Despite a spectacular increase in size and productiveness under domestication, which helped make corn the basic food plant of the pre-Columbian cultures and civilizations of America, there has been no substantial change in 7,000 years in the fundamental biological characteristics of the corn plant."[10]

Thus the long-sought-for proof has been found: the domestication of maize took place in Mexico where, quite logically, one of the first American high cultures was then able to develop. The North American Indians took over this domesticated plant, which in the course of centuries spread northward until at last a hoard of corn hidden by the Indians was discovered by the almost desperate Pilgrim Fathers in Massachusetts after their landing in 1620, and helped them through their terrible first winter.

"Love and cherish your corn as you love and cherish your women," the Zuñis of New Mexico say today—and no doubt their ancestors said it thousands of years ago.

Book Four

14

Discovery of the Mounds

From Wisconsin to the Gulf of Mexico, from Mississippi to the Appalachians, but especially in the state of Ohio, rise tens of thousands of artificial hills. Some of them are still well preserved, some have been partly blown away by the winds of a thousand years, torn up by the plows of farmers, disfigured and pillaged by grave robbers.

Among these hills are some shaped like pyramids!

The word instantly calls to mind the largest stone structures of all ages, and principally the three huge Egyptian monuments near Gizeh in the vicinity of Cairo. Only the temple pyramids of the Mayas and Aztecs in Central America and Mexico are comparable to these. Let us be careful. The North American mounds perhaps cannot be called pyramids in the mathematically strict sense. Nor are they made of stone. Rather, they are sometimes small, but sometimes gigantic heaps of earth, artificial hills. In fact, one of them covers an area larger than the Egyptian pyramid of Cheops.

In spite of all these qualifications, it is astonishing, in fact inexplicable, how few people know of these mounds or are aware that there are more than 100,000 of them in the

United States. Many of them are in no way like pyramids and are so fantastically shaped that they defy description. The usual term for them is "mounds." The word is a bit on the vague side: it does not refer specifically to a burial mound or temple base, but is rather an overall term that ultimately came to be attached to a postulated people, of whom little is known, namely the Mound Builders.

Whoever they were, these relics of their existence command respect. It has been estimated that one mound near Miamisburg, Ohio, must contain no fewer than 311,353 cubic feet of earth. Another, in Ross County, Ohio (there are some 500 mounds in this county alone), was heaped up of 20,000 wagonloads of earth. That is a farmer's unit of measurement, for the Indians had no wagons; they used only their hands, baskets, and sacks made of hides. Anyone who does not like such rough-and-ready estimates can take the word of two modern archaeologists, who made the most careful studies, including aerial photographs and soil tests, to determine the cubic contents of the mounds at Poverty Point in northern Louisiana. In 1956 James A. Ford and C. H. Webb announced that some 530,000 cubic yards of earth had been moved by the Indians. Of the largest mound Ford says, "It can be estimated that the finished mound required something over three million man-hours of labor."[1]

The North American mounds exist in far greater numbers than the Egyptian pyramids, and taken all together, as the organized expenditure of labor by a "primitive" people, go far beyond the Egyptian achievement in its totality.

It was inevitable that these monuments, which the first settlers encountered as they advanced westward, should have inspired the pioneers to the wildest imaginings.

"Through the battle, through defeat / Moving yet and never stopping / Pioneers! O Pioneers!" Walt Whitman hailed these men, who certainly had no thought of archaeological research but were simply fighting for their lives. It thus could never have occurred to them to connect these structures with the wild, roaming Red Men, the dashing mounted Sioux or Apaches or whatever their names were, Indians who seemed to have nothing in mind but warfare and hunting and who had the deepest scorn for any sort of slavish work.

Even the first erudite people who came on the scene were perplexed. Mounds of this sort must surely have been raised by some legendary ancient race, some enormously superior civilization, they thought.

It makes for a certain neatness that scientific investigation of the East began almost 100 years before that of the Southwest, if we date the archaeology of the latter with Bandelier around 1880, or of the former with Thomas Jefferson around 1780. In between, the American Antiquarian Society was founded as early as November 19, 1812, with its meeting place the Exchange Coffee House in Boston. Its constitution read: "Its immediate and peculiar design is, to discover the antiquities of *our own continent;* and, by providing a fixed and permanent place of deposit, to preserve such relicks of American antiquities as are portable."

But this dignified body took no part in the scientific and unscientific controversies concerning the mounds that raged for an entire century, and it did not attempt to come to grips with the wildly fantastic theories concerning the Mound Builders.

In 1827 a book was published in Heidelberg, Germany, entitled *Nachrichten über die früheren Einwohner von Nordamerika und ihre Denkmäler* ("Accounts of the Early Inhabitants of North America and their Monuments"). Its author was Friedrich Wilhelm Assall, who had come to the United States as a miner in 1818, served as a soldier for nine months, and then settled in Ohio and Pennsylvania, where he eventually became Head Mining Officer of the State of Pennsylvania. In 1823 he returned to Germany on a visit and informed Franz Joseph Mone, a Heidelberg professor, of the mysterious Indian monuments he had seen, especially in Ohio. Mone was extremely interested, for only three years earlier the University of Göttingen had offered a prize for a critical comparison of American and Asiatic monuments. He strongly urged Assall to write up his observations.

Assall did more than that. He looked into all the writings on the subject that he could find, weighing these against his own observations, which were frequently better, sounder geographically and ethnologically than those of his predecessors. Assall had his own theories about the mounds, both as to their age and their origins, at a time when there was almost no critical discussion of the subject in America. (Caleb Atwater's *Description* had been published a bare seven years earlier.) Assall's monograph had an additional importance in that it was probably the first in Europe that attracted the attention of the German scholarly world to monuments in North America. But we also mention this book because it seems to have gone unnoticed by those American scholars who have put together the story of the *discovery* of the Mound Builders. By a lucky chance the badly battered volume of 160 pages fell into my hands. I have so far not found it in any archaeological library in the United States. In fact, not even the Library of Congress possesses a copy!

As we have already related in the Prelude to this book, Thomas Jefferson had formulated certain basic principles in 1781 when he carried out the first stratigraphic excavation of a mound. But he was not the only President of the United States to take a lively interest in the Mound Builders. William Henry Harrison had already won a place for himself in American military history as the hero of many Indian battles, including some fought against the legendary chief Tecumseh, whose uprising of 1810 he crushed at the Tippecanoe River. "Old Tippecanoe" made steady progress in his military and political career. Like Jefferson, he came from Virginia, but was noted for the extreme simplicity of his life. Perhaps it was this that won him his unusually lopsided victory. He became the ninth President of the United States, but held office for only one month—from March 4 to April 4, 1841. Then he died of pneumonia, perhaps also as a result of the strain of adjusting to his new status.

His interest in the Mound Builders had begun in 1829. In 1838 he published his *Discourse on the Aborigines of the Valley of the Ohio*. But unlike the scientifically schooled Jefferson, he saw the mounds through a romantic haze. Old soldier that he was, to him a mound could only have been a fortress. Or else the base of some heathen temple where frightful scenes of human sacrifice took place amidst clouds of sinister smoke. Nevertheless, he was hardheaded enough to conclude that the Mound Builders must have been farmers.

Our oldest descriptions of the mounds, however, do not stem from such comparative latecomers but again from the Spanish conquistadors. Hernando de Soto landed in Florida in 1539, made his way northward, and happened on many mounds. He saw both old *and* new ones! Here are a few quotations from the old sources:[2]

"The governor [de] Soto opened a large temple in the woods, in which were buried the chiefs of the country, and took from it a quantity of pearls. . . ."

"The caciques of this country make a custom of raising near their dwellings very high hills, on which they sometimes build their houses."

"The Indians try to place their villages on elevated sites, but inasmuch as in Florida there are not many sites of this kind where they can conveniently build, *they erect elevations themselves* in the following manner. . . ."

"The chief's house stood near the beach upon a very high *mount made by hand for defense.*"

". . . a town of 400 houses, and a large square, where the cacique's house stood upon a mound made by art."

If the archaeologists of the nineteenth century had been historically schooled and had looked into the Spanish accounts, the innumerable fantasies about the Mound Builders would never have arisen. It did not occur to the Spaniards to invent some legendary ancient race, for they could see Mound Builders still at work, although on a modest scale.

In the East, however, all sorts of speculations flourished. One of the more sober theories was that the mounds in the South must have been fortifications erected by the Spanish soldiers. Wilder explanations were given for the mounds in the West. To be sure, the reports by the first travelers and pioneers who ventured into the vast stretches beyond the Mississippi were extremely vague. Few expeditions were as well conducted as that of Meriwether Lewis and William Clark, who had the benefit of a set of directives from President Jefferson (Lewis had previously been his secretary). Lewis and Clark brought back an enormous amount of information from their adventurous two-and-a-half-year journey across the breadth of the continent to the Pacific Ocean—but they were unusual men.

George Catlin, too, was certainly an unusual man. This lawyer, who suddenly wished to be a portrait painter, also discovered that he had a bent for adventure. He fulfilled both drives by wandering through Indian country for eight years and brought back not only a host of paintings and sketches, but also voluminous notes that testified to the keenness of his eye and the sharpness of his mind. To the shame of his native land, Europe recognized his creative achievements before America. His extraordinary two-volume book, containing more than 300 excellent engravings, had to be printed in London at his own expense in 1841.[3]

We could draw up an endless list of those who contributed valuable material toward our knowledge of the Mound Builders. We will mention only a few of these informants, who were often picturesque characters in their own right.

The Moravian missionary David Zeisberger went to Ohio with a group of Christianized Indians and there founded the town of Schönbrunn in 1772. For years he had lived among the Onondagas and Delawares. In Ohio he saw the mounds and described them in his *History of the American Indians,* thereby providing what was probably the first significant account of the mounds.

General Rufus Putnam was a veteran of the Revolutionary War and founder in 1786 of the Ohio Company, which aimed, as was frankly announced, at acquiring vast landholdings at bargain prices. He secured the services of a sturdy man of the cloth, one Reverend Manasseh Cutler, who became what we would today call his lobbyist. Cutler

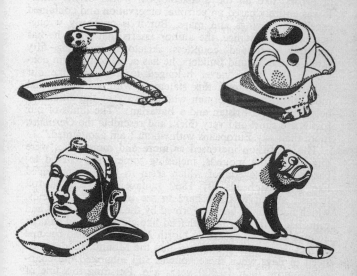

The Mound Builders had developed the art of making pipes, shaped from clay or carved out of soft stone, to a degree not to be attained in Europe until centuries later.

prevailed on the government, then situated in New York, to grant land to the Ohio Company. In 1787–88 he and Putnam founded Marietta in the heart of a district of countless mounds. And oddly enough, these hardheaded businessmen showed the right instincts as far as archaeology was concerned: they prevented senseless destruction of the ancient monuments. Putnam, familiar with military surveying, prepared maps of the mound area, which remained for more than a century the best to be had. And the Reverend Cutler, improbable though it sounds, anticipated Dr. Douglass's tree-ring dating by some 140 years. Of course, the method he used was rough-and-ready, but the significant thing is that he employed it to date a historical monument. After felling one of the gigantic trees on a Marietta mound, he counted the annual rings and determined that (in 1798) the mound must be at least 463 years old!

Another interesting figure was Caleb Atwater, who rose from postmaster to Commissioner of Indian Affairs under President Jackson. In 1829 he published a book that is usually referred to as "a classic," although I have found it full of errors, like all the archaeological works of his time.[4] It was entirely based on personal observation and contained excellent drawings and maps. But it is curiously wrongheaded. For instance, the author asserts that while he has carefully examined countless skeletons, including fifty skulls of the Mound Builders, he has come to the firm conviction that they "never belonged to a people like our Indians." He follows this statement with a remark that must surprise any German who is aware of the difference between, say, a Frisian and a Bavarian: "The limbs of our fossils are short and very thick, and resemble the *Germans,* more than any Europeans with whom I am acquainted."

The confusion increased as more and more relics were dug out of the mounds, including some finely carved tobacco pipes, several of which seem to have been shaped like elephant heads. By 1860 fantasy had received full license, and it was not hard to see that several mounds, which had simply been deformed by the action of wind and rain, had originally been shaped like elephants and camels, animals that had existed in North America but had become extinct. From this it followed that the Mound Builders had lived in days when these animals still inhabited the continent—more than 10,000 years ago. Pursuing this line of reasoning a little further, Frederick Larkin in 1880 theorized that the Mound Builders had not only tamed the mammoth, but actually domesticated it. He argued that only the enormous mammoths, those bulldozers of the ancient world, could have moved the mountains of earth that went into a mound.

Fowke and Moore also must have been two remarkable characters.

Gerard Fowke had been a cavalry officer during the Civil War. He journeyed throughout the East, visiting every mound he heard about. In addition, he sought out the private collectors, of whom there were more and more, to wangle rare finds out of them (we shall describe the nature of such finds in the chapter after next). He also found time to publish several totally serious books about his researches. One curious aspect of his travels was that he went everywhere, thousands of miles, *on foot;* for while he was still a cavalry officer he had vowed that once the war was over he would never mount a horse again. After being in a minor accident he also did not trust the railroad. He lived long enough to see something of the advantages of the automobile—and despised it! Hibben relates that as late as the 1920's he would see this tall man, wearing cavalry boots that came above his knees, tramping the roads of Ohio, Indiana, and Illinois.[5]

The wealthy cotton trader Cyrus Moore seems to have been merely a collector, and a predatory one at that; never-

Wooden mask, called the Deer Dancer, from Spiro Mound, Okla.

theless, he has left us quite a few useful descriptions and illustrations of archaeological finds. Summer after summer for many years he set out, accompanied by twenty-five sturdy lads, on a specially constructed houseboat, touring the waters of the Mississippi and Ohio, stopping wherever he saw a mound (and he could easily see thousands of them) to have his men dig into it and pillage it. Laden with Indian artifacts that would have made the heart of any scientist pound, he sailed down to New Orleans in the fall. Evenings, Hibben recounts, he sat in the stern of his boat, in a specially made easy chair, playing the banjo.

There were hordes of other "pothunters" like him, although most of them had to operate on a more modest scale. There can be no objection in principle to these digging amateurs to whom science has owed so much in the past and who still make valuable contributions—if they will call in the nearest professional without delay. Amateur clubs and local historical societies are constantly springing up and have flourished especially since the end of the last war. Associations of this sort train their members in the techniques of digging and make them aware of their responsibility to science. A debt of gratitude is owed the director of the Bronson Museum of the Massachusetts Archaeological Society, who has written an excellent handbook for amateurs that every "Sunday pothunter" should carry in his pocket.[6]

State laws now protect most mounds from pillaging, so that nowadays the sort of thing that happened to the Spiro Mound in Oklahoma would be virtually impossible. In the nineteenth century a farmer plowing at the edge of a mound turned up an artfully carved tobacco pipe of red-

One of the first recorded finds of the Mound Builder period—long ago described by Alexander von Humboldt and published by Squier and Davis in 1848. The provenance of this small pipe, carved out of green sandstone, is uncertain.

dish stone. He showed it to friends who had heard that foolish people in the East paid high prices for such things. After the farmer had harvested his crop, they themselves went to the mound, first chopped down all the trees growing on it (thereby destroying any chance for dating it), and began pothunting. And they found plenty, more than plenty; they found things wherever they drove their shovels into the ground: pottery, hammered copper plates, many more pipes, whole necklaces of stone, bones, shells. The treasure seemed inexhaustible, and the collectors flocked to the site and paid good prices. As a result, the news spread. The University of Oklahoma sent experts to save whatever remained. But the cunning farmers had meanwhile set up a registered mining company; they could claim that the mound was the property of this company and would not allow the archaeologists the slightest say.

Helplessly, the scientists had to look on as the farmers now began to attack the mound with dynamite. The destruction proceeded and went on until a state ordinance finally prohibited further havoc. Not until 1935 did the University of Oklahoma try to salvage something from the ruins of Spiro—and actually turned up more finds in that fantastic mound.

When research has accumulated so much material that an overview has become well-nigh impossible, an urgent need arises for a great classifier or a great compiler. The history of science shows that these classifiers or compilers are often not professionals, perhaps rarely can be, for their outstanding trait must be the ability to eliminate and omit —which horrifies the specialist with his passion for completeness. Consequently these men are frequently not "field" workers at all; they may be bookworms, or even pure amateurs, though they have to be extraordinary specimens of that breed.

In the course of 120 years of Mound Builder research, three works of classification that may justly be called standard texts have appeared. The very first was the work of amateurs, although they did not write only from their armchairs but also made significant field researches. Along with these three books there were, of course, innumerable publications by others, whose work no archaeologist can ignore, such as that of the highly interesting Cyrus Thomas. But none of these scholars produced a "standard text."

Ephraim George Squier, born in Bethlehem, New York,

in 1821, worked as a journalist in various cities until he finally settled down in Chillicothe, Ohio, the very heart of mound country. He published a local newspaper and served also as clerk of the Ohio House of Representatives; but these occupations left him ample time to pursue his passion for Indian antiquities. A Chillicothe physician, Dr. E. H. Davis, also had this passion. The two joined forces and started investigating mounds. For years. They actually dug into more than 200 of these artificial hills and located some 100 ancient Indian earthwork enclosures, which are frequently found among groups of mounds. Then they published jointly—though Squier contributed the major share —the book that is regarded as one of the classics of North American archaeology: *Ancient Monuments of the Mississippi Valley: Comprising the Results of Extensive Original Surveys and Explorations.*

The ponderous folio volume has 306 pages, 19 chapters, 48 plates, most of them maps that were the result of excellent survey work, and 297 wood engravings. The book created an immediate stir—did so, in fact, even in manuscript. For Squier had submitted it to an institution that assigned a committee to examine it, and such were the merits of the book that the decision was made to launch a new series of publications, of which this book was to be the first. It therefore appeared as Volume I of the Smithsonian Contributions to Knowledge, printed in the "City of Washington" in 1848.

This publication thus represented one of the first major scholarly contributions of the Smithsonian Institution, which in the future was to lend tremendous support to American archaeology and to become the repository of the very largest scientific collections in America. Its founder was an Englishman.

James Smithson was born illegitimately in France and died in Italy. He was a cultivated man, educated at Oxford and enormously wealthy. When he died in 1829, he left his entire fortune to a nephew. But his will provided that if the nephew died without issue, the fortune would devolve to the United States of America, "to found at Washington, under the name of the Smithsonian Institution, an establishment for the increase and diffusion of knowledge among men."

The nephew did indeed leave no issue when he died in 1835, and in 1838 the clipper ship *Mediator* sailed to Philadelphia with a huge chest full of gold sovereigns. These

to America. But before and after Mather the question
ained an open one. How did these people fit into God's
ation as it was outlined in the Bible, the sole true
rce? Evidently they did not fit at all unless one took a
mendous mental leap and accounted for them as de-
endants of the "ten lost tribes of Israel." The leap was
ken. This theory, whose proponents scarcely bother to
onsider how and by what route these tribes could have
ade the tremendous voyage from Palestine, has been held
own to our present century.[1] However, this is not, as is
commonly thought, one of the tenets of the Church of
Jesus Christ of Latter-day Saints. The Mormons do not
believe that the ten lost tribes migrated to America. Rather,
they believe that there were two other Israelite migrations
to America—for so it was revealed in 1827 to the founder
of their religion, Joseph Smith, by Moroni, a "resurrected
personage," upon gleaming gold plates in a hieroglyphic
script To be specific, Mormon doctrine holds that after the
tower of Babel had to be discontinued because of the confusion of tongues, a tribe of Jaredites set out to populate
America but came to a miserable end. Undeterred, other
Israelites set out for America in the year 600 B.C., under
the leadership of a man named Lehi. One group of these,
the Nephites, became the founders of the great states in
Central America and the Andes, but died out by 324 B.C.
The other, a more primitive nomadic group, became the an-
ccstors of the North American Indian tribes. At the period
in which Joseph Smith received his revelation archaeology
certainly had no such facts or dates remotely at its disposal. Nor does it today. (The *Book of Mormon*, first English edition, was published in Palmyra, New York, in 1830.)

Two other by no means irresponsible thinkers of the
eighteenth and nineteenth centuries, who started from the
premise that the Indians had migrated from Asia, still tried
to reconcile their views with the biblical story. Caleb Atwater, mentioned above in connection with the Mound
Builders, attempted this in 1820, and James Adair, who had
raded in Indian territories for some forty years, worked up
is theory as early as 1775.[2]

Thomas Jefferson falls in the period between these two
en. He alone saw the problem in purely scientific terms
d was one of the first to hold that the immigration of the
dians from Asia had taken place by way of the far north.
s theory is recorded in his *Notes on Virginia*.

Before and since it has been proposed that the Indians

were promptly reminted into American coinage, yielding
the sum of $508,318.46.

The testament remains a puzzle to this day. For Smithson
had never been in America, nor had he ever shown any
particular interest in America. But his money proved a
blessing to the United States. The Institution was officially
founded on August 10, 1846, although many voices were
raised urging that the gift be rejected, or asserting that the
federal government had no legal right to accept it.

But to return to our standard texts.

No fewer than eighty-two years passed before another
man, Henry Clyde Shetrone, ventured to work his way
through the thickets of the literature that had accumulated in the interval, to subject the enormous collections to
critical study, and to take up the spade himself wherever he
felt more knowledge was wanted. In 1930 he published his
book, *The Mound Builders: A Reconstruction of the Life
of a Prehistoric American Race, through Exploration and
Interpretation of Their Earth Mounds, Their Burials, and
Their Cultural Remains.* The book has 508 pages and 300
illustrations. Shetrone introduced himself as "Director and
Archaeologist, the Ohio State Archaeological and Historical
Society." In his foreword he says: "The 'Mound Builders'
is dedicated to the average man and woman who, although
fully awake to the human interest in their story, lack time
and opportunity for digesting the rather extensive but often
unavailable literature on this subject." And he continues:
"If the professional prehistorian also finds the book a handy
companion of the archaeology of the general mound area,
its publication will be more than justified."

His hope has been fulfilled. His book and that of Squier-
Davis are classics that no student of Indian archaeology
can overlook. The need for them has lately been confirmed;
both books, the former in 1964 and the latter in 1965, were
reprinted photomechanically and sold at high prices because
the originals had become so rare.

Both books contain errors. Neither adequately answers
the questions of who the Mound Builders really were, how
long they built, when they began, and when they so mysteriously disappeared. Actually, it was only after 1930,
through a great number of studies utilizing modern methods
of dating, that these questions were really clarified. And
once again it was an amateur who had made a name for
himself as an author of juveniles and popular articles on
the Red Man, who ventured to treat the subject in its

entirety. In a synthesis that fully measures up to scientific standards he at last presented the *real* picture of those hard-working peoples—for various peoples were involved—stripped of all mysticism. In 1968 Robert Silverberg's *Mound Builders of Ancient America* was published. The subtitle sets forth his point of view: "The Archaeology of a Myth."

But before we briefly sketch the cultures of the Mound Builders, before we come to grips with this particular myth, something must be said about the fantastic notions that float about concerning the Indian peoples in general and their origins—notions for which there is only the most slender basis, but which stubbornly refuse to die. A trustworthy person tells me that right now in America there are some 300,000 persons who firmly believe that not only early American culture, but all cultures, come from the land of Mu. The adherents of the Atlantis theory are beyond counting. But as the great Austrian novelist Robert Musil remarked, "Certain errors are stations on the way to truth."

15

Wild Theories from
Atlantis to Mu

THE newcomers to the New World naturally pondered the origins of these numerous "red" tribes. As we have already noted, some of the clergy in particular were of the opinion that the Indians were not human beings at all, since there was no mention of them in the Bible. This view was extremely convenient in economic terms, for it permitted unscrupulous exploitation of the natives. Nevertheless, it did not last, especially after the relations between the soldiers and the Indian girls proved the opposite in a short time. (Incidentally, though, it was not until that the white man's Congress in Washington declared Indians were citizens of the United States, with all appropriate rights and obligations.)

Cotton Mather, the mighty preacher from Boston, was probably the spiritual father of the terrible Salem trials of 1692, adopted a simple and clear attitude to the problem. In 1702 he asserted, not metaphorically but literally, that *the devil in person* had brought

were descendants of Scandinavians, Ethiopians, Chinese, Moluccans, Scythians, Polynesians, Hindus, Egyptians, Phoenicians, the legendary Atlanteans, or the even more mythical population of the land of Mu.

Some may wonder why a simple though equally fallacious idea was scarcely ever advanced: the thesis that the Indians had not come from somewhere, but had been in the American continents from the beginning. This may be somewhat accounted for by the belief in the Bible that we have already discussed, the Bible excluded such a possibility. But there was also the fact that no one was thinking in terms of a theory of evolution until that momentous November 24, 1859, when Darwin published *The Origin of Species*. The idea that the Indians, like man elsewhere in the world, had developed from lower forms to *Homo sapiens,* could not have crossed anyone's mind.

What was involved, too, was the concept of historical time, which had to be totally recast. We will remember that in 1750 the Irish Archbishop James Ussher computed on the basis of the Bible that the creation of the earth had taken place at nine o'clock in the morning on October 26 in the year 4004 B.C.[3] In 1599, without such precise computations, Shakespeare had already said in *As You Like It:* "The poor world is almost six thousand years old." Only in the light of such ideas can we realize how tremendously Darwin changed men's view of the universe and of the human race and why all theories of evolution were regarded as a dire assault upon the Bible. As late as 1925, in the famous "Monkey Trial" at Dayton, Tennessee, the schoolteacher John Scopes was found guilty and fined $100 for having taught Darwin's theory to his classes The city of Dayton and the state of Tennessee became the laughingstock of the world, but did that change anything inside the so-called Bible Belt? The ban on the teaching of any theory of evolution remained on the lawbooks until very recently in three states, Tennessee, Alabama, and Mississippi. In 1966 Susan Epperson, a biology teacher in Alabama, challenged this law—and on November 12, 1968, the United States Supreme Court at last ruled that any law against teaching the theory of evolution was unconstitutional.[4]

There was still another idea that might have arisen about the Indians. A freethinker, at any rate, could have entertained it. Instead of assuming that the Indians came from the Old World, he could have decided that they represented the primitive human race, from which he himself was descended. But European arrogance would not permit any such speculation.

For many years specialists have been divided over the question of possible contacts between the Indian cultures in North and South America and civilizations on the other continents. Those who argue that there were such contacts are defenders of the "diffusion" theory. But before we take up this question, we must mention two more fantastic stories concerning the origin of the Indians, according to which all Indian culture is derived from extra-American sources. For like all wrong tracks, such theories are part and parcel of the history of a science. They must be given their due; by contrast with their specious glitter, the light of science shines all the more brightly.

The question of Atlantis, for example, has provoked fierce controversy ever since antiquity. Along with serious efforts to substantiate the story, there have been the wildest theories, which have sprung from pure imaginings. The concept of Atlantis goes back to two dialogues by the Greek philosopher Plato, the *Timaeus* and the *Critias*. According to these, Solon the Lawgiver, who lived about two centuries before Plato (c. 640–560 B.C.) heard about Atlantis from Egyptian priests. It was described as a rich and powerful island "beyond the Pillars of Hercules" inhabited by a highly civilized but warlike people. Nine thousand years before his time—according to Solon—this land had vanished beneath the waves in a great natural catastrophe.

As Plato tells the story, it is equally probable and improbable. Aristotle, who was Plato's pupil, called the account a fable without historical value. Still, there is no reason why there would not have been an island, inhabited by a people as civilized as the times allowed, that had been wiped out by a catastrophe. There have been examples of such. Nor is it folly to search for this land. Heinrich Schliemann did something similar when he looked for legendary Troy, and Arthur Evans when he searched for the equally legendary Palace of Minos. They took their clues from ancient sources that scarcely seemed believable but which were magnificently verified when these places came to light.

So far, however, all searches for Atlantis have been in vain. In the course of time it has been "located" in Spain, in the Canary Islands, at the mouth of the Niger River, in Mexico, and in Scandinavia.

In the 1950's the German pastor Jürgen Spanuth claimed that he had found Atlantis and actually dived down to it; it lay submerged in the North Sea, near the island of Helgoland.[5] And as these lines are being written, James W. Mavor, Jr., is just as positive that Atlantis was situated near one of the Cyclades Islands in the Aegean Sea.[6]

There is no reason to call off this search. Still, it has become somewhat ridiculous, for even if a sunken island with traces of civilization were to be found, there would be no way of proving its identity with Plato's Atlantis; the data in the classical sources are simply too imprecise.

But if a certain suggestion of fraudulence has clung to Atlantis research over the centuries, it is because of the mythmaking that has gone along with it. The most fanciful forms of civilization have been attributed to Atlantis, and ultimately a fabulous tale has grown up of a prehistoric "Atlantean culture" towering over all others. Legend has in fact made the island the very source of all human cultures.

We cannot go into all these fantasies here. A brief example may suffice. It comes from the book by the anthroposophist Rudolf Steiner, whose creed still has followers all over the world: *Our Atlantean Forefathers.*[7]

"Just as today the power of heat is extracted from coal and transformed into kinetic energy in our vehicles, so the Atlanteans knew how to place the germinal powers of living organisms at the service of their technology. . . . In Atlantean times plants were not only raised as food, but also to utilize the forces slumbering within them for transportation and industry. Thus the Atlanteans had devices which transformed the germinal force of seeds into technically exploitable power. Thus the floating vehicles of the Atlanteans were propelled a short distance above the ground."

In addition to all that, we are asked to believe that the American cultures were of course of Atlantean origin (to the large groups of Rosicrucians, Theosophists, and Anthroposophists this idea is gospel). It is strange, though, that the Indians remembered so very little of this civilization, which allegedly surpassed our own in technical perfection, and that they were not even able to preserve the wheel, let alone writing

Nevertheless "Two sages, Plato of Athens and Donnelly of Minneapolis, have made Atlantis a household word,' wrote William Churchward in 1890. He was right, for ten years previously the book *Atlantis: The Antediluvian World* by Ignatius Donnelly, whom he so blithely links with Plato, had gone into no less than eighteen editions and to this day is still read in America as an honored "classic" on this subject.

Donnelly knew exactly where Atlantis was situated, more exactly than Plato. According to him, the drowned island lies in the Atlantic Ocean, west of the Azores. And this is the location accepted by the majority of those who believe at all in Atlantis.

Nevertheless, the Atlantis theory is modesty itself compared with another theory born in our century. Its herald is Colonel James Churchward (not to be confused with the above-mentioned William), who in 1931 announced that he had rediscovered the land of Mu.

In contrast to Atlantis, Mu lay in the Pacific Ocean and was, according to Churchward, much larger than Plato's island. It covered an area from Easter Island to the Carolines, from Hawaii in the north to the Cook Islands in the south. This continent, which, given such a size it may well be called, had 64 million inhabitants. Fifty thousand years ago a civilization had developed there that was "in many respects superior to our own and far in advance of us in some important essentials which the modern world is just beginning to have cognizance of."[8] The creation of man also took place in Mu. "The oldest records of man are not to be found in Egypt or the Valley of the Euphrates, but *right here in North America* and in the Orient where Mu planted her first colonies!"

These assertions are based on a number of "Naacal tablets," which Churchward, so he relates, found some fifty years before the publication of his book "in certain Monasteries in India and Tibet whose names are withheld by request." Unfortunately. According to Churchward, many years later William Niven found corresponding stone tablets in Mexico. The Naacal tablets are supposed to be 15,000 years old, the Mexican tablets a good 12,000 years. This would mean there was writing in Mexico at a time in which—according to the general view of archaeologists —Tepexpan man, one of the earliest primitive American hunters, was pursuing his mammoths and would, as the anthropologist Robert Wauchope pithily put it, "have had some difficulty signing his name with an X."[9]

Churchward had heard of the existence of these tablets from a priest of the Indian monastery and had pleaded for six months before he was allowed to see them. The tablets had lain untouched in vaults since time immemorial. Of course, the clay tablets were written in a secret script, but fortunately the priest still had the key to it in his possession. And he taught Churchward what he knew. "Months of intense concentration in translating the tablets followed, but the reward justified the effort. The writings described in detail the creation of the earth and of man, and the place where he first appeared—Mu!" Whatever details were lacking from these Indian tablets were supplemented by the Mexican texts. This is a mere sample of the Mu theory. It is hard to say how many followers Churchward has today; there must be a great many of them. I personally have known only two, both mystics devoted to the wisdom of the Orient. Not long ago, one of them sent a postcard to an Indian guru of his acquaintance asking whether he was doing right to sell his house. Anyone who is interested in Churchward's astonishingly detailed texts can easily obtain them. By 1961 *The Lost Continent of Mu* had reached its twentieth edition. What is more, there is now a paperback edition as well.

The fascination of these books for the layman is based on their seeming to solve innumerable problems, problems that intrigue him but which he has never investigated in a serious way, so that he has no notion of the underlying elements and difficulties. These books—and this is the secret of their success—do not solve the problems by stripping away veils and seeking that clarity which is the scientist's aim. Instead, they festoon the problem with all sorts of romantic folderol, bathe the whole in a false dusk of mysticism and pretend to sell the reader a key that will instantaneously make him one of the elite, a member of a group possessing special secrets, and *by that fact alone* able to grasp all the hidden truths that the scientist, working "only" with his impoverished intellect, cannot possibly understand.

To be sure, no scientist can manage without emotions. Inspirations, glimmerings, blind gropings, trials and errors are essential features of the history of scientific research. It should be evident that the true test of the archaeologist in particular is whether he can so animate his material by the power of his imagination that he can bring the past to life. ("Imagination is the fire of discovery," the great British archaeologist Flinders Petrie has said.) Nevertheless, we must remember that science must ultimately be conceived of as a *method* that keeps imagination under control, that its touchstone is always a fact which can be verified, that although it works with hypotheses, it never tries to make theses of them until proof is forthcoming. Naturally, this is the ideal. Science makes mistakes, of course; that is part of the human condition. Even scientific theories are historically conditioned and subject to revision, but the principle holds true.

This principle involves the very opposite of that pseudo-science which is practiced by "crackpots." Highly intelligent, often amazingly well-read and diligent in the pursuit of whatever will serve their cherished systems, most of them are harmless enough, although on occasion they can do enormous damage, as the cases of Houston Stewart Chamberlain and Alfred Rosenberg demonstrate. The crackpot has an obsession. Rosenberg's obsession was a peculiarly repulsive one and proved to be highly contagious. His book, *The Myth of the Twentieth Century,* laid the foundations for Nazi National Socialism.

The anthropologist Robert Wauchope has made a special study of the crackpots in American archaeology.[10] He describes, for instance, their aggrieved attitude toward the professional scientists: "One cannot help but see some regularity in these attitudes. The typical advocate of the 'wild' theories of American Indian origins begins his book with the underdog appeal; he points out that he has been personally scorned, ridiculed, or at best snubbed by the professionals Then he predicts that his writings will in turn be ill received or ignored, and he proceeds to attack the thickheaded bigotry of the men in universities and museums Frequently he implies that they are not only hopelessly conservative and jealous of any scholarly inroads by amateurs, but also that they are actually dishonest, and when confronted with conflicting evidence they will suppress or if necessary destroy it. Still, though blasting the professionals as ignorant, incompetent, and unethical, the pseudo-scientists almost invariably take pride in any real or (more often) fancied approval they obtain from these misguided Phuddy Duddies "

Here we have a new word This amusing coinage is not yet widely known. Phuddy Duddy is a portmanteau word compounded of "fuddy duddy" (in the familiar sense of ultraconservative) and the academic title Ph.D. "They do not sleep with their windows open for fear that a new idea might fly in,' said Harold S. Gladwin, who gave the new word currency. Yet Gladwin was an amateur archaeologist who himself financed worthwhile excavations and has much to his credit. But since several of his theories were not fully accepted, he felt himself to be a crusader against the professionals, whom he snipes at as hopeless Phuddy Duddies.[11] It is rather amusing to note that a Phuddy Duddy in one field can be a crackpot in another. Thus Leo Wiener, though a Harvard professor of Slavic and a philologist who knew more than fifty languages, offered a theory on the African origins of the Central American cultures. His attitude was even more aggrieved than Gladwin's. "Unquestionably," he wrote, "the archaeological dogs will continue to bay at the moon. . . ."[12]

Wauchope concludes with words to which we can fully subscribe: "The amateurs will always hate the Phuddy Duddies, and the professionals will forever scorn the Crackpots."

16

Solving the Riddle
of the Mounds

THE city of Newark, Ohio, thirty miles from the state capital of Columbus, can boast one of the most unusual golf courses in the United States. At first glance a newcomer to the area might notice nothing. There are a few broad, flattened hills, but hills are common to golf courses. The hills of Newark, however, are prehistoric mounds. And the golfer's white ball skims over historical monuments more than 1,000 years old.

The once walled "avenues" from one mound to another extend over some four square miles. Much has been destroyed; only the Great Circle, a walled area 1,200 feet in diameter, with Eagle Mound in its center, has been preserved. One might wonder that the inhabitants of Newark had no compunctions about building a golf course here. But we must remember that for Ohio people a mound is nothing special; they live among them, and several farmers have their homes right on top of them. For as we have said, there are tens of thousands. At only a few of these sites can we recapture the feelings that overcame Squier more than a century ago when he first tramped over these places:

"Here, covered with the gigantic trees of a primitive forest, the work presents a truly grand and impressive appearance; and in entering the ancient avenue for the first time, the visitor does not fail to experience a sensation of awe, such as he might feel in passing the portals of an Egyptian temple, or in gazing upon the silent ruins of Petra of the desert."[1]

Even the Great Serpent Mound, which is probably the most famous of them, does not appear so very impressive when you walk along it or stand in front of it, although it is a curious sight. It is best seen from the lookout tower or

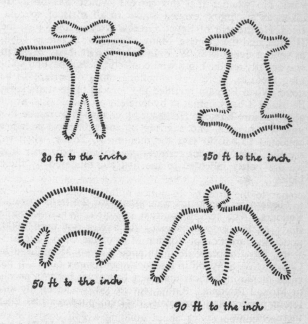

80 ft to the inch

150 ft to the inch

50 ft to the inch

90 ft to the inch

Effigy mounds in Wisconsin. Top left, a mound of 150 feet shaped like a two-headed man. The second figure may represent a frog or a turtle. Above left, is a small bear, 56 feet long, and finally a bird with wings half spread.

a helicopter, for only then can we appreciate the amount of labor that must have gone into its making. And in fact most of the pictures of it are aerial views. Even Squier, who in 1848 had no way of taking aerial photographs, realized what was needed. In his book he presents an amazingly precise drawing of the Great Serpent in bird's-eye perspective, and calls the mound "probably the most extraordinary earthwork thus far discovered in the West."[2]

The Great Serpent is situated in Adams County, Ohio, and throughout its length follows the bends of a small stream, Bush Creek. But it is raised 150 feet above the water level. The head is at the highest point, the mouth opened; the tail twists several times. "The entire length," Squier wrote, "would not be less than one thousand feet" (actually it is 1,330 feet). The average height of the body is about one yard. No wonder that this serpent, which was promptly taken as a symbol, excited Squier to all sorts of speculations. He thought of Egypt, Greece, Assyria, the Celts, the Hindus, and the Chinese. Many years later, as late as 1883, as solid a figure as F. W. Putnam of the Peabody Museum was equally tempted into wild conjectures. But beyond spinning theories, there was something more important to be done. When Putnam revisited the Serpent three years later, he found it badly damaged by amateur archaeologists, probably treasure hunters. He headed a campaign to rescue this unique structure, and a group of energetic Boston ladies collected $5,880 to save the monument. Today, when we see the Great Serpent restored, we should remember that we are partly indebted to the first aid rendered by these ladies.

Modern archaeologists do not care for the term "Mound Builders." The reason for that is simple. When scientific study of the mounds began, which was not until 1900, under the direction of William Mills of the Ohio State Museum, Fay-Cooper Cole in Illinois, Warren Moorehead in Georgia, W. S. Webb in Kentucky, and many others, it became increasingly clear that there had never been "a people of Mound Builders." Rather, several peoples at totally different periods and for totally different purposes had built these mounds.

For example, in the northern Mississippi Valley the mounds are hump-shaped and rarely higher than thirty feet. But almost all of them were burial mounds, full of skeletons. Farther to the south, however, we find mounds that are more like pyramids. These square or rectangular hills, generally flattened at the top, rise from St. Louis to the Gulf of Mexico. Even today we can still discern that a staircase or a ramp led up to them. Why and to what? Undoubtedly to a temple that stood on the top. Thus these hillocks have been called temple mounds.

The mounds created in the shape of animals have proved especially difficult for the archaeologists to classify. We have already described the Great Serpent Mound. Most of those remaining can be seen in Wisconsin, but there are also some in Ohio. They come in the form of eagles, tortoises, bears, foxes, elks, buffaloes, even people, and so far as I know such earthworks are unique in the world.

The archaeologists call these "effigy mounds." The remarkable feature of these mounds, most of them animal forms, is their tremendous proportions, so that the shapes cannot be grasped at eye level.

Once again the greatest difficulty facing the archaeologists was the matter of dating. For in the case of the mounds, tree-ring dating proved relatively unsuccessful. In 1937 Dr. Florence Ellis, a pupil of Dr. Douglass, came to the central Mississippi Valley and spent four years trying

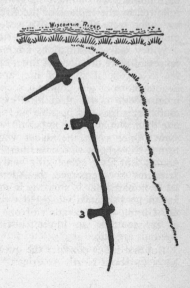

A typical effigy mound group, the Lower Dells Group in Sauk County, Wis. The lowest of the three birds had a wingspread of 240 feet. The most amazing thing about all these earthworks is their intellectual concept, for the whole creation could be properly seen only from the air—which the creators could never achieve.

to find suitable specimens for her dating method. Years later Robert E. Bell worked on the same problem in Kincaid, Illinois. He was able to collect 500 samples of wood, but only twenty of these in the end proved suitable for analysis. The results were, naturally, rather sparse.[3] The climate of the woodlands and river valleys of the East differed too greatly from that of the bone-dry Southwest. Fire or the dampness of the ground had left few wooden structures intact. In addition, the fluctuations in the weather over the centuries had been so small that the tree rings showed few differences. Hence it was hardly possible to obtain an "overlapping" (see Chapter 9).

Here is a general survey of the chronological conclusions the archaeologists have arrived at, according to Gordon R. Willey.[4]

1000–300 B.C.	Burial Mound Period I
300 B.C.–A.D. 700	Burial Mound Period II
A.D. 700–1200	Temple Mound Period I
A.D. 1200–1700	Temple Mound Period II

Of course there were human beings before the Mound Builders in these vast spaces. The so-called Paleo-Indians, pure nomads who hunted big game 10,000 years ago, were followed by the Indians of the Archaic Period, up to 1000 B.C., who were already partly sedentary. But we will have more to say about these early periods later on.

Willey makes distinctions among these "periods," which represent mere divisions of time, the "traditions," which refer to a general style of life, and the "cultures," which denote more or less coherent social groups that developed independent modes of cultural expression. Actually, many more categories are possible and some are current; but to cite them would only hamper our effort to obtain a general view. (Once again, the reader who wants more detail may turn to Silverberg, who omits hardly a single scientific viewpoint.) But after painstaking analysis of the minutiae, two "cultures" soon emerged, the Adena and the Hopewell. The latter in particular is amazing in many respects. And amazing things happened while Hopewell culture was being dug up. During the excavation of one Hopewell burial mound an archaeologist was himself buried.

But first let us consider the question everyone asks when he hears about North American "pyramids": Which is the biggest? There is no one simple answer to that, since it depends on whether by "biggest" we are referring to height or the size of the base or the whole area, which frequently includes earthen walls and subsidiary mounds.

Usually, the Cahokia Mound, which is in Illinois, is called the biggest. It is sometimes referred to as Monk Mound because Trappist monks once grew vegetables on one of its terraces. This flattened pyramid is over 100 feet in height, 1,080 feet long and 710 feet wide. The largest Egyptian pyramid, that of Pharaoh Cheops at Gizeh, is 480 feet high; the four regular sides are each 756 feet long. This would mean that the base of the American pyramid is nearly 200,000 square feet *larger than the biggest Egyptian pyramid!* But there is also the group around the American pyramid to consider. The Cahokia Mound was once the center of more than a hundred smaller, likewise flat-topped mounds, and within an area of seven miles around it there are another three hundred!

The Miamisburg Mound near the city of the same name in Ohio is still 78 feet high. And the Grave Creek Mound in Moundsville, Ohio, is still 70 feet high, with a diameter at the base of more than 320 feet.

If we take the size of the outlying structures into our reckoning, the long avenues that often connected groups of mounds, or the enclosures of earth built for defensive purposes, once topped by long rows of palisades, comparisons of size become virtually impossible.

One of the most interesting burial mounds was Seip Mound in Ross County, Ohio, named after the Seip brothers, who were the "owners." (Somehow one puts this word in quotation marks. It would go equally against the grain to say that a certain Mohammed was the "owner" of the pyramid of Cheops, or a Mr. DuBois owns the cathedral at Chartres.) This mound is a good 30 feet high, 250 feet long and almost 150 feet wide. It is composed of a mass of earth that has been estimated at no less than 20,000 cubic yards. It was here that an archaeologist found an astonishing treasure—and buried himself.

Henry Clyde Shetrone worked at the Seip Mound for three summers, from 1926 to 1928. He reports his accident casually, with a scientist's modesty: "It may interest the reader to know that in the exploration of the mound a serious accident occurred."[5] He had dug a probe trench into the mound, producing a wall thirty feet high. When he started to measure and photograph it, the upper part began to sway; a tremendous mass of earth toppled down, burying him. His helpers were numbed by shock for a moment, then rushed to the spot with picks and shovels. When they dug Shetrone out, he seemed dead but was only unconscious. After he came to, they took him to the nearest hospital, where he was found to have several broken bones. But he had come out of it alive and "made a complete recovery."

This mound held not only ninety-nine skeletons, but also an amazing quantity of treasure. Shetrone relates:

"The most striking feature of the examination was the finding of an interior sepulcher or vault, constructed of logs and timbers, in which reposed four adult skeletons, placed side by side and extended on their backs, while lying at their heads, transversely, were the skeletons of two infants. Whether or not this was a family tomb or a sepulcher devoted to the 'royalty' of the community, it is indisputable that the occupants were of the elect. The burials were accompanied by a rich array of artifacts, some of which were unique. There was *thousands of pearls,* from which circumstance newspaper reports at the time designated the interments as the *'great pearl burial.'* Implements and ornaments of copper, mica, tortoiseshell, and silver were found in profusion."[6]

This hoard of pearls strikes a strange note. They were, however, river pearls of various sizes. The tourist or museum visitor will always ask their value. Questions of value are difficult to answer. What value can be placed on a copper axe weighing no fewer than twenty-eight pounds, which was found at the same site—undoubtedly a religious object intended for a chief or a medicine man? Such items rightly go to museums, do not find their way into commerce, and hence are not placed on price lists. But pearls can be compared with the marketable variety, and Professor Frank C. Hibben of the University of New Mexico has ventured to give an estimate. By modern standards, he says, those pearls are worth $2,000,000 or more.[7]

But to return to the two "cultures" that today are recognized as the most impressive: the Adena and Hopewell cultures. Almost at once controversies over their dating flared up among the scholars. It was agreed relatively quickly that the Adena culture was the earlier, simply because the Hopewell culture displayed refinements in certain arts that the Adena people had only adumbrated. At first the Adena

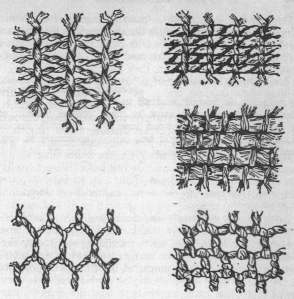

Textiles of the Hopewell Mound Builders, before
A.D. *500.*

people were thought to have been contemporaries of the
pueblo builders, but a number of scholars insisted that they
were considerably older, although a few crackpots would
have it that they had been a mythic primeval race or direct
descendants of the Welsh Prince Madoc, who is supposed
to have sailed to America in the twelfth century. (There
were a good many other such poetic tales that attached
themselves to the Mound Builders.) But even by the end
of the thirties the scientific discussion "ended in nothing
but a succession of frustrating estimates and furious de-
bates," as Frederick Johnson remarks.[8]

This situation changed abruptly when Libby came to the
rescue with his radiocarbon dating. Or rather, he first confused the issues more than he clarified them. The first few
measurements, interpreted much too hastily, seemed to indicate that the previous verdict of the archaeologists must
be turned upside down, that is, that Hopewell should be

placed *earlier* than Adena. Instead of going into details here, and in the interest of being cautious, as the scholars themselves must be cautious, we quote Frederick Johnson of the Peabody Foundation once more. His preliminary conclusion in 1967 runs:

". . . the total number of dates available is inadequate to date these cultures which, in various forms, were distributed over most of eastern North America and represent more than 1000 or 1500 years of cultural development and degeneration. Assignment of the figures to one culture or another varies, depending on details of classification by several authors, who do not always agree concerning assignment of traits to one culture or the other. Very broadly, however, *Adena ranges from about 500 to 900* A.D., and *Hopewell, especially in the north, existed from about 900 to 1150* A.D."[9]

Today, there is scarcely any doubt that Adena came before Hopewell. But we are still far from being able to give a date for the building of every mound—as we can so frequently tell the date to the year in the case of the Southwestern pueblos. What is more, we have many theories but as yet no certainty about where the *round-headed* (a term used by physical anthropologists to describe races of people) Adena people came from and why and where they went to when one day they left the area, above all, the Ohio Valley. And the long-headed Hopewell people remain equally enigmatic. The "where from" and "where to" are still the subject of much scientific discussion. Nevertheless, from the vast quantities of artifacts found in the mounds we are able to draw up a fairly accurate picture of both cultures.

The Adena Mounds near Chillicothe are named after the estate of a former governor of Ohio, Thomas Worthington. William C. Mills dug there in 1901, discovering among other things the famous "Adena pipe" in the form of a human figure, and gave the culture its name. But as late as 1930 Shetrone could give only two pages in his great book to this culture, with five more brief mentions, so little was known about it as yet. Two years later, however, Emerson F. Greenman identified seventy Adena Mounds, and thirteen years later, in 1945, William S. Webb and Charles E. Snow were able to publish their substantial report, *The Adena People.*[10] Webb, incidentally, headed the archaeological salvage work that had become necessary when the building of big dams threatened to flood the ruins. Webb and Snow identified another 103 Adena structures; by 1957 the number had risen to 222!

WILLIAM CULLEN BRYANT
(1794–1878)

Poet, journalist, and reluctant lawyer, he published his first book of verse at the age of fourteen. Though he sounds extremely puritanical today, he was highly esteemed in his time. The mounds inspired his muse more than once. The following verses are part of the poem "The Prairies," published in *Poems*, 1832.

As o'er the verdant waste I guide my steed,
Among the high rank grass that sweeps his sides,
The hollow beating of his footsteps seems
A sacrilegious sound. I think of those
Upon whose rest he tramples. Are they here—
The dead of other days? and did the dust
Of these fair solitudes once stir with life
And burn with passion? Let the mighty mounds
That overlook the rivers, or that rise
In the dim forest crowded with old oaks,
Answer. A race that long has passed away
Built them; a disciplined and populous race
Heaped, with long toil, the earth while yet the Greek
Was hewing the Pentelicus to forms
Of symmetry and rearing on its rock
The glittering Parthenon.

The Adena people were the first in eastern America to unite the three important elements that make a culture possible: the cultivation of maize, the production of pottery, and organized community work. Did the idea of building mounds come from Mexico? Perhaps, but the point cannot be proved. Adena Mounds were burial mounds, whereas the Mexican peoples had built chiefly temple mounds. Obviously Adena culture had a social hierarchy; one can easily tell the graves of distinguished persons from those of no special rank. The bodies of the latter were usually cremated. Something very curious was discovered on some of the skeletons. We quote Willey:

"Bodies were placed on their backs in an extended possition, apparently when the body was still in the flesh or, at least, in an articulated condition. Many bones have been recovered *stained with red ocher*. Either the skeleton was

*Map of the most important Adena and Hopewell mounds,
built between 800 B.C. and A.D. 500. By 1957, 222 Adena
mounds had been identified; there are thousands of both
types.*

stripped of flesh before the red pigment was poured over it,
or there was a period of exposure to decay after which the
ocher was applied to the bones. The latter possibility would
mean that some time elapsed between the time the body
was placed in the tomb and the tomb was sealed."[11]

All this suggests an extraordinary amount of labor. Another curious factor is that these people lived in very small
village communities of rarely more than five houses. If we
accept the estimate that thousands of Indians had to labor
for at least five years to build some of the larger mounds,
the problem of organization is perplexing. How were so
many people assembled and how were they provisioned?
Yet they also had time for producing all sorts of artifacts,
especially ornaments. Small stone or clay tablets, of a size
that can be conveniently held in the hand and little more
than half an inch thick, engraved with fantastic patterns,
sometimes stylized birds, sometimes pure abstract ornamentation, have prompted a good deal of guesswork on the

part of the archaeologists. The only reasonable explanation so far suggested is that these were printing blocks for Adena "textiles."

Whatever the Adena people possessed can be found in finer form in Hopewell culture. The name derives from the property of a Captain Hopewell, on whose farm there were more than thirty mounds. In the general eagerness to present some evidence of American antiquity at the Chicago World's Fair of 1893, Warren K. Moorehead dug at Hopewell's farm, and brought the choicest of his findings to the fair. Thus the name became fixed.

The long-headed Hopewells poured into the territory of the Adena people. Did they overpower them? Drive them away? Mingle with them? Did they take over their predecessors' burial rituals or bring their own ideas with them? So many questions, so few answers. In four paragraphs Silverberg sums up what we know today about their methods of burial:

A carved stone pipe from an Adena mound. The bowl of the pipe is between the figure's feet, the mouthpiece in the head.

Mother and child— a sculpture from a Hopewell burial mound in Illinois.

"The Hopewell Mounds are the most visible evidence of the complex cult of the dead that these people observed. Here the sacred rites and ceremonies were performed; here the tribal notables were laid to rest with what must have been remarkable pomp and circumstance. Some three fourths of the Hopewell dead were cremated; tomb burial in the flesh was seemingly the privilege only of a high caste.

"The Hopewell funeral activities centered about mortuary houses built on specially prepared sites. First of all trees and underbrush were cleared from the area where the mound was to rise; loose topsoil was removed, and the subsurface usually was plastered with tough clay. Next, a layer of sand or fine gravel an inch or more in depth was strewn over the clay floor, and on this was erected a large wooden structure. The walls of these mortuary houses consisted of rows of single palisades. Some of the buildings were so big that they probably did not have roofs, but were stockades open to the sky; smaller, roofed apartments were often arranged around the inside of the main wall.

"Burials of several kinds took place in the same mortuary house. Cremations were carried out in rectangular clay-lined crematory pits dug in the prepared floor; the bodies had first been stripped of flesh through exposure and decay or by cleaning. After the burning, ashes and bone fragments were gathered up and placed in log crypts on platforms near the crematory pits, or else were left in the pits themselves.

"In an adjoining chamber, burials in the flesh were prepared. A rectangular tomb of log cribbing was built up on a low clay platform on the floor of the mortuary house; the dead lay within, extended full length, surrounded by grave goods that had been ceremonially 'killed,' or broken, presumably to liberate their spirits so that they could accompany the deceased into the afterworld. These log tombs were similar to those of the Adena folk; the chief difference between Adena and Hopewell burials lies not in the preparation of the tombs but in the greater richness and quality of the Hopewell accompanying grave goods."[12]

That is a sober, objective description. There must surely have been elaborate ceremonies accompanying these funerals. For these we must call our imagination into play. But what pictures can we conjure up? The colors are faded, the cries and incantations stilled; no account has come down to us of the rituals the medicine men performed upon those mounds 1,500 years ago.

The individuality of this culture seems to have crystallized in Illinois first of all. From there it spread to Ohio and Indiana, to Michigan, Wisconsin, Iowa, and Missouri —all this during the first centuries of the Christian era.

What particularly distinguishes the Hopewell people is their fondness for ornament. They actually adorned their whole bodies from head to foot; often they even affixed copper noses to their skeletons. To obtain rare materials they set up a procurement network over the whole of eastern America and westward as far as the Rocky Mountains. To what extent they engaged in "trade" we have no way of knowing. They obtained copper from Lake Superior, shells, alligator and shark teeth from the Gulf of Mexico. From the far west they imported obsidian, the black volcanic glass from which they made their cult knives. From the Rocky Mountains they imported the teeth and claws of the dangerous grizzly bears. Other shells came from the Atlantic Coast, and glittering disks of mica from the Carolinas.

Their most prized ornaments were the softly gleaming river pearls. These have been found not only in Seip Mound. Rare though they were, they have been found *by the gallon* in other graves of notables. Single strings of pearls are today valued at several thousand dollars—truly royal ornaments, especially since some skeletons were decked with not one but many strings.

They scarcely used gold and silver; their metal was copper, which they pounded and hammered into tools, ornaments, and a kind of armor plate. But it must be noted that they were *not* familiar with the process of smelting and hence of pouring metal; at best they could temper metal by the process called "annealing." Such is the accepted archaeological view. In total defiance of it, the engineer Arlington H. Mallery arrived at a fantastic theory, which he presented in book form in 1951. We may gather its essence from the subtitle of this work: "The Story of Iron-Age Civilization prior to Columbus."[13] In the space of 238 pages, Mallery seemingly proved irrefutably, on the basis of innumerable pictures, radiocarbon dates, microscopic and metallurgical analyses, that North America had had an iron age. At first glance the wealth of "evidence" was so arresting that no less an authority than Matthew W. Sterling, director of the Bureau of American Ethnology of the Smith-

Hopewell warrior, with necklace of disc shell beads with halves of human mandible as pendants, a spearhead and small rings of shell, and hawk claws. The other objects and dress elements are taken from warrior statuettes or are hypothetical, as is the arrangement of hawk's claws and shell rings on the breechcloth. Reconstruction from the principal skeleton (No. 4), Long Tomb 2, Whitnah Mound 54.

sonian Institution, contributed a preface to the book. In it he wrote:

"It will be difficult to convince American archaeologists that there was a pre-Columbian iron age in America. This startling item, however, is one that should not long remain in doubt. The detailed studies of metallurgists and the new Carbon 14 dating method should be sufficient to give a definite answer on this point."

This is hard to account for. Haury comments: "Sterling, I'm sure, took the position in writing the introduction for the book that he was not endorsing the content, but rather it was a recognition of the fact that out of the minds of men like Mallery a new and challenging idea may be spawned." On the book itself he remarks tersely: "Mallery's book, of course, is sheer nonsense, as you point out."[14]

What did Hopewell man look like? Thanks to the particularly fine labors of Thorne Deuel, director of the Illinois State Museum, we now have many reconstructions, based chiefly on diggings in Illinois. Deuel has provided answers to museum visitors' questions not by presenting an imaginary Hopewell man, but men and women within a wide variety of "social occasions." He has even been able to reconstruct hair styles.[15] We present a few pictures, which are more vivid than words. The most splendiferous person in Hopewell times was undoubtedly the Ohio warrior. It would seem that army officers the world over show peacock-like tendencies. The Hopewell warrior wore his breastplates of hammered copper like armor. A helmet, often supplemented with horns or other ornaments, adorned his proud head. Thin layers of mica refracted the sunlight. Like the rest of his people, he must also have worn earrings, bracelets, and necklaces, and he certainly had a pipe about his person, often carved with remarkable artistry in the form of a rabbit, a squirrel, or a duck. One that is exceptionally beautiful shows a duck sitting on the back of a fish. Pipe production was not only highly artistic but also on a large scale; in the Trapper Mound in Ohio alone 136 pipes carved out of stone were found.

And yet they vanished, this people who perhaps had come closer than the Pueblo tribes to the threshold of a high culture within a relatively short span of time. They must have had a strongly developed hierarchic structure with a ruling class holding considerable spiritual and secular power, such as the Pueblos never had. (The latter, as we have noted before, possessed a markedly democratic and above all peace-loving social structure.) There is even one rather bold theory that argues for a hereditary monarchy among the Hopewell people, on the basis of a single anthropological point. Silverberg puts it this way: "It has recently been found that many of the Ohio Hopewell skulls found in the richest burial deposits show bony growth known as exostoses along the inner ear canals. This is an extremely rare human trait, and it is genetically transmitted; so the supposition is that the Hopewell chieftains whose graves these are belonged to the same family—a hereditary aristocracy, in essence."[16]

In any case, a new people stepped upon the stage of history. And once more they were Mound Builders. But they did not begin at once to build beside and among the works of their predecessors, as the Hopewells had done when they invaded the Adena people's Ohio valley. Instead, they erected their structures farther to the south along the

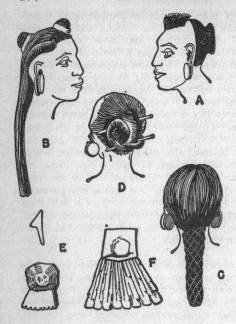

Male (A) and fe-
male (B) hairdo of
Hopewell people. C
shows the hairdo of
a nursing mother,
E and F are bustles,
Indian forerunners
of a cul-de-Paris,
made from turkey
tail feathers.

mighty highway of the Mississippi. They started in the delta and gradually conquered the more northerly provinces.

We call this people the Temple Mound Builders. For their structures were no longer primarily burial mounds but often tremendous bases for temples. They built flat-topped pyramids meant as thrones of the gods. Visible from a great distance, these resemble more the Mesopotamian ziggurats than the Egyptian royal tombs. For the Egyptian pyramids were tombs for a single pharaoh, something we constantly tend to forget because of their enormous size. Perhaps the temple mounds bear comparison with the Mexican and Central American temple pyramids of the Aztecs and Mayas, though they are built of earth rather than stone. Although Central American influences upon the Adena and Hopewell cultures remain debatable and were certainly limited, in the case of the Temple Mound Builders they are patent. The function of the mounds is the same. And exactly as in Mexico, the mounds are scarcely ever single;

they always appear in groups of sometimes as many as forty mounds, constituting ceremonial centers with large areas for processions or assemblies in the middle. And there is another similarity; they were not conceived from the first by an architect to be of a certain shape and size. Rather, they grew up layer by layer; as many as a dozen such layers have been counted. How long did the building take? Did the builders operate, like the Mayas, by a fifty-two-year calendar? Did they have a calendar at all? What was the origin of the impulse? Who gave the order to heap up a new layer, to embark on more years of toil?

Ramps or stairways led to the top, to the temple. Sometimes the inclines were so steep that, as a traveler in 1790 remarked, cattle could not have been driven up them. Unfortunately, none of these temples has been preserved, for they were made of wood and have long since disappeared. There are indications, however, that the priests kept a sacred flame in the temples, to which the people bowed down and where perhaps human sacrifices were offered, as in Mexico.

These mounds were seldom used for burials; normally burial took place in cemeteries around the ceremonial centers. It was in these that archaeologists have made the finds that prove this people's high degree of craft and artistic talent, in no way inferior to that of the Hopewells. They

Skull of a Hopewell man, adorned with a copper helmet imitating antlers. Along with the helmet were found strings of river pearls and copper breastplates.

also indicate to what a great degree religious feelings determined their lives and thought. They also incised their drawings in copper, shells, and stone, scratched or pressed them into their pottery. But their subjects are far more than the expression of a pure impulse to ornamentation; most of the motifs are religious, perhaps allusions to grim ceremonies. For we can see not only priests decked out extravagantly in feathers, but also lopped-off hands, human skulls, arms with bones protruding from them, and human hearts. All this, as well as the innumerable vessels, implements, and knives whose purpose was evidently purely ceremonial, has prompted archaeologists to speak of a highly developed cult of the dead that must have obsessed the Temple Mound Builders. We owe the first clear development of this idea to A. J. Waring, Jr., and Preston Holder, followed by James A. Ford and Gordon R. Willey.[17]

Although the first descriptions of the Temple Mounds come from the Spanish, and although by the end of the eighteenth century there were further accounts of them by travelers from the north, they did not receive serious attention nearly as early as the mounds in Ohio and Illinois. Strictly speaking, their scientific study did not really begin until the excavation of the Ocmulgee Group, east of Macon, Georgia, from 1933 on. This dig lasted for eight years. In 1938 its first director, A. R. Kelly, published a preliminary description.[18] He was able to demonstrate no less than six successive occupations of this site. The first primitive, undecorated pottery appears between 2000 and 1500 B.C., while the first real temple site comprised three large and four small mounds.

There is a longer history behind the excavation of the Etowah Group in the vicinity of Cartersville in northern Georgia. When the Spaniards saw it, the group of mounds was almost leveled and overgrown with vegetation. In 1819 the Reverend Elias Cornelius wrote a good account of it. Archaeological investigations began in 1871, although they were in no way comparable to the systematic work in Ocmulgee fifty years later. Cyrus Thomas worked on the Etowah Group, followed by W. H. Holmes of the Bureau of Ethnology in 1890. From 1925 on, the aged, magnificent veteran of mound research, Warren K. Moorehead, spent three winters there; thirty-four years previously he had excavated the *original* Hopewell Mound. It was Moorehead who, after numerous finds, came out strongly for the theory that the Temple Mound Builders had not been merely influenced by Mexico; rather, they had immigrated from there. So far this theory remains unproved.

One day the culture came to an end. Around A.D. 1500 the cult of the dead seems to have assumed extreme and possibly barbarous forms. Perhaps the arrogance of the priests led to a rebellion of the oppressed masses; perhaps there were warlike thrusts from outside; perhaps an epidemic struck the people. Perhaps—but once again we do not know why this culture perished. In any case, by the time the first white men arrived, the great period of the Temple Builders was past. But here and there old rituals were preserved for a while among the tribes of the Chocktaws, Chickasaws, Creeks, and Natchez. By this time we have written records. We must include some observations about these tribes and their social structure, first, because that structure is totally unique among the North American Indians between the two oceans and, second, because the ways of these tribes may well be a direct link to the traditions of the last of the Temple Mound Builders.

We have excellent accounts concerning the Natchez from Frenchmen who lived among them from 1698 to 1732 in the seven small villages along St. Catherine Creek, near the present city of Natchez, Mississippi. The center for the group was Emerald Mound, more than thirty-five feet high;

A shell gorget from a Missouri mound, 4½ inches in diameter. A warrior or priest is forcing another person to the ground. The symbolism of the objects held in the standing figure's mouth and hand is not clear.

but in addition every village had its own mound and—this is highly unusual—a special residential mound for the chief.

The Natchez people lived in a four-class society under an *absolute monarchy*. The ruler was called the Great Sun and enjoyed divine honors. He was too exalted even to touch another member of his tribe; if he wanted to hand someone something, he kicked the thing away from him. He was also too fine ever to walk even the shortest distance. Splendid in his royal crown of swan's feathers, he was always carried in a litter. Should he after all have to set foot on the ground, mats were spread before him. He had unlimited power over his subjects and ruled them despotically.

The members of the highest class were also called Suns and enjoyed aristocratic privileges as the king's sole confidants. The next class were the Nobles. Below them stood the larger group of Honored Men. Then came the common people.

And probably nowhere in the world except India, with its Untouchables, has a ruling class so frankly proclaimed its contempt for the laboring folk as among the Natchez. The people were simply called "the Stinkers" or "Stinkards." Stinkers were completely at the mercy of the higher classes.

We must interject here that class society has been the mark of every high culture in the history of mankind. Only since Rousseau and Marx has it been argued that this need not *necessarily* be the case. Thus we should hardly be surprised that the first comprehensive *Archaeology of the United States,* written in 1856, stated with disarming simplicity that the Natchez "were the most civilized of the North American aborigines."[19]

Whether or not this is true, the Natchez social order had one remarkable feature that set it totally apart from all the feudal orders of Europe: it provided for a systematic mingling of blood among the classes. Thus every Great Sun was by tradition forced to marry a Stinker. Royal hereditary succession did not exist; a son of the Great Sun could never himself become Great Sun, but fell to the rank of a Noble. The children of these Nobles were in their turn obliged to marry Stinkers. If a Noblewoman married a Stinker, the children became Nobles; but if the father was a Nobleman who married a Stinker woman, the children slid one class lower, becoming Honored Men. If a female Sun married a Stinker, which was possible, the husband

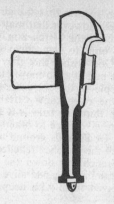

Unusually fine example of a polished stone axe (after A.D. 1200) from Moundsville, Ala.

had fewer rights than a European prince consort. He was not permitted to eat with his wife and had always to stand in her presence like any other Stinker, for that was what he remained. And if his wife decided that he no longer pleased her, she could have him killed and take another Stinker for her husband.

All of this of course added up to an extremely complicated social order, but the Indians obviously mastered its intricacies. The basic characteristic of this social structure was that the men ruled, but that rank was determined solely by descent from the woman. The female Sun also chose the new Great Sun.

There is much dispute as to what extent, if at all, this social order devolves from that of the earlier Temple Mound Builders. I myself regard it as an extreme development of the late period; it does not seem likely that such an order could have been sustained for approximately a thousand years. But this does not exclude the possibility that the early Temple Builder societies might have been monarchies.

The first careful observers, the French, had already noticed the "natural" decline of the Natchez. This was, they thought, the will of God, but they did not overlook the devastating effects of diseases like smallpox and measles, imported by the whites, that proved fatal to the Indians. With the Natchez, as with other Indian peoples, it is impossible to find a single explanation for their decline. One observer even reports that the girls and women employed contraceptives. However that may be, a certain de la Vente, who lived among the Natchez in 1704, writes:

"I cannot omit to remark to you, it is that it appears visibly that God wishes that they yield their place to new peoples." He puts it even more plainly: "What is certain is that our people in the six years in which they have been descending the river know certainly that the number has diminished a third, so true is it that it seems God wishes to make them give place to others."[20]

Evidently God's mills ground too slowly for the Frenchmen. In 1729 the Natchez rebelled against French exploitation. The French put down the uprising so bloodily that only a few families escaped alive to other tribes, who, so it is said, received them with deep respect and treated them very well.

Thus ended the last of the Mound Builders, the constructors of North America's pyramids. If they were indeed descendants of the first Burial Mound Builders, they had had a continuous history of over 2,700 years. These were the people who ever since the days of Jefferson have been a stimulus to the imagination and a riddle to science.

17

The American Goliath

In this chapter we shall conclude the portion of our book that deals with North American "cultures," and move on to an older world, a totally different one, in whose existence most anthropologists and archaeologists did not believe until 1926.

Whatever the word "culture" in reference to prehistoric peoples is taken to mean, it is certainly valid to speak of a Basket Maker culture, a culture of the Pueblo peoples, of the Hohokam, of the various groups of Mound Builders. For we must conceive of all these peoples as living in differentiated societies based upon the domestication of maize. These all present an enormous contrast to the life of the roaming hunters who inhabited the continent thousands of years earlier, small groups struggling for sheer survival, battling with prehistoric animals, the mighty woolly mammoth, the bison, and the giant sloth.

Fossils of these ancient animals were found in abundance, but for a long time it was assumed that no traces of man's activity would ever turn up in conjunction with them. Only in the Old World, the premise was, had man been so ancient a resident.

In this book we have laid considerable stress on the wrong paths science has taken, as well as the right ones, to illustrate the point that science is in the most literal sense a quest for knowledge. In the same spirit, therefore, we shall tell "the True, Moral and Diverting Tale" of the Cardiff Giant, also known as the American Goliath. The story has its humorous aspects, for it is concerned with a gigantic hoax; but inasmuch as it happened in America the hoax was on a larger scale than elsewhere, and the forged fossil involved was also larger than life. The episode is also evidence of how little science knew about human fossils a century ago.[1]

The story opens in 1866, and oddly enough begins as a theological dispute between a tobacco farmer and a minister in a small town in Iowa. The Reverend Turk obstinately insisted that there were giants in the old days, for so it stood in the Bible, and whatever was in the Bible had to be true. George Hull, farmer and cigar manufacturer, regarded both the assertion and the reasoning as sheer nonsense. In present-day terminology we might call the antagonists a Fundamentalist and an agnostic—names unknown to the persons involved. Views such as Hull's were first characterized as agnosticism in 1870 by Thomas Henry Huxley, and Fundamentalism as a conservative religious movement did not really begin to rally significant numbers of followers in the United States until after the First World War.

In any case, the agnostic Hull became so riled at the minister that he decided on a stupendous act of revenge. If Turk believed in giants, Hull would give him one!

Hull took his time. In June, 1868, he and a friend were seen at the gypsum quarries near Fort Dodge, Iowa, where they cut a gigantic block and with extreme care and many security measures carted it away. To inquiries of what it was for, he said either that it was for a Lincoln memorial or that he was bringing it to Washington, where it was to be exhibited as a sample of the "best building stone in the world."

Hull went to an enormous amount of trouble to transport this five-ton block. He broke several wagons just on the forty miles of poor road to the nearest railroad station and caused one bridge to collapse under the weight. There were further difficulties at the railroad station, but Hull succeeded in bringing the block intact to Chicago, where the stonemason Edward Burckhardt went to work on it. The result was a recumbent figure 10 feet 4½ inches long, weighing a mere 2,990 pounds.

Hull then "treated" the sculpture. With a special hammer studded with spikes he pounded "pores" into the huge body. Then he washed the stone in acids to give it the appearance of venerable age and transported it farther by railroad, in an iron-bound chest, and by wagon, by way of Detroit and Syracuse to the small town of Cardiff, south of Syracuse, New York. He took it to the farm of his relative, William C. Newell, who was in on the conspiracy. There the giant was buried. This whole affair, springing from the quarrel with the minister, had so far cost Hull no less than $2,200.

On the morning of October 16, 1869, one year after the "burial," Mr. Newell casually ordered two of his hired hands to dig him a well behind the barn. At a depth of three feet the men came across a human foot, and ran terror-stricken into the house. Within a few hours the whole neighborhood had heard about the find; within a few days thousands, literally thousands, of persons poured into the area to see the giant, which had been carefully unearthed and was now presented to view in all its great size and bleached beauty.

From the very first moment opinions were divided. But by and by the rather vague views of a respected business-man prevailed: "This is not a thing contrived of man, but the face of one who lived on earth, the very image and child of God." Someone else opined that it was a forgotten monument to George Washington. A third suggested that it was a statue put up by the first Jesuits in the country and meant to frighten the Indians. But more and more persons maintained that it was undoubtedly thousands of years old and the fossilized body of a gigantic primitive man, which, of course, was what Hull wanted them to think. Controversy broke out among the learned when James Hall, the respected director of the New York State Museum, declared the giant "the most remarkable object yet brought to light in this country." That was true enough. Two Yale professors categorically sneered: "Humbug!" All this provided a field day for the newspapers. And Hull and Newell found themselves in business overnight. They charged admission fees for the privilege of seeing the "American Goliath." Booths sprang up around the farm, and an extra horse omnibus had to be placed in service from Syracuse to bring all the curiosity seekers. On one day alone there were 3,000 visitors! A man from New York offered $100 for "a very small piece of the giant." Within a few weeks two new restaurants were opened in the area, the Giant Saloon and Goliath House, where three different broadsides were sold, each offering the "only authentic and reliable" descriptions of the giant.

To make a long story short, it cannot be said that American science, young though it was, was altogether deceived by the giant. From the start sharp questions were asked, and after a relatively brief period serious people came to the conclusion that the giant was a giant humbug. But the amazing fact is this: when Hull broke down and revealed the true story, the voices of those who insisted that the giant was a fossilized primitive man were by no means silenced. No less a personage than Oliver Wendell Holmes, the great physician and essayist, bored a hole behind the ear of the gypsum figure and reported that it displayed marvelous anatomical detail. The philosopher Ralph Waldo Emerson announced that the giant was beyond his depth, "very wonderful and undoubtedly ancient." Perhaps neither had heard of Hull's public confession. And the same may be true for the Yale student who wrote a seventeen-page paper arguing that the giant was an ancient image of the Phoenician god Baal. He had even discovered hieroglyphs between the elbow and shoulder, though no one else ever saw these.

The end of the story sounds like something from the commedia dell'arte. Phineas T. Barnum, the great circus tycoon, offered $60,000 for the gypsum giant. After some spirited bidding, another impresario won the contest. He brought the giant to New York and exhibited it on Broadway—only to discover, a few days later, that the clever Barnum had the effrontery to present in Wood's Museum, a few blocks away, an exact copy of the giant, a forgery of the forgery, which he shamelessly billed as "the original of all Cardiff Giants." Naturally, the owner of the first figure tried to sue. But the outraged public now turned against both giants; the pavements of New York became too hot for the exhibitors, and the "genuine" giant began his travels. He was put on show until interest faded. Then he was forgotten for decades, "dug up" once more for a movie, *The Mighty Barnum* (1934), and finally found a well-deserved rest in the Farmer's Museum in Cooperstown, New York.

Anyone seeing him resting there (a few years ago a tractor and ten men were needed to move him into another room) may have his laugh. At this date the "giant" seems an appealing, rather touching figure who could not possibly deceive anybody. But at the time he was fashioned, scientific study of fossils was only about thirty years old in Europe and had few practitioners in America.

It is not surprising, therefore, that there could be still other cases of this sort—not such colorful ones, but interesting enough to merit reporting. One was the case of the Calaveras Skull, of which a daily newspaper in 1866 wrote as follows:

"A human skull has been found in California, in the Pliocene formation. This skull is the remnant not only of the earliest pioneer of this state, but *the earliest known human being*. . . . The skull was found in a shaft 150 feet deep, two miles from Angels in Calaveras County, by a miner named James Watson, who gave it to Mr. Scribner, a merchant, who gave it to Dr. Jones, who sent it to the State Geological Survey. . . .

The published volume of the State Survey of the Geology of California states that man existed here contemporaneously with the mastodon, but *this fossil proves that he was here before the mastodon was known to exist.*"

In fact, Professor Josiah D. Whitney of the State Geological Survey confirmed this view in 1880. As he reported—but he examined the circumstances of the find as a geologist and not as an archaeologist—the skull had unquestionably been located in geological strata of the last epoch of the Tertiary, the Pliocene, hence was older than the Ice Ages, several millions of years old. If that were true, man had been present in America earlier than in Asia, Africa, or Europe! Interestingly enough, it was not a scientist but a writer who scoffed a bit at this theory, namely, Bret Harte, then already world-famous as a master of the short story.

In 1907, some years after these lines were written, the anthropologist Aleš Hrdlička, who was equipped with far more knowledge than his predecessors, published the truth about the Calaveras man. It could only have been a prank; someone had planted this skull in a geological stratum from which it could not possibly have originated.[2]

The European world of scholarship can ill afford to smile at the backwardness of American science because of such an incident. There was, after all, the scandal of the Piltdown skull, which took place much later, in our own century, when the science of anthropology was already well advanced. Yet that fraud was not exposed until 1953. In 1908

BRET HARTE (1836–1902)

SPEAK, O man, less recent! Fragmentary fossil!
Primal pioneer of pliocene formation,
Hid in lowest drifts below the earliest stratum
    Of volcanic tufa!

Older than the beasts, the oldest Palaeotherium;
Older than the trees, the oldest Cryptogami;
Older than the hills, those infantile eruptions
    Of earth's epidermis!

Eo—Mio—Plio—whatsoe'er the "cene" was
That those vacant sockets filled with awe and wonder,—
Whether shores Devonian or Silurian beaches,—
    Tell us thy strange story!

Or has the professor slightly antedated
By some thousand years thy advent on this planet,
Giving thee an air that's somewhat better fitted
    For cold-blooded creature?

—"To the Pliocene Skull"
(A Geological Address)

The poem has eight more stanzas; it is quoted here from the edition of 1899. It appeared in the section entitled "Parodies" in the volume *Poems and Two Men of Sandy Bar*

the lawyer Charles Dawson found fragments of a skull in Hastings, England, and fitted the pieces together. His reconstruction caused a tremendous sensation; for almost five decades virtually all important European anthropologists were at loggerheads over it. For the skull represented a species that did not fit at all into the theory of evolution. Nor could it have. In 1953 chemical tests proved that the skull had been contrived with extraordinary cleverness out of two skulls! The cranium was old, but the jawbone came from a modern orangutan. Even the British House of Commons discussed this Piltdown scandal. The mystery of who constructed this ingenious forgery has never been solved.

But to return to America. Every so often there were a few small, enigmatic finds, on the basis of which scientists went on hoping that the New World, too, would yield traces of a human being who could be regarded as the "ancestor" of America's oldest known inhabitants—those peoples who in the first millennium B.C. suddenly appeared on the scene as organized societies. The general opinion was, however, that the "first American" could scarcely have lived earlier than 3,000 or 4,000 years ago. Back in 1810 Baron Cuvier, the great French zoologist and paleontologist, had declared categorically: "Fossil man does not exist!" He was speaking of Europe. And just as categorically American scientists of repute declared even as late as the 1920's: an American Ice Age man does not exist. They were wrong. But if man had existed in Ice Age America, where were his traces?

The first answer came via a black cowboy. And his discovery leads us into the really *pre*historic age, the strange, wild world of the Early Hunters.

Book Five

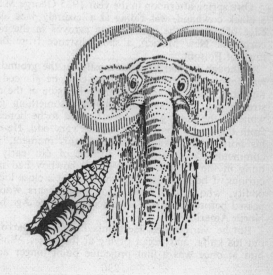

18

Folsom Man

ONE spring afternoon in the year 1925 George McJunkin, a black cowhand, was riding at a leisurely pace along the edge of one of the innumerable arroyos in the northeast corner of New Mexico, a short distance from the small town of Folsom.

Although he had his eyes mostly on the ground, for he was following the track of a lost cow, he glanced around now and then, and across to the other side of the dried-up stream bed. And suddenly he saw something glittering white in the blazing sun, what seemed to be bones jutting from the bank. That struck him as very odd. He drew up his horse and looked harder. "At this moment," Hibben comments, "a considerable portion of our early history hung in the balance."[1] For if this cowboy had not been curious, if he had not dismounted to get a close look at the oddity, who knows how many more years would have passed before there was any proof of an Ice Age hunter in North America?

But he *was* curious. He climbed across the arroyo, took out his knife, and began prying at the bones. What struck him at once was a flint projectile point longer and more

290

carefully worked than any he had ever seen before. And he was familiar enough with Indian arrowheads, for there were many of them lying around in this country. Once he had scraped a whole bone clear, he realized that he had never seen such a bone either. In shape it was rather like a cattle bone but could not have been one, for it was much more massive than the bones of any cattle. Did the cowboy at once see some connection between the flint point and the bleached bone? Certainly he had no inkling that he had just made the most important discovery in the field of North American prehistory. He used his knife a while longer, dislodged a few more pieces of bone, which he pocketed, then went on with his hunt for the lost cow, and finally rode home, for the sun was going down.

How word of his find got around is obscure. In any case, that same summer J. D. Figgins, director of the Colorado Museum of Natural History in Denver, heard about it. Pieces of the bone were sent to him, and he was able to identify them. The cowboy had been right to think them unusual. They belonged to a bison that had become extinct about 10,000 years ago—an animal which, unlike the buffaloes hunted by Buffalo Bill, had long horns and was considerably larger: the *Bison taylori* or, as zoologists now prefer to call it, the *Bison antiquus figginsi*.

Was it true that a flint projectile point had been found with this bone, really cheek by jowl, in the *same* stratum? The possibilities were so exciting that by the summer of 1926 the museum had organized the first systematic excavation of the site, with Figgins directing. Two points were found, and near them, close to the bones of *Bison antiquus*, a broken point. Was that proof enough? Not for the skeptics. Not yet.

Elated, Figgins went to several museums with his finds to show them to experts. He was soon sadder and wiser. The old warning was invoked: the weapons and the bones might have been brought together in the same stratum by outside influences. Only the scientists at the American Museum of Natural History encouraged Figgins to go on digging, which he did. And in the summer of 1927 he had more luck than before. He found *proof* that the weapon and the skeleton of the extinct animal belonged together. This time he left the projectile point in place, without moving it a fraction of an inch—*in situ*, as the archaeologists call it—and invited his colleagues to see for themselves.

And they came in droves; nobody wanted to miss this extraordinary discovery. Among them was Frank H. H. Roberts, Jr., the noted anthropologist. He happened to be at the annual Pecos Conference with Kidder when the telegram reached him. What he saw at Folsom immediately convinced him. He fetched Kidder, who was likewise convinced. Roberts later reported:

"Arriving at the fossil pit, on September 2, he [Roberts is speaking of himself in the third person] found Director Figgins, several members of the Colorado Museum Board, and Dr. Barnum Brown, of the American Museum of Natural History, New York, on the ground. The point, which became the pattern and furnished the name for the type, had just been uncovered by Dr. Brown. There was no question but that *here was the evidence of an authentic association.* The point was still embedded in the *matrix between two of the ribs of the animal skeleton.*"[2]

On the type of the weapon he adds: "Furthermore, it was ascertained that the points were *totally different from the ordinary types* scattered over that portion of the Southwest."

Next year, under the direction of Dr. Barnum Brown, more finds were made. Nineteen Folsom points, as they were already being called to distinguish them from all other early weapons, were discovered. Roberts, summing up the situation in 1928, reports: "Some of the most skeptical critics of the year before became enthusiastic converts. The Folsom find was accepted as a reliable indication that man was present in the Southwest at an earlier period than was previously supposed."

Seldom has a bit of archaeological news stirred so much public interest as the report of the Folsom find. It intensified America's interest in her past. Newspapers spoke of the discovery of an American Neanderthal man (anthropologically, a ridiculous comparison). Not until the initial excitement had died down somewhat was the crucial question asked: Where was the *human being* who had propelled this missile? Propelled with a spear thrower or hurled by hand —for given the length of the points, from one to three inches, they could only be spearheads or javelins, not arrowheads. Besides, by 1928 scientists were fairly sure that bow and arrow had been invented by the late Basket Makers. *Not a single human bone* was found at Folsom! And we may as well anticipate: to this day not a bone, not a skull, let alone a whole skeleton, has ever been found in *direct* association with a Folsom point.

But the by now incontrovertible fact that reasoning men, *Homo sapiens,* had been at work here was proved by other signs besides the skillfully worked projectile points. For every single one of the bison skeletons lacked the tailbone. There could be only one explanation for this: the bisons had been skinned, for in the course of skinning the tail remains attached to the hide. Why were they skinned? The answer is easily deduced: the hides would have been needed for clothing, for draping the cave entrance, for comfortable rugs, or for all these purposes together. And, in fact, near the spearheads a few blunt chipped stones were found, undoubtedly the scrapers, the tools with which Folsom man had scraped the flesh and sinews from the hides.

Some of the bones showed notches that could only have been made by a knife, a stone knife, of course. It was clear that the hunter had cut up his meat on the spot. Curiously, most of the skeletons were preserved whole; only occasionally was a leg missing. Had these early men only carved out a few steaks? Had they carried away nothing from those huge carcasses, which would have fed them for weeks? Did this mean that they had no fixed abode, no permanent camp?

Gradually, more things were clarified. Here, where the bisons had been killed, there must have been a small lake, or at least a large pond. Once upon a time lush grass had grown in this now parched country; dark streaks of humus in the bank where the cowboy found the first bones testified to this. The huge beasts had come here to drink; the men had closed in on them and butchered them all in a veritable orgy of killing.

Once again we ask: How was it that none of the hunters was injured during this slaughter, none killed? It must have been a dangerous business to attack the huge bisons with nothing but spears. But Folsom man had evidently mastered the technique.

When had this hunting party taken place? We have already said: about 10,000 years ago. In 1928 that estimate was based solely on geological stratigraphy. But geological measurements are generally very rough. By and by, other estimates were offered. Some scientists thought the Folsom bison grave might be as much as 15,000 years old; others would concede it no more than 7,000 years. To be sure, there was still no way of telling *how long* Folsom man had hunted through North America. As we shall see, he left his weapons in many other places. But radiocarbon dating could fix the time of various individual sites. Thus, investigation of one site in Colorado yielded an age of 10,000 ± 375 years.

It seemed as if the First American had been discovered. But soon there would be other finds that would challenge his priority. Some scientists, arguing against the existence of Ice Age man in America, had pointed out that no traces of such early men had ever been found in America's numerous caves—and to judge by the evidence of Europe, Ice Age man had lived in caves.

As it turned out, the next discovery of weapons, which until recently appeared to predate all others, took place in a cave.

19

Sandia Man

THE same year that Folsom man was discovered, a group of Boy Scouts, Troop Number 13 from Albuquerque, New Mexico, set out on a treasure hunt high up in the nearby Sandia Mountains. They tramped in thin air, 7,250 feet above the Rio Grande.

One cave seemed more alluring than others because it was so difficult of access. But when the boys were in it and had started digging through layers of dust, they soon found their shovels striking fallen rocks. Discouraged, they gave up on the whole enterprise. Had they persevered, they would indeed have found a treasure, though one of a special kind. As it was, they missed one of the most important discoveries in American prehistory.

By the spring of 1936, almost ten years later, Folsom man had long since been acknowledged as the earliest American, and no one was counting on finding traces of a still earlier ancient man. But the cave was visited again by a student at the University of New Mexico in Albuquerque named Kenneth Davis. Today there is another cave in the area named after him. Davis came upon signs of that still earlier party of Boy Scouts, matches, and similar debris, and dug about as far as the Scouts had before they lost interest. But he was more methodical than they, and by careful sifting found a few objects in the top layer of dust. What he found was nothing extraordinary for the region: an arrowhead, part of a deer's antler that had been made into a tool, remains of a prehistoric coiled basket, and a few shards of pottery. Packing these odds and ends into a cigar box, he brought them all down to the university. The professor of anthropology at the time was Frank C. Hibben, who had also studied zoology—a circumstance that was to be of value. Hibben decided, quite literally, to get to the bottom of the matter.

In 1941, five years later, he wrote his scientific report. But this created far less of a stir than another article of his, a colorful popular account written for *The Saturday Evening Post* in 1943, at a time when he was serving as a lieutenant in the Navy. In the rather brash manner typical of mass-circulation magazines, the *Post* introduced Hibben's article as follows:

"Until recently we thought the Folsom man, of 10,000 years ago, was our earliest citizen; now we have evidence of another ancient, a mighty hunter, who makes the Folsom chap seem like a Johnny-come-lately."[1]

As a matter of fact, if strict scientific standards are applied, the question of the age of Sandia man, whose discovery Hibben then proclaimed, has not been definitely settled to this day. We must realize that there was not yet anything like radiocarbon dating, which could unequivocally (or at any rate, approximately) establish the dates of the relics found in the various strata. When Hibben made his amazing discovery, he was dependent on the relative datings of the strata to one another—for he did at once find several clear strata. The pottery finds on the surface were the only items that could be dated with fair certainty: he recognized them as typical Pueblo and estimated their age at about 500 years. That age was in itself highly interesting, but as the excavation proceeded, the whole project became more and more exciting.

It was not easy digging at all. The cave that seemed the most promising, because of its situation, was more of a tunnel than a cave, and this tunnel extended 153 yards into the cliff, with a downward slope of twenty-five yards. Though the tunnel was some ten feet wide, it was almost choked by the great heaps of dust, accumulations of rubble, and masses of fallen rock, which in some places blocked the passage right up to the ceiling. Under Hibben's direction the diggers—most of them student volunteers—had to make do with the simplest equipment: flashlights, spades, shovels, trowels, picks. Most of the time they had to work crawling on their bellies. But the greatest handicap was the dust; at the slightest touch it billowed up from the floor. If a spade was thrust into it, it rose in such dense clouds that the flashlights were as good as useless. Breathing was so difficult that the workers had to spell one another more and more frequently. Under these circumstances, with the problems constantly mounting, the team would probably have given up but for a sudden discovery about 150 yards from the entrance.

The discovery came about by chance. One of the diggers disturbed a swarm of bats, who fluttered clumsily, squeaking loudly, all about him. Shying away, he stumbled back against a heap of broken rock, fell, and as he did so grasped something that he immediately recognized as unusual, although he was groping in almost total darkness. He stuffed it quickly into his collecting bag and crawled toward the exit. As Hibben tells the story:

"There in the daylight of a New Mexico afternoon, the group of men gathered around to see what they had. Even then they weren't sure. The object was, indeed, a piece of bone, but certainly it was no ordinary bone from any ordinary animal. In shape, it was like the short curved blade of a Turkish dagger. It looked vaguely familiar. It was the bony core of the claw of a giant ground sloth, which has been extinct these last 10,000 years."[2]

From other excavations the giant sloth was quite familiar. Today reconstructions of these huge animals, which attained several times the size of species now living, can be seen in a good many American museums. With its dirty yellow color, its sluggishly menacing movements, it must have been a weird sight; its motion had a strangely crippled quality, for it walked on the back of its hands because of the extraordinary length of its claws. Yet it was a harmless vegetarian, and with its clumsy gait must have been easy prey for the prehistoric hunters. Easy and rewarding: some 1,500 pounds of edible meat! For there are other finds of bones along with weapons, like the Folsom find, which prove that the early Indians hunted and ate this animal.

Since the giant sloths became extinct toward the end of

the last Ice Age, about 10,000 years ago, the find could with good conscience be dated "more than 10,000 years old."

Although this was not the first such find, it was extremely significant. It indicated that this cave had at least served the giant sloth as a temporary shelter 10,000 years ago. But there was another possibility. Might pieces of a sloth have been carried into the cave? For the whole skeleton was not found, as would have been the case if a sloth had crawled in here, sick, to die alone. Might the cave hold traces of a contemporary man? That was now the exciting prospect. *Contemporary* is the operative word, for those earlier finds by Davis had shown that men had been here at some later period and left arrowheads and pottery behind.

"Here," Hibben says, "was a golden opportunity to make a discovery of sweeping significance."[3]

The time had come to put the project on a more serious basis. A camp was established at the foot of the canyon, and dust masks were added to the equipment. But even these masks were not sufficient protection against the swirling clouds of dust which settled in the lungs so persistently that some of the diggers suffered severe bronchial illnesses. It took months before an effective measure was worked out: a kind of gigantic vacuum cleaner was installed, and long rubber hoses reaching deep into the cave sucked the dust out of the air.

Thanks to all this, it proved possible to dig the first pit into the ground of the cave. The situation was highly promising. Most of the Folsom excavations had been conducted along river beds, where the stratigraphy was difficult to interpret because of washouts, infalls, and replacements. But in the Sandia Cave everything was arranged in neat strata. As Hibben puts it:

"Groupings of the strata within the cave necessarily are referable mainly to periods represented only by phenomena occurring within the cave. However, the problem of exterior factors such as stream erosion or accidental wash into or through the cave is practically eliminated. All objects and matter in the cave appear to have been deposited there originally. There was no deposition from the outside nor were original internal deposits redistributed by such factors as stream wash, solifluction, faulting, or other natural agencies of disturbance. These deposits, then, may be regarded as primary and may be judged in their relative positions."[4]

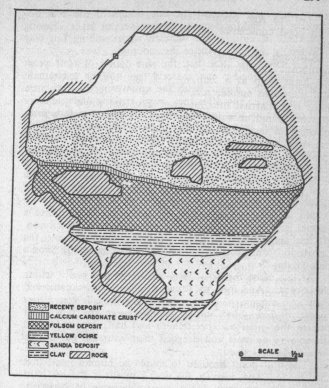

Cross section of Sandia Cave, N. Mex., at a depth of ten meters.

There were six strata. Here is a brief list (the appended drawing shows them plainly). On top lay the stratum of dust, heavily mixed with the bat excrement of several hundred years. Then followed a thin but extremely hard calcium carbonate crust; it was the hardness of this that had discouraged the Albuquerque Boy Scouts from continuing their treasure hunting. The diggers now had to attack it with jackhammers. The third layer, which they called the "Folsom deposit" because of the finds, came next. Then there was a layer of yellow ocher. Beneath this came the most important stratum, the one that held the real discovery: the Sandia deposit. It was the last layer showing any signs of culture, for beneath were nothing but clay and finally the solid rock of the mountain.

This somewhat drab list, the summation of four years of toilsome digging, can scarcely transmit the excitement that stirred the diggers with the uncovering of each new layer and especially after they began making finds of more and more relics that pointed thousands and more thousands of years back into the American past. Hibben again:

"Through the dust and leaves and other debris near the entrance to the cave, the first excavated pit was begun. Down several feet beneath the surface we began to come upon bone fragments and teeth and even pieces of hoofs and horns of animals which we knew to be extinct. The thick-walled bones of the mammoth and the mastodon we could identify at a glance. And there was the hoof of a camel, and here the jaw of a large, straight-horned bison. It has been many centuries since the mammoth and the mastodon roamed the foothills and canyons of the Sandia Mountains."[5]

At last came the great moment of the first really telling discovery: "And then we found it! There it was, cemented fast in a magma of camel and bison bones. *It was a flint point of undoubted human manufacture*. The flint point meant that man had been there and had seen and killed those very animals and dragged them into this cave. This was evidence indeed.

"The flint point brought to mind the human hand that had made it and, in turn, the man himself. It was not hard to visualize this man, the original cave man of America. He must have sat on this same stone at the cave mouth and watched the herds of bison and camel in the canyon below. What did he look like? We had the flint point he made; *now for the hunter himself!*"[6]

The spearhead that they found in the Folsom stratum was so patently of the familiar Folsom type that there seemed no possibility of doubt. The age, too, appeared certain; at present the age of Folsom man is estimated at about 10,000 years, at most 11,000. But Folsom man himself seems to have become extinct along with the animals he hunted. The diggers in the Sandia Cave kept hoping that they might find a cultural transitional form, traces of a man who lived after Folsom man and would establish the connection to the much later Basket Makers. This hope—

fortunately, as it turned out—was far too modest. For, incredibly, they did not find the traces of a more recent, but of a still earlier man.

Under the Folsom stratum was the layer of yellow ocher. After they had penetrated that, they found, in the fifth stratum, no fewer than nineteen projectile points, together with badly encrusted remnants of bones which, however, could be identified by the preserved teeth as remains of the horse (*Equus excelsus*), bison, camel, mastodon, and mammoth. The layer of ocher separated the weapons so clearly from the Folsom stratum that here there could not be the doubts that were to rise at other sites—at least no doubts for the time being—that here were traces of human hunters who had lived *before* Folsom man.

This discovery was a scientific sensation almost as great at the Folsom find of 1925. What is more, the Sandia points differed clearly from the Folsom points. They were longer on the average, not nearly so well worked, and clearly indicated a more primitive stage of culture.

The diggers at once began indulging in bold speculations. "Many were the evenings around the campfire, after we had washed off the cave dust at the end of the day of digging, that we speculated until bedtime about Sandia man. We usually ended these speculations with the remark that Sandia man probably looked as modern as ourselves. If he had been dressed in a Homburg hat and a modern business suit, you probably wouldn't have turned to look at him if he had passed you on the street."[7]

Every good excavator allows himself such fancies. But here imagination seems to have run far ahead of the facts. For what had happened in the case of the Folsom find happened again: the weapons were found, and the animals the man had killed for food. There were even two hearths at which Sandia man had certainly squatted. In other words, there was no doubt about his existence. But not a trace of the man himself was found, not a fragment of bone, not one of his teeth that had bitten into the mammoth flesh.

Nevertheless, the discovery was a momentous one. It proved that the cultural history of North American man had begun even earlier than had hitherto been assumed. But how much earlier? How much time was represented by that layer of ocher separating the Folsom stratum from the Sandia stratum underneath it?

At the time, without radiocarbon dating, there was no direct means for attacking this supremely important question. Only geology could throw some light on the matter. And the geologist who came to the rescue was Professor Kirk Bryan of Harvard University.

The report that Bryan drew up after a careful study of Sandia Cave is nineteen pages long and is soberly titled, "Correlation of the Deposits of Sandia Cave, New Mexico, with the Glacial Chronology." It was published as an appendix to Hibben's scientific article in 1941.

Glacial chronology is the science of the succession of Ice Ages. It has long been known that as many Ice Ages passed over North America as over Europe and Asia. The great glaciers came in waves, advancing and then receding. Kirk Bryan, after examining the cave in 1939 and 1940, during the last phase of the excavation, detected signs of alternate wet and dry periods in the strata—a reflection of the advancing Ice Ages and the accompanying climatic changes, for the ice itself never reached the vicinity, let alone the altitude, of the Sandia Mountains.

To let Dr. Bryan speak for himself, we quote from the opening of his report:

"The excavator of the cave, Dr. Frank C. Hibben, has described and discussed the cultural and animal remains and their archaeological relationships. Hence the following paper is concerned mainly with the geologic aspects of the cave and an attempt to correlate the deposits with the glacial chronology.

"This correlation leads to the conclusion that the artifact-bearing cave deposits were laid down during the time of greater moisture corresponding to the last ice advance of the Wisconsin stage of glaciation. The climax of this episode is represented by the sterile ocher deposits, which therefore have a nominal date in the accepted chronology of 25,000 ± years. People of the Folsom culture lived in the cave just later than, and those of the Sandia culture just previous to, this nominal date."[8]

This method of dating has since been subject to widespread criticism. In order to clarify the method, we also quote Hibben's brief summary:

"We did have, however, undeniable evidence of a Sandia man living before a Folsom man. Not only that, but there was additional evidence that the cave had been dry at first, then wet, then dry again, then wet, and finally dry—which is the way it was when the excavation was made. Professor

Bryan readily explained the why of these successive wet and dry periods.

"During the time of the last great continental glaciations, the ice is known to have moved out in successive tongues, or advances. Over a period of several thousand years, these tremendous masses of continental ice moved out and then melted back, or retreated, several times. When the continental ice advanced, the climate was wet, rainy and humid, as well as cold. When the ice retreated, it became dry, with less rainfall than before. The wet and dry periods of Sandia Cave, then, were sympathetic with the advances and retreats of the continental glaciers to the north."[9]

According to Bryan, then, Sandia man is supposed to have lived, hunted and dwelt in this cave 25,000 years ago!

This was a dating that overthrew all hitherto accepted views on the appearance of first man in America—the views of archaeologists, at any rate. But Bryan spoke for a different science, and therefore archaeologists were shy about questioning his conclusions even though, and this must be stressed, Bryan himself by no means took a dogmatic tone. Rather, he offered his opinions with all the circumspection of a specialist who does not feel so very competent to speak on a different discipline. Thus, he quickly follows up his verdict on the 25,000 years with the following reservation:

"Such a line of argument has obvious and unescapable faults. If the sequence of events within the cave deposits is unassailable, the interpretation of the deposits in terms of climate may be faulty. If the latter is correct, it is always possible that the correlation with the general climatic rhythm is incorrect. Furthermore, our knowledge of the climatic rhythm, the number, length and amplitude of its fluctuations, is still imperfect."[10]

In fact, archaeologists of repute very soon expressed their doubts. These doubts remained even after Hibben later appealed to radiocarbon datings that seemed to corroborate the age of 25,000 years. I had the opportunity to query him in person in the autumn of 1965, at which time he insisted on this dating. But several archaeologists challenged these radiocarbon datings on a variety of grounds. Gordon R. Willey of Harvard University wrote in 1966: "No reliable radiocarbon dates have yet been established on either the Folsom or Sandia level of the Sandia cave."[11] He refers to recent studies by G. A. Agogino, who even calls into question the seemingly so convincing separation of the two strata by the layer of ocher and considers it possible that the Folsom points and the Sandia points were originally positioned in the same stratum.

In addition, during the thirties the Clovis point (named after the site) was found, a fluted point like the Folsom type, but considerably larger, in fact the largest of all the points that have been found (some of them reached five inches). Conclusive radiocarbon datings have assigned the Clovis point to 9200 B.C., the Folsom point to 9000–8000 B.C.

Frederick Johnson cautiously sums up the Sandia problem as follows: "Sandia points, it seems to me, are old in North America, possibly as old or older than Clovis and Folsom points, but the age is not yet certain. This is not to say that they are the oldest points in the continent or that they are part of the inventory of tools of the First American. Recent discoveries in Washington, Oregon, and British Columbia and the Northwest Territories testify to the distinct possibility that man is older in North America than Sandia and Folsom."[12]

Today, in fact, there is scarcely an archaeologist other than Hibben who would ascribe an age of more than 10,000 to 12,000 years to the Sandia points. But what about the other points that have been found?

20

The World of the Early Hunters

THERE is something eerie about the Early Hunter in North America. His spirit hovers over the forests of the East, the prairies and deserts of the West, from northern Alaska to northern Texas. He has left his traces behind everywhere, above all his weapons, and also the hacked bones of the giant beasts he killed, and the hearths at which he roasted their meat.

But where is he himself? Just as with Folsom man, archaeologists have utterly failed to find Sandia man, or the hand, the arm, that hurled the deadly weapons. Whenever they thought they had at last come upon human traces, bits of skulls or skeletons from those faraway times, so many doubts arose about the chronological placing of the accompanying weapons that no agreement could be achieved. Still and all, in the next chapter we have a few revelations to make.

We must recall once more that up to the Folsom find in 1925, up to 1927,[1] in fact, it was generally accepted that the

305

First American could scarcely have been more than 4,000 years old and that Ice Age inhabitants of America were out of the question.

One person in particular, Aleš Hrdlička of the Bureau of Ethnology in Washington, blocked all research into the remote past for a whole generation. A man of considerable merits in many fields, he showed incredible obstinacy in this matter. He was an odd bird in other respects also. For example, he made it a rule that all his associates had to will their skulls to science, but in his own last will he stipulated that he was to be cremated, his ashes mingled with those of his first wife and deposited in an urn in the Smithsonian Institution.

He was ruthless in enforcing his dominance upon younger men. Kirk Bryan, the geologist, once told his students during Hrdlička's "reign": "If you ever find evidence of human life in a context which is ancient, bury it carefully, but do not forget about it."[2]

Frank H. H. Roberts, Jr., suggests the power Hrdlička wielded and the way this affected the course of research well into 1940 when he remarks that every young anthropologist, geologist, or paleontologist of the period would have been imperiling his career if he opposed this dictator in the slightest way.[3] Even in 1928, by which time the importance of the Folsom find was clear to everyone, Hrdlička had the temerity to decree at a meeting of the New York Academy that there could not have been a Paleo-Indian (as we call the people who hunted the now extinct animals). "With his back to the wall, Hrdlička was denying everything to maintain his position that man could be anything, anything at all, but not ancient in America," Wilmsen says.[4] But eventually the finds accumulated to such an extent that even the skeptics had to bow to the evidence.

Back in 1939, when H. Marie Wormington of the Denver Museum of Natural History attempted to summarize the existing knowledge about the Early Hunters, she was able to do this in the space of eighty pages, listing ninety-two references. In 1957, after an interval of eighteen years, she published a new edition of her by then famous reference work, *Ancient Man in North America*. In doing justice to the newly discovered material, she produced a book of 322 pages, this time with 586 references, and this after rigorous compression.

But what has been written *by now* on the problem of

North American Paleo-Indians, based upon innumerable excavations, has grown beyond all measure. A comprehensive scientific study, one that considers *everything*, is no longer possible; the time has come for incisive surveys. And it is significant that the first person who boldly ventured a broad but highly readable compilation was once again an outsider: Kenneth Macgowan, Broadway theater man, Hollywood producer, author of an excellent history of the movies—and also a passionate archaeologist. His book, *Early Man in the New World*, was at first treated coolly by the professionals; but it received their blessing when, shortly before his death, it was republished in a revised and reasonably priced edition in 1962 by the American Museum of Natural History. At that time the museum's curator provided it with a foreword, and the anthropologist Joseph A. Hester carefully and painstakingly edited it.

What sets the Folsom find apart from all others is the way it was repeatedly confirmed within a short time. The archaeologists' greatest stroke of luck was the discovery of the Lindenmeier site in northern Colorado. The name comes from the owner of the land. In 1934 two brothers reported to the Smithsonian Institution the sensational discovery of a campsite of Folsom man. Frank H. H. Roberts, Jr., regarded as a specialist since his participation in the original Folsom excavation, rushed to the spot. And in fact there was even more to see there than at Folsom.

The campsite had obviously been frequented by Folsom

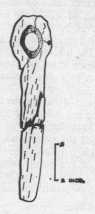

A curious bone implement found at Murray Springs, Ariz., in 1967, together with mammoth bones. It dates from the period of the Clovis hunters, and probably served for smoothing spear shafts.

man for years. Once again their was tangible evidence of those Early Hunters: a spear point still embedded in the vertebra of a *Bison antiquus*. But that was the merest beginning. In five years of work Roberts brought to light no fewer than 6,000 stone implements and other remains.

When we gaze over this parched, dreary landscape today, we wonder why men should have pitched their camp here of all places. But first, they did not live permanently at this place; they were nomadic hunters and probably assembled here only at certain seasons. Secondly, the geologists have shown that this region was damp and fertile 10,000 years ago.

Roberts found flint knives and razor-sharp blades, choppers, fine bones polished to needle sharpness, and heavy stone hammers. There were also bone awls, undoubtedly for punching hides, and carefully sliced disks of bone. Since these disks had no holes by which they could have been strung into necklaces or bracelets, they may have been America's first gambling chips![5]

When it became possible, long after the discovery, to take the first radiocarbon measurements, these items were dated to 8820 B.C., a brilliant corroboration of the estimate made by the first Folsom excavators on the basis of purely geological stratification.

Meanwhile, however, there had been another find that brought to light a different type of man, or more precisely, this man's weapons. But these finds, again spear points, differed distinctly from the Folsom points. The first examples turned up as early as 1931, but the decisive find was made in 1932 near Clovis, New Mexico, close to the Texas border. It may seem a bit tiresome to relate that once again two amateurs found the first traces. But so it was, and these two outsiders once again must be commended for promptly reporting their discovery to a professional, this time Edgar B. Howard of the University of Pennsylvania Museum. For four years Howard, followed by John L. Cutter, searched the shores of ancient dried-out lakes. Herds of giant beasts as well as the long-since-extinct camels and horses once must have roamed the grasslands here. The weapons of the Early Hunters were found strewn over many miles. And here, too, some of the points were lodged between the ribs of the animals in such a way that there could be no doubt about the contemporaneity of man and animal. The points

Spearheads of the Early Hunters. The elegantly fluted Folsom point found in 1925 provided the first clue to the existence of this people. Then followed the discovery of Clovis and Sandia points. The Folsom points were one to three inches long

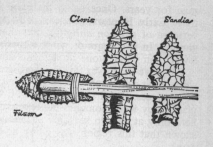

were longer than the Folsom type, averaging between two and five inches.[6]

The excavations were continued by E. H. Sellards during three seasons from 1949 to 1951. His work furnished proof that the Clovis point must be older than the Folsom point. The stratigraphic record told a plain tale: in the two uppermost layers there were incontestable Folsom artifacts; in the lowest layer equally incontestable Clovis remains. The Clovis hunters had brought down no fewer than four mammoths at this site; the skeletons were completely preserved.

The geologists assign a maximum age of about 13,000 years to the Clovis stratum. Thus the Clovis "culture" appeared to be intermediary between Sandia and Folsom. However, there are some archaeologists who maintain that the three cultures overlapped in time. And in saying this we come to the dispute over dates that has so far not been settled.

In the early fifties workmen under the supervision of Emil W. Haury unloaded an unusual burden at the University of Arizona in Tucson. It was a plaster block a cubic yard in size. Embedded in this block were the ribs, vertebrae, and scapula of a mammoth, and in among the bones five of the projectile points that had killed the huge animal. Back at the site the bones and weapons had been wrapped with plaster-soaked canvas until the whole hardened into a transportable block.

The find came from the Naco site, named after a place in Arizona near the Mexican border. It had been discovered in 1951, once more by amateurs, and had been investigated systematically by Haury from 1952 on.

Map of the chief campsites of the Early Hunters, who pursued bison and mammoth more than 10,000 years ago.

The geologist Ernst Antevs, after studying the stratification of the site, came up with an estimate of 10,000 to 11,000 years or more for the age of the bones. Other geological estimates went as high as 13,000 years. But the university's radiocarbon laboratory later said 9,250 years.

Haury did not feel really satisfied with any of these dates, but he predicted that more mammoths would be found in the vicinity, thus providing additional material for dating. And he was proved right.[7] Only two years later the rancher Edward F. Lehner, looking over some land he wanted to buy eleven miles northwest of the Naco site, on the San Pedro River, discovered gigantic bones. He informed Haury, who was later to pay tribute to the hospitality and helpfulness of Lehner and his wife. They bought the farm and were to remain closely connected with the subsequent excavations. In 1955–56 the Lehner site yielded thirteen Clovis points (some not quite definitely identified as such), eight stone tools that had evidently been used for butchering, two hearths with charcoal remains (the best material for radiocarbon dating), and the skeletons of nine mammoth calves. There were also remains of bison, horse, and tapir. Haury had good luck; heavy rainstorms in 1955 washed many items to the surface. Still, that was not enough; to clear the whole area, Haury had thousands of tons of soil moved by a bulldozer.

And what was the dating situation here?

Once again the geologists had first chance. And once more Antevs arrived at a very great age: between 10,000 and 15,000 years. His final conclusion: "The mammoth hunts of the Lehner and Naco sites are assigned an age of 13,000 or more years."[8] But the physicists disagreed. Radiocarbon datings were obtained from no fewer than three universities—Tucson, Michigan, and Copenhagen—of materials from the same stratum, from three hearths close together. And the results were staggering.

Haury writes tersely: "At least three of the Arizona laboratory dates, 7205 ± 450 for Hearth 1 and 7022 ± 450 and 8330 ± 450 for Hearth 2 are not acceptable. . . . *Obviously* something is wrong."[9]

But what? The problem is very simple: the first two dates show the relative contemporaneity of the hearths, but the second hearth yields two dates *1,308 years apart*. No one hearth site could possibly have been in use for such a length of time! And worse was to come. For now the dates from Copenhagen and Michigan arrived. And Copenhagen reported an age of 11,180, Michigan of 11,290 years!

The only explanation is that the samples for the first tests had somehow become contaminated, or at least some of them had. The scientists developed a method for removing the contaminations and undertook new tests. This time they obtained ages of 10,900 years for one specimen and 12,000 years for another.

Here we have an almost classic case of the difficulties that beset C-14 dating, such as we have indicated in the chapter "The Tick of Time." When such problems arise, the archaeologist must draw on his experience and knowledge for the final verdict. And so Haury cautiously sums up the matter:

"It seems to us that a date of from 11,000 to 12,000 years ago for the time of the kills is probably not far from the truth, although this time range is short of Antevs' estimate."[10]

All these dates for the Early Hunters range between 9,000 and 13,000 years ago. The question arises: Were there still earlier hunters? And what about the time span between these hunters and the later cultures, closer in time to us, those cultures which knew agriculture and had fixed abodes, or the still later Pueblos and Mound Builders? A period of several thousand years still remains to be bridged.

There are some answers.

At the end of our discussion of Sandia we quoted Frederick Johnson, who points to the possibility of a greater age for Stone Age man in America. In 1933 Fenley Hunter, on a field trip for the American Museum of Natural History, found promising bones near Tule Springs in southern Nevada. "With the bones was found an obsidian flake, produced by man and bearing scars that appeared to have resulted from use."[11] Between 1933 and 1955 Mark R. Harrington investigated this site several times. In 1955 charcoal remains were dated by Libby, the inventor of the C-14 method, to more than 23,800 years—though how much more he could not say. A hearth was found where there were indications that a camel had been cut up into steaks and roasted. A few years later a new radiocarbon dating yielded still a greater age: 26,000–28,000 years!

That was sensational, of course, and was reported by the press throughout America. We may as well say here that of late such reports have been appearing in the press almost every year—most prematurely. It would be well to put such dates aside, to wait for confirmation, for new investigations, which unfortunately often turn out as did the case of Tule Springs. Even the cautious H. Marie Wormington had credulously accepted the remote date for Tule Springs at first. But in 1962 and 1963 Richard Shutler, Jr., with a team of specialists from other disciplines, made new excavations and checked the old ones. And Wormington corrected her view:

"It became apparent that the samples used for the earlier radiocarbon assays were mixed with materials collected from two deposits of quite different ages, although on the basis of the first limited excavations it had been entirely reasonable to believe that a single deposit was represented. *Dates obtained from such a mixture are, of course, meaningless.*" What was the new result? "In a unit dated at 9250 B.C. to 8000 B.C. the only incontrovertible evidence of human occupation was found. It consisted of a scraper and some flakes."[12]

Thus one hope was buried, but another had already appeared. Oddly, this second find was made on an island.

It was Santa Rosa Island, forty-five miles off the coast of southern California. The enigma here was how early man had crossed such an expanse of water. But the geologists showed that during the last Ice Age the water level must have been much lower. Although there was still no land bridge, the distance to the mainland had probably diminished to two miles, which certainly could have been crossed on a tree trunk. Such a primitive means of transportation points to unquenchable curiosity on the part of early man.

The remains of hundreds of small mammoths were found. These were obviously a variety of dwarf mammoth, easy to hunt, and once more there were many indications that men had systematically butchered them. For example, the skulls were shattered, obviously to get at a delicacy, the brains. In 1956 and 1960 Phil C. Orr reported on the radiocarbon dating.[13] The results were: 29,650 years—although with the unusually high uncertainty factor of ± 2,500 years. But—one piece of decayed cypress wood that lay *underneath* two mammoth skeletons showed only 15,820 years.

The dance of dates goes on. Many archaeologists are still extremely skeptical about all these remote datings, particularly those going beyond 20,000 years. But the evidence in favor of man in America at so early a period is gradually mounting, as we shall see in the next chapter.

Probably it will remain for the next generation of archaeologists to establish a really continuous sequence from the Paleo-Indians of the Ice Age who hunted big game to the Pueblo Indians and Mound Builders. But some of the outlines have already been traced.

As the masses of ice upon the continent receded toward the north, as the climate changed and the big animals began dying out, there may have been some or several waves of fresh immigrants from Asia, although some members of the first immigration may have adjusted to the new conditions. Undoubtedly, the big-game hunters did not live solely by hunting; they surely ate fruits, berries, nuts, and roots.

"Man in fact unites within himself the two extreme dispositions of the mammal, and therefore he is not sure, all his life long, whether he is a sheep or a tiger," Ortega y Gasset remarks in his sardonic manner.[14] But it is equally clear that in the following millennia "food gathering" acquired greater importance. The clans and tribes became more settled; more and more caves were occupied as fixed abodes, or at any rate men resorted more consistently to the same *buen retiros* during the harsher seasons of the year. By 1962 Baldwin could list: "Danger Cave, Gypsum Cave, Fort Rock Cave, Roaring Springs Cave, Ventana Cave, Bat Cave, Catlow Cave, Deadman Cave, Promontory Cave, Black Rock Cave, Paisley Cave, Fishbone Cave, Lovelock Cave, Raven Cave, Juke Box Cave."[15] There are many others.

Inside these caves, and just outside their entrances, the refuse piles up, layer upon layer, a treasure trove for the stratigraphers. And alongside were the charcoal remains of hearths—providing the best of materials for the radiocarbon daters. One example of such a treasure trove is Danger Cave in western Utah, so called because in 1941 a huge boulder suddenly came hurtling down from the roof, almost killing the first excavators. Here the finds provided evidence for the use of the cave for 11,000 years, right down to the Christian era.

A definite picture of ancient man was emerging. Finds proved that the first basketry, flexible baskets, and the first leather moccasins appeared at a very early date. In Fork Rock Cave L. S. Cressman found so many sandals woven of shredded sagebrush bark that archaeologists spoke of the "oldest shoe factory in the world." There were nearly a hundred of these moccasins, 9,000 years old. Ultimately, Cressman and Jesse D. Jennings of the University of Utah found continuous strata extending from very ancient times to 1400 B.C.—strings, ropes, nets, and baskets made of plant fibers. In Ventana Cave in southern Arizona Emil W. Haury found a continuous occupation of 10,000 years, which, as we learned in Chapter 12, provides a transition to Mogollon and perhaps to Hohokam. And from 6,000 to 7,000 years ago there are multitudinous traces of the animal that appeared some 3,000 years earlier in the Old World as the first of all domesticated animals: the dog.

It is a rather unfortunate choice of words to call these modes of human life, whose traces are concentrated chiefly in and around caves, "desert cultures."

The person who has thrown particularly bright light into these caves was a most unusual individual. Mark R. Harrington, born in 1882, took as deep an interest in modern Indians as in their ancient forefathers. He lived among twenty-three Indian tribes and dug for antiquities virtually all over America. Inevitably, he had to leave a few of his projects uncompleted. The Borax Lake site, for instance, which he had worked first, was not finally interpreted and dated until 1970.[16] He undertook one of his scientifically most interesting excavations in Nevada, sixteen miles from the gambling paradise of Las Vegas. "The story of this discovery is an excellent illustration of the detective methods used by archaeologists," Wormington remarks.[17]

Harrington had visited Gypsum Cave for the first time in 1924 but did not start digging systematically until 1929. We have stressed the point that for the archaeologist every single scrap of material can be valuable. In this case, the first thing that stirred Harrington's curiosity was a curious mass which could only be taken for one thing. It consisted of feces, blobs of dung of such size that only an unusually large animal, an animal now extinct, could have produced them. Analyses showed that the dung was that of an herbivorous animal. The shape of the cave was such—it was 300 feet long, with five successive chambers—that only an animal that could *crawl* on all fours could possibly have entered it. The deduction of the archaeological detectives was that only a giant sloth could have lived here.

The deduction proved correct. Harrington found remains of the sloth. He found not only the skull but also—and this was a treasure for the paleontologists—well-preserved claws and bits of the coarse hair, still showing its original reddish coloration.

Alongside the animal there turned up once again the weapons of the man who had done the killing here. "The next step, of course, would be to actually prove the killing; but if we can show that Mr. Man ever met Mr. Sloth, little additional proof is necessary, for Man has always had a very bad reputation for assisting his neighbors, human and otherwise, into the great Hereafter," Harrington remarks.[18] The projectile points that had killed this sloth were entirely different from any found hitherto; they were lozenge-shaped and had small tapering stems. As was customary, they were given the name of the site: Gypsum points.

But probably the most significant fact about this cave was that it had been inhabited, or at least visited, down to historic times, in fact right down to the present. The oldest sloth dung tested in the radiocarbon laboratory gave an age of 10,455 ± 250 years, the more recent, in a higher stratum, 8,527 ± 250 years. The cave yielded weapons of the Paleo-Indians, relics of the Basket Makers and the Pueblo Indians, and, finally, remains of the still living Paiute Indians. And to crown all the strata, resplendent in the very top layer, was a tin can! It had once contained beans. Here, certainly, was an impressive example of continuity: from the roaming cave hunter to the resting cowboy.

21

When the Great Beasts Died

"To find an answer, one must first have sufficient knowledge to formulate the question." With these words, H. Marie Wormington closes her book, *Ancient Man in North America*.

Halvor L. Skavlem had that knowledge. For many years he had tramped the fields of his country house near Kaw-Ray-Kaw-Saw-Kaw (more generally known as White Crow) on the shore of Lake Koshkonong in Wisconsin, looking for arrowheads, stone tools, and other Indian relics for his collection. But not until 1912, by which time he was sixty-seven years old, did he ask himself the crucial question: If I were an Indian, how would I sharpen this broken stone implement I have just found?

Answering this question turned into an avocation that lasted for seventeen years. The question itself broadened into: How did the Indians make their weapons? How did they produce and how did they use their stone tools?

Skavlem had with him an intelligent boy, Alonzo W. Pond, who helped him and who later, with perfect consistency, studied archaeology. In 1930 Pond, together with the now eighty-five-year-old Skavlem, published a book that

317

for the first time described all the methods of transforming stone from the natural raw material into a well-shaped arrowhead or tool.[1] But as early as 1923 the first long article about "this charming old arrow-maker of Lake Koshkonong" appeared, and many visitors had the privilege of watching him at work.

Even as they watched, the majority certainly did not realize that with every blow upon a piece of flint he was shattering a prejudice that had already hardened into a myth: the notion that the ancient Indians must have known some "secret of stone," a mysterious method of working stone which the white man must have lost hundreds of years ago. For otherwise, even some archaeologists argued, the tremendous quantity of spearheads, arrowheads, and stone implements, more and more of which were being dug up all the time, simply could not be explained. It was seriously asserted that the Indians had worked patiently for weeks or months before they succeeded in manufacturing a few points out of raw stone and that the labor of polishing a really "elegant" stone must have required several generations.

It is true that even before Skavlem there had been more sensible opinions. But this Norwegian-American was the first person to investigate *all* the aspects of early weapon-and-tool manufacture by testing every possibility. Thus he discovered that there was no need to use harder stone for working softer stone. Rather, it was possible to break away flakes from steel-hard flint by *pressing* with rounded bones or sticks of wood. He experimented with the way the stone had to be held, where the pounding or impact or pressure had to be applied. And most important of all, he demonstrated that a practiced Indian of the Stone Age could make an arrowhead in an incredibly short time—not in days, let alone weeks, but in a few minutes. He needed no more than a few hours even for a neatly polished stone axe. He also demonstrated the utility of such tools. For example, it took him only ten minutes to fell a tree three inches in diameter with a stone axe.

His experiments also answered the question of why the Early Hunters treated their weapons so casually, why when butchering animals they did not pull out their spearheads for reuse, or cut them out when the shaft had broken off. They simply had no need to do so; they could make new points because the process took only a few minutes.

When we examine these early weapons in museums—and every museum in the United States has a collection of them—we find them labeled "projectile points" instead of the more specific "spearhead" or "arrowhead."

There is good reason for this. Only the oldest points can be definitely identified by their size as spearheads. And we know that bow and arrow did not appear until the first millennium B.C. But in the transitional period from Early Hunters to food gatherers and house builders, points were made in such assorted sizes and above all in such a variety of shapes that it is often impossible to determine their exact purpose.

Such a multitude of shapes has turned up since the Folsom find that several archaeological conferences have been called solely to establish a generally accepted classification. In the course of these conferences it turned out that classifications already introduced and based on only one type of point proved to be superfluous or simply wrong. Thus, for example, the "Yuma Culture," to which whole chapters in the older literature have been devoted, is a term no longer used by archaeologists. A conference held in 1948 agreed to abolish the concept.

We do not need to set down all the names—from Eden to Plainview—that have been given to the various types. But one term calls for special mention. For although all the other types of weapons devised by Stone Age man were developed in much the same shapes the whole world over, this one seems to be a purely North American invention. It is the fluted point, which appears in its most elegant form in the Folsom point.

This fluted spearhead is shaped like a long, narrow leaf that has been cut diagonally through the middle. It is frequently shaped with the characteristic flutings running from base to apex on both sides, and merely to take such a point in one's hand provides aesthetic pleasure. These points are the first small masterpieces of early man. In making them he *must* have had more than mere utility in mind. Of course it is evident that a fluted point would sit more securely in a cleft spear shaft than an unfluted point. But spears obviously held their points quite well without the fluting, as the vast numbers of variant points from later and earlier times indicate. What, then, prompted Folsom man to undertake this additional labor?

Before Skavlem showed them how relatively easy it is

North American man's first "secret weapon." Long before the invention of bow and arrow the Early Hunter used this spear thrower, the atlatl, for felling the great beasts.

to make weapons, and even "elegant" weapons, everyone wondered at the artistry and—so it was thought—the infinite pains that had apparently gone into shaping Folsom points. But pains or not, the invention of the doubly fluted spearhead, that most shapely of all the stone implements of early man, must be credited to the North American Indian.

At a much later period the Indian once again showed his artistry in the fashioning of many types of *arrow*heads. Some are so perfect in their form that one wonders whether their utility matches their beauty. But one of the perceptions of our twentieth century, particularly of the Bauhaus school, is that technical perfection is always identical with aesthetic appeal.

In this book I have referred several times to the importance of original invention. What is probably the most *poetic* explanation for the invention of bow and arrow (which, it is worth repeating, did not appear in North America until the first millennium B.C.) has been offered by the famous Spanish philosopher Ortega y Gasset:

"It is not improbable, and would be in full accord with early man's mentality, that the arrow represents a *materialized metaphor*. When the hunter saw the animal fleeing

Here is perhaps the most remarkable item of pictorial documentation in North American archaeology. The picture shows a mound excavation conducted by Dr. Montroville Dickeson and is a detail from a painting on muslin by I. J. Egan done around 1850. The painting, 348 feet long and 7½ feet high, is a gigantic panorama entitled *Monumental Grandeur of the Mississippi Valley*. Too fragile to be shown nowadays, it is preserved in the City Art Museum of St. Louis. The painting shows scenes of De Soto's burial in 1542, the effects of a tornado, the massacre at Fort Rosalie, the pursuit of a farmer by wolves (once lauded as a "humorous scene"), and many other matters. The vast painting was meant to be rolled up on two poles, so that it could be exhibited even in small halls by Dr. Dickeson, who traveled through all of America with it, unrolling it like a movie strip. Dickeson, a physician and amateur archaeologist, claimed to have excavated some 1,000 ancient Indian monuments and mounds, in the course of which he collected 40,000 Indian curiosities that may still be seen at the University of Pennsylvania.

Two of the mounds as they were pictured about 1848 and were seen by the thousands by nineteenth-century travelers. Today many mounds have been leveled. The upper one shows Grave Creek Mound near Wheeling, W. Va., which has a circumference of 1,000 feet at the base and is 50 feet high. The lower picture portrays one of the mounds in Marietta, Ohio.

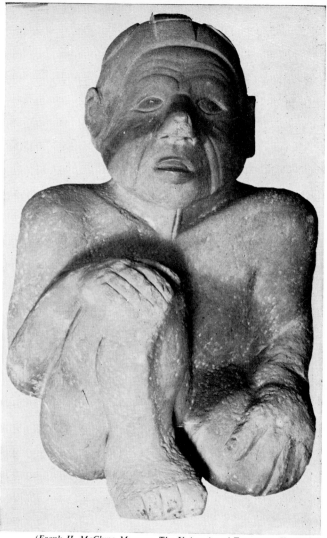

An 18-inch-tall sandstone figure made by the Mound Builders. Found in Wilson County, Tenn.

The drawing, by archaeologists Squier and Davis in 1848, made the serpent famous.

The Great Serpent Mound in Adams County, Ohio: 1,330 feet long.

(Both photos from The Mound Builders, copyright 1926, renewed 1956 by H. C. Shetrone, by permission of D. Appleton and Co.)

Skulls from two Mound Builder graves. The upper one comes from Point Washington, Fla., and was protected by an urn. Below, a man and woman from the largest mound of the Hopewell group south of Columbus, Ohio. Bizarre ornamentation, including copper noses, were set into both skulls.

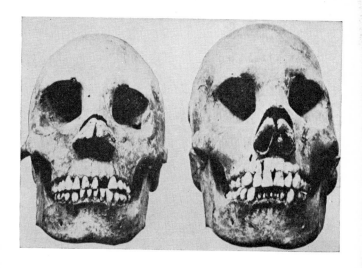

Double grave in a mound of the Hopewell group, Ohio. The man's skull is surmounted by a copper plate, and a copper axe lies between his feet. Both man and woman wear copper bracelets.

(*From* The Mound Builders, *copyright 1928, renewed 1956 by H. C. Shetrone, by permission of D. Appleton and Co.*)

(United States Department of the Interior)

The painstaking excavation of this temple mound near Macon, Ga., one of the Ocmulgee group, began in 1930. The temple, which once crowned the uppermost platform, was destroyed hundreds of years ago. The pyramid is more than 40 feet high; probably more than a million baskets of earth were carried in its construction.

(Field Museum of Natural History)

Model of a temple mound from the Mississippi Valley. The "pyramid" was a religious center and the only "architecture" of these peoples, whose homes were merely primitive huts. A wooden ladder leads to the apex here, but frequently the pyramids were built with steps or ramps. Not a single one of the small temples that once topped these mounds has survived.

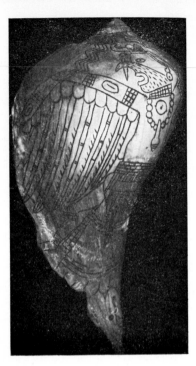

Specimen of the craftsmanship of the Temple Mound Builders: an artistically ornamented shell from a mound in Le Flore County, Okla.

(Museum of the American Indian, Heye Foundation)

The drawing shows the entire etching as it would look were it rolled flat.

Workmen laying to final rest in the Farmer's Museum in Cooperstown, N.Y., the biggest forgery in the history of North American archaeology—the fake "antediluvian giant" known as the Cardiff Giant or the "American Goliath."

(New York State Historical Association)

The most sensational archaeological find of the twenties: a cowboy found a spearhead between the ribs of a *Bison antiquus,* an animal extinct for 10,000 years—proof that man lived in North America during the Ice Age. The so-called Folsom point is the elegantly shaped weapon of the Early Hunter.

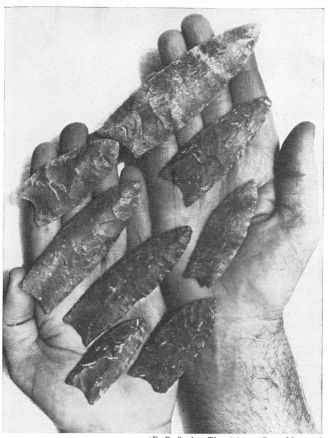

These eight points of the Clovis type killed a mammoth around 12,000 years ago. They were excavated in Naco, Ariz., by Emil W. Haury in 1951. Two of the points were still fixed between the ribs of the huge, long-extinct animal; one of them appears to have made a fatal cut of the spinal cord.

Careful exhumation of a mammoth skeleton in New Mexico. The Early Hunter set off to kill animals of this size armed with two weapons: the spear and fire.

(Dick Kent)

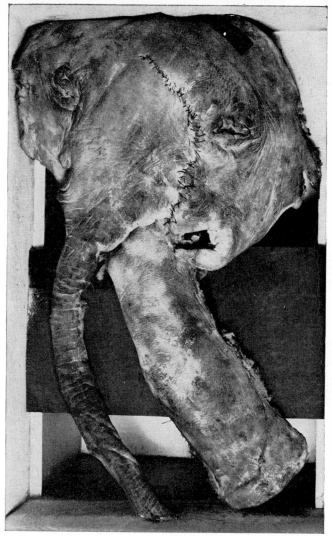

Well-preserved head and leg of young mammoth, exhumed from the frozen soil of Alaska.

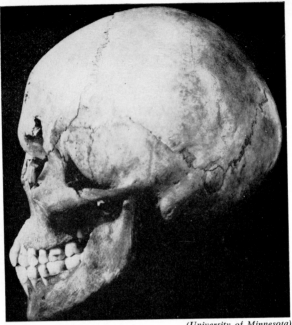

(University of Minnesota)

Two skulls that provoked fierce controversies among American archaeologists and anthropologists. To this day, their age has not been satisfactorily clarified (see Chapter 23). Although both are called "man," they are the skulls of two girls. Above, one named jokingly "Minnesota Minnie"; below, the "Midland girl," whose skull was patched from 60 pieces.

(Museum of New Mexico, courtesy University of Texas Press)

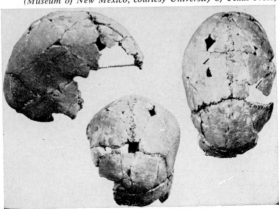

Ishi, North America's last Stone Age man, in 1911, shortly after he was found, almost starved to death, in California.

Ishi after he had become a museum janitor and learned 400 words of English. Here, in the wilderness, he shows his friends, the anthropologists Alfred L. Kroeber and T. T. Waterman, how his people made a harpoon.

(*Lowie Museum of Anthropology, University of California, Berkeley*) unattainably beyond his reach, he would have thought that a bird with its wings could easily catch it. Since he was not a bird and also had none at hand—it is surprising how little primitive man bothered about birds—he finally attached a beak to one end of a small stick and feathers to the other end. In other words, he created the *artificial bird,* the *arrow,* which flies swift as lightning through space and pierces the flank of the fleeing deer."[2]

The much older invention of the atlatl must have been scarcely less ingenious. The atlatl was the decisive weapon against the giant beasts and represents man's first great achievement in the technology of arms.

An atlatl is a spear thrower. The Aztec word was *at'-lat-l;* it has come down to us from the Spaniards, who saw the weapon in action. It consists of a short length of hardwood, at most two feet long. A loop attached to one end provides a grip for the fingers; at the other end there is a deep notch. A short spear is placed in this notch. Then the atlatl, which thus constitutes a prolongation of the arm, is swung in an arc from back to front—and at the climax of the movement the spear flies off with considerably more impetus than an ordinary javelin can attain. What is involved is the exploitation of centrifugal force, and if that cannot be called a significant invention by Stone Age man, I do not know what "invention" means.

Naturally, the Stone Age Edison who conceived it will remain forever nameless. We do not even know *where* the atlatl was invented. Like the bow and arrow, it was probably thought up more or less at the same time in several different places throughout the inhabited world. Some of Edison's inventions, too, were being duplicated at the same time in other countries.

Nevertheless, when we take these narrow points into our hand, it is hard to imagine that the Early Hunters could have used them successfully against mammoth and bison. Unfortunately, the points cannot tell us as much about these early men as pottery can about the later Indians. We learn a good deal when we establish, purely statistically, that Folsom points are found chiefly in the ribs of bison, the older Clovis points chiefly in the ribs of mammoths. But it takes a good deal of imagination to visualize the life, the daily struggle for sheer survival, of these Early Hunters.

Quite a few archaeologists have ventured to give vivid descriptions of such early hunting scenes. It is absolutely essential to call upon the aid of the imaginative faculty. The spearhead in the museum tells us nothing if we cannot picture it driving with fatal effect into the backbones of a mammoth or a bison. Here is how John M. Corbett reconstructs a bison hunt:

"Ten thousand years ago, a small band of weary, footsore, hungry hunters cautiously approached a few bison which they had managed to stampede away from the main herd. Ten in number, the bison had finally paused to drink at a small spring in a rincon of the canyon wall and to graze upon the thick, tall grass. For a day and a half, the hunters had carefully followed the large, hairy mammals, hoping the beasts would lose their sense of danger and allow themselves to be boxed into a place where the hunters could approach close enough to kill them.

"At last the moment was at hand! Warily, two hunters crawled along the slope of the canyon wall from opposite sides, seeking places from which they could throw large rocks upon the animals or hurl their spears with devastating force. Patiently, five more hunters waited below, concealed by the tall grass or behind convenient boulders. When the first two were in place, the leader gave the signal. Rocks came tumbling down on the startled bison; spears whistled through the air and thudded into soft flesh; one or two missed, but most found their targets. Shouts and cries filled the air. The bison, caught by surprise, whirled and milled around the waterhole for a moment, then several broke for the open country. One was wounded, the spear in its flank bobbing like a wave-tossed spindle. On this animal the hunters concentrated; three more spears found their target, and the great beast went down thrashing wildly. Two other animals lay maimed at the waterhole; one young calf, hobbling painfully, tried to get away to the open country but was quickly dispatched. The remaining six bison disappeared through the thickets and tall grass to the west."[3]

We can expand the details of this prehistoric scene, can see the hunters tearing and hacking at the carcasses, probably devouring such inner parts as the heart, kidneys, and liver then and there, loading juicy portions on their shoulders to carry to their campsite, while others were busy stripping the precious hides. We can imagine the welcome of women and children when the successful hunters reached the campsite. . . .

The procedure in mammoth hunts must have been much the same. Man, that largely hairless, relatively weak and, of all mammals, the most defenseless, had a developed hand, and this hand held a spear!

We can scarcely assume that a small group of hunters confronted a herd of mammoths in the open fields, that would have been suicidal. Undoubtedly, the men turned the conditions of the terrain to their advantage, building traps, pits covered with vegetation, which would collapse under the weight of the great beasts. But more often they must have tracked the animals to low-lying springs in the many damp canyons whose entrances could be blocked by stones and tree trunks, and they would then attack the mammoths from a safe distance, keeping up the assault until the bloody end. We also have plenty of examples of their having driven both bison and mammoths over the brink of cliffs, so that the animals lay helpless at the bottom, with broken legs, exposed to lances and thrown stones. But *how* were they driven?

The answer must be: by the one weapon of the Early Hunters that we have hitherto not mentioned—man's most terrible weapon since earliest times, and the one against which all animals were helpless.

Fire.

This leads us to the question that may have troubled the reader as he has come upon repeated references to extinct animals: *Why* did these animals die out? And why did man not die with them?

We may as well state at once that there are innumerable theories and no solution as yet. In 1965 a congress of specialists addressed itself to this question, and the results were published in 1967.[4] What emerges first of all is the wide variety of opinions.

Geologists call the epoch in which the giant animals lived together with man the Pleistocene. This was the time of advancing and receding masses of ice, which were accompanied by significant climatic changes. In view of this, the earliest theory, which can be supported by a good many arguments, held that the climatic conditions prevented the survival of the huge animals who needed enormous quantities of plant food. But not only the big animals died. The llama-sized camel and the horse also became extinct, as well as some small animals: a variety of rabbit; three species of antelope.

Other scientists were partisans of a catastrophe theory. They held that tremendous earthquakes and volcanic erup-

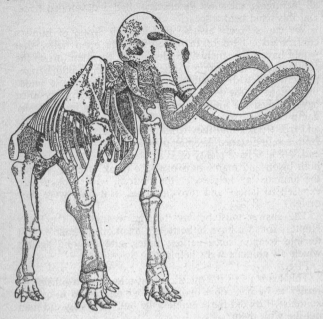

American elephants were all of the genus Mammuthus. *They included the woolly mammoth, which also ranged the Old World, and the imperial, confined to North America. This skeleton of one imperial variety, called the Columbian, stands 12 feet high at the shoulder.*

tions must have wiped out the animals within a short time. This view had considerable tradition behind it, for we must remember that only a generation ago the extinction of animals was seen in *dramatic* terms. These great convulsions were generally supposed to have taken place "ten thousand years ago." But this view received its death blow in 1968, when Jesse D. Jennings assembled all available radiocarbon datings of skeletal finds of animals. It turned out that the animals had by no means died out at the same time. Some, the mammoth, for example, probably survived until as late as 4000 B.C., longer than the horse. And the *Bison antiquus* was still roaming the prairies while the modern bison was slowly taking possession of the same terrain—around 6000 to 5000 B.C.[5]

Finally, there was the theory of unknown diseases, animal epidemics that supposedly decimated the herds. But, we must then ask, why were only a certain relatively small group of animals affected? Or again, a gigantic wave of suicides among the animals was predicated—with references to the lemmings, which supposedly take the mysterious balance of nature into their own paws, so to speak, by plunging into the sea in hordes at certain intervals.

The science of ecology is still only in its beginnings, and there is certainly an unsolved problem here—as is indicated by the perplexity of the inhabitants of the Florida coast in January, 1970, when 150 whales suddenly swam up on the beach. When stouthearted men used ropes to drag them back into the waves, the whales once more stormed up on the beach—to certain death.[6]

Here I should like to point out a matter that I feel needs rethinking. The Spanish philosopher Ortega y Gasset, whom we have already quoted twice, touches upon this problem in his brilliant essay *"Prólogo a un Tratado de Montería"* ("Prologue to a Treatise on Hunting"). He says: "The prehistorians are accustomed to assuring us that the various ice ages and post-ice ages were a hunter's paradise. They give us the impression that priceless game swarmed everywhere in dreamlike quantities, and as we read, the predator that slumbers in every good hunter feels his incisors sharpening and his mouth watering. But such statements are imprecise and summary."[7]

Ortega y Gasset goes on to cite evidence from many different stages of history to show that game animals were *always rare*. If this is so, it is by no means improbable that *man* exterminated the now extinct animals. One writer, to be sure, repeatedly asserts that 40 million large animals roamed through North America 10,000 years ago; but he presents no proof whatsoever for this figure.

As we give more thought to the theory of "Pleistocene overkill," as Martin has called it, its plausibility increases. First and foremost, there were the hunting methods of Ice Age men. In order for them to kill any member of a bison or elephant herd "it was necessary to kill them all . . . by driving them over a cliff."[8] (The word "elephant" can validly be applied both to the mammoth proper and the smaller mastodon; both of these animals existed in North America.) And how would man have created stampedes of this sort? By his possession of the dread secret of making fire. We do not know to what extent he was able to control the fires once he had set them. But as the flames swept through forests and over prairies, they would have destroyed thousands of animals, although the hunting horde could make use of only two or three. And these wholesale killings must have had dire effects. For replacements were scanty. Since the Early Hunter undoubtedly preferred young animals for his game—he found it easier and less risky to pursue them than older animals, and their meat was surely tastier—the reproductive capacity of the species was cut down. What is more, elephants have a gestation period of from eighteen to twenty-two months and bear only a single calf. At this rate they could not easily maintain their numbers in the face of ruthless slaughter by that newcomer to the evolutionary scene, man.

Why did *man* survive? After all, he was not only a hunter but also prey. When he crept up upon a herd of bison at the spring, the saber-toothed tiger might well be lurking in the underbrush. The giant bear also came to the water hole, and perhaps the wolf prowled hungrily about. Man survived because of his brain, because he is omnivorous, and because he can adapt to climatic changes. He not only survived; he developed. He left behind a bloody trail until he became a tiller of the soil and a dweller in houses, until he created civilization and culture, until the days he himself, as *man*, became man's greatest enemy.

I hope that in this book I have thoroughly refuted the notion—particularly widespread in Europe—that North American archaeology is concerned solely with flints. But in order to provide some small refreshment after the surfeit of flints in the last few chapters, and before we turn from weapons to the weapon maker himself, from spearheads to the skeletons of the First Americans, I now present an intermezzo drawn from the romantic period of American archaeology.

22   INTERMEZZO

The Towers of Silence

THE scientific report had been written long ago and published in the professional journal, *American Antiquity*. During the Second World War the author, Frank C. Hibben of the University of New Mexico, served as a lieutenant in the Navy. Reflecting upon his most interesting archaeological discoveries, he then wrote: "It is only since I have been in the Navy and have stood long hours of watch that I have had time to think that there might be a human-interest side to this work."

It is astonishing that this had not occurred to him earlier. But at any rate, the outcome of his ruminations was a "human-interest" article, "The Mystery of the Stone Towers."[1] It was published in 1944 by the now extinct *Saturday Evening Post*, whose circulation was nearly 3,500,000 in those days.

It seems to have been Hibben's fate that his discoveries and his reports on them arouse controversies among the specialists. A year before, as we have already mentioned, the *Post* had published his popular account of the discovery of Sandia Cave; and his opinions on "Sandia man" remain controversial to this day. His colleagues are similarly divided about what to make of the Gallina discovery. There is a degree of unity on the question today; most archaeologists agree that it is not particularly important. But the matter is so interesting that we certainly would not want to suppress it. For "this was a story of violence and bloodshed without a beginning and without an end."

Once more it was an outsider who made the actual discovery. In 1933 a rancher named Joe Areano was prospecting for gold along the Gallina River in the farthest corner of northern New Mexico. Suddenly, to his utter amazement, he saw before him a tall, rectangular stone tower. Then he realized that there were several, not just one.

We must consider that at the time this part of New Mexico was hardly explored, let alone surveyed. Only Navajo Indians roamed the area, and possibly no white man had ever set foot there before Areano. The landscape is desolate, almost inaccessible, but grandiose. It is high country covered with wooded mesas, cleft by deep, wild canyons, a land of glittering light and blackest shadows, the cliffs glowing in the richest colors from bright yellow to intense blues and purples.

Nothing could seem more improbable than suddenly to come upon such massive stone towers in this remote wilderness. Areano reckoned their height at twenty-five to thirty feet. He promptly dubbed them *torreónes* (fortress towers). Since he found a few ancient slag heaps in the vicinity, he decided that someone must have smelted gold here at one time. But fortune was not good to him; he found no gold, and therefore contented himself with picking up eight obviously very ancient but still brightly painted earthenware bowls that lay at the foot of one tower. They struck him as pretty, and he thought they might be salable. For this purpose, he went to Santa Fé. Here he learned that he had broken a law; it was illegal to remove, let alone sell, any antiquities found on land belonging to the state. Consequently, the pretty bowls were taken from him for the museum. The museum people listened to his story about the *torreónes*, but did not give it credence right away. It sounded too improbable. Again and again they asked him whether he had not seen old pueblo ruins. But no, he insisted that these towers were just as he described them, and he had seen not just one stone tower but several; they had looked like the ruins of medieval castles he had seen in pictures, absolutely not like a pueblo.

It was clear that the matter had to be pursued. That same year an expedition headed by Frank C. Hibben, with a number of student volunteers, set out over the difficult terrain. In their heavily laden car they could drive only as far as the entrance to Gallina Canyon. There they had to commandeer a wagon in order to penetrate into the wilderness of cliffs, which in winter is absolutely inaccessible. But it was the middle of June, and so they were able to make progress along the bed of the Gallina River, which was already completely dried out.

They saw the first tower after squeezing through a place in Gallina Canyon so narrow that the hubs of the wheels scraped the cliffs on both sides. Suddenly, after they had forced this narrow passage, a basin opened up before them, about a mile long and 200 or 300 yards wide. Hibben describes it vividly:

"The cliffs on both sides were cut into a series of long, jagged points that jutted out on both sides of the basin, like the jaws of a great steel trap spread wide open. The wagon lurched out onto a low terrace at the upper end of the basin, and there we saw our first *torreón* against a blue sky.

"The tower was perched on top of one of these rocky pinnacles, close to one side of the encircling cliffs. Even though it was high above us, we could see that it was artificial, even though it apparently grew out of the rock on which it stood. Outlined against the dazzling sky, as we viewed it from the floor of the canyon below, the tower looked medieval."

They stopped their wagon, took their binoculars, and scanned the edges of the canyon. They saw a second, then a third tower, then many, isolated or in whole groups, every single one on some pinnacle. It was exactly as Areano had said: "They looked like castles along the rimrock."

"Our thoughts and speculations," Hibben says, "ran riot."

It was obvious that these were not ordinary pueblos. But what kind of structures were they? Who had built them? And when? The archaeologists began an extensive study. They took photos, made maps, rode miles deep into the canyons to the south and north. And they found—we can anticipate the result here—no fewer than 500 *torreónes* in an area of perhaps thirty-five by fifty miles.

That could not have been the work of a small tribe. A whole people must have lived here. For lack of any authentic name, Hibben and his group called them the Gallina people. And 500 towers—that was more than any single generation could have built.

The studies went on for several summers. The wild beauty of the mountains was overwhelming. But there were several aspects of the region that made the expedition extraordinarily difficult. For example, there was the shortage of water. Only one tiny spring was found, and its water contained a high percentage of gypsum, alkali, and Epsom salts. Its effects on the stomachs and intestines of the exploring party were devastating. One wit among the students put up a sign beside the spring: "Before the days of gin and beer, Gallina man drank water here, God rest his soul!" Then there was a type of black fly there that descended in clouds. Its bites or stings caused blisters and sores, so that the members of the party looked as if they were suffering from an incurable poison-ivy infection.

But none of this could deter the explorers. Everyone was burning to see what was inside the towers. They chose for investigation the group of eight towers on the pinnacle that they had first seen. As chance would have it, the first tower they approached later proved to be quite typical. (Most of the towers were rectangular; only a few had the corners so curved that they appeared to be almost round.) The building was between twenty-five and thirty feet high. The walls were of sandstone blocks, roughly cut, jointed with adobe mortar, that mixture of clay and straw the Pueblo Indians ordinarily used to make bricks. At the base, the walls were no less than six feet thick.

The top actually resembled a European castle, even to a parapet for the defenders. The tower had no door; the only way to enter it was by means of a ladder to the roof and then through a hatchway to another ladder into the interior. Hibben and his party found the remains of such ladders in the interior when they dug their way through the collapsed roof beams, loosened blocks, and the refuse of centuries.

Inside, a surprise awaited them. Those rude, defiant towers, seemingly built solely for defense, proved to be richly ornamented and finished on the interior. The inner walls were smoothly plastered and covered with drawings of plants, birds, flowers, and "pennant-like flags," which might have been tokens of victories.

The floor of the tower chamber was about twenty by twenty feet and paved with "massive slabs of carefully fitted sandstone." All around were stone or adobe benches, which were hollow, so that they must have served as bins for storage. A neatly built hearth was also found, and an airshaft let into the thickness of the wall. In the bins they found the first traces of the mysterious people who had inhabited these rooms. When they opened the bins, "the puff of centuries-old air that came out was like the breath from an Egyptian tomb." They found themselves looking upon whole collections of utilitarian and ornamental objects, reposing there as if someone's hand had arranged them only the day before.

There were leather pouches containing the colored powders used for ceremonies, ornamented seashells, brightly painted wooden prayer sticks, amulets, and good-luck symbols, deerhide articles of clothing, featherwork, cane arrows and flint arrowheads, dance masks, and horns. These are all objects still used by the Indians. Consequently, they could not have been *age-old*.

And then there was the most surprising thing of all.

"What fairly made us gasp as we carefully uncovered them was the occupants of the tower itself. They were still here, and their story was with them. In all, scattered about the tower in various positions and attitudes, were sixteen people!"

Excavators, who must breathe deep of the air of the past, frequently fight off its numbing chill by a kind of swagger, just as medical students are apt to tell jokes as they perform autopsies. The young scientists quickly established an easy relationship with their finds. They gave the bodies names, calling one Itchy Fingers, another Big Bruiser, a third, the body of a woman, Bold Titania.

But to top it all off was the discovery of a drama. These people had not died natural deaths. They had been struck down in battle with an enemy. Careful study showed incontrovertibly what had happened. The wooden roof of the tower had been set ablaze by flaming arrows. The fire had then spread to the ladders and everything else that was flammable. Roof beams had collapsed into the interior, carrying down parts of the stone parapet along with the defenders posted on it. And the extremely dry climate of the Southwestern plateau country, together with the charring effects of heat and the protection of the rubble that fell on top of the people, had preserved some of the bodies so well that they were in better condition than many Egyptian mummies.

"Here was the body of a woman sprawled backward over one of the storage bins. She had been crushed by falling stones from the top of the wall, but her body was remarkably preserved, even to a look of intense agony on her somewhat flattened face. Studded in her breast and stomach were the charred ends of sixteen arrows of cane with flint heads. She still clutched in her left hand a bow, even with a part of the string still on one end. It was a short bow, powerful looking, of oak wood, and yet the body was undoubtedly that of a woman.

"In the center of the floor of the tower, where they had apparently fallen when struck from the roof, were two men, one crosswise on top of the other. In the hands of one were three bows, two of oak and one of juniper wood, and in his other hand was a bundle of twenty-seven arrows. Evidently this man had been passing the ammunition when he was struck down.

"The other man, too, was a warrior, and had met the same harsh end. A stone ax with a jagged edge was embedded in his skull over his left eye, clear to the middle of the blade, and still stuck there. Another woman had apparently been fighting at the same time. These were remarkable people, these Gallina warriors, the women as well as the men. This woman had an arrow in her shoulder, and possibly others. It was difficult to tell, as the falling roof had crushed her badly. Her hair-do was in perfect shape, however, and looked remarkably modern. She had very carefully parted her hair in the middle and swept it down on either side in three braids. These three braids on each side were looped up again and worked into a little knot at the very back of her head. The looped braids, which drooped down to about her shoulder, were fixed with little pieces of painted buckskin in a very modern manner. Her scalp along the part of her hair was painted red."

Even their clothing was partly preserved.

"A whole cluster of warriors had apparently fallen or been thrown down the hatchway where the ladder had entered the house from the roof. Their feet were still shod with finely woven yucca sandals, tied with thongs around the instep and ankle. They looked remarkably like modern beach shoes, and even had designs woven into their soles in a sort of nonskid effect. One man had a buckskin breech clout hanging down from a twisted belt on either side of his waist. Another had buckskin breeches that covered his whole lower body, and charred remnants of the porcupine quilling that had ornamented them still adhered to the stiff leather."

But the most striking discovery, which instantly brought the whole scene to life, came when they examined the air shaft. Here they found the body of a boy of perhaps fifteen or sixteen, long thin locks of hair still on his head. He must have been alive when he fell down with the collapsing roof. Evidently he had tried, with his last strength, to crawl into the narrow shaft, and had become stuck there. The burning brands that had fallen with him had reached and charred only the lower part of his body. But an arrow, fired from behind, was still sticking in his hip. "You could almost read on the dried and mummified face the look of terror and fear that it still held, centuries after the boy had crowded himself into the hole, trying to get away from the heat."

Until the outbreak of the Second World War, Hibben and his assistants continued their explorations. Ultimately, they cleared the interiors of seventeen towers, and all seventeen told the same story. In one, five defenders remained, in another, eleven, among them another woman with weapon in hand. Every tower had been destroyed by fire, and in each the defenders had fought to the last. The questions became more and more insistent. Who had built these towers? Who had defended them? Who had attacked and destroyed them?

A fourth question, and one of the key ones—how old the towers were—could be answered with some precision. Dendrochronology helped. There were enough roof beams remaining to permit tree-ring datings. According to the analyses (we are still citing Hibben), the trees for these beams had been cut between 1143 and 1245. This meant that all these Gallina towers had been erected over the span of a century, some 700 years ago and 250 years before the Spanish arrived.

Who the builders were remains a mystery. All the objects and weapons found with them, as well as the physical characteristics of the skeletons and bodies found in some of the towers, differ sharply from the remains of Pueblo Indians. The pottery shows quality alien to the Southwest; it resembles types found in Nebraska and the Mississippi Valley. Hibben further determined that the tower builders had cultivated a variety of corn and a special type of squash that hitherto had been thought typical only of Iowa and the Missouri Valley. These were clues, but puzzling ones. Hibben sums up:

"On a basis of many bits of evidence, of which these are

just a few, we concluded that the Gallina people had entered the Southwest at a very early date, possibly several hundred years before they were destroyed. They came from the plains, possibly as far east as the Mississippi Valley itself, and brought with them a number of their characteristic traits. What caused them to move into the Southwestern area, we do not know, but it seems that they found it already populated by others—which possibly explains why they picked the rough but beautiful Gallina country for their home. Where they got the trait of building towers is not known. Possibly they found some other peoples who built towers for defense; possibly they invented this type of architecture themselves, when the need arose to protect themselves."

Among the modern surveys of the whole of North American archaeology, several do not mention the Gallina problem at all. John C. McGregor in his standard *Southwestern Archaeology,* published in 1965, merely praises the varied pottery of a "Gallina phase," and acknowledges the uniqueness of the towers. But he leaves open all questions of "who" and "where from."

There remains the question of who attacked this redoubtable people, which had set up such excellent defenses, and exterminated them—only, apparently, to move on or to return home, for there was no attempt to occupy the ruins. All the evidence points to an extremely bellicose nomad people—but the tribes that answer this description, the Navajos and the Apaches, say, did not invade these highlands until some 200 years after the slaughter at Gallina, at least so far as we know. The arrows found in the bodies of the victims provide one hint. They, however, point to the Pueblo Indians, who used exactly this type of arrow with narrow, triangular flint points. The whole thing is contradictory and bewildering.

23

The First American, or
The Girls from Midland
and Laguna

THE reader may have wondered—and the scientists have repeatedly posed the same question—why we have found such vast numbers of weapons in America made by early man, who lived long before the Mound Builders and the Pueblo people, but for so long have never come across the remains of man himself. There have been, as a matter of fact, a few finds. But many of the "incontrovertible" discoveries—the newspapers rush into print with premature accounts of such every year—have proved to be highly doubtful when examined under the specialist's magnifying glass.

That was what happened with so-called Nebraska man, whose discovery was once hailed in banner headlines. His extreme age, determined on the basis of a tooth, seemed undeniable. Until it turned out that the tooth was that of an extinct species of peccary.

One case unclarified to this day is that of "Minnesota Minnie." That was what journalists dubbed the remains of a girl, probably fifteen years old, whose skull was turned up in Minnesota by a bulldozer in 1931. Naturally, ten feet of strata were destroyed in the process. It may be that this girl actually fell or was pushed into glacial Lake Pelican some 8,000 to 10,000 years ago and drowned. But it may also be that she was a Sioux girl, perhaps of the last century, who for some obscure reasons was buried in such a deep grave.

At any rate, more and more skeletal remains are available for consideration at the present time. There is no longer any doubt that these first Americans were immigrants, and also no doubt that they were already members of the human race, that is to say, they belonged to the final stage of the long evolution toward man. They were members of *Homo sapiens,* the group to which we ourselves belong. (The scientific name *sapiens,* which means "rational, intelligent," can also mean "wise," but even today, after some 40,000 years of prehistory and history, this meaning is seldom applicable.)

Some years ago there were two skeletal finds vying for the honor of being the First American: Midland man and Tepexpan man, the former found near Texas, the latter near Mexico City. The two finds, and what was done with them, present an extreme contrast. The excavaton of Midland man is to this day viewed as a model of beautiful, accurate teamwork. The heads of the expedition were Fred Wendorf of the Laboratory of Anthropology at Santa Fé, Alex D. Krieger of the University of Texas at Austin, Claude C. Albritton of Southern Methodist University at Dallas, and T. D. Steward of the United States National Museum, a branch of the Smithsonian Institution.[1] On the other hand, Jesse D. Jennings of the University of Utah has branded the excavation of Tepexpan man "a masterpiece of vague reporting."[2]

Midland "man" was really a woman, aged about thirty, whose bones were found in 1933 by the amateur Keith Glasscock. He immediately called upon the specialists— and Jennings praises him for that: "May Keith's tribe increase!" But in spite of all the care of the investigators, the skeleton can be dated only vaguely: older than 10,000 years, *perhaps* as much as 20,000 years old. This would mean, if the maximum age could be accepted, that the Midland girl is indeed the oldest American. But this extreme date is unfortunately too uncertain.

Tepexpan man, male and of considerably riper years, with teeth almost worn down to the jawbone, has been set down with fair certainty as 10,000 years old, or just a little older.

However that may be, the question of the oldest, the first American, has not yet been unequivocally answered. Once again we quote Gordon R. Willey, who in a lecture to the American Philosophical Society in Philadelphia in 1956 voiced what may be considered for the time being the last word on the subject:

"Little doubt now exists that the first man to enter the New World crossed the Bering Strait from Asia to Alaska during the Pleistocene. It is also virtually certain that these first Americans belonged to the genus *Homo sapiens* and highly likely that they were of the Mongoloid racial stock. Beyond these basic agreements, the particular time at which they came and the cultural heritage which they brought with them *are highly controversial.*

"The hard facts of the matter are that man was definitely in the New World by 10,000 B.C. At this time he was a hunter of large, now extinct, mammals, including the mammoth, and he pursued these beasts with lances or darts tipped with finely flaked, stone projectile points that were characteristically fluted.

"Now in the opinion of some archaeologists man had first entered the Americas only shortly before 10,000 B.C., and had brought with him, from Asia, Upper Paleolithic blade and projectile-point-making techniques from which he developed the characteristic American fluted forms.

"A counter-opinion holds that man came to the New World long before this, perhaps as far back as 30,000 or 40,000 or more years ago. Coming at this time he brought with him a much simpler tool kit. It included no blades or projectile points but was, rather, in the tradition of the ancient Lower or Middle Paleolithic Chopper-Chopping Tool Industry of Southeast Asia. From this tradition he developed in the New World, over the millennia, and independent of additional Old World stimuli, the lanceolate, fluted projectile points of 10,000 B.C.

"Neither of these hypotheses is entirely satisfactory—at least in our present state of knowledge."[3]

On the whole these words are still valid today, but a few

new finds have come along in the interval, and above all there has been a successful new dating of an old find. If that dating really proves accurate, it will justify the banner headlines that appeared in the newspapers from Los Angeles to New York early in 1969: "LAGUNA GIRL" DATED.

Before we go into the findings we must clarify one point: the story of *man*, including his predecessors, the ancestors of *Homo sapiens*, is far, far older than any traces of him in America.

The best known of man's predecessors is probably Neanderthal man, whose skeleton was found in a cave near Düsseldorf, Germany, in 1856. At first he was thought to be either a misshapen idiot of modern times or even a lost Cossack from the Russian army that pursued Napoleon in 1812. I. C. Fuhlrott first recognized the skeleton as that of a prehistoric man. Today he is thought to be about 50,000 years old. But these and all the following dates on ages are quite vague and are repeatedly disputed by the scholars. Moreover, the designations represent great spans of time, so that to identify a given find as Neanderthal, for instance, and then to place it in time, says nothing about how long this type existed *before* and *after* the given date. In the case of the Neanderthal man it is fairly well agreed that he represents a kind of blind alley in the study of human evolution; he died out, and our real ancestor came from another race.

The discovery of Java man leads us much farther back into the past; an age of 500,000 to 1,000,000 years has been assigned to him. The same is true for Heidelberg and Peking man; the latter is dated at between 200,000 and 500,000 years. In 1959 the African finds of Louis S. B. Leakey, curator of the Coryndon Museum in Nairobi, Kenya, aroused excitement. In Olduvay Gorge in Tanzania (then Tanganyika) he found human remains that apparently went back 600,000 years, and subsequently other remains to which he assigned the fantastic age of 1,750,000 years.

More pertinent to our purposes, however, is the discovery of Cro-Magnon man, made in 1868 in a cave in the French Dordogne. Along with the remains of mammoths and wild horses lay the skeletons of three men, a woman, and a fetus. Cro-Magnon man is indubitably our nearest ancestor; he is dated to the period between 30,000 and 40,000 years ago. Long-skulled, narrow-nosed, high-browed, very broad-shouldered, his face was still rather flat. But while there is not yet agreement over whether Neanderthal man and pre-Neanderthal man were already members of *Homo sapiens* (and most scientists think they were not), it is now generally accepted that Cro-Magnon man was.

What is the difference between the two?

Oswald Spengler once remarked cynically that you could run into Neanderthal man today in any gathering of the common people. By way of contrast, the French archaeologist Henry de Lumley, while digging up remains of a 200,000-year-old human campsite near Nice, was asked this question by a reporter, and answered wryly:

"If you were riding in the subway and a Cro-Magnon chap got on, you probably wouldn't notice him. If a pre-Neanderthaler hung on the next strap, you'd look at him twice!"

"And probably get off at the next station," the reporter surmised.[4]

The man who emigrated to America ages ago was human in the fullest sense of the word—*Homo sapiens* armed with fire, weapons, and tools, driven by curiosity and the hunger for game-filled land.

To turn now to the strange Laguna girl, whose travels thousands of years after her death probably exceeded any in her lifetime.

In 1933 seventeen-year-old Howard Wilson and a friend went treasure hunting. Wilson already had a handsome collection of spearheads, arrowheads, and other such things. The two boys dug a short distance from their home, at what is now St. Ann's Drive, Laguna Beach, California. Poking with a screwdriver in places where the ground was soft and sandy, they came upon a bone which they immediately decided was human. That excited them. But the next layer of earth was hard, and the next after that was still harder. One of the boys ran back home and fetched a pickaxe. They began grubbing away. A skull came to light. At this their eagerness overcame them—they hacked more violently and less cautiously, and one of the blows struck the skull. Fortunately, it did not shatter, but henceforth it bore the clear mark of an amateur's excavation. That fact was later to prove important.

Wilson took the find home and showed it to his mother. She said tersely that he ought to throw the bones into the garbage can at once. But Wilson—praise be his disobedience!—put the skull away in a shoebox. There it remained for the time being.

Wilson kept up his interest in Indian relics, and two years later he took another look at the skull. It struck him that this one was very different from the skulls he had seen in the course of his museum visits, and he decided to pursue the matter. He wrote to the Southwest Museum in Highland Park, California, enclosing a careful drawing. The reply he received was that his skull was undoubtedly prehistoric, "but not especially a primitive type."[5]

Wilson did not give up, and now the skull's wanderings began. It was sent to Dr. D. B. Rogers of the Museum of Natural History in Santa Barbara, who identified it as fairly old and assumed that it could be attributed to the Oak Grove people, the oldest known Indians of California.

As yet no one suspected the truth.

After several months' study of the skull at the University of Southern California in 1937, Ivan A. Bopatin sent a letter to Wilson in which he stated his conclusions: "After close visual examination and comparison with other skulls in our laboratory, I am able to say only that the skull under consideration *does not differ from that of an average California Indian.*"[6]

The skull went back into the shoebox. And only its finder continued to believe there was something unusual about it. After the passage of *sixteen years* he placed it at the disposal of the sculptor George Stromer. Stromer was a specialist in making sculptures of prehistoric men for a museum.

And now, incongruous though it sounds, the next estimate of the skull's age went all the way to the other extreme. Stromer showed it to Dr. J. J. Markey, who took it with him to the great European center of anthropology in Paris, the famous Musée de l'Homme. The scientists there imagined that they had found embedded in the skull fossil shellfish that had been extinct for *100,000 years!* Could the skull then be 100,000 years old? This seemed totally incredible.

Dr. Markey, now fascinated by the mystery of this skull, carried it with him to Rome, Madrid, Brussels, and the British Museum. It certainly cannot be said that the skull was ignored; but the judgments that leading anthropologists handed down were anything but definitive. (We must remember that radiocarbon dating did not exist before 1947.)

After a journey of eight years the skull finally came home to its finder.

Then, after more years had passed, a lucky chance suddenly altered the situation. Early in 1967 the world-famous archaeologist Louis S. B. Leakey, excavator of those oldest human remains in Olduvay Gorge mentioned above, was on a lecture tour in California. Through the good offices of someone who knew Leakey, the stubborn Wilson, who had meanwhile become a successful building designer in South Laguna but who still had archaeological ambitions and still believed in the special nature of his find, arranged a meeting with Leakey. The famous man consented to give the amateur ten minutes—but after Leakey was shown the skull and heard the circumstances of the find, their conversation continued for three quarters of an hour. Then Leakey decided that the skull must be sent at once to Dr. Berger at the University of California for radiocarbon dating.

Dr. Rainer Berger, former assistant to Libby, the inventor of C-14 dating, who was now working at the Institute of Geophysics and Planetary Physics, tackled this long-unsolved problem. He subjected the skull to a most careful investigation by the latest methods. The amazing result, which, as we have mentioned, made headlines everywhere, was summed up by Berger in the following dry report:

"Radiocarbon date of the skull: Portions of the skull, parietal and temporal bones, were dated by the collagen method as follows: 78.5 g of bones were extracted continuously with ether for several days to remove any organic substances introduced by handling the skull. Then the mineral matrix of the bones was destroyed by dilute cold hydrochloric acid treatment. Finally humic acids of different specific activity were extracted with dilute, cold sodium hydroxide. The remaining organic portion was dated and found to correspond to an age of 17,150 ± 1,470 years."[7]

This plus-or-minus figure is unusually large and indicates great caution. If the measurement is correct, it means that the long underestimated Laguna skull is between 18,620 and 15,680 years old.

A truly amazing age!

Dr. Berger refused to be content with his initial results. He checked the authenticity of the skull. Was what he had in the laboratory really the same skull Wilson had found—after so many trips through so many museums? Fortunately, proof was available. At the time the find was still new, a local newspaper had published a picture of it. And on this picture was plainly visible the gouge that the impetuous Wilson had made with his pickaxe. The gouge was at the same spot on the skull in the laboratory.

Other analyses were undertaken. In particular, the bone Wilson had found in conjunction with the skull was also tested. There was a purely anthropological study by Dr. D. Stewart, the Smithsonian Institution expert, who decided that the skull was in all probability that of a woman—hence "Laguna girl." In addition, Wilson was asked whether he could identify the site of the find. He could, and during 1968 an extensive excavation was undertaken at St. Ann's Drive. Would it not be possible to find other bones?

But the results were disappointing, and doubts sprang up. The excavation turned up a few animal bones and shells, but no more human remains. What was more perplexing, at a depth of about two feet California mussel shells were found, which were dated by the C-14 method at 8,950 ± 80. But at a depth of about six feet more shells were found that yielded a date of 8,300 ± 80 years.

Here was confusion compounded. Not only were the younger mussel shells at a lower depth than the older, contrary to all the rules of stratigraphy, but according to Wilson's statements the skull had lain *between* them.

How can a 17,000-year-old skull have found its way between two strata 8,000 and 9,000 years old?

Dr. Berger and the archaeologist J. R. Sackett explain that this puzzling situation is not so puzzling if the special geographical conditions of the area are considered. We need not go into their detailed expositions. It is enough to know that displacements of the earth, which can lead to the strangest stratigraphic relationships, are extremely common in the area—as the canyon dwellers in the vicinity of Los Angeles well know, for in 1968 many of them had to jump out of their windows when huge masses of earth suddenly started moving and threatened to overwhelm their houses.

Nevertheless, doubts remain on the part of the overcautious archaeologists, who have learned caution from a great many disconcerting experiences. They no longer regard a single dating as sufficient. They insist on double and triple proofs, and lay special weight on the oldest method of proof in their profession: stratigraphy.

Nevertheless, "L. S. B. Leakey is satisfied with the appearance and the C-14 age of the skull," Berger writes. And he adds: "It is thus the oldest direct evidence of Man in the Americas."[8]

There are still other sites to mention, but let us leave them to the specialists. In any case, there is ample evidence that North American archaeology has been progressing at a furious rate during the past ten years, not only in its methods, but also in the number of finds. (Leakey labored in Africa for thirty years but turned up only three sites of importance.) It is an old experience in the history of all the sciences that each new discovery sets off a chain reaction. Suddenly the scientist's eye sharpens and perceives what he had previously overlooked. I therefore believe that we are on the verge of a great many fresh discoveries. And perhaps Leakey or someone else will one day be able to prove what he now suspects only on the basis of inconclusive finds: that man is far, far older in America than previously assumed.[9]

In 1968 Leakey uncovered extremely primitive stone tools, so-called pebble choppers, in the course of a California excavation. In an interview he dated them at 40,000–50,000 years, perhaps even as old as 80,000–100,000. Most archaeologists, however, still doubt that his finds represent tools at all; they consider them chance sports of nature. In 1965 Emil W. Haury bet Leakey $100 that within the next fifteen years he would not be able to actually *prove* that man in North America is between 50,000 and 100,000 years old. So far, Haury is still the winner.

The layman with an interest in science is apt to turn to the specialist for ultimate, unequivocal answers. "What am I to tell my son when he asks how old the oldest American is?" one father asked. Well, we have given the answer here —*as exactly as it is possible to do so today*. If all the thousands of years we have tossed back and forth makes the matter a little hard to understand—what does the father answer if his son asks him to explain the theory of relativity?

24

The Way Across
Bering Strait

MISTS, fog, drifting ice floes—nothing more could be seen by the man in the crow's nest of the small ship that was painfully fighting its way northward through the strait that would subsequently bear the captain's name: Bering Strait. The date was August, 1728. On orders from Tsar Peter, Vitus Bering had set out to explore the northern frontiers of the gigantic Russian Empire. When he passed through the strait, he did not know for certain that he was sailing between two continents, although both shores would have been plainly visible on a clear day—for at its narrowest spot the strait is only about fifty-six miles wide. But he took that on trust; his seaman's instinct told him that these cold waters separated Siberia from Alaska. And he was right. Only—that had not always been the case.

Today Bering Strait is twenty-four fathoms deep. To whalers and seal hunters its aspect is as harsh as it has been for thousands of years. For the greater part of the year the temperature of the air does not rise above 32 degrees Fahrenheit, that of the water above 48 degrees. The range of the tides is small; the strait would be totally blocked by polar ice were it not for the constant northward current from the Pacific. In the middle of this dreary passage lie two equally dreary tiny islands, the Diomedes. Since the strait is so narrow, Eskimos can cross it in their kayaks, and they do so every so often.

But the people who crossed it from Siberia to Alaska more than 10,000 years ago followed the big game animals, and just like the animals, they walked *on dry land*.

William Howells of Harvard sums up: "They did not know that this particular neck of land would be covered as the sea rose much later, when the glaciers melted. They

The immigration route of the Early Hunters across Bering Strait.

did not know they were entering a whole new world, splendid with game animals: mastodons, mammoths, horses, camels, long-horn bisons, musk-oxen and such oddities as the giant sloth, to say nothing of elk, moose, caribou and deer. They did not know they were the first Americans."[1]

And they also did not invade the new continent in great wild hordes. No vast migration of whole peoples ever took place here, as happened very much later several times between Asia and Europe. "Peoples" who could have emigrated from Siberia to Alaska did not exist. There were just the early Siberian hunters of Mongoloid race, who lived in small tribes, always following the tracks of the big animals that served as their main food. They *trickled* into North America—and once again, at the end of our book, we must discuss the question of *when*.

Several Ice Ages passed over North America, as over Europe and Asia. Half the continents were covered with mighty sheets of ice—but four times the ice advanced and four times it receded, each time accompanied by massive climatic changes. The process must not be viewed dramatically. Earthquakes are dramatic, but Ice Ages unfold at an "epic" pace, extending over spans of time that seem beyond the human scale. Yet geologists are fairly certain that the glaciers, by binding vast quantities of water, so lowered the level in the Bering Sea and the Arctic Ocean that Bering Strait became a land bridge. With all due caution they further assert that there were occasions when the conditions for Siberian hunters to conquer the American continents were especially favorable, from 20,000 to 40,000 years ago, and from 12,000 to 13,000 years ago.

In 1967 David M. Hopkins, who devoted many years to studying Bering Strait, wrote:

"Eighteen years ago, stormbound at Wales village, I studied the mist smoking over a turbulent Bering Strait and wondered who, on this violent day, might be shouldering the wind on the Asian shore to share my search for traces of the past. Near me rose a peaty mound, the midden left by generation upon generation of Eskimos dwelling at the western tip of North America; behind me rose Cape Mountain, scarred by ancient glaciers, carved by ancient waves. Perhaps someone was at that moment sheltering his Cyrillic notes from the mist as he huddled on a terrace on East Cape, at the eastern tip of Siberia—or in an Eskimo burial ground at Uelen, Siberia's easternmost village."[2]

Hopkins wrote this in his capacity as editor of the many papers which were delivered in 1965 by twenty-seven scientists from six nations (for the first time Russian scholars were included) at the Seventh Congress of the International Quaternary Association. These papers all concerned a single theme: the Bering land bridge.

It is significant that scholars no longer discuss the question of whether the first Americans came from Siberia; today that is regarded as conclusive. The theory has been around for a long time; the first to suggest the possibility of immigration from Asia was probably the monk José de Acosta in 1590. But the present certainty rests on a rather indirect type of proof: the fact that all other theories have been eliminated either as wrong or—for example, the theories of the "ten lost tribes of Israel," of Atlantis and Mu—as simply nonsensical.

Of course, the immigration probably took place in several waves; that is the prevailing view today. We also cannot entirely exclude the possibility that there may have been *chance* immigrations by ship or raft across the Pacific or the northern Atlantic before Columbus and possibly even before the Vikings. Such visits would account, some say, for the multiplicity of Indian languages and for racial differences. Nevertheless, is it conceivable that a few tribes in a relatively few thousand years increased to millions and scattered themselves from Bering Strait to the southern tip of South America? For many years that question went unanswered.

There is really something mysterious about the urge to reach the south, which must have inspired these people. For a long time the simplest explanation seemed to serve, a "natural impulse to follow the sun," a kind of prehistoric "Southward, Ho!" as it were. But if that were the case, why did the Asiatic tribes wander northward into the cold and darkness? And why did the Eskimos, the latest prehistoric immigrants to America, not obey this impulse? Instead, they acclimatized themselves to the harshest of conditions, conditions barely endurable for human beings.

As far as the increase in numbers of the first immigrants is concerned, some interesting calculations have been made. These were reported by C. Vance Haynes, Jr., in 1966.[3] According to Haynes, a tribe of only thirty mammoth hunters could in 500 years increase from a population of 800 to 12,500 persons, or from 26 to 425 tribes. Haynes makes these extrapolations on the basis of the Clovis hunters, who immigrated 12,000–13,000 years ago, and whose characteristic spearheads are found widely distributed over the continent. He further calculates that these tribes would have been able to produce in the same span of time from 2 million to 14 million spearheads!

There remains the pace of expansion. Haynes calculated that if the Clovis hunters moved only four miles to the south every year, they could easily have wandered from the Bering land bridge to their southernmost hunting grounds in New Mexico within 500 years. That is a realistic view. One unrealistic theory runs as follows:

"If a single nomadic hunting group, starting from Bering Strait, moved its camp but three miles southward each week, week after week, month after month, the extreme southern end of South America could be reached in only seventy years."[4]

That is unrealistic because for a people of hunters, who must constantly follow their big animals up and down their terrain, such a continuous journey to the south is entirely out of the question. But whatever the case, *these first hunters took possession of North and South America.*

The diffusion theory can in no way affect this fact. The diffusionists hold that several cultural invasions must have taken place—perhaps from Egypt, from Mesopotamia, or even from China. As evidence they point to linguistic similarities, the building of pyramids, certain mythological notions, and other parallels. As far as the resemblance of Indian languages to those of the Old World goes, Willey flatly stated as recently as 1966: "At present no such relationships have ever been satisfactorily demonstrated."[5] Nevertheless, both he and many other modern archaeologists are prepared to believe that there might have been cultural influences from the Old World, especially in Central and South America. But if these occurred, they occurred in *historical* times, millennia after the first Early Hunters roamed the lonely plateaus of the North American Southwest, tracking down the now extinct animals. And these Early Hunters, the real First Americans, came across the Bering land bridge, plucky, curious, to a certain extent, inventive. Why they did not develop such advanced civilizations in North America as those of the Mayas, Aztecs, and Incas in Central and South America will probably remain a riddle forever.

The Story of Ishi

THE story begins at the fence of a slaughterhouse two or three miles outside the town of Oroville, California, at dawn on August 29, 1911. Oroville, then a town of some 3,800 people, is about seventy miles northeast of Sacramento.

The dogs began barking so madly that a few sleep-sodden butchers came out to see what was the matter. Leaning against the fence was a man whom they at first took to be a drunken tramp. Then they saw that he was almost naked; only around his shoulders was there a scrap of cloth resembling a poncho. And his face was obviously that of an Indian, but of a type they had never seen before. The poor creature's black eyes glittered with a hunted look of terror.

The baffled butchers could think of nothing better to do than to summon the sheriff. He arrived, approached the stranger with drawn gun, and ordered him to come along. The response was a series of incomprehensible sounds. To be on the safe side, the sheriff handcuffed the fellow—who meekly accepted whatever was done with him but continued to show signs of intense fear—and took him to the Oroville jail, where he locked him in a cell normally reserved for the mentally ill.

At this point the sheriff realized that his prisoner was utterly exhausted. The man was undoubtedly an Indian, but his skin was somewhat lighter than that of the tribes the sheriff knew. All attempts at communication proved fruitless, even when a Mexican tried Spanish and a few Indians were fetched who spoke several Indian dialects.

The sheriff was unhappy about the whole affair, for within a short time word of the "wild man" had got around, and more and more curiosity seekers kept coming to have a look at him. At last the reporter of the local newspaper arrived. The "wild man's" picture appeared in the newspaper next day, and the next day the story made banner headlines in the San Francisco papers. There, at the Anthropological Museum of the University of California, Alfred L. Kroeber and Thomas T. Waterman saw them.

It was lucky for Ishi—we may as well give the wild man his name—and lucky for science that Kroeber and Waterman not only read the newspaper articles but also guessed at once that this might represent a unique case. If the strange man actually spoke an unknown language, might he not be one of the last survivors of a supposedly vanished tribe? That seemed a totally fantastic hope on the part of the two anthropologists. Nevertheless, on August 31, two days after Ishi had appeared, Kroeber sent the following telegram to Oroville: "Sheriff Butte County. Newspapers report capture wild Indian speaking language other tribes totally unable understand. Please confirm or deny by collect telegram and if story correct hold Indian till arrival Professor State University who will take charge and be responsible for him. Matter important account aboriginal history."[1]

The reply came promptly, and on that very day Waterman set out for Oroville and Ishi.

The anthropologists' hope had but a single and perhaps flimsy basis. It was known that the country around Oroville had formerly been the territory of the Yana Indians, who had spoken various dialects. The languages of the two northern tribes had been preserved. The last survivors, a man named Batwi and called Sam, and a woman named Chidaimiya, Christianized as Betty Brown, had dictated an extensive vocabulary. But not a word of the language of the southern tribe, the Yahi, had ever been recorded; the tribe was considered extinct. If by a miracle Ishi were a Yahi, there would certainly be difficulties in communication, but what a coup for science it would be.

We can imagine the suspense with which Waterman, his Yana word list in hand, first approached Ishi in his cell. He opened the "dictionary," pointed to objects, and pronounced the words, repeating them with varying intonations because he could not be sure about his pronunciation. Ishi sat hunched, impassive, weak; he had refused food because, as came out later, he thought the white men were trying to poison him. He merely stared at Waterman with an unfathomable look. Waterman began to lose heart; he was approaching the end of his list. Finally he pointed at the wood of the cot and said, *"Siwini,"* which means yellow pine. And suddenly Ishi straightened up. *"Siwini,"* he repeated. And then the two were seized by excitement; they wildly tapped the wood again and again, exclaiming with beaming smiles, *"Siwini, siwini!"* They understood one another.

It took hours before Waterman found other intelligible words, before he ascertained that Ishi was indeed a Yahi and that the language of this southern tribe was closely akin to the partly known dialect of the north, until he began to see the links and learn how to modify the pronunciation, until sentences formed and suddenly the moment came when Ishi asked his first question—a question, Waterman realized at once, to which he could give only one answer if he were to win the wild man's trust. The question was *"I ne ma Yahi?"* (Are you of our tribe?) And Waterman, looking into those black eyes, said, "Yes."

From that moment on Ishi emerged from the Stone Age into the world of modern man. But a few technical problems had to be solved first. The sheriff did not know what to do. Ishi was clearly neither insane nor dangerous, so what reason was there for keeping him in prison? On the other hand, what would become of him if he were released into a world that he could regard only as hostile and frightening?

The sheriff shifted the responsibility to Waterman, who gladly assumed it. Telegrams passed back and forth between Oroville and Kroeber in San Francisco. But this case was unprecedented; the Indian Bureau in Washington had to be consulted. After forty-eight hours the matter was finally settled. The sheriff signed a document that was probably unique in the annals of the law: a prisoner was turned directly over to a museum.

And then Ishi's second life began.

Here we must turn the clock back to understand the kind

of world from which Ishi had emerged and why his case
was such a piece of good fortune for science. For Ishi's life
had followed the curve of a tragedy of almost classical
Greek proportions, the tragedy of a whole people's downfall.

From archaeological finds it can be more or less estimated that before the white immigration into California
perhaps 150,000 Indians lived in what is now that populous
state. They consisted of twenty-one nations, which were divided into more than 250 subgroups, tribes and families in
which 113 different dialects were spoken. Some of these
dialects differed no more than Boston English from that of
New Orleans, but many were as far apart as French and
English. The Yanas constituted a sizable group. There were
2,000 or 3,000 of them scattered east of the Sacramento
River as far as Mount Lassen. About a thousand years before they had retreated to the highlands and evolved into a
predatory people. There were actually four tribes of them,
of which the southernmost, the Yahi, lived in the vicinity
of Mill Creek and Deer Creek. Linguistically, they belonged
to the Hokan family. One curiosity, very rare throughout
the world, was that men and women spoke a different dialect. The boys, for example, who were raised by the women,
did not learn the male language until around their tenth
year. And brothers and sisters addressed one another in the
second person plural, making the respectful distinction that
Frenchmen convey by *tu* and *vous*.

They lived the life of hunters, fishermen, and gatherers
of fruits and roots; their basic food was acorn flour. They
had no pottery but wove baskets for all purposes.

Their tragedy began with the California gold rush in
1849.

The land had drifted along under Mexican ownership. In
1848 it fell to the United States, and as a result of the gold
rush there ensued a period of total lawlessness. In 1849
alone 80,000 prospectors poured by sea and land into the
river valleys and mountains, tough men with a high percentage of scoundrels among them. Ships were abandoned
in the harbors, farms deserted, and whole villages were depopulated, while on the other hand innumerable rough-and-
ready temporary prospectors' settlements sprang up out of
the ground. Only eight per cent of the population was
female, and in the mining regions only two per cent. During
the ten years to 1860 the white population increased to
390,000. It may be mentioned here only as an ornamental
detail that among these people was one destined to enter

history as the most famous archaeologist of his time, the future excavator of Troy, Heinrich Schliemann. He could not stand California for long; manners and morals were too rude for him. The deeds and misdeeds of those years have undergone a romantic transfiguration; they have become legendary. Later it was said that they showed the American character at its best and at its worst. The group that suffered the most during that time were the Indians.

The aboriginals were driven back step by step. When they defended themselves with their few and poor weapons, when in their hunger they attacked wagon trains or plundered ranches, frightful reprisal campaigns were waged against them. Early in the sixties panic swept the country east of Sacramento when Indians, probably Yahi, killed five white children. But in the years 1862–67 the whites had killed between 3,000 and 4,000 Indians. One detail alone suggests the senseless cruelty of the times: *the whites introduced scalping,* which was unknown to the California tribes. Waterman relates: "On good authority I can report the case of an old prospector-pioneer-miner-trapper of this region, who had on his bed even in recent years a blanket lined with Indian scalps. These had been taken years before. He had never been a government scout, soldier, or officer of the law. The Indians he had killed purely on his own account. No reckoning was at any time demanded of him."

Ishi grew up during this period. As far as could be deduced, he must have been born around 1862. It may be that he never saw a white man close up, for his group was constantly in flight. And fear of the white man was burned into him from earliest childhood, when he heard stories of the latest massacres in which the remnants of his tribe had fallen. For the Yahis had struck back. Robbed of the land that had nourished them, driven by hunger from the parched wilderness to which they had retreated, they had attacked a ranch in August, 1865, killing three white men. One moonless night, under the leadership of two legendary Indian killers, Anderson and Good, both already proud possessors of many scalps, seventeen white men surrounded the small Yahi village on Mill Creek and slaughtered men, women, and children. "Many dead bodies floated down the rapid current." More such butchery was repeated in 1867 and 1868 and climaxed north of Mill Creek, where in a cave near Camp Seco thirty-three Indians were surrounded, killed, and scalped by only four white men, all heavily armed. During the massacre they shifted from their heavy rifles to revolvers because the rifles, as the white participant Norman Kingsley later remarked, "tore them up so bad"—especially the infants.

After this slaughter the white settlers thought they had exterminated the Yahis once and for all. But then something mysterious happened. When several cowboys visited the cave a few days later, they found that the thirty-three corpses had vanished. This meant that there must be a few survivors, who had given their dead the last rites (these Indians practiced cremation). But these survivors did not reappear. They vanished without a trace into the wilderness for twelve years, from 1872 to 1884.

Theodora Kroeber, the great anthropologist's wife, has displayed such empathy in her description of this period of concealment under threat of death that it would be a pity not to quote her:

"The twelve years from 1872 to 1884 were without incident or rumor. The concealment for those twelve years was complete. No horses or stock were hunted, no cabins were rifled, no grain stolen; not a footprint, not a telltale bit of ash, or wisp of smoke from a fire was seen; not a single broken arrowshaft or a lost spear point or a remnant of a milkweed rope snare was found on a forest or meadow floor as a sign that Indians were about. . . .

"The years of Ishi's total disconnection from history were most of the years of his life: a long interlude of stillness. The senses strain to understand what must have been the waking and sleeping of that time; and if Ishi could not light up for us its traumas and tragedies, he could and did describe and reënact for us, something of its day-to-day living.

"The hidden ones fished with the harpoon and the net, and hunted with the bow and arrow, and by setting snares—silent weapons all. They gathered acorns in the autumn, enough if possible to see them through the winter. They ate green clover in April, and brodiaea bulbs in early summer. In midsummer they went to Waganupa, four nights' journey, to its cooler air and deeper shade and more abundant game. For the rest, they lived on upper Mill Creek in small houses camouflaged so that from above, the only direction from which they could have been seen, the bent branches which covered them looked like nature's work. Nearby were storage shelters disguised in the same way, and containing drying frames, baskets of dried meat and fish and acorns, and utensil baskets, tools, and hides. They traveled sometimes for long distances by leaping from boulder to boulder, their bare feet leaving no print; or they walked up or down stream, making of their creeks a highroad. Each footprint on the ground was covered over with dead leaves, obliterated. Their trails went under the heavy chaparral, not through it, and they traveled them on all fours. A cow could not find such trails; even deer sought more open ones. If a branch was in the way it was gradually bent back farther and farther, and if need be severed by charring and wearing through with a crude tool made from splitting a boulder, a slow but silent process. They never chopped, the sound of chopping being the unmistakable announcement of human presence. They kept their fires small so that the smoke dissipated harmlessly through the brush without rising beaconwise above the bay tree canopy, and they covered the site of a camp-fire with broken rock as soon as the fire was out. They went up and down the perpendicular cliffs of Mill Creek cañon on ropes of milkweed fiber—a quick and safe way down, since the cañon was well screened by trees that overhung its rim. They could bring up a catch of fish or a basket of water, or let themselves down for a swim with far less trouble and time than it took to scramble up and down the little branching trails which led to the water's edge. Also, they preferred to use these trails sparingly so that they would not become too plainly marked but continue to appear to be no more than the runways of rabbits or weasels. They ground their acorns to flour on smooth stones and made the staple mush, cooking it in baskets. They wore capes of deerskin and wildcat, occasionally of bearskin. And they slept under blankets of rabbitskins. Ethnologists are agreed that they pursued a way of life the most totally aboriginal and primitive of any on the continent, at least after the coming of the white man to America."[2]

Under such circumstances Ishi grew to manhood. News of the last Yahis suddenly began to leak out in 1884. There was little to go by, no more than rumors. Here and there an Indian had been seen and had vanished like a shadow; here and there a cowboy's depot of foodstuffs had been plundered, but only dim traces of bare feet remained. These observations reached the newspapers, eked out with all kinds of journalistic imaginings. Today we know that Ishi was still living with four members of his tribe. Their last abode was *wowunupo mu tetna*, "the grizzly bear's hiding place."

"The site of Wowunupo is a narrow ledge . . . five hundred or more feet above the creek, the only place where even the simplest of shelters could imaginably be built anywhere on the steep cañon wall. Trees grow tall along this ledge, shading it and screening it from below and from the other side. From the ledge to the rim of the cañon, another two hundred feet, is bare cliff, sheer and impassable, which provided the village with a sheltered rear wall and perfect protection from above."

And yet it was not safe enough. The whites were coming closer. First two of them, then a single man, caught sight of an Indian—and was driven back by an arrow. In 1908 Wowunupo was discovered. What the party of whites found was an ancient sick Indian woman, covered with mats, as if her relatives had tried to hide her at the approach of the whites. Food and blankets were also found. When the whites returned next day, the old woman had also vanished. Later it was learned that Ishi had lived there with his mother, his sister, one old and one young man. By the time the camp was found, the younger man was already dead; the others dispersed in terror and died in the wilderness. Only Ishi survived. The last of his tribe, he hunted alone through the woods for another three years, until he could no longer find anything to eat. Then, half starved, for the first time in his life he crawled up to the dwellings of the whites and was found that morning by the slaughterhouse fence.

Ishi arrived at the museum on Labor Day, September 4, 1911, and next morning was taken to Kroeber. Ishi's status was not entirely clear. Was he, for example, an American citizen with the right to vote? The question was in fact officially submitted to Washington but was then tacitly dropped. Who would pay for Ishi's support? Kroeber found the solution by putting the savage on the payroll as assistant janitor, and to everyone's astonishment it turned out that Ishi fully satisfied the requirements of the job. He cleaned and swept with care and devotion.

The influx of the curious exceeded all expectations. Not only reporters and photographers but circus directors and vaudeville managers flocked to the museum. They wanted to hire Ishi, and one of them had the effrontery to ask Kroeber to join the Indian in a two-man show. Record companies wanted Ishi to sing for them, and movie companies (that was the year of birth for Hollywood as a film capital) wanted to have him appear in documentary and entertainment films. He even received a marriage proposal.

The anthropologists were fascinated by two different aspects of the case. First, how would a Stone Age man behave in the civilized world of the twentieth century; and second, what would he have to tell about his own world?

The "civilizing" of Ishi took place swiftly, and with some surprising results. He instantly accepted the clothing that was offered him—except for the shoes, which he put on only for special occasions. He who had run naked all his life now absolutely refused to be photographed without clothes; it was only some time later, on an outing to the wilderness, that he allowed it once more. He was extremely neat and orderly. Every day he took a bath—but then he had also done that in the wild. In this respect he was probably cleaner than the average white inhabitant of the West. The anthropologists took him to restaurants and to the theater. He was shy but immediately learned the use of knife and fork and "did not attract attention."

In the theater he was fascinated by the audience, but showed no interest in what was taking place on the stage, not even at a performance of acrobats. They had noticed the same thing when they took him to the ocean. To their surprise the ocean, too, made no impression on Ishi, whose eyes were again riveted on the "audience," that is, the swarms of white people on the beach. For most of his life Ishi had known no more than a dozen other human beings; only during the raids of the later years had he learned of the existence of the white men, but he had had no conception of their numbers, and it was this that now overwhelmed him. Incidentally, Ishi could count from two to twenty, and when his wages were paid in half-dollars he was quite aware of the difference between twenty and forty. In order to cash checks he had to sign his name. He learned to do that.

On his first walks wagons and cars did not startle him (although even the wheel lay quite outside his ken). But the railroad trains made a deep impression, for he was seeing them for the first time, although he had known of their existence. On his wanderings he had often heard them in the distance and regarded them as evil demons. Yet he now had no objection to using trains when accompanied and was soon riding on the trolley alone. The tall houses did not strike him as marvelous; the cliffs in the canyon had been higher, he remarked.

"Remarked" is the word, for in the course of time he

learned English and soon possessed a vocabulary of about 500–600 words, not appreciably less than many European first-generation immigrants. There was only one time when he reacted with sheer horror. That was in the nearby hospital, where he had struck up a friendship with Dr. Saxton Pope, who regularly examined him and treated his frequent colds. By chance Ishi wandered into the morgue. He quailed at the sight of the dead bodies and stammered about spirits and evil demons.

Regular visiting times for him were set, Sundays from 2 to 4:30. At the first reception he attended a thousand persons showed up. Ishi was a model of dignified bearing, shaking hands with everyone who was brought over to meet him, each time smiling pleasantly. He also made a great effort to recognize persons he had seen before. Interestingly, he applied his own tribal name, "Yana," to a Chinese, whereas the whites remained "Saltu," the "Others." That might be taken as a convincing piece of evidence for the Asiatic descent of all Indians, but of course its basis could also have been quite superficial. Still, it is worth noting that Ishi, like the Chinese, could not pronounce the American r and substituted l for it.

All his friends, Kroeber, Waterman, and Pope in particular, had the impression that Ishi felt "at home" in the museum. But none of them had realized just how much it had come to mean to him. For when the plan arose to undertake a long journey of exploration into Yana country with Ishi, he was utterly dismayed. Far from wanting to see his homeland again, he belabored his friends with descriptions of the hardships they would encounter. There would be terrible storms. Snakes and mountain lions were a perpetual menace. They could expect hunger and thirst; there would be no soft beds for them at night. Were they going to subject themselves to all that just to get to know his wilderness? He pointed to the bath, to the heating, to the chairs and chests of drawers. It seemed to him insane to give up all these comforts, even if only for a few weeks!

At this point we must relate what Ishi taught and not only what he learned. He taught his friends everything he knew and could do. He began with his language, gradually dictating his entire vocabulary. But he also sang his songs and imitated the countless calls of wild animals and birds, a trick he used in hunting. He demonstrated the manual skills by which a Stone Age man was able to survive in the wilderness. For Dr. Pope's records he narrated forty different stories, tales of the woodland world, a tissue of dreams and spirits, fear and love. In the museum garden he built a hut such as he had had in Yana land. But he did not make baskets because he either could not or would not, for that was women's work. A man's task was to produce implements for hunting. In that realm he displayed abilities that were priceless to the scientists. Here was a chance to *watch* how a man chipped a spearhead out of a piece of obsidian 1,000 or 10,000 years ago. Ishi needed thirty minutes to produce a perfectly formed, deadly, needle-sharp point. Before the scientists' eyes he made harpoons, fishing tackle and nooses, and wove ropes out of milkweed fibers or deer sinews. And as his crowning feat, he made a bow and arrow. This was a drawn-out task, for the wood had to be repeatedly dried at various stages of the work, and in addition certain mystic rites had to be observed. Dr. Pope became his eager pupil and subsequently published several treatises on the art of wielding a bow. Waterman was less fortunate. He watched attentively as Ishi produced sparks and kindled a fire by means of a wooden drill and a piece of softwood. Somewhat too hastily, Waterman told his anthropology students that they could not pass the course unless they learned to use a fire drill like Ishi. He would show them the technique, he said, whereupon he turned and turned the drill without producing the slightest spark.

In May, 1914, Kroeber prepared the expedition to Yana land in spite of Ishi's lack of enthusiasm for the trip. And now the scientists could see him in his own world. He led them to all the places he remembered because of some special occurrence—the site of a massacre during his childhood, the place where a cremation had been held, the spot made unforgettable by a lucky arrow or a battle with a cinnamon bear. And in Wowunupo, the grizzly bear's hiding place, they relived the end of the last members of his tribe.

Here also they saw him using his wonderful bow. He shot a bird in flight, rabbits at five yards, and deer at distances up to forty yards. They watched him gliding with perfect noiselessness through the thickets but could never manage to imitate his silent movements any more than they could master the acrobatic art with which he swung over the canyons cliffs on a rope he had made himself. They eagerly took notes as he gradually identified more than 200 plants and explained their uses as food or medicine. And they were deeply moved by the stoic patience with which he would lie in ambush for hours, if need be, not moving a muscle, waiting for game to emerge from hiding, for he recognized its presence with absolute infallibility.

All through this time the scientists kept expecting that their friend Ishi would turn away from them emotionally, that he would want to stay in the wilderness where he had grown to manhood. But nothing of the kind happened. Instead, Ishi kept begging them to go home, and "home" was his room in the museum. When the Bureau of Indian Affairs once more raised the question of whether Ishi should not be sent to live among his own kind on a reservation, Kroeber had to transmit the proposal to him. Ishi replied: "I will live like the white man for the remainder of my days. I wish to stay here where I now am. I will grow old in this house, and it is here I will die."

And that was how it was.

In 1915 Ishi fell sick, and his condition steadily worsened. Soon there could be no doubt that he had tuberculosis. He spent a long time in the hospital under the care of his friend Dr. Pope. Then he asked to be taken "home" to die, and once again he meant his museum. His wish was granted. And there, on March 15, 1916, the last wild Indian of North America died.

Ishi was given a handsome funeral that showed the sentimental attachment, in the best sense of the word, that his friends had formed toward him over the years—those scientists who had initially been interested in him only as a case. When the question arose of releasing his body for autopsy for scientific purposes, Kroeber, who happened to be in New York at the time, telegraphed: "Science can go to hell." He added: "We have hundreds of Indian skeletons that nobody ever comes near to study. The prime interest in this case would be of a morbid romantic nature!" But since Kroeber was not on the spot, a compromise between science and sentiment was arranged. The autopsy was held; then Ishi's body was cremated in the manner of his ancestors and his ashes placed in an Indian vase. Along with him were buried his bow, five arrows, a basket of acorn meal, some obsidian points, and other small items.

Kroeber, later asked for a brief characterization of Ishi, replied: "He was the most patient man I ever knew. I mean he had mastered the philosophy of patience, without trace either of self-pity or of bitterness to dull the purity of his cheerful enduringness."

And Dr. Pope provided this obituary: "And so, stoic and unafraid, departed the last wild Indian of America. *He closes a chapter in History.* He looked upon us as sophisticated children—smart, but not wise. We knew many things, and much that is false. He knew nature, which is always true. His were the qualities of character that last forever. He was kind; he had courage and self-restraint, and though all had been taken from him, there was no bitterness in his heart. His soul was that of a child, his mind that of a philosopher."

Ishi was soon forgotten, not by his friends, but by the world. But many notes were made about him, and these have been preserved. However, when interest in Ishi revived belatedly in 1957 and the wax cylinders on which his voice, songs and vocabulary had been recorded were brought out from storage, it turned out that all the machines that could take the cylinders were broken. Not a single one of the old gramophones could be made to work. Finally an ingenious student managed to put together a single usable machine out of several old gramophones, and so some of the cylinders could be replayed. But things proved even worse when the old rolls of films were opened. For museum purposes the California Motion Picture Corporation had shot some 5,000 feet of film on Ishi. But the film had been stored for four decades in a room near heating pipes, of all places. When the cans were opened, their contents proved to be shapeless lumps of melted celluloid.

Bibliography and References

THIS bibliography lists all the principal scholarly books and articles consulted for this book. But it also includes a number of items that will not be found in scholarly bibliographies—literary and journalistic works of value for our special purposes.

An asterisk—which is not intended to be evaluative—calls attention to introductions and general surveys useful to a reader who seeks a broader view of the field. Wherever possible, the latest editions of books have been cited. This is the more practicable course, since such books as, for instance, the 1924 edition of Alfred V. Kidder's *An Introduction to the Study of Southwestern Archaeology* can scarcely be located today, whereas the paperback edition of 1963 is obtainable and doubly useful because Irving Rouse has provided it with an excellent summary of developments in Southwestern archaeology since the first edition. Similarly, I list many original articles by their later publication in anthologies that can be found in every fairly good library. For a catalogue of documentary movies on Indian cultures see Owen, Deetz, and Fisher, *The North American Indians; A Sourcebook.* There the sources for 251 films are listed. However, these films deal almost exclusively with Indians in the twentieth century.

American Heritage Publishing Co. *The American Heritage Pictorial Atlas of United States History.* New York, 1966.

Andrews, Ralph W *Indian Primitive.* New York: Bonanza Books, 1960.

Antevs, Ernst. "Geological Age of the Lehner Mammoth Site." *American Antiquity,* 25, No. 1 (July, 1959).

Archaeology in American Colleges. New York: Archaeological Institute of America, 1967.

Ascher, Robert. "Teaching Archaeology in the University." *Archaeology*, 21, No. 4 (October, 1968).

Assall, Friedrich Wilhelm, *Nachrichten über die früheren Einwohner von Nordamerika und ihre Denkmäler herausgegeben mit einem Vorbericht von Franz Joseph Mone*. Heidelberg, 1827.

Atwater, Caleb. *Description of the Antiquities Discovered in the State of Ohio and Other Western States*. Transactions of the American Antiquarian Society, Archeologia Americana, 1 (1820).

* Bakeless, John. *The Eyes of Discovery: The Pageant of North America as Seen by the First Explorers*. New York: Dover Press, 1961.

* Baldwin, Gordon C. *America's Buried Past: The Story of North American Archaeology*. New York: G. P. Putnam's Sons, 1962.

Bandelier, Adolph F. *Historical Introduction to Studies Among the Sedentary Indians of New Mexico: Report on the Ruins of the Pueblo of Pecos*. Papers of the Archaeological Institute of America, American Series I, Boston, 1881.

———. "The Romantic School in American Archaeology." Read before the New York Historical Society, February 3, 1885. New York: Trow's Printing and Bookbinding Company, 1885.

———. "Cibola." Sunday editions, May, June, July, October, 1885, and January, February, 1886, of the German-language *Staatszeitung*, New York.

———. *Contributions to the History of the Southwestern Portion of the United States: Hemenway Southwestern Archaeological Expedition*. Papers of the Archaeological Institute of America, American Series V, Cambridge, 1890.

———. *Final Report of Investigations Among the Indians of the Southwestern United States, Carried on Mainly in the Years from 1880 to 1885*. Papers of the Archaeological Institute of America, American Series No. 3, Part 1, Cambridge, 1890; No. 4, Part 2, Cambridge, 1892.

———. *The Delight Makers*. New York: Dodd, Mead & Co., 1918.

Bandelier, Fanny. *The Journey of Alvar Nuñez Cabeza de Vaca*, translated from his own narrative. New York: Allerton Book Co., 1922.

Bandi, Hans-Georg. *Eskimo Prehistory*. College: University of Alaska Press, 1969.

Bannister, Bryant. "The Interpretation of Tree-Ring Dates." *American Antiquity*, 27, 1962.

———. *Tree-Ring Dating of the Archaeological Sites in the Chaco Canyon Region, New Mexico*. Southwestern Monuments Association, Technical Series 6, Part 2 (1965).

Belknap, William, Jr. "20th-Century Indians Preserve Customs of the Cliff Dwellers." *National Geographic*, 125, No. 2 (February, 1964).

* Benedict, Ruth. *Patterns of Culture*. Boston: Houghton Mifflin, 1934.

Benfer, Robert A. "A Design for the Study of Archaeological Characteristics." *American Anthropologist*, 69, No. 6 (December, 1967).

Berger, Rainer and Sackett, James R. "Final Report on the Laguna Beach Excavation of the Isotope Foundation." Publication of the University of California, February 10, 1969.

Biek, Leo. *Archaeology and the Microscope: The Scientific Examination of Archaeological Evidence*. New York and London: Frederick A. Praeger, 1963.

Binford, Lewis R. "Archaeological Systematics and the Study of Culture Process." *American Antiquity*, 31, No. 2, Part 1 (October, 1965).

Binford, Sally R., and Binford, Lewis R. *New Perspectives in Archaeology*. Chicago: Aldine Publishing Co., 1938.

Birdsell, Joseph B. *The Problem of the Early Peopling of the Americas as Viewed from Asia*. Papers on the Physical Anthropology of the American Indian, Wenner-Gren Foundation for Anthropological Research, New York, 1951.

Boas, Franz. *General Anthropology*. New York: Johnson Reprint Corp., 1970.

Bolton, Herbert Eugene, *Coronado, Knight of Pueblos and Plains*. Albuquerque: University of New Mexico Press, 1964.

Book of Mormon. An Account Written by the Hand of Mormon Upon Plates taken from the Plates of Nephi. Salt Lake City: Church of Jesus Christ of Latter-day Saints, 1950.

Boswell, Victor R. "Our Vegetable Travellers." *National Geographic*, 96, No. 2 (August, 1949).

Braunschweig, Johann Daniel von. *Ueber die Alt-Americanischen Denkmäler*. Berlin: Reimer, 1840.

Brew, J. O., ed. *One Hundred Years of Anthropology*. Cambridge: Harvard University Press, 1968.

* Brothwell, Don, and Higgs, Eric. *Science in Archaeology: A Comprehensive Survey of Progress and Research*. rev. ed. New York: Frederick A. Praeger, 1970.

Bryan, Kirk. "Correlation of the Deposits of Sandia Cave, New Mexico, with the Glacial Chronology" in Frank C. Hibben, "Evidences of Early Occupation in Sandia Cave, New Mexico, and Other Sites in the Sandia-Manzano Region." *Smithsonian Miscellaneous Collections*, 99, No. 23, Washington, D.C., 1941.

Bryant, William Cullen. *Poems*. New York: Oxford University Press, 1914,

Burland, Cotty. *North American Indian Mythology*. London: Paul Hamlyn, 1965.

Burroughs, Carroll A. "Searching for Cliff Dweller's Secrets." *National Geographic*, 116, No. 5 (November, 1959).

* Bushnell, G. H. S. *The First Americans: The Pre-Columbian Civilizations*. New York: McGraw-Hill, 1968.

Butcher, Devereux. "Exploring Our Prehistoric Indian Ruins: The National Archaeological Monuments of the United States." National Parks Association, Washington, 1965.

Butzer, Karl W. *Environment and Archaeology: An Introduction to Pleistocene Geography*. Chicago: Aldine Publishing Co., 1964.

* Caldwell, Joseph R., ed. *New Roads to Yesterday: Essays in Archaeology*. New York: Basic Books, 1966.

Campbell, Bernard G. *Human Evolution: An Introduction to Man's Adaptations*. Chicago: Aldine Publishing Co., 1966.

Carlson, Roy L. *Basket Maker III Sites Near Durango, Colorado*. University of Colorado Studies, Series in Anthropology, No. 8, Boulder, June, 1963.

Cartier, Raymond, *L'Europe à la conquête de l'Amérique*. Paris: Librairie Plon, 1956.

Catlin, George. *Illustrations of the Manners, Customs and Condition of the North American Indians: In a Series of Letters and Notes written during eight years of Travel and Adventure among the wildest and most remarkable Tribes now existing. With three hundred and sixty Engravings, from the Author's Original Paintings.* London: Henry G. Bohn, 1845.

Chapman, Kenneth M. *The Pottery of Santo Domingo Pueblo: A Detailed Study of Its Decoration.* Memoirs of the Laboratory of Anthropology, 1, Santa Fé, 1953.

Childe, V. Gordon. *A Short Introduction to Archaeology.* New York: Collier Books, 1962.

Churchward, Colonel James. *The Lost Continent of Mu.* New York: Crown Publishers, 1931.

Clarke, David L. *Analytical Archaeology.* London: Methuen, 1968.

Coblentz, Stanton A., ed. *The Music Makers.* New York: Bernard Ackermann, 1945.

Collier, John. *Indians of the Americas.* New York: New American Library, 1947.

Colton, Harold S. *The Sinagua: A Summary of the Archaeology of the Region of Flagstaff, Arizona.* Museum of Northern Arizona, Bulletin 22, Flagstaff, 1946.

———. *Black Sand: Prehistory in Northern Arizona.* Albuquerque: University of New Mexico Press, 1960.

Cone, Cynthia A., and Pelto, Pertti J. *Guide to Cultural Anthropology.* Glenview: Scott, Foresman, 1969.

Coon, Carleton S. *The Story of Man.* New York: Alfred A. Knopf, 1965.

Coon, Carleton S., and Hunt, Edward E., eds. *Anthropology A–Z.* New York: Grosset & Dunlap, 1963.

Corbett, John M. *Aztec Ruins.* National Park Service Historical Handbook Series No. 36, Washington, D.C., 1962.

Coze, Paul. "Kachinas: Masked Dancers of the Southwest." *National Geographic,* 107, No. 2 (August, 1957).

Cummings, B. "The Ancient Inhabitants of the San Juan Valley." *Bulletin of the University of Utah,* 3, No. 3, Part 2, Salt Lake City, 1910.

Cushing, Frank Hamilton. *My Adventures in Zuñi.* Santa Fé: Peripatetic Press, 1941 (original edition published in 1882–83). This volume also includes *Zuñi and Cushing* by E. DeGolyer and *An Aboriginal Pilgrimage* by Sylvester Baxter.

* Daniel, Glyn. *The Idea of Prehistory: The Origins and Development of the Study of Man's Past Before the Recorded Word.* Cleveland and New York: World Publishing Co., 1963.

———. "Archaeology and the Origins of Civilization." *The Listener,* December 1, 1966.

Darwin, Charles. *On the Origin of Species by Means of Natural Selection, or the Preservation of Favoured Races in the Struggle for Life.* London: John Murray, 1859.

Day, A. Grove. *Coronado's Quest: The Discovery of the Southwestern States.* Berkeley and Los Angeles: University of California Press, 1964.

De Camp, L. Sprague. "The End of the Monkey War." *Scientific American,* 220, No. 2 (February, 1969).

———. *The Great Monkey Trial.* New York: Doubleday, 1967.

* Deetz, James, *Invitation to Archaeology.* Garden City: Natural History Press, 1967.

———. "Archeology as a Social Science," in *Current Directions in Anthropology.* Bulletin of the American Anthropological Association, 3, No. 3, Part 2, Washington, D.C., September, 1970.

* Deuel, Leo, ed. *Conquistadors Without Swords: Archaeologists in the Americas: An Account with Original Narratives.* New York: St. Martin's Press, 1967.

———. *Flights into Yesterday: The Story of Aerial Archaeology.* New York: St. Martin's Press, 1967.

Dittert, Alfred E., and Eddy, Frank W. *Pueblo Period Sites in the Piedra River Section, Navajo Reservoir District.* Museum of New Mexico Papers in Anthropology, Museum of New Mexico Press, Santa Fé, 1963.

Dockstader, Frederick J. *Indian Art in America: The Arts and Crafts of the North American Indian.* Greenwich: New York Graphic Society, 1967.

Dodge, Natt N., and Zim, Herbert S. *The Southwest: A Guide to the Wide Open Spaces.* New York: Golden Press, 1960.

Douglass, Andrew Ellicott. "The Secret of the Southwest Solved by Talkative Tree Rings." *National Geographic,* 46, No. 12 (December, 1929).

Driver, Harold E. *Indians of North America.* Chicago: University of Chicago Press, 1961.

Dubos, René. *So Human An Animal.* New York: Charles Scribner's Sons, 1968.

Ducrocq, Albert. *Atomwissenschaft und Urgeschichte.* Rowohlts Deutsche Enzyklopädie. Hamburg, 1957.

Dunn, James Taylor. "The True, Moral and Diverting Tale of the Cardiff Giant or the American Goliath." *New York History* reprint, July, 1948.

Dutton, Bertha P., ed. *Indians of the Southwest.* Southwestern Association on Indian Affairs, Santa Fé, 1963.

Eggan, Fred. *Social Organization of the Western Pueblos.* Chicago and London: University of Chicago Press, 1963.

———. *The American Indian: Perspectives for the Study of Social Change.* Chicago: Aldine Publishing Co., 1966.

Eiseley, Loren. *The Unexpected Universe.* New York: Harcourt, Brace & World, 1969.

Elting, Mary, and Folsom, Michael. *The Mysterious Grain: Science in Search of the Origin of Corn.* New York: Evans & Co., 1967.

Erdmann, James A.; Douglas, Charles L.; and Marr, John W. *Environment of Mesa Verde, Colorado.* Archaeological Research Series 7-B, Wetherill Mesa Studies, National Park Service, U.S. Department of the Interior, Washington, D.C., 1969.

Erdoes, Richard. *The Pueblo Indians.* New York: Funk & Wagnalls, 1967.

Every, Dale van. *Disinherited: The Lost Birthright of the American Indian.* New York: William Morrow, 1966.

Fagan, Brian. *Introductory Readings in Archaeology.* Boston: Little, Brown, 1970.

Farb, Peter. *Man's Rise to Civilization as Shown by the Indians of North America from Primeval Times to the Coming of the Industrial State.* New York: Dutton, 1968.

Fergusson, Erna. *New Mexico: A Pageant of Three Peoples.* New York: Alfred A. Knopf, 1951.

Fewkes, J. W. "A Report on the Present Condition of a Ruin in Arizona Called Casa Grande." *Journal of American Ethnology and Archaeology,* 2, Cambridge, 1892.

Fisher, Reginald G. *Some Geographic Factors that Influenced the Ancient Populations of the Chaco Canyon, New Mexico.* University of New Mexico Bulletin. Archaeological Series, 3, No. 1 (May 15, 1934).

Ford, James A. *A Comparison of Formative Cultures in the Americas: Diffusion or the Psychic Unity of Man.* Smithsonian Contributions to Anthropology, 2, Smithsonian Institution Press, Washington, D.C., 1969.

Ford, James A., and Webb, Charles H. *Poverty Point: A Late Archaic Site in Louisiana.* American Museum of Natural History, Anthropological Papers, 46, No. 1 (1956).

Ford, James A., and Willey, Gordon R. "An Interpretation of the Prehistory of the Eastern United States." *American Anthropologist,* 43, No. 3, 1941.

Freneau, Philip M. *Poems.* Princeton: Princeton University Press, 1902.

Gardin, Jean-Claude. "Probleme der Dokumentation." *Diogenes,* 11–12, Cologne, 1956.

* Gehlen, Arnold: *Urmensch und Spätkultur.* Bonn: Athenäum-Verlag, 1956.

———. *Anthropologische Forschung.* Rowohlts Deutsche Enzyklopädie, Hamburg, 1961.

Giddings, J. Louis. *Ancient Man of the Arctic.* New York: Alfred A. Knopf, 1967.

Gilbert, John P., and Hammel, E. A. "Computer Simulation and Analysis of Problems in Kinship and Social Structure." *American Anthropologist,* 68, No. 1 (February, 1966).

Gillmore, Frances, and Wetherill, Louisa Wade. *Traders to the Navajos: The Story of the Wetherills of Kayenta.* Albuquerque: University of New Mexico Press, 1965.

Gladwin, Harold S. *Men Out of Asia.* New York: McGraw-Hill, 1947.

* Gladwin, Harold S.; Haury, Emil W.; Sayles, E. B.; and Gladwin, Nora. *Excavations at Snaketown: Material Culture.* Reprint. Tucson: University of Arizona Press, 1965.

Gould, Richard A. "Chipping Stones in the Outback." *Natural History,* 77, No. 2 (February, 1968).

Grahmann, Rudolf, and Müller-Beck, Hansjürgen. *Urgeschichte der Menschheit.* Stuttgart: Kohlhammer, 1966.

Grant, Bruce. *American Indians Yesterday and Today: A Profusely Illustrated Encylopedia of the American Indian.* New York: E. P. Dutton, 1958.

Greengo, Robert E. "Obituary: Alfred Vincent Kidder, 1885–1963," *American Anthropologist,* 70, No. 2 (April, 1968).

* Griffin, James B., ed. *Archaeology of the Eastern United States.* Chicago and London: University of Chicago Press, 1964.

———. "Eastern North America Archaeology, a Summary: Prehistoric Cultures Changed from Small Hunting Bands to Well-Organized Agricultural Towns and Tribes." *Science,* 156, No. 3772 (April 14, 1967).

Guernsey, Samuel J. *Exploration in Northeastern Arizona.* Papers of the Peabody Museum of American Archaeology and Ethnology, 12, No. 1, Harvard University, 1931.

Guide to Departments of Anthropology 1969–70. Bulletin of the American Anthropological Association, Washington, D.C., 1970.

Guthe, Carl E. *Pueblo Pottery Making: A Study at the Village of San Ildefonso.* Papers of the Phillips Academy, Southwestern Expedition, No. 2, New Haven, 1925.

Haberland, Wolfgang. "Bat Cave," in *Tribus,* Veröffentlichungen des Linden-Museums, No. 15, August, 1966.

———. *Nordamerika.* Baden-Baden: Holle Verlag, 1965.

Hampton, Jim. "On the Anasazi Trail." *The National Observer,* June 5, 1967.

Hargrave, Lyndon L. *Oraibi: A Brief History of the Oldest Inhabited Town in the United States.* Museum Notes, Museum of Northern Arizona, 4, No. 7 (January, 1932).

——. "Turkey Bones from Wetherill Mesa." Memoirs of the Society for American Archaeology, No. 19, *American Antiquity,* 31, No. 2, Part 2 (October, 1965).

Harrington, Mark R. "Gypsum Cave, Nevada," in Leo Deuel, *Conquistadors Without Swords.*

Harris, Marvin, and Morren, George E. B. "The Limitations of the Principle of Limited Possibilities." *American Anthropologist,* 68, No. 1 (February, 1966).

Harte, Bret. *Poetical Works.* Boston: Houghton Mifflin Co., 1899.

Haury, Emil W. "A Possible Cochise-Mogollon-Hohokam Sequence." *Proceedings of the American Philosophical Society,* 86, No. 2, Philadelphia, 1943.

——. *The Stratigraphy and Archaeology of Ventana Cave, Arizona.* Albuquerque: University of New Mexico Press, 1950.

——. "Artifacts with Mammoth Remains, Naco, Arizona." *American Antiquity,* 19, No. 1, 1953.

——. ed. *American Anthropologist, Southwest Issue,* 56, No. 4 (August, 1954).

——. *Post-Pleistocene Human Occupation of the Southwest.* Tucson: University of Arizona Press, 1958.

——. "Snaketown, 1964–1965." *The Kiva: Journal of the Arizona Archaeological and Historical Society,* 31, No. 1 (October 1, 1965).

——. "First Masters of the American Desert: The Hohokam." *National Geographic,* 131, No. 5 (May, 1967).

Haury, Emil W.; Sayles, E. B.; and Wasley, William W. "The Lehner Mammoth Site." *American Antiquity,* 25, No. 1 (July 1, 1959).

Haven, Samuel F. *Archaeology of the United States, or Sketches, Historical and Bibliographical of the Progress of Information and Opinion Respecting Vestiges of Antiquity in the United States.* Smithsonian Contributions to Knowledge, Washington, 1856.

Hawkes, Jacquetta, ed. *The World of the Past.* New York: Alfred A. Knopf, 1963.

Hawley, Florence, *Tree Ring Analysis and Dating in the Mississippi Drainage.* University of Chicago Publications in Anthropology, Occasional Paper No. 2, 1941.

Hayes, Alden C. *The Archaeological Survey of Wetherill Mesa.* Archaeological Research Series No. 7-A, National Park Service, Washington, 1964.

Haynes, C. Vance, Jr. "Elephant Hunting in North America." *Scientific American,* 214, No. 6 (June, 1966).

Haynes, C. Vance, and Agogino, George. *Geologic Significance of a New Radiocarbon Date from the Lindenmeier Site.* Denver Museum of Natural History, Proceedings No. 9, 1960.

* Heizer, Robert F., ed. *The Archaeologist at Work: A Source Book in Archaeological Method and Interpretation.* New York: Harper & Brothers, 1959.

Hellmann, Geoffrey T. *The Smithsonian: Octopus on the Mall.* Philadelphia: J. B. Lippincott Co., 1967.

Helm, June, ed. *Pioneers of American Anthropology: The Uses of Biography.* Seattle: University of Washington Press, 1966.

Heydecker, J. "Die Phönizier waren schon vor 3000 Jahren in Amerika," *Die Tat,* Zürich, June 1, 1968.

Hibben, Frank C. "The Gallina Phase." *American Antiquity,* 4, No. 2, 1938.

———. "Evidences of Early Occupation in Sandia Cave, New Mexico, and Other Sites in the Sandia-Manzano Region," with Appendix on "Correlation of the Deposits of Sandia Cave, New Mexico, with the Glacial Chronology" by Kirk Bryan. *Smithsonian Miscellaneous Collections,* 99, No. 23, Washington, 1941.

———. "We Found the Home of the First American." *Saturday Evening Post,* April 17, 1943.

———. "The Mystery of the Stone Towers." *Saturday Evening Post,* December 9, 1944.

———. *Treasure in the Dust: Exploring Ancient North America.* Philadelphia and New York: J. B. Lippincott Co., 1951.

———. *Digging Up America.* New York: Hill and Wang, 1960.

*———. *The Lost Americans.* New York: Thomas Y. Crowell, 1968.

Hodges, Henry. *Artifacts: An Introduction to Primitive Technology.* New York and London: Frederick A. Praeger, 1964.

Holand, Hjalmar Rued. *A Pre-Columbian Crusade to America.* New York: Twayne, 1962.

Hole, Frank, and Heizer, Robert F. *An Introduction to Prehistoric Archaeology.* New York: Holt, Rinehart & Winston, 1966.

Holmes, W. H. *Report on the Ancient Ruins of Southwestern Colorado, Examined During the Summers of 1875 and 1876.* Tenth Annual Report of the U.S. Geological and Geographical Survey of the Territories, 1876, Washington, 1878.

———. *Biographical Memoirs of Lewis Henry Morgan, 1818–1881.* National Academy of Science, Biographical Memoirs, 6, 1909.

* Hopkins, David M., ed. *The Bering Land Bridge.* Based on a symposium held at the Seventh Congress of the International Association for Quaternary Research, Boulder, Colorado, August–September, 1965. Stanford: Stanford University Press, 1967.

Horgan, Paul. *Conquistadors in North American History.* Greenwich: Fawcett Publications, 1965.

Howe, Sherman S. "The Story of the Aztec Ruins." *The Basin Spokesman,* Farmington, New Mexico, 1955.

Howells, William. *Back of History: The Story of Our Own Origins.* Rev. ed. New York: Natural History Library, 1963.

Hrdlička, Aleš. *Skeletal Remains Suggesting or Attributed to Early Man in North America.* Smithsonian Institution, Bureau of American Ethnology, Bulletin 33, Washington, D.C., 1907.

———. *Recent Discoveries Attributed to Early Man in America.* Bureau of American Ethnology, Bulletin 66, Washington, D.C., 1918.

Huddleston, Lee Eldridge. *Origins of the American Indians: European Concepts, 1492–1729.* Institute of Latin American Studies, Latin American Monographs, 11. Austin and London: University of Texas Press, 1967.

Huizinga, Johan. *Homo Ludens: A Study of the Play Elements in Culture.* Boston: Beacon Press, 1955.

Hulbert, Archer Butler. *Historic Highways of America,* Vol. 1, *Paths of the Mound-Building Indians and Great Game Animals.* Reprint. Cleveland: Frontier Press, 1967.

Ingstad, Helge. *Die erste Entdeckung Amerikas: Auf den Spuren der Wikinger.* Berlin: Ullstein, 1966.

Jackson, William Henry. *Time Exposure.* New York: G. P. Putnam's Sons, 1940.

Jacob, Heinrich Eduard. *Six Thousand Years of Bread.* Translated by Richard and Clara Winston. New York: Doubleday, 1944.

Jefferson, Thomas. *Notes on the State of Virginia.* In Saul K. Padover, ed., *The Complete Jefferson.* New York: Books for Libraries, 1943.

Jennings, Jesse E. "Danger Cave." Anthropological Papers, No. 27, University of Utah, 1957.

*———. *Prehistory of North America.* New York: McGraw-Hill, 1968.

Jennings, Jesse D., and Norbeck, Edward, eds. *Prehistoric Man in the New World.* Chicago and London: University of Chicago Press, 1964.

Johnson, Frederick. "Radiocarbon Dates from Sandia Cave, Correction." *Science,* 125, No. 3241, 1957.

———. "Archaeology in an Emergency: *The Federal Government's* Inter-Agency Archaeological Salvage Program Is Twenty Years Old." *Science,* 152, No. 3729 (June 17, 1966).

———. "Radiocarbon Dating and Archaeology in North America." *Science,* 155 (January 13, 1967).

Jones, Evan. " 'Dig-It-Yourself' Archaeologists." The New York *Times Magazine,* February 16, 1958.

Jones, Gwyn. *The North Atlantic Saga, Being the North Voyages of Discovery and Settlement to Iceland, Greenland, America.* London: Oxford University Press, 1964.

Josephy, Alvin M., Jr. *The Patriot Chiefs: A Chronicle of American Indian Leadership.* New York: The Viking Press, 1961.

*———. *The Indian Heritage of America.* New York: Alfred A. Knopf, 1968.

Judd, Neil M. *The Bureau of American Ethnology: A Partial History.* Norman: University of Oklahoma Press, 1967.

———. *Men Met Along the Trail: Adventures in Archaeology.* Norman: University of Oklahoma Press, 1968.

Jung, C. G. *Memories, Dreams, Reflections.* Edited and recorded by Aniela Jaffé. Translated by Richard and Clara Winston. New York: Pantheon Books, 1963.

Kelly, A. R. *A Preliminary Report on Archaeological Explorations at Macon, Georgia.* Smithsonian Institution, Bureau of American Ethnology, Bulletin 119, Washington, D.C., 1938.

Kidder, Alfred Vincent. "The Pueblo of Pecos." Archaeological Institute of America, Papers of the School of American Archaeology, No. 33, Santa Fé, 1916.

*———. *An Introduction to the Study of Southwestern Archaeology.* 2d ed. With a preliminary account of the excavations at Pecos and a summary of Southwestern archaeology today by Irving Rouse. New Haven and London: Yale University Press, 1963.

———. "Sylvanus Griswold Morley, 1883–1948." *El Palacio,* 55, Santa Fé, 1948.

Kidder, Alfred Vincent, and Guernsey, Samuel J. *Archaeological Explorations in Northeastern Arizona.* Bureau of American Ethnology, Bulletin 65, Washington, D.C., 1919.

Klein, Bernard, and Icolari, Daniel. *Reference Encyclopedia of the American Indian.* New York: B. Klein & Co., 1967.

Krieger, Alex D. "Early Man in the New World." In *Prehistoric Man in the New World,* edited by Jesse D. Jennings and Edward Norbeck.

* Kroeber, A. L. *A Roster of Civilizations and Culture.* Chicago: Aldine Publishing Co., 1962.

———. *Anthropology: Biology and Race.* New York: Harcourt, Brace & World, Harbinger Book, 1963.

*———. *Anthropology: Culture Patterns and Processes.* New York: Harcourt, Brace & World, Harbinger Book, 1963.

———. *An Anthropoligst Looks at History.* Berkeley and Los Angeles: University of California Press, 1963.

Kroeber, Theodora. *Ishi in Two Worlds: A Biography of the Last Wild Indian in North America.* Berkeley and Los Angeles: University of California Press, 1965.

Krutch, Joseph Wood. *The Voice of the Desert: A Naturalist's Interpretation.* New York: William Sloane Associates, 1954.

———. *The Desert Year.* New York: The Viking Press, 1964.

* La Farge, Oliver. *A Pictorial History of the American Indian.* New York: Crown Publishers, 1965.

Lamb, Charles. *The Essays of Elia and the Last Essays of Elia.* Garden City: Doubleday, Dolphin Books, n.d.

Lange, Charles H., and Riley, Carroll L. *The Southwestern Journals of Adolph F. Bandelier 1880–1882.* Santa Fé: University of New Mexico Press, 1966.

Las Casas, Bartolomé de. *A Relation of the First Voyages and Discoveries Made by the Spaniards in America with an Account of their unparallel'd Cruelties on the Indians, in the destruction of above Forty Millions of People.* London: Printed for Daniel Brown at the Black Swan & Bible without Temple-Bar and Andrew Bell at the Crosskeys and Bible in Cornhil near Stocksmarket, 1699.

Lawrence, D. H. *Mornings in Mexico.* London: Secker, 1927.

Leakey, L. S. B. "Finding the World's Earliest Man." *National Geographic,* 118, No. 3 (September, 1960).

———. "Exploring 1,750,000 Years into Man's Past." *National Geographic,* 120, No. 4. (October, 1961).

Leakey, L. S. B.; Simpson, Ruth de Ette; and Clements, Thomas. "Archaeological Excavations in the Calico Mountains, California: Preliminary Report." *Science,* 160 (May 31, 1968).

Lee, Richard B., and DeVore, Irven, eds. *Man the Hunter.* Chicago: Aldine Publishing Co., 1968.

Lehner, Ernst and Johanna. *How They Saw the New World: A Most Revealing and Wonderful Collection of Over 200 Rare Woodcuts and Engravings of Old Maps, the Natives, Plants, Views, Towns and Curious Animals of the Newly Discovered Land.* New York: Tudor, 1966.

Lévi-Strauss, Claude. *Structural Anthropology.* New York: Doubleday, 1967.

Lewis, John. *Anthropology Made Simple.* Garden City: Doubleday, 1961.

Libby, Willard F. *Radiocarbon Dating.* Chicago and London: University of Chicago Press, 1955.

Lister, Robert H. *Contributions to Mesa Verde Archaeology: I Site 499, Mesa Verde National Park, Colorado* (with a chapter on pottery by Florence C. Lister). University of Colorado Studies, Series in Anthropology, No. 9, University of Colorado Press, Boulder, September, 1964.

———. "Archaeology for Layman and Scientist at Mesa Verde." *Science,* 160, No. 3827 (May 3, 1968).

Lister, Robert H. and Florence C. *Earl Morris and Southwestern Archaeology.* Albuquerque: University of New Mexico Press, 1968.

Lommel, Andreas. *Die Welt der Frühen Jäger: Medizinmänner, Schamanen, Künstler:* Callwey, 1965.

London, Jack. *Before Adam*. New York: Macmillan, 1907.
———. *The Star Rover*. New York: Macmillan, 1915.
Longacre, William A. "Current Thinking in American Archeology," in *Current Directions in Anthropology*. Bulletin of the American Anthropological Association, 3, No. 3, Part 2, Washington, D.C., September, 1970.
Longfellow, Henry Wadsworth. *The Complete Poetical Works*. Boston: Houghton Mifflin Co., 1922.
Lummis, C. F. "A Hero in Science." *The Land of Sunshine*, 13, August, 1900.
———. "Death of Bandelier an Irreparable Loss," *El Palacio*, 1, 6–7, Santa Fé, April–May, 1914.
———. "In Memory." In Adolph F. Bandelier, *The Delight Makers*.
Lyons, Richard D. "How Man Came to the Americas." New York *Times*, April 23, 1967.
* Macgowan, Kenneth, and Hester, Joseph A., Jr. *Early Man in the New World*. New York: Natural History Library, 1962.
MacNeish, R. S. "1964 Archaeological Excavation and Comparisons" in *Investigations in Southwest Yukon*. Papers of the R. S. Peabody Foundation, 6, No. 2, Andover.
Mallery, Arlington H. *Lost America: The Story of Iron Age Civilization Prior to Columbus*. Columbus, Ohio: Overlook Co., 1951.
Mangelsdorf, Paul C.; MacNeish, Richard S.; and Galinat, Walton C. "Domestication of Corn." In Joseph R. Caldwell, *New Roads to Yesterday*.
Mangelsdorf, Paul C., and Reeves, R. G. "The Origin of Maize: Present Status of the Problem." *American Anthropologist*, 47, No. 2, 1945.
Manley, Frank. "Horseleg Mountain: A Transitional Palaeo-Indian Site." *Archaeology*, 21, No. 1 (January, 1968).
Manners, Robert O., and Kaplan, David. *Theory in Anthropology: A Sourcebook*. Chicago: Aldine Publishing Co., 1968.
Martin, Paul S. *Digging Into History: A Brief Account of Fifteen Years of Archaeological Work in New Mexico*. Chicago Natural History Museum, Popular Series, Anthropology, No. 38, Chicago, 1963.
———. *The Last 10,000 Years: A Fossil Pollen Record of the Southwest*. Tucson: University of Arizona Press, 1970.
———. "Pleistocene Overkill." *Natural History*, December, 1967.
* Martin, Paul S.; Quimby, George I.; and Collier, Donald. *Indians Before Columbus: Twenty Thousand Years of North American History Revealed by Archaeology*. Chicago: University of Chicago Press, 1962.
Martin, Paul S., and Wright, H. E. "Pleistocene Extinctions: The Search for a Cause." *Proceedings of the Seventh Congress of the International Association for Quaternary Research*, No. 6, New Haven and London: Yale University Press, 1967.
Matson, Frederick R., ed. *Ceramics and Man*. Chicago: Aldine Publishing Co., 1965.
Matthews, William H. *Fossils: An Introduction to Prehistoric Life*. New York: Barnes & Noble, 1962.
Mavor, James W. *Voyage to Atlantis*. New York: G. P. Putnam's Sons, 1969.
Mazess, Richard B., and Zimmerman, D. W. "Pottery Dating from Thermoluminescence." *Science*, 152, No. 3720 (April 15, 1966).
McGregor, John C. *The Pool and Irving Villages: A Study of Hope-*

well Occupation in the Illinois River Valley. Urbana: University of Illinois Press, 1958.

———. Southwestern Archaeology. 2d ed. Urbana: University of Illinois Press, 1965.

McNitt, Frank. *Richard Wetherill: Anasazi.* Albuquerque: University of New Mexico Press, 1966.

* Mead, Margaret, and Bunzel, Ruth L., eds. *The Golden Age of American Anthropology.* New York: George Braziller, 1960.

Meighan, Clement W. *Archaeology: An Introduction.* Los Angeles: University of California Press, 1966.

Merve, Nikolaas, J. van der. *The Carbon-14 Dating of Iron.* Chicago: University of Chicago Press, 1969.

Meyer, Jerome S. *World Book of Great Inventions.* Cleveland and New York: World Publishing Co., 1956.

Michels, Joseph W. "Archaeology and Dating by Hydration of Obsidian." *Science,* 158, No. 3798 (October 13, 1967).

Mindeleff, Victor. *A Study of Pueblo Architecture in Tusayan and Cibola.* Eighth Annual Report of the Bureau of Ethnology, 1886–1887, Washington, 1891.

Moore, Ruth. *Man, Time and Fossils.* New York: Alfred A. Knopf, 1953.

Moorehead, W. K., and Taylor, J. L. B. *The Cahokia Mounds.* University of Illinois Bulletin, 26, No. 4, Urbana, September, 1928.

Morris, Ann Axtell. *Digging in the Southwest.* Garden City: Doubleday, Doran & Co., 1933.

Morris, Earl H. "The Excavation of a Ruin Near Aztec, San Juan County, New Mexico." *American Anthropologist,* 17, No. 4, 1915.

———. "Discoveries at the Aztec Ruin." *American Museum Journal,* 17, No. 3, New York, 1917.

———. "The Aztec Ruin." Anthropological Papers of the American Museum of Natural History, 26, Part 1, New York, 1919.

———. "Mummy Cave." *Natural History,* 42, No. 2, New York, September, 1938.

Mühlmann, Wilhelm E. *Geschichte der Anthropologie.* Bonn: Universitäts-Verlag, 1948.

Müller-Beck, Hansjürgen, "Paleohunters is America: Origins and Diffusion." *Science,* 152, No. 3726 (May 27, 1966).

———. "On Migrations of Hunters Across the Bering Land Bridge in the Upper Pleistocene." In David M. Hopkins, ed., *The Bering Land Bridge.*

Oakley, Kenneth P. *Man the Tool-Maker.* Chicago: University of Chicago Press, 1964.

———. *Frameworks for Dating Fossil Man.* Chicago: Aldine Publishing Co., 1968.

Orr, Phil C. "Radiocarbon Dates from Santa Rosa Island, I." Santa Barbara Museum of Natural History, Anthropological Bulletin No. 2, 1956, and "Radiocarbon Dates from Santa Rosa Island, II," Santa Barbara Museum of Natural History, Anthropological Bulletin, No. 3, 1960.

Orr, Phil C., and Berger, Rainer. "The Fire Areas of Santa Rosa Island, California." *Proceedings of the National Academy of Sciences,* 56, No. 5–6 (November–December, 1966).

Oretga y Gasset, José. *Prólogo a un Tratado de Montería.* Madrid, 1944.

Osborne, Douglas. "Solving the Riddles of Wetherill Mesa." *National Geographic,* 125, No. 2 (February, 1964).

* Owen, Roger C.; Deetz, James J. F.; and Fisher, Anthony D. *The North American Indians: A Sourcebook*. New York: Macmillan, 1967.

Oxenstierna, Eric. "The Vikings." *Scientific American*, 216, No. 5 (May, 1967).

Padover, Saul K. *The Complete Jefferson*. New York: Books for Libraries, 1943.

Parker, William E., and Viles, Jonas. *Letters of Thomas Jefferson*. New York, 1905.

Peckham, Stewart. *Prehistoric Weapons in the Southwest*. Santa Fé: Museum of Mexico Press, 1965.

Pfeiffer, John. "When Homo Erectus Tamed Fire, He Tamed Himself." New York *Times Magazine*, December 11, 1966.

Piggott, Stuart, ed., *The Dawn of Civilization*. London: Thames & Hudson, 1961.

Pinkley, Jean M. "The Pueblos and the Turkey: Who Domesticated Whom?" Memoirs of the Society for American Archaeology, No. 19, *American Antiquity*, 31, No. 2, Part 2 (October, 1965).

Poggie, John J., Jr. "A Note on Lewis Henry Morgan." *American Anthropologist*, 68, No. 2, Part 1 (April, 1966).

Pond, Alonzo W. *Primitive Methods of Working Stone Based on Experiments of Halvor L. Skavlem*. Logan Museum, Beloit College, Beloit, 1930.

Poole, Lynn and Gray. *Carbon-14 and Other Science Methods that Date the Past*. New York: McGraw-Hill, 1961.

Pope, G. D., Jr. *Ocmulgee National Monument, Georgia*. National Park Service Historical Handbook, Series No. 24, Washington, D.C., 1961.

Pourade, Richard F., and Rogers, Malcolm J., eds. *Ancient Hunters of the Far West*. San Diego: Union-Tribune Publishing Co., 1966.

Priestley, J. B., and Hawkes, Jacquetta. *Journey Down a Rainbow*. New York: Harper & Brothers, 1955.

Prudden, T. Mitchell. "An Elder Brother to the Cliff-Dweller." *Harper's Monthly*, 95, No. 565 (June, 1897).

Prufer, Olaf H. "Ohio Hopewell Ceramics: An Analysis of the Extant Collections." Museum of Anthropology, Anthropological Papers No. 33, University of Michigan, Ann Arbor, 1968.

Rainey, Froelich. "New Techniques in Archaeology." *Proceedings of the American Philosophical Society*, 110, No. 2, Philadelphia, April 22, 1966.

Ress, Paul Evan. "Beach Boys on the Riviera, 200,000 B.C.," *Life*, May 2, 1966.

Robbins, Roland Wells, and Jones, Evan. *Hidden America*. New York: Alfred A. Knopf, 1959.

Robbins, Maurice, with Irving, Mary B. *The Amateur Archaeologist's Handbook*. New York: Thomas Y. Crowell, 1965.

Roberts, Frank H. H., Jr., "A Folsom Complex." *Smithsonian Miscellaneous Collections*, 94, No. 4, Washington, D.C., 1935.

Rust, Alfred. *Über Waffen- und Werkzeugtechnik des Altmenschen*. Neumünster: Karl Wachholtz Verlag, 1965.

Sanders, William T., and Marino, Joseph P. *New World Prehistory: Archaeology of the American Indian*. Englewood Cliffs: Prentice-Hall, 1970.

Sapir, E. *Time Perspective in Aboriginal American Culture: A Study in Method*. Geological Survey of Canada, Anthropological Series No. 13, Ottawa, 1916.

Scheele, William E. *Prehistoric Man and the Primates.* Cleveland and New York: World Publishing Co., 1957.

Schmeck, Harold M., Jr. "The Oldest American." New York *Times,* June 4, 1967.

Scholte, Bob. "Epistemic Paradigms: Some Problems in Cross-Cultural Research on Social Anthropological History and Theory." *American Anthropologist,* 68, No. 5 (October, 1966).

Schwartz, Douglas W. *Conceptions of Kentucky Prehistory: A Case Study in the History of Archaeology.* Lexington: University of Kentucky Press, 1967.

Schwarz, Georg Theodor. *Archäologen an der Arbeit: Neue Wege zur Erforschung der Antike.* Berne and Munich: Francke Verlag, 1965.

Sellards, E. H. *Early Man in America: A Study in Prehistory.* Austin: University of Texas Press, 1952.

Shepard, Anna O. *Ceramics for the Archaeologists.* Washington, D.C.: Carnegie Institution of Washington, 1956.

* Shetrone, Henry Clyde. *The Mound Builders: A Reconstruction of the Life of a Prehistoric American Race, through Exploration and Interpretation of Their Earth Mounds, Their Burials, and Their Cultural Remains.* Port Washington: Kennikat Press, 1930.

Silverberg, Robert. *Home of the Red Man: Indian North America Before Columbus.* Greenwich: New York Graphic Society, 1963.

*————. *Mound Builders of Ancient America: The Archaeology of a Myth.* Greenwich: New York Graphic Society, 1968.

Skelton, R. A.; Marston, Thomas E.; and Painter, George D. *The Vinland Map and the Tartar Relation.* New Haven and London: Yale University Press, 1965.

Slotkin, J. S., ed. *Readings in Early Anthropology.* Chicago: Aldine Publishing Co., 1965.

Smithsonian Institution. *The Smithsonian Institution.* Washington, 1964.

Spanuth, Jürgen. *Atlantis.* Tübingen: Grabert Verlag, 1965.

Squier, E. G., and Davis, E. H. *Ancient Monuments of the Mississippi Valley: Comprising the Results of Extensive Original Surveys and Explorations.* Smithsonian Contributions to Knowledge, 1, City of Washington, 1848.

Stallings, W. S., Jr. *Dating Prehistoric Ruins by Tree Rings.* Tucson: University of Arizona Press, 1960.

Steefel, Lawrence. Review of Erik Wahlgren, *The Kensington Stone: A Mystery Solved* in *The Minnesota Archaeologist,* 27, No. 3, 1965.

Steiner, Rudolf. *Unsere altantischen Vorfahren.* Berlin, 1918.

Stirling, Matthew W., ed. *National Geographic on Indians of the Americas.* Washington, D.C. National Geographic Society, 1965.

Stoutenburgh, John L., Jr. *Dictionary of the American Indian.* New York: Philosophical Library, 1960.

Stuart, George E., and Gene S. *Discovering Man's Past in the Americas.* Washington, D.C.: National Geographic Society, 1969.

Stubbs, Stanley A. *Bird's-Eye View of the Pueblos: Ground Plans of the Indian Villages of New Mexico and Arizona, with Aerial Photographs and Scale Drawings.* Norman: University of Oklahoma Press, 1950.

Suess, Hans E. "Die Eichung der Radiokarbonuhr." *Bild der Wissenschaft,* No. 2, February, 1969.

Swanton, John R. *Indian Tribes of the Lower Mississippi Valley.*

Smithsonian Institution, Bureau of Ethnology, Bulletin 43, Washington, D.C. 1911.

Taylor, Walter W. *A Study of Archaeology.* American Anthropological Association Memoir No. 69, Menasha, Wis., 1948.

Terra, Helmut de. *Urmensch und Mammut: Alte Kulturen im Boden Mittelamerikas.* Wiesbaden: Brockhaus, 1954.

Terrell, John Upton, *Journey into Darkness: A True Account of Cabeza de Vaca's Remarkable Expedition Across the North American Continent, 1528–1536.* New York: William Morrow, 1962.

———. *The Man Who Rediscovered America: A Biography of John Wesley Powell.* New York: Weybright & Talley, 1969.

Ucko, Peter J., and Dimbleby, G. W., eds. *The Domestication and Exploitation of Plants and Animals.* Proceedings of a meeting of the research seminar in archaeology and related subjects held at the Institute of Archaeology, London University. Chicago: Aldine Publishing Co., 1969.

* Underhill, Ruth M. *Red Man's Religion: Beliefs and Practices of the Indians North of Mexico.* Chicago and London: University of Chicago Press, 1965.

Verrill, A. Hyatt, and Ruth. *America's Ancient Civilizations.* New York: G. P. Putnam's Sons, 1953.

Wahlgren, Erik. *The Kensington Stone: A Mystery Solved.* Madison: University of Wisconsin Press, 1958.

Washburn, Sherwood L., ed. *Social Life of Early Man.* Chicago: Aldine Publishing Co., 1961.

Watson, Don. *Cliff Dwellings of the Mesa Verde: A Story in Pictures.* Mesa Verde Museum Association, Colorado, n.d.

———. *Indians of the Mesa Verde.* Mesa Verde Museum Association, Colorado, 1961.

Watson, Patty Jo. "Prehistoric Miners of Salts Cave, Kenucky." *Archaeology,* 19, No. 4 (October, 1966).

Wauchope, Robert. *Lost Tribes and Sunken Continents: Myth and Method in the Study of American Indians.* Chicago and London: University of Chicago Press, 1962.

———. "Alfred Vincent Kidder 1885–1963." *American Antiquity* 31, No. 2, Part 1 (October, 1965).

Weaver, Kenneth F. "Magnetic Clues Help Date the Past." *National Geographic,* 131, No. 5 (May, 1967).

Webb, William S., and Snow, Charles E. *The Adena People.* University of Kentucky Reports in Anthropology and Archaeology, 6, Lexington, 1945.

Wedel, Waldo R.; Husted, Wilfred M.; and Moss, John H. "Mummy Cave: Prehistoric Record from Rocky Mountains of Wyoming." *Science,* 160, No. 3824 (April 12, 1968).

Wells, Calvin. *Bones, Bodies and Disease: Evidence of Disease and Abnormality in Early Man.* London: Thames & Hudson, 1968.

Wendorf, Fred; Krieger, Alex D.; and Albritton, Claude C. *The Midland Discovery: A Report on the Pleistocene Human Remains from Midland, Texas.* Austin: University of Texas Press, 1955.

Wendt, Herbert. *Es begann in Babel: Die Entdeckung der Völker.* Rastatt: Grote, 1958.

Wheat, Joe Ben. *Introduction to the Earl Morris Papers,* University of Colorado Studies, Series in Anthropology No. 8, Boulder, Colorado, June, 1963.

————. *Prehistoric People of the Northern Southwest*. Grand Canyon Natural History Association, Bulletin No. 12, Grand Canyon, 1963.

* Wheeler, Sir Mortimer, *Archaeology from the Earth*. New York: G. P. Putnam's Sons, 1962.

White, Leslie A., ed. *Pioneers in American Anthropology: The Bandelier-Morgan Letters 1873–1883, I–II*. Albuquerque: University of New Mexico Press, 1940.

Wilkins, Thurman. *Clarence King*. New York: Macmillan, 1958.

Willey, Gordon R. "New World Archaeology in 1965." *Proceedings of the American Philosophical Society*, 110, No. 2, Philadelphia, 1966.

————. *An Introduction to American Archaeology*, Vol. 1, *North and Middle America*. Englewood Cliffs: Prentice-Hall, 1966.

* Willey, Gordon R., and Phillips, Philip. *Method and Theory in American Archaeology*. Chicago: University of Chicago Press, 1965.

* Wilmsen, Edwin N. "An Outline of Early Man Studies in the United States." *American Antiquity*, 31, No. 2, Part 1 (October, 1965).

Woolley, Sir Leonard. *Digging Up the Past*. London: Penguin Books, 1952.

* Wormington, H. Marie. *Ancient Man in North America*. The Denver Museum of Natural History, Popular Series No. 4, Denver, 1964.

————. "When Did Man Come to North America?" in James S. Copley, ed., *Ancient Hunters of the Far West*.

Zeuner, Frederick E. *Dating the Past: An Introduction to Geochronology*. London: Methuen, 1952.

Notes

Preface

1. From a lecture at William Marsh Rice University, 1962, entitled "Early Man in the New World," printed in *Prehistoric Man in the New World*, ed. Jesse D. Jennings and Edward Norbeck (Chicago: University of Chicago Press, 1954).
2. John C. McGregor, *Southwestern Archaeology*, 2nd ed. (Urbana: University of Illinois Press, 1965).
3. Sir Mortimer Wheeler, *Archaeology from the Earth* (New York: G. P. Putnam's Sons, 1962).
4. Gordon C. Baldwin, *America's Buried Past* (New York: G. P. Putnam's Sons, 1962).
5. H. Marie Wormington, *Ancient Man in North America*, Denver Museum of Natural History, Popular Series, No. 4 (Denver, 1964).
6. Henry Clyde Shetrone, *The Mound Builders* (Port Washington: Kennikat Press, 1930).

PRELUDE / *The President and the Mounds*

1. Wheeler, *Archaeology from the Earth*.
2. William E. Parker and Jonas Viles, *Letters and Addresses of Thomas Jefferson* (New York, 1905).
3. All the following quotations from the *Notes* are taken from Saul K. Padover, *The Complete Jefferson* (New York: Books for Libraries, 1943).

1 / *Columbus, the Vikings, and the Skraelings*

1. Quoted from Margaret Mead and Ruth L. Bunzel, eds., *The Golden Age of American Anthropology* (New York: George Braziller, 1960).

381

2. R. A. Skelton, Thomas E. Marston, and George D. Painter, *The Vinland Map and the Tartar Relation* (New Haven and London: Yale University Press, 1965). The following quotations are also taken from this book.

3. Lawrence Steefel, review of *The Kensington Stone: A Mystery Solved*, by Erik Wahlgren, *The Minnesota Archaeologist*, 27, No. 3 (1965). This review goes far beyond the book under discussion and gives an excellent account of the entire Kensington problem.

4. Eric Oxenstierna, in *"Die Welt der Literatur"* (Hamburg, January 19, 1967).

5. Helge Ingstad, *Die erste Entdeckung Amerikas* (Berlin: Ullstein, 1966).

6. Gwyn Jones, *The Norse Atlantic Saga* (London: Oxford University Press, 1964).

7. Ingstad, *Die erste Entdeckung Amerikas.*

8. Oxenstierna, in *"Die Welt der Literatur."*

2 / The Seven Cities of Cibola

1. All quotations from Bartolomé de las Casas, *A Relation of the First Voyages and Discoveries Made by the Spaniards in America* (London, 1699).

2. Quoted from A. Grove Day, *Coronado's Quest* (Los Angeles: University of California Press, 1964). Also available in Herbert Eugene Bolton, *Coronado* (Albuquerque: University of New Mexico Press, 1964).

3. "The Seven Cities of Cibola," by Lewis Henry Morgan, published in the *North American Review* in 1869, is merely a preliminary study.

4. John Upton Terrell, *Journey into Darkness* (New York: William Morrow, 1962).

5. *The Journey of Alvar Nuñez Cabeza de Vaca,* trans. Fanny Bandelier (New York: Allerton Book Co., 1922).

6. Bandelier, *Journey of de Vaca.*

7. Terrell, *Journey into Darkness.*

8. Terrell, *Journey into Darkness.*

9. Bandelier, *Journey of de Vaca.*

10. Wilhelm Wundt, *Völkerpsychologie* (1911–24), Vol. 1.

11. Adolph F. Bandelier, "Fray Marcos of Nizza," Papers of the Archaeological Institute of America, American Series V (Cambridge, 1890).

12. Adolph F. Bandelier, "Fray Marcos."

13. Adolph F. Bandelier, "Fray Marcos."

14. Adolph F. Bandelier, "Fray Marcos."

15. Adolph F. Bandelier, "Fray Marcos."

16. Adolph F. Bandelier, "Fray Marcos."

17. Paul Horgan, *Conquistadors in North American History* (Greenwich: Fawcett Publications, 1965).

18. Horgan, *Conquistadors.*

19. Horgan, *Conquistadors.*

20. Day, *Coronado's Quest.*

21. Day, *Coronado's Quest.*

22. Day, *Coronado's Quest.*

3 / Hymn to the Southwest—From Bandelier to Kidder

1. Charles F. Lummis, "In Memory," in Adolph F. Bandelier, *The Delight Makers*, 3rd ed. (New York: Dodd, Mead & Co., 1918).
2. A spate of books and articles appeared commemorating the hundredth anniversary of this expedition. The biography of Powell by John Upton Terrell, *The Man Who Rediscovered America* (New York: Weybright & Talley, 1969) is worth reading because it emphasizes Powell's merits as a staunch friend of the Indians and advocate of their few remaining rights.
3. Frank Hamilton Cushing, *My Adventures in Zuñi*, ed. E. De-Golyer (Santa Fé: Peripatetic Press, 1941), first published 1882–83.
4. Joseph Wood Krutch, *The Desert Year* (New York: The Viking Press, 1964. This book contains the essay, "He was There Before Coronado," but it is not a contribution to our subject. Krutch speaks of the scorpion, which has inhabited the Southwest somewhat longer than our Indians—around 2,000,000 years.
5. Charles F. Lummis, "Death of Bandelier an Irreparable Loss," *El Palació* (April–May, 1914).
6. Leslie A. White, ed., *Pioneers in American Anthropology: The Bandelier-Morgan Letters 1873–1883*, 2 vols. (Albuquerque: University of New Mexico Press, 1940).
7. Lummis, "Death of Bandelier."
8. Alfred V. Kidder, "Sylvanus Griswold Morley, 1883–1948," *El Palacio*, 55 (1948).
9. Quoted from the obituary by Robert E. Greengo: "Alfred Vincent Kidder, 1885–1963," *American Anthropologist*, 70, No. 2 (April, 1968).
10. John Witthoft, "Continuity and Change in American Archaeology," *Bulletin of the American Anthropological Association*, Abstracts of Papers, 1, No. 3. In his summary he goes so far as to say that Kidder and a few others "were the first to affect the anti-intellectual bias of early archaeologists. The techniques of the pioneers led to the development of *schema* of local cultural evolution. These *schema* were antagonistic to the tradition of the American frontier and to American rationalizations about aborigines. American social theory, based upon economics in the American scene, required that anthropology relegate the savage to a position of non-evolving elemental culture with no culture history. Thus early American academic archaeology accepted the bias of the white frontiersmen and strove to defend it. Not until the time of the archaeological pioneers could Jefferson's ideas and ideals surface again in the American mind, and then only because the frontier was extinct, the Indian lost and of no economic significance. The diffusion of scientific archaeology from the pioneer areas to marginal regions was slow. . . . The old reactionary antagonisms to the development of scientific archaeology are part of the American myth of the frontier. Now that the aborigines are gone and we have taken over their economic resources, we can indulge in pity for them and we can afford to understand their cultural evolution and the themes of their lives. It took a Jefferson to do this in earlier times."
11. Greengo, "Alfred Vincent Kidder."
12. From a letter to the author dated July 13, 1970.

13. This and the five following quotations are from Alfred Vincent Kidder, *An Introduction to the Study of Southwestern Archaeology*, with an introduction on Southwestern archaeology today by Irving Rouse (New Haven and London: Yale University Press, 1963).

14. Basket Maker I is dropped in Roberts's Modification because this period is purely hypothetical. Roberts calls the Basket Maker group III "modified"—not the most felicitous word—because it shows not only change but a higher level of culture that clearly suggests the transition to the first Pueblo era. He speaks of Kidder's Pueblo I and Pueblo II periods as "developmental" because they lead into the era of the "Great Pueblo," which has also been called the "Classical Age" or the "Golden Age" of the Pueblos. That lasted—to anticipate a date which at the time of Kidder's work had not yet been determined—until one of the periods of great drought, which must have scourged the Southwest like the wrath of God from A.D. 1276 to 1298. Calling Pueblo IV "regressive" again does not seem a very happy formulation. Irving Rouse, for example, who has provided so excellent a commentary on Kidder's classic books, holds that this period still retained some of the brilliance of the "Golden Age."

It is inherent in rapidly advancing research that the scholars are continually having to modify their views. This can be extremely confusing to the reader who approaches the subject as an outsider. Consequently, we shall follow the established Kidder classification, especially later on, when we attempt some characterization of the different periods. As late as 1963 this practice has been followed by McGregor whenever he goes into detail in his widely praised *Southwestern Archaeology*—although he presents a classification of his own to embrace the history of the *entire* Southwest.

4 / The Rise and Fall of Pueblo Azetc

1. Sherman S. Howe, "The Story of the Aztec Ruins," *The Basin Spokesman* (1955), published in Farmington, New Mexico.
2. John M. Corbett, *Aztec Ruins,* National Park Service Historical Handbook Series, No. 36 (Washington, D.C., 1962).
3. Joe Ben Wheat, *Introduction to the Earl Morris Papers,* University of Colorado Studies, Series in Anthropology, No. 8 (Boulder, 1963).
4. Florence C. Lister and Robert H. Lister, *Earl Morris and Southwestern Archaeology* (Albuquerque: University of New Mexico Press, 1968).
5. Corbett, *Aztec Ruins.*

5 / Mummies, Mummies . . .

1. Ann Axtell Morris, *Digging in the Southwest* (New York: Doubleday, 1933).
2. Morris, *Digging in the Southwest.*
3. Morris, *Digging in the Southwest.*
4. Morris, *Digging in the Southwest.*

6 / What Is Archaeology, and Wherefore Do We Study It?

1. Hortense Powdermaker, *Hollywood, the Dream Factory; An Anthropologist Looks at the Movie-Makers* (Boston: Little, Brown, 1951).
2. Robert Ascher, "Teaching Archaeology in the University," *Archaeology*, 21, No. 4 (October, 1968).
3. Douglas W. Schwartz, *Conceptions of Kentucky Prehistory: A Case Study in the History of Archaeology*, Studies in Anthropology, No. 6 (Lexington: University of Kentucky Press, 1967).
4. A. L. Kroeber and C. Kluckhohn, "Culture: A Critical Review of Concepts and Definitions," Papers of the Peabody Museum of American Archaeology and Ethnology, 47, No. 1 (Cambridge, 1951).
5. Wheeler, *Archaeology from the Earth.*
6. The student of North American anthropology or archaeology will want to acquaint himself with discussions that have arisen only in very recent years—for example, with philosophical interpretations of the various concepts of culture. He will also have to look into the remarkable results that have been achieved by application of modern statistical methods. On these matters, William A. Longacre has contributed a brief but highly instructive survey. See the bibliography.
7. Paul S. Martin, *Digging Into History, A Brief Account of Fifteen Years of Archaeological Work in New Mexico,* Chicago Natural History Museum, Popular Series, Anthropology, No. 38 (Chicago, 1959).

7 / Strata and Shards

1. Morris, *Digging in the Southwest.*
2. Wheeler, *Archaeology from the Earth.*
3. Professor Frederick Johnson has rightly reminded me that stratigraphy has taken great strides in the eastern United States, partly as a consequence of the WPA program. In fact, he regards this development as so important that he actually speaks of "WPA archaeology."
4. Emil Haury in his introduction to the first report: Harold S. Gladwin et al., *Excavations at Snaketown* (1938; reprint ed., Tucson: University of Arizona Press, 1965).
5. Waldo E. Wedel, Wilfred M. Husted, and John H. Moss, "Mummy Caves: Prehistoric Record from Rocky Mountains of Wyoming," *Science*, 160, No. 3824 (April 12, 1968).
6. Stuart Piggott, ed., *The Dawn of Civilization* (London: Thames and Hudson, 1961).
7. Gordon R. Willey, "New World Prehistory," in *New Roads to Yesterday,* ed. Joseph R. Caldwell (New York: Basic Books, 1968).
8. See Carl E. Guthe, *Pueblo Pottery Making: A Study at the Village of San Ildefonso,* Papers of the Phillips Academy, Southwestern Expedition, No. 2 (New Haven, 1925). The times given here are taken from Paul S. Martin, George I. Quimby, and Donald Collier, *Indians Before Columbus* (Chicago: University of Chicago Press, 1947).
9. Johan Huizinga, *Homo Ludens: A Study of the Play Element in Culture* (Boston: Beacon Press, 1955).

10. E. T. Hall, "Dating Pottery by Thermoluminescence," in *Science in Archaeology*, rev. ed., ed. Don Brothwell and Eric Higgs (New York: Frederick A. Praeger, 1970).
11. Morris, *Digging in the Southwest*.
12. Anna O. Shephard, *Ceramics for the Archaeologists* (Washington, D.C.: Carnegie Institution of Washington, 1956).

8 / The Tick of Time

1. Froelich Rainey, "New Techniques in Archaeology," *Proceedings of the American Philosophical Society*, 110, No. 2 (Philadelphia, 1966).
2. Brothwell and Higgs, *Science in Archaeology*.
3. Told to the author by Dr. Rainer Berger, Willard Libby's former assistant.

9 / The Endless Tree

1. Frederick E. Zeuner, *Dating the Past: An Introduction to Geochronology*. 3rd ed. (London: Methuen, 1952).
2. Andrew Ellicott Douglass, "The Secret of the Southwest Solved by Talkative Tree Rings," *National Geographic*, 46, No. 12 (December, 1929).
3. Morris, *Digging in the Southwest*.
4. Bryant Bannister, *Tree-Ring Dating of the Archaeological Sites in the Chaco Canyon Region, New Mexico*, Southwestern Monuments Association, Technical Series, 6, Part 2 (1965).
5. Bannister, *Tree-Ring Dating*.
6. Hans E. Suess, "Die Eichung der Radiokarbonuhr," *Bild der Wissenschaft*, No. 2 (February, 1969).

10 / Along the Road . . .

1. Quoted from McGregor, *Southwestern Archaeology*. McGregor provides the best surveys and the most concentrated accounts of the individual phases. This "summa," which he calls merely an "introduction," runs to almost 500 pages. But since 1965 the research material has increased by leaps and bounds, so that it is scarcely possible any longer for one individual to survey it. Unlike McGregor, I do not include Pueblo II and III under one heading, but rather I and II.
2. McGregor, *Southerwestern Archaeology*.
3. These informative pamphlets cannot ordinarily be bought in bookshops, but can be ordered from the Superintendent of Documents, Washington, D.C. A separate series of publications is devoted to Mesa Verde, for example, since a permanent archaeological station with a staff of several scientists is located there.
4. Harold S. Colton, *Black Sand* (Albuquerque: University of New Mexico Press, 1960).
5. Stanley A. Stubbs, *Bird's-Eye View of the Pueblos* (Norman: University of Oklahoma Press, 1950). Ground plans of the Indian villages of New Mexico and Arizona, with aerial photographs and scale drawings.
6. C. G. Jung, *Memories, Dreams, Reflections*, ed. Aniela Jaffé (New York: Pantheon Books, 1963).

7. Richard Erdoes, *The Pueblo Indians* (New York: Funk and Wagnalls, 1967).
8. Kidder, *Southwestern Archaeology*.
9. J. B. Priestley and Jacquetta Hawkes, *Journey Down a Rainbow* (New York: Harper & Brothers, 1955).
10. D. H. Lawrence, *Mornings in Mexico* (London: Martin Secker, 1927).
11. Morris, *Digging in the Southwest*.

11 / The Inquisitive Brothers of Mesa Verde

1. Priestly and Hawkes, *Journey*.
2. Don Watson, *Indians of the Mesa Verde*, Mesa Verde Museum Association (Colorado, 1961).
3. T. Mitchell Prudden, "An Elder Brother to the Cliff-Dweller," *Harper's Monthly*, 95, No. 565 (June, 1897).
4. Frank McNitt, *Richard Wetherill: Anasazi*, rev. ed. (Albuquerque: University of New Mexico Press, 1966).
5. William Henry Jackson, *Time Exposure* (New York: G. P. Putnam's Sons, 1940). A typical Jackson piece can be found in Leo Deuel's excellent anthology, *Conquistadors Without Swords: Archaeologists in the Americas* (New York: St. Martin's Press, 1967).
6. This happened in Canyon del Muerto, but also elsewhere—including Mesa Verde; New York *Times*, January 12, 1967.
7. McNitt, *Richard Wetherill*.

12 / Those Who Have Vanished: Cochise, Mogollon, and the Hohokam

1. McGregor, *Southwestern Archaeology*.
2. Emil W. Haury, "A Possible Cochise-Mogollon-Hohokam Sequence," *Proceedings of the American Philosophical Society*, 86, No. 2 (1943).
3. Martin, *Digging Into History*.
4. Kenneth P. Weaver, "Magnetic Clues Help Date the Past," *National Geographic*, 131, No. 5 (May, 1967).
5. Gordon R. Willey, *"New World Prehistory,"* in *New Roads to Yesterday*, ed. J. R. Caldwell (New York: Basic Books, 1966).
6. However, Haury comments on this name: " 'Those who have vanished' is the romanticized interpretation of the word, but 'Hohokam' actually means something that is 'all used up.' A blown-out automobile tire is 'Hohokam.' An old abandoned village is also 'Hohokam' or used up." (Information in a letter from Emil W. Haury to the author.)
7. Harold S. Gladwin, "Approach to the Problem," in *Excavations at Snaketown*.
8. Martin, *Digging Into History*.
9. Gladwin, *Excavations*.
10. Emil W. Haury, "First Masters of the American Desert: The Hohokam," *National Geographic*, 131, No. 5 (May, 1967).
11. Haury, "First Masters."
12. Text from Weiditz's album in the Germanisches Museum, Nuremberg. Cf. C. W. Ceram, *March of Archaeology* (New York: Alfred A. Knopf, 1958), picture on page 258.

13. B. H. McLeod of the Inspiration Copper Company has demonstrated by careful analysis that these little bells were *cast*—for which process a melting temperature of 2066° F. is needed. Could the Hohokam have been capable of producing such temperatures? See App. III in Gladwin, *Excavations at Snaketown*.
14. Haury, "First Masters."
15. Haury, "First Masters."

13 / The Story of Maize

1. Jerome S. Meyer, *World Book of Great Inventions* (Cleveland and New York: World Publishing Co., 1956).
2. Jean M. Pinkley, "The Pueblos and the Turkey: Who Domesticated Whom?" Memoirs of the Society for American Archaeology, No. 19, *American Antiquity*, 31, No. 2, Part 2 (October, 1965).
3. Pinkley, "The Pueblos and the Turkey."
4. Pinkley, "The Pueblos and the Turkey."
5. Pinkley, "The Pueblos and the Turkey."
6. Lyndon L. Hargrave, "Turkey Bones from Wetherill Mesa," Memoirs of the Society for American Archaeology, No. 19, *American Antiquity*, 31, No. 2, Part 2 (October, 1965).
7. Ivan L. Schoen reports in "Contact with the Stone Age," *Natural History*, 78 (1969), on a stay with the Wama tribe in northeastern South America: "The only pets we saw in the village were four half-grown *wild* turkeys, which followed their owner wherever she went. The Indians had instructed us not to touch them." Perhaps Pinkley's account has elements of humorous exaggeration. J. Stokley Ligon, for example, speaks of quite different experiences in his *History and Management of Merriam's Wild Turkey* (Albuquerque: University of New Mexico Press, 1946).
8. Victor R. Boswell, "Our Vegetable Travellers," *National Geographic*, 96, No. 2 (August, 1949).
9. Frank S. Hibben, *Digging Up America* (New York: Hill and Wang, 1960).
10. Paul C. Mangelsdorf, Richard S. MacNeish, and Walton C. Galinat, "Domestication of Corn," in *New Roads to Yesterday*, ed. Joseph R. Caldwell (New York: Basic Books, 1966).

14 / Discovery of the Mounds

1. James A. Ford and Charles H. Webb, *Poverty Point: A Late Archaic Site in Louisiana*, American Museum of Natural History Anthropological Papers, 46, No. 1 (1956).
2. Quoted from Cyrus Thomas, *The Problem of the Ohio Mounds* (Washington: Smithsonian Institution, Bureau of Ethnology, 1889).
3. George Catlin, *Illustrations of the Manners, Customs and Condition of the North American Indians: In a Series of Letters and Notes written during eight years of Travel and Adventure among the wildest and most remarkable Tribes now existing. With three hundred and sixty Engravings, from the Author's Original Paintings.* (London: Henry G. Bohen, 1841). By 1845 this book had already reached its fifth edition.

4. Caleb Atwater, *Description of the Antiquities Discovered in the State of Ohio and other Western States*, Transactions of the American Antiquarian Society, Archaeologia Americana, 1 (1820).
5. Hibben, *Digging Up America*.
6. Maurice Robbins with Mary B. Irving, *The Amateur Archaeologist's Handbook: A Complete Guide for Digging into America's Past* (New York: Thomas Y. Crowell Company, 1965).

15 / Wild Theories from Atlantis to Mu

1. In 1970 many newspapers published accounts of a find purporting to prove that groups of Jewish refugees reached America shortly after the great defeats the Romans inflicted upon rebellious Judaea in A.D. 70 and 133. This theory, which has been advocated particularly by Cyrus H. Gordon of Brandeis University, is based upon an inscribed tablet found in Tennessee in 1885, beneath a skeleton in a burial mound. Gordon has read the text: "For the land of Judah." The tablet was photographed at the Smithsonian Institution in 1894, but unfortunately the photo was published upside down, so that no one recognized its possible meaning. Gordon first learned of the tablet's existence in August, 1970. As corroborative evidence for his theory, he points to the curious tribe of Melungeons in eastern Tennessee, "who are neither Indian nor Negro, who are Caucasian but not Anglo-Saxon." (Quoted from the article, "Credits Jews for Discovery of America," Chicago *Tribune*, October 19, 1970.) The future will determine whether Gordon's thesis meets with scientific acceptance. But there is scarcely any doubt that after the conquest of the American continents by Mongoloid nomads from Siberia, landings by European, African, Near Eastern, and perhaps Chinese or Japanese peoples were possible. The youngest generation of American archaeologists has been gathering more and more material tending to show that such landings did in fact take place. In terms of art history, this theory has recently received support from Alexander von Wuthenau of the University of the Americas in Mexico City, in his book *The Art of Terra-cotta Pottery in Pre-Columbian Central and South America* (New York: Crown, 1970). His studies indicate that certain cultural influences, weakened by the passage of centuries, might have diffused to North America.
2. James Adair, *History of the American Indian* (London, 1775). The passages from Caleb Atwater and James Adair important for our purposes are reprinted in *The Golden Age of Anthropology,* ed. Margaret Mead and Ruth L. Bunzel.
3. James Ussher, *Annalis Veteris et Novi Testamenti* (1650–1654).
4. L. Sprague de Camp, "The End of the Monkey War," *Scientific American*, 220, No. 2 (February, 1969).
5. Jürgen Spanuth, *Atlantis* (Tübingen: Grabert Verlag, 1965).
6. James W. Mavor, Jr., *Voyage to Atlantis* (New York: G. P. Putnam's Sons, 1969).
7. Rudolf Steiner, *Unsere atlantischen Vorfahren* (Berlin, 1918).
8. James Churchward, *The Lost Continent of Mu* (New York: Crown Publishers, 1931).

9. Robert Wauchope, *Lost Tribes and Sunken Continents* (Chicago: University of Chicago Press, 1962).
10. Wauchope, *Lost Tribes.*
11. Harold S. Gladwin, *Men Out of Asia* (New York: McGraw-Hill, 1947).
12. Leo Wiener, *Mayan and Mexican Origins* (Cambridge: by the author, 1926).

16 / Solving the Riddle of the Mounds

1. E. G. Squier and E. H. Davis, *Ancient Monuments of the Mississippi Valley* (City of Washington, 1848).
2. Squier and Davis, *Ancient Monuments.*
3. Florence Hawley, *Tree Ring Analysis and Dating in the Mississippi Drainage,* University of Chicago Publications in Anthropology, Occasional Paper No. 2, 1941. See also: Robert E. Bell, "Dendrochronology in the Mississippi Valley," in *Archaeology of the Eastern United States,* ed. James B. Griffin, 3rd ed. (Chicago: University of Chicago Press, 1964).
4. Gordon R. Willey, *An Introduction to American Archaeology,* Vol. 1 (Englewood Cliffs: Prentice-Hall, 1966).
5. Shetrone, *The Mound Builders.*
6. Shetrone, *The Mound Builders.*
7. Hibben, *Digging Up America.*
8. Frederick Johnson, "Radiocarbon Dating and Archaeology in North America," *Science,* 155 (January 13, 1967).
9. Johnson, "Radiocarbon Dating."
10. William S. Webb and Charles E. Snow, *The Adena People,* University of Kentucky Reports in Anthropology and Archaeology, 6 (Lexington, 1945).
11. Willey, *American Archaeology.*
12. Robert Silverberg, *Mound Builders of Ancient America: The Archaeology of a Myth* (Greenwich: New York Graphic Society, 1968).
13. Arlington H. Mallery, *Lost America* (Columbus: Overlook Co., 1951).
14. Emil W. Haury in a letter to the author dated November 10, 1969.
15. Thorne Deuel, "Hopewellian Dress in Illinois," in Griffin, *Archaeology of the Eastern United States.*
16. Silverberg, *Mound Builders.*
17. James A. Ford and Gordon R. Willey, "An Interpretation of the Prehistory of the Eastern United States," *American Anthropologist,* 43, No. 3 (1941).
18. A. R. Kelly, *A Preliminary Report on Archaeological Explorations at Macon, Ga.* Smithsonian Institution, Bureau of American Ethnology, Bulletin No. 119 (Washington, D.C., 1938).
19. Samuel P. Haven, *Archaeology of the United States,* Smithsonian Contributions to Knowledge (Washington, D.C., 1856).
20. John R. Swanton, *Indian Tribes of the Lower Mississippi Valley,* Smithsonian Institution, Bureau of Ethnology, Bulletin No. 43 (Washington, D.C., 1911).

17 / The American Goliath

1. All quotations on Goliath from James Taylor Dunn, "The True, Moral and Diverting Tale of the Cardiff Giant or the American Goliath," *New York History* reprint (July, 1948).

2. Aleš Hrdlička, *Skeletal Remains Suggesting or Attributed to Early Man in North America*, Smithsonian Institution, Bureau of American Ethnology, Bulletin No. 33 (Washington, D.C., 1907).

18 / Folsom Man

1. Frank C. Hibben, *The Lost Americans* (New York: Thomas Y. Crowell, 1968).
2. Frank H. H. Roberts, Jr., "A Folsom Complex," *Smithsonian Miscellaneous Collections*, 94, No. 4 (Washington, D.C., 1935).

19 / Sandia Man

1. *Saturday Evening Post*, April 17, 1943.
2. Frank C. Hibben, "We Found the Home of the First American," *Saturday Evening Post*, April 17, 1943.
3. Hibben, "Home of the First American."
4. Frank C. Hibben, "Evidences of Early Occupation in Sandia Cave, New Mexico, and Other Sites in the Sandia-Manzano Region," *Smithsonian Miscellaneous Collections*, 99, No. 23 (Washington, D.C., 1941).
5. Hibben, "Home of the First American."
6. Hibben, "Home of the First American."
7. Hibben, "Home of the First American."
8. Kirk Bryan, "Correlation of the Deposits of Sandia Cave, New Mexico, with the Glacial Chronology." Appendix to Hibben, "Evidences of Early Occupation in Sandia Cave."
9. Hibben, "Evidences of Early Occupation in Sandia Cave."
10. Bryan, "Correlation of the Deposits of Sandia Cave."
11. Willey, *American Archaeology*.
12. In a letter to the author dated November 5, 1968, which he has kindly released for publication.

20 / The World of the Early Hunters

1. In the technical literature the reader will often find the dates 1926 or 1927. It depends on whether the author is referring to the actual discovery by the black cowboy, the first inspection by the scientists, or the first excavation.
2. Quoted by Frederick Johnson in "Radiocarbon Dating and Archaeology in North America," *Science*, 155 (January 13, 1967).
3. Other examples are given in Edwin N. Wilmsen, "An Outline of Early Man Studies in the United States," *American Antiquity*, 31, No. 2, Part 1 (October, 1965).
4. Wilmsen, "An Outline of Early Man Studies." This remark refers to the dispute between Hrdlička and Albert E. Jenks over the "Minnesota mummy."
5. But these interpretations must be offered cautiously. There is a whole series of finds that cannot be explained, for example, the "cogged stones," actual cogwheels carved out of stone, which have been found in Orange County, California. They range in diameter from two and a half to more than six inches and have

as many as twenty-two teeth, which are cut out with machine-like precision. It is a total enigma what men of 8,000 years ago—that has been the age assigned to them—could have done with these objects. They could scarcely have been weapons or tools, for several are carved out of such soft stone that any kind of vigorous use would break the teeth. Were they perhaps toys? Religious utensils? There are many theories, all lacking any solid proofs.

6. As we remark in the text, the best list of all points, arranged by sites, is given by H. Marie Wormington in *Ancient Man in North America.*

7. Emil W. Haury, "Artifacts with Mammoth Remains, Naco, Arizona," *American Antiquity,* 19, No. 1, (1953).

8. Ernst Antevs, "Geological Age of the Lehner Mammoth Site," *American Antiquity,* 25, No. 1 (July, 1959).

9. Emil W. Haury, "The Lehner Mammoth Site," *American Antiquity,* 25, No. 1 (July, 1959).

10. Haury, "The Lehner Mammoth Site."

11. Wormington, *Ancient Man.*

12. H. Marie Wormington, "A Summary of What We Know Today," in *Ancient Hunters of the Far West,* ed. James S. Copley (San Diego: Union-Tribune Publishing Co., 1968).

13. Phil C. Orr, "Radiocarbon Dates from Santa Rosa Island I," and "Radiocarbon Dates from Santa Rosa Island II," Museum of Natural History Anthropological Bulletin Nos. 2 and 3 (Santa Barbara, 1956, 1960).

14. José Ortega y Gasset, *Prólogo a un Tratado de Montería* (Madrid, 1944).

15. Baldwin, *America's Buried Past.*

16. Clement W. Meighan and C. Vance Haynes, "The Borax Lake Site Revisited," *Science,* 167, No. 3922 (February 27, 1970).

17. Wormington, *Ancient Man.*

18. Mark R. Harrington, "Gypsum Cave, Nevada," in Leo Deuel, *Conquistadors Without Swords.*

21 / When the Great Beasts Died

1. Alonzo W. Pond, *Primitive Methods of Working Stone Based on Experiments of Halvor L. Skavlem,* Logan Museum, Beloit College (Beloit, 1930).

2. Ortega y Gasset, *Prólogo a un Tratado de Montería.*

3. Corbett, *Aztec Ruins.*

4. P. S. Martin and H. E. Wright, Jr., eds., "Pleistocene Extinctions: The Search for a Cause," *Proceedings of the 7th Congress of the International Association for Quaternary Research,* 6 (New Haven: Yale University Press, 1967).

5. Jesse D. Jennings, *Prehistory of North America* (New York: McGraw-Hill, 1968).

6. "A Place to Die," *Time,* January 26, 1970.

7. Ortega y Gasset, *Prólogo a un Tratado de Montería.*

8. Paul S. Martin, "Pleistocene Overkill," *Natural History* (December, 1967).

INTERMEZZO 22 / *The Towers of Silence.*

1. Frank C. Hibben, "The Mystery of the Stone Towers," *Satur-*

day Evening Post, December 9, 1944. All further quotations in this chapter are taken from this article.

23 / The First American, or The Girls From Midland and Laguna

1. Fred Wendorf et al., *The Midland Discovery* (Austin: University of Texas Press, 1955). Helmut de Terra, *Urmensch und Mammut* (Wiesbaden: Brockhaus, 1954).
2. Jennings, *Prehistory of North America.*
3. Gordon R. Willey, "New World Archaeology in 1965," *Proceedings of the American Philosophical Society,* 110, No. 2 (Philadelphia, 1966).
4. Paul Evan Ress, "Beach Boys on the Riviera, 200,000 B.C.," *Life,* May 2, 1966.
5. Rainer Berger and James R. Sackett, "Final Report on the Laguna Beach Excavation of the Isotope Foundation," Publication of the University of California (Los Angeles, February 10, 1969).
6. Berger and Sackett, "Laguna Beach Excavation."
7. Berger and Sackett, "Laguna Beach Excavation."
8. Berger and Sackett, "Laguna Beach Excavation."
9. L. S. B. Leakey et al., "Archaeological Excavations in the Calico Mountains, California: Preliminary Report," *Science,* 160 (May 31, 1968).

24 / The Way Across Bering Strait

1. William Howells, *Back of History* (New York: Natural History Library, 1954).
2. David M. Hopkins, ed., *The Bering Land Bridge* (Stanford: Stanford University Press, 1967).
3. C. Vance Haynes, Jr., "Elephant Hunting in North America," *Scientific American,* 214, No. 6 (June, 1966).
4. Baldwin, *America's Buried Past.*
5. Willey, *American Archaeology.*

EPILOGUE / The Story of Ishi

1. This and all other quotations in this chapter from Theodora Kroeber, *Ishi in Two Worlds* (Los Angeles: University of California Press, 1965).
2. Stone Age Indians lived in *South* America; that is, up to the past decade they knew no other tool but the stone axe. These Amarakaeri and Isconahua in eastern Peru and the Xetá in southern Brazil have meanwhile either died out or have replaced their stone by iron axes brought to them by missionaries. In June, 1968, however, remnants of the Wama tribe in Surinam, northeastern South America, were rediscovered. They are still using stone axes and know nothing of agriculture. These Indians may be regarded as the last real primitives in the American continents. See the foreword by Robert L. Carneitor to Ivan L. Schoen, "Contact with the Stone Age," *Natural History,* 78, 1969.

Credits for Drawings

Index

MENTOR Titles of Related Interest

☐ **AMERICAN INDIAN MYTHOLOGY by Alice Marriott and Carol K. Rachlin.** A collection of myths, legends and contemporary folklore from some twenty North American tribes, this profusely illustrated volume is one of the most comprehensive studies of Indian lore in America. (#MW1376—$1.50)

☐ **AMERICAN EPIC: The Story of the American Indian by Alice Marriott and Carol K. Rachlin.** A full yet compact history of the origins, cultures and destinies of all the major American Indian tribes. (#MW1503—$1.50)

☐ **THE DEATH OF THE GREAT SPIRIT: An Elegy for the American Indian by Earl Shorris.** A comprehensive history of the American Indian, from Sitting Bull to the Red Power Radicals of today. (#MW1355—$1.50)

☐ **INDIANS OF THE AMERICAS (abridged) by John Collier.** The first book to paint the full panorama of the Red Indian from the Paleolithic Age to the present. (#MY1273—$1.25)